D1528363

Chinese Englishes
A Sociolinguistic History

This book explores the history of the English language in China from the arrival of the first English-speaking traders in the early seventeenth century to the present. Kingsley Bolton brings together and examines a substantial body of historical, linguistic and sociolinguistic research on the description and analysis of English in Hong Kong and China. He uses early wordlists, satirical cartoons and data from journals and memoirs, as well as more conventional sources, to uncover the forgotten history of English in China and to show how contemporary Hong Kong English has its historical roots in Chinese pidgin English. The book also considers the varying status of English in mainland China over time, and recent developments since 1997. With its interdisciplinary perspective, the book will appeal not only to linguists, but to all those working in the fields of Asian studies and English studies, including those concerned with cultural and literary studies.

KINGSLEY BOLTON is an Associate Professor in the Department of English at the University of Hong Kong, where he lectures on sociolinguistics and World Englishes. He has published a number of books and articles on sociolinguistics, Asian Englishes, Hong Kong English, Chinese pidgin English and Chinese secret societies. From September 2003, he will be Professor in the Department of English at Stockholm University.

Chinese Englishes

STUDIES IN ENGLISH LANGUAGE

The aim of this series is to provide a framework for original work on the English language. All volumes are based securely on empirical research, and represent theoretical and descriptive contributions to our knowledge of national varieties of English, both written and spoken. The series will cover a broad range of topics in English grammar, vocabulary, discourse, and pragmatics, and is aimed at an international readership.

Already published

Christian Mair
Infinitival complement clauses in English: a study of syntax in discourse

Charles F. Meyer
Apposition in contemporary English

Jan Firbas
Functional sentence perspective in written and spoken communication

Izchak M. Schlesinger
Cognitive space and linguistic case

Katie Wales
Personal pronouns in present-day English

Laura Wright (editor)
The development of standard English, 1300–1800: theories, descriptions, conflicts

Charles F. Meyer
English corpus linguistics: theory and practice

Stephen J. Nagle and Sara L. Sanders (editors)
English in the Southern United States

Chinese Englishes
A Sociolinguistic History

KINGSLEY BOLTON

CAMBRIDGE
UNIVERSITY PRESS

PUBLISHED BY THE PRESS SYNDICATE OF THE UNIVERSITY OF CAMBRIDGE
The Pitt Building, Trumpington Street, Cambridge, United Kingdom

CAMBRIDGE UNIVERSITY PRESS
The Edinburgh Building, Cambridge, CB2 2RU, UK
40 West 20th Street, New York, NY 10011–4211, USA
477 Williamstown Road, Port Melbourne, VIC 3207, Australia
Ruiz de Alarcón 13, 28014 Madrid, Spain
Dock House, The Waterfront, Cape Town 8001, South Africa

http://www.cambridge.org

First published 2003
Third printing 2005

Printed in the United Kingdom at University Press, Cambridge

Typefaces Ehrhardt 10/12 pt. and Melior   *System* LaTeX 2_ε [TB]

A catalogue record for this book is available from the British Library

ISBN 0 521 81163 5 hardback

For my parents, Enid Vilna Elias (1915–1991) and Douglas Ronald Bolton (1916–2002)

Contents

Maps

Illustrations

Tables

Preface

This book sets out to bring together and make sense of a substantial body of historical, linguistic and sociolinguistic research on the description and analysis of English in Hong Kong and China. My starting point was my own disciplinary background in sociolinguistics, a subject broadly defined as 'the study of language and society'. However, as my research progressed, I found it necessary to consider other approaches to the subject as well. I have therefore attempted to draw broadly, and I hope appropriately, from a range of other disciplines, including anthropology, history and sociology.

On 1 July 1997, British colonial Hong Kong ceased to exist. Hong Kong island, the Kowloon peninsula and the New Territories hinterland, together comprising an area of some 400 square miles with a population of some 6.5 million, was reunited politically with the People's Republic of China (PRC), with 1.3 billion citizens spread over almost 3,700,000 square miles, and the largest population of any nation-state in the world. In this process, a much-vaunted enclave of international capitalism was being placed under the control of what was, notionally at least, the largest surviving communist regime in the world. Hong Kong was now reinvented as the Hong Kong Special Administrative Region (HKSAR), whose future would be ensured by a series of diplomatic agreements guaranteeing the enclave a high degree of autonomy, and the continuation of its capitalist system.

As an educator and academic researcher who witnessed many of the events (albeit at varying degrees of distance) which determined Hong Kong's future in the period of late colonial rule, part of my motivation for carrying out this research was to explain many of the language-related issues in the territory, both to my students and myself. In time, this led into a deepening engagement with the linguistic history of both Hong Kong and China. A major theme which I hope emerges from this volume is that English in China has a long and barely remembered history, which can be traced back to the beginnings of British maritime trade with Canton (Guangzhou) and Macao. This early contact was the beginning of a long process of cultural, political and linguistic interaction that would connect in turn with such later developments as the opium trade at Canton, the 'semi-colonialism' of nineteenth-century treaty-port China, the fall of the Qing (Ch'ing) dynasty and the creation of modern China.

It is this history that I have attempted to recover, and come to terms with, in this study, while siting it in the wider context of the study of Asian Englishes. Chapter 1 attempts to provide a critical overview of current approaches to research within the field of Asian Englishes, 'new Englishes' and World Englishes, including English studies, corpus linguistics, the sociology of language, applied linguistics, pidgin and creole studies, lexicography and critical linguistics. I also assess the relevance of such perspectives to the discussion of English in Hong Kong and China, partly in order to clear the way for the description and analysis which follows in the succeeding chapters.

Chapter 2 deals with the sociolinguistic description of English and other languages in Hong Kong, where the discussion of language issues is grounded in the sociopolitical detail of the final years of British colonialism (from approximately 1980 until 1997, the year of the Hong Kong 'handover'). The earlier sections of the chapter deal with the sociopolitical history of Hong Kong in these years, describing the development of an immigrant refugee society, dramatic population growth and the creation of an Asian miracle economy. It is also the story of a distinct Hong Kong identity, reflected in the cosmopolitan and hybrid cultures of film, television, music, and print media. Above all, perhaps, it is a story of unremitting social and political change. The later sections of the chapter deal with the language background to Hong Kong society, from a historical as well as a contemporary perspective, in order to explain the particular dynamics of Hong Kong as a multilingual society.

Chapter 3 was researched and written in order to understand (what I came to think of as) the 'forgotten past' of English in southern China. This in turn involved me in the 'archaeology' of English, a research method for which I would now claim an important role in investigating the history of World Englishes. Essentially, the core components of this method are historical and textual: historical in the sense that the method requires an examination of extant historical research on western trade and settlement in China (as well as primary historical sources where available), and textual in that many of the source materials provided instantiations of earlier written, and sometimes spoken, forms of the language. More specifically, many of the texts I studied were the records of early maritime trading voyages to China, accounts of Canton trade, and the diaries and other writings of China missionaries and colonial officials. I was also able to uncover a substantial number of English and American glossaries of 'pidgin' and 'China Coast' English from nineteenth- and early twentieth-century sources, which were useful not only in revealing processes of language change, but also in shedding light on the discourses of Chinese pidgin English. In addition, I gained access to a number of Chinese-authored glossaries and dictionaries of English from the same period, which in turn proved to be invaluable sources of historically relevant sociolinguistic information. All of which has helped me uncover a history of English in South China which begins in the early seventeenth century, continues with the 'Canton jargon' of the late eighteenth and early nineteenth centuries, and reaches to the 'Hong Kong English' of the present.

Chapter 4 returns to the present day with a discussion of the status, functions and features of English in the contemporary HKSAR. This chapter surveys the sociolinguistic background to the recognition of Hong Kong English, and the arguments in favour of a 'paradigm shift' to open up more creative possibilities for the language. After a discussion of the criteria necessary to the recognition of Hong Kong English, I also consider the ideologies of English in Hong Kong and the weight of the local complaint tradition in the discussion of language issues. The later sections of the chapter discuss the variety's creativity in literary as well as less formal contexts. I argue that the case for the recognition of Hong Kong English rests not only on the recognition of features of language, but also on the acceptance of a new space, or spaces, for the discourses associated with English in Hong Kong.

In the final chapter, chapter 5, I endeavour to connect the history of English in Hong Kong and southern China with that of the People's Republic of China. Here I provide a survey of English-language teaching in the PRC from the late Qing period to the present. From this it is evident that mainland China has its own history of Englishes to tell, from the self-strengthening era of the late Qing, through the Christian colleges of Republican China and the turbulent educational history of the post-1949 era, to the sometimes unexpected present of today. At a time when the PRC is moving towards full membership of the World Trade Organisation and the further opening of trade and other contacts with the world (including the 2008 Beijing Olympics), much more might be said about the possible futures of Chinese Englishes. That however would be the subject of another study, one which would deal with the contemporary and unfolding story of the continuing 'interface' between the world's largest two language cultures, both in China and throughout diasporic Chinese communities worldwide.[1] For now, it may be enough to begin to recover the past, a past with a history of almost 370 years of Chinese-English linguistic contact.

---

[1] I am grateful to Professor Tom McArthur for suggesting the use of the term 'Chinese–English interface' to refer to the complex cultural and linguistic interactions between the Chinese languages and World Englishes at a seminar on this topic at the University of Hong Kong in March 2000 (McArthur 2000).

Acknowledgements

I owe a major debt to a number of people who have commented on various sections of this book, or who have contributed to my research in various ways, by discussing ideas and information, providing access to research materials, pointing me to archival sources, or by encouraging and supporting this project in many other ways. I am sure that the following list is only partly adequate, and apologise for any omissions, obvious or otherwise. In Britain, I wish to thank Guy Cook, Alan Davies, Colin Dunk, Roy Harris, Jeffrey Henderson, Paul Kerswill, Alistair McIntosh, Frederick Payne, Martha Pennington, Rudy Smet, Peter Trudgill and Robert J. C. Young. Very special thanks are due to Tom McArthur for his encouragement of this book from the very outset. In Sweden, I am very grateful to Gunnel Melchers and Gunnar Persson for their long support since my earliest days as a university teacher, and in Germany I am equally grateful to Edgar Schneider for his collegiality and solid support in recent years. In the USA, warmest thanks go to Braj and Yamuna Kachru, and to Larry Smith, for countless kindnesses, intellectual inspiration, and much more. In Australia, I would like to thank Susan Butler, James Lambert, Richard Tardif and all the *Macquarie Dictionary* team for their unique spirit and special contribution to the study of Asian Englishes. I am also very grateful to Emma Cotter, who read through this book in draft and made so many helpful suggestions. In the Philippines, I would like to thank Ma. Lourdes S. Bautista, Andrew Gonzalez from De La Salle University, and Ian Gill of the Asian Development Bank. In Macao, I wish to thank Nara Barreto, Alan Baxter, Glenn Timmermans and Paul Van Dyke; in the People's Republic of China, Yin Qiping and Chen Shubo; and, in Japan, Andrew Moody. In Hong Kong, I have so many to thank, including colleagues and former colleagues from the University of Hong Kong, as well as others working elsewhere in the community. These include Bob Adamson, John Bacon-Shone, Phil Benson, James K. Chin, Susanna Chow, Jonathan Grant, John E. Joseph, Sussy Komala (Xu Xi), Wilma Komala, Agnes Lam, Jacqui Lam, Zoë Law, Cedric Lee, Gregory Lee, Monique Lee, Ian Lok, Kang Kwong Luke, Kerrie MacPherson, Christopher Munn, Cathy Nancarrow, Owen Nancarrow, Gerald Nelson, Stephen Selby, Anthony Sweeting, Davina To, Q. S. Tong, Geoff Wade and Michelle Woo. I am very grateful to Shirley Geok-Lin Lim for all her advice, comments and warmth. Sincere thanks are due to my colleagues Christopher Hutton and Daniel R. Davis for reading through and commenting on early drafts of the book. Very special thanks go to Johan and Åsa for all their support and encouragement over the past years.

I would also like to thank those who have given me permission to reproduce copyright material for inclusion in this book. These are: Tribal DDB Hong Kong (for the advertisement from the *South China Morning Post*, 3 July 1989, in chapter 2), the Bodleian Library (for the illustration of 'Mundy's Chinese' in chapter 3), Jardine Matheson Limited (for the photograph of Tong King-sing in chapter 3), the Syndics of Cambridge University Library (for permission to reproduce the *Punch* cartoon, 'A Chanson for Canton' in chapter 3), the People's Educational Press of Beijing (for permission to reproduce the textbook illustrations in chapter 5) and the British Library (for permission to reproduce the *Redhaired glossary*, 15346.b.12 in appendix 4).

China and Hong Kong

1   New Englishes and World Englishes: pluricentric approaches to English worldwide

> English is no longer the possession of the British, or even the British and the Americans, but an international language which increasing numbers of people adopt for at least some of their purposes, without thereby denying . . . the value of their own languages.   (Halliday, MacIntosh and Strevens 1964: 293)

> A working definition of English linguistic imperialism is that the dominance of English is asserted and maintained by the establishment and continuous reconstitution of structural and cultural inequalities between English and other languages.
> (Phillipson 1992: 47)

> [T]he pluricentricity of English is overwhelming, and unprecedented in linguistic history. It raises issues of diversification, codification, identity, creativity, cross-cultural intelligibility and of power and ideology. The universalization of English and the power of the language have come at a price; for some, the implications are agonizing, while for others they are a matter of ecstasy.   (Kachru 1996: 135)

In this chapter, I hope to link the study of World Englishes and 'new' Englishes to a number of related disciplines – including English studies, English corpus linguistics, the sociology of language, applied linguistics, pidgin and creole studies, lexicography and critical linguistics – with the dual purpose of siting my own research within the tradition of research into World Englishes that has developed over the last twenty years or so, and of investigating how far the World Englishes paradigm may help clarify research on English in Hong Kong and China.

New Englishes

Over the last twenty years, the term 'new Englishes' has been used to refer to the 'localised' forms of English found in the Caribbean, West and East Africa, and parts of Asia. One possible assumption here is that the occurrence of hybridised varieties of English dates from only the last two decades, although, in fact, contact language phenomena involving hybridisation between European and Asian languages have a relatively lengthy history, as long as the movements of European trade and colonialism in Asia themselves. 'New English' in Asia was predated by

1

'new Portuguese' for at least a hundred years, and there is clear textual evidence to suggest that we can speak meaningfully about the origins of 'Asian English(es)' from at least the seventeenth century onwards.[1] For the purposes of this chapter, however, I intend to place such questions on hold and to reserve historical scepticism. I accept, therefore, that in the early 1980s in various branches of linguistics, including English linguistics, sociolinguistics and applied linguistics, there was a relatively sudden interest in 'new Englishes' which took hold among language scholars and even gained recognition among the British and American general public through the popularised accounts of international English(es) in print and on television. Within the academic world at least it seems reasonable to accept Kachru's (1992) claim that a major 'paradigm shift' in the study of English in the world began to take place at the beginning of the 1980s.

Before 1980, there was a general assumption within Britain, the United States and many other societies where English was taught, that the primary target model was 'English' in a singular, or perhaps 'plural singular', sense, which included the 'standard English' of Britain and the 'general American' of the United States of America. During the 1980s, however, interest grew in the identification and description of global varieties of English. This shift in focus was based largely on a recognition of 'Englishes' in the plural, and the identification and recognition of geographical 'varieties' of English throughout the world as 'international Englishes', 'World Englishes' or 'new Englishes'. Tom McArthur (1992a) defines 'new Englishes' as: 'a term in linguistics for a recently emerging and increasingly autonomous variety of English, especially in a non-western setting such as India, Nigeria, or Singapore' (1992a: 688–9).[2]

The last two decades have seen the publication of a vast number of journal articles about 'new Englishes', many of which have been published by three journals, *English World-Wide* (1980 onwards, edited by Manfred Görlach); *World Englishes*

---

[1] Issues of colonialism, imperialism, race and modernity played a major role in the encounters of the European powers (including the Portuguese, Spanish, Dutch, French and English) with the colonial others of the Americas, Africa and Asia. Language was central to these encounters, as the contact between European travellers, traders, armies and colonial officials with the peoples of these 'new' worlds entailed 'languages in contact', almost always with unexpected and to this day only partly understood consequences, both for the history of linguistics and for the history of intellectual thought. The central issue here, however, is the problematic use of the term 'new' in association with 'Englishes'. It may also be argued that English itself is a relatively 'new' language. First, it has a history said to begin a mere 1,500 years ago, in comparison, for example, to Chinese, for which many scholars would claim a history of 4,000 years. Second, it is a new language in the sense that its structure and forms were created through a process 'something like – but *not* – creolization . . . in medieval England' as Anglian encountered Old Norse, French, Latin and Greek, a process that McArthur refers to as 'waves of hybridization' (McArthur 1998: 175–6).

[2] One of the first references to the term 'new English' is in an article by Braj Kachru entitled 'The new Englishes and old models', published in 1977. In addition to the two books by Pride (1982) and Platt *et al.* (1984), the term 'new Englishes' also occurs in another chapter by Kachru (1980), in a chapter of Kachru's book on Indian English (1983), and in the final chapter of McCrum, Cran and MacNeil's popularised account of *The Story of English* (1986). Later in the same decade came *New Englishes: the Case of Singapore* (Foley 1988).

(1981 onwards, edited by Braj Kachru and Larry Smith); and *English Today* (from 1985, edited by Tom McArthur). *World Englishes* is worth particular note in this context, as its original title of *World Language English* was changed to *World Englishes* when Kachru, together with Larry Smith, took over the editorship in 1985. The use of the term 'Englishes' to refer to 'varieties of English' is again of recent popularity. The *MLA* (Modern Language Association) *Bibliography*, for example, has only one reference to 'Englishes' before 1980, but 292 references for the years 1980–2002; similarly, the *LLBA* (Linguistics and Language Behaviour Abstracts) *Index* has one reference to 'Englishes' before 1980 and 985 for the period 1980–2002.

One reason for the rapidly increasing use of the term 'new English(es)' has been the increased recognition accorded to 'international varieties' of English. In the Asian region, these varieties are said to include such 'dialects' of English as Indian English, Malaysian English, Philippine English and Singapore English. A plethora of terminology has come into use in such societies: 'English as an international (auxiliary) language', 'global English(es)', 'international English(es)', 'localised varieties of English', 'new varieties of English', 'non-native varieties of English', 'second-language varieties of English', 'World Englishes' and 'new Englishes'. At the time of writing, those terms currently enjoying greatest popularity are 'World English', 'World Englishes', 'global English' and 'new Englishes'.

One way to exemplify the distinction between 'World English' and 'World Englishes' is at the level of vocabulary. Susan Butler, writing as a lexicographer, claims that in most contexts where English is establishing itself as a 'localised' or 'new' English, '[t]here are two major forces operating at the moment . . . The first is an outside pressure – the sweep of American English through the English-speaking world' which Butler regards as synonymous with *World English*, because '[t]his force provides the words which are present globally in international English and which are usually conveyed around the world by the media' (Butler 1997a: 107). The second dynamic which Butler identifies, and which operates through *World Englishes*, is 'the purely local – the wellspring of local culture and a sense of identity' (1997a: 109). Thus at the level of lexis, items like *cable TV*, *cyberpunk*, *high five* and *political correctness* might be identified with 'World English', whereas items like *bamboo snake*, *outstation*, *adobo* and *sari-sari store* would be items found in 'World Englishes', more specifically 'Asian Englishes'.

When Kachru and Smith took over the editorship of the journal *World Language English* in 1985 it was retitled *World Englishes* (subtitled *A Journal of English as an International and Intranational Language*). Their explanation for this was that *World Englishes* embodies 'a new idea, a new credo', for which the plural 'Englishes' was significant:

> 'Englishes' symbolizes the functional and formal variation in the language, and its international acculturation, for example, in West Africa, in Southern Africa, in East Africa, in South Asia, in Southeast Asia, in the West Indies, in the Philippines, and in the traditional English-using countries: the USA,

the UK, Australia, Canada, and New Zealand. The language now belongs to those who use it as their first language, and to those who use it as an additional language, whether in its standard form or in its localized forms. (Kachru and Smith 1985: 210)

McArthur (1987) also talks about the core of 'World Standard English', against which localised 'English languages' are ordered. A synoptic view of these two terms can be formulated thus: 'World English' generally refers to the idealised norm of an internationally propagated and internationally intelligible variety of the language, increasingly associated with the American print and electronic media, while 'World Englishes' refers to localised varieties of English used intranationally in many 'ESL' societies throughout the world, such as Nigeria, Kenya, India, Singapore and the Philippines. In many instances, however, we may be referring to the spread of English at either or both levels; so in my discussion in this chapter I frequently use the term 'World Englishes' to include varieties in both senses.

The term 'global English' can for the present be regarded as roughly synonymous with 'World English'; and the term 'new Englishes' is broadly similar to 'World Englishes'; although there is a difference of emphasis, as the following discussion of the origin and use of the term suggests. McArthur (1992b) notes that Pride (1982) was the first to use *New Englishes* as a book title. This volume comprised fifteen papers on English in Africa and Asia, in societies such as Cameroon, Nigeria, India, Sri Lanka, Malaysia, Singapore and the Philippines. The topics covered include the sociolinguistic description of English in Africa and Asia, bilingualism and biculturalism, language education and the classification and description of 'new varieties' or 'nativized varieties' of English. The term 'new Englishes' is dealt with only parenthetically, however, in spite of its choice as a title for the book. Pride's introduction to the volume, entitled 'The appeal of the new Englishes', fails to define the term itself, but instead discusses the range of issues contiguous to the volume's contents, including 'linguistic imperialism', the 'neutrality' of English in former anglophone colonies and extant discussions of 'integrative' versus 'instrumental' motivations in such contexts (Pride 1982: 1–7). Also of interest in the same volume is the article by Richards, 'Rhetorical and communicative styles in the new varieties of English', which discusses the emergence and importance of new Englishes:

> The new varieties of English, described variously as 'indigenous', 'nativized', and 'local' varieties of English ... are now asserting their sociolinguistic legitimacy ... [T]he rapidity with which the new varieties of English have emerged and the distinctiveness of the new codes of English thus produced raise interesting questions of typology and linguistic change that call for adequate theoretical models and explanations. (Richards 1982: 227)

Platt, Weber and Ho's (1984) volume, *The New Englishes*, surveyed a number of issues related to the Englishes of Asia, including India, Singapore and the Philippines, and West Africa, notably Nigeria and Ghana. The authors suggest a number of criteria which identify a new English including:

- its use in educational systems (particularly those where English is a second language);
- its development in an area where a 'native variety' of English is not a majority language;
- its use for a range of functions, in a particular country or society; and
- linguistic evidence, at the levels of 'sounds', 'words' and 'sentence structures' of 'localised' or 'nativised' features. (1984: 2)

In addition they also mention the importance of political and related factors:

> Looking at New Englishes in more general terms, one can see that they have many things in common. When we consider their present-day functions, they often have a high status in the nations where they are used as official or second language. Many of them . . . are used by groups within the country as a regular language for communication in at least some areas of everyday activity. (1984: 6)

The books by Pride (1982) and Platt *et al.* (1984) are typically regarded as first and founding studies in this field. Although these were both 'centrist' publications as they were printed by US and British publishers, by the early 1980s work on new varieties of English was also underway at universities on the academic 'periphery' of Africa and Asia in those societies where such varieties were actually emerging. Kachru published an early study of Indian English in the mid-1960s (Kachru 1965), and Llamzon published a study of 'Standard Filipino English' in the late 1960s (Llamzon 1969). Noss (1983) includes a number of descriptions of Asian varieties of English including Wong on 'Malaysian English', Gonzalez on 'Philippine English', Tay and Gupta on 'Standard Singapore English', Nababan on 'English in Indonesia' and Sukwiwat on 'the Thai variety of English'.

Noss's (1983) book also included a number of position papers, including one by Llamzon on the 'Essential features of new varieties of English', which today might be read alongside Platt *et al.*'s (1984) set of criteria for defining 'new Englishes'. According to Llamzon, new varieties of English are identifiable through four essential sets of features: ecological features, historical features, sociolinguistic features and cultural features (Llamzon 1983: 100–4). *Ecological features* are a product of a linguistic environment where verbal behaviour involves 'polyglossic' linguistic choice, code-switching and code-mixing, and lexical shift (lexical borrowing from the local language). *Historical features* typical to new varieties of English relate to 'their comparatively brief historical development from the parent variety', and the fact that, in addition, 'the structural descriptions of the new varieties of English [are] . . . all fairly recent' (Llamzon 1983: 101). The most important *sociolinguistic features* relate to the use of the variety in the more intimate domains of home, friendship and recreation. Does 'sociolectal-switching' take place, that is, do speakers vary their 'rhetorical' and 'communicative' styles according to context, for example to indicate social distance or intimacy? Finally, Llamzon discusses *cultural features* with reference to creative writing and a local literature in English, arguing that:

> works by novelists, poets and playwrights have demonstrated that the English language can ... be used as a vehicle for the transmission of the cultural heritage of Third World countries. The appearance of this body of literary works signals that the transplanted tree has finally reached maturity, and is now beginning to blossom and fructify. (1983: 104)

Llamzon's reference to the importance of creative writing and literatures in this context is significant. In many Asian societies, including India, Singapore and the Philippines, there is a body of creative writing in English that reaches back five decades and more. In Llamzon's own society there are poets and novelists such as Nick Joaquin, F. Sionil Jose and many others who enjoy both national status and international acclaim.

Since at least the early 1980s, Commonwealth and postcolonial writers from a range of developing societies have increasingly won acclaim from the literary world in the form of the Booker Prize and other awards, and have also gained recognition within the western academy (particularly within the field of postcolonial studies). The emergence of 'new Englishes' in the early 1980s thus overlapped with, and was influenced by, these 'new literatures' (see, for example, King 1974; Hosillos 1982; Lim 1984). The end of the decade saw the publication of *The Empire Writes Back* (Ashcroft, Griffiths and Tiffin 1989). By 1993, the title of their book had been appropriated for a *Time* magazine cover story and feature article (Iyer 1993) detailing the successes of Booker nominees and prize-winners such as Salman Rushdie and Vikram Seth (both of Indian parentage), Kazuo Ishiguro (Japanese), Timothy Mo (Anglo-Chinese), Michael Ondaatje (Sri Lankan), Ben Okri (Nigerian) and Nobel prize-winner Derek Walcott (Trinidadian).

Iyer describes these writers as 'transcultural', because 'they are addressing an audience as mixed up and eclectic and uprooted as themselves [in ...] a new postimperial order in which English is the lingua franca' (1993: 48). According to Iyer, publishing is becoming de-centred and new presses are being set up in Australia, India and Singapore. He quotes Robert McCrum: 'There is not one English language anymore, but there are many English languages ... each of these Englishes is creating its own very special literature, which, because it doesn't feel oppressed by the immensely influential literary tradition in England, is somehow freer' (1993: 53).

As we can see, then, the last twenty years or so have seen a rapid growth of interest in the study of the 'new Englishes' as well as a number of related fields. With thousands of academic articles on these topics, at least three international academic journals devoted primarily to this branch of linguistics and increasing numbers of books on the topic, some taxonomy of the literature may be required. From my own reading of the literature, I suggest that a number of discernible, yet overlapping, approaches to research (and publications) in the field of 'World Englishes', 'new Englishes' or 'new varieties of English' may be identified. These approaches include those of:

- English studies;
- sociolinguistics;
- applied linguistics;
- lexicography;
- 'popularisers';
- critical linguistics; and
- futurologists

On a cautionary note, it has to be stated that the classifications I am suggesting here are by no means discrete, as work in certain categories obviously overlaps greatly with work in others. For example, in the first category of 'English studies', I place linguists such as Tom McArthur and Manfred Görlach, but their work, in some instances, is not simply restricted to this category alone. McArthur, for example, also has done much in the fields of applied linguistics and language pedagogy. Similarly, Görlach's work on World Englishes also displays a strong interest in sociolinguistics, as many of the articles published in his journal *English World-Wide* indicate. Trudgill and Crystal are similarly wide-ranging. Trudgill and Hannah's (1982) influential book on *International English* was partly designed for teaching purposes and thus could be categorised as 'applied linguistics' (whereas I have categorised it under 'sociolinguistics'). Crystal's work might be judged by some to belong to the field of English studies, but I prefer to discuss it beneath the heading of the 'populariser approach' to World Englishes. Braj Kachru's work is another case in point, as he has published a great deal on the teaching of World Englishes, and many might see his work as 'applied linguistics'. For various reasons, not least his connection with J. R. Firth and his description of his own work as engaging in 'socially realistic' linguistics, I prefer to categorise his contributions as belonging more to the field of sociolinguistics, more specifically, the 'sociolinguistics of World Englishes'.

The English studies approach

The 'English studies' approach to varieties of English is the approach favoured by the 'description of English' tradition, which arose partly from English philology and the study of the history of English, and partly from the study of phonetics in the late nineteenth and early twentieth century. More recently, this approach has been exemplified by the work of contemporary British linguists, such as Robert Burchfield, David Crystal, Sidney Greenbaum, Tom McArthur, Randolph Quirk and John Wells.

Randolph Quirk was one of the first in the contemporary period to discuss 'varieties' of English and the notion of 'standards' of World English in his 1962 book, *The Use of English*.[3] Quirk later (1990) assumed the role of a guardian of international 'standards' of English and was drawn into a celebrated debate with Braj Kachru on 'liberation linguistics'. In the mid-1980s, a number of books on World Englishes in the 'English studies' tradition were published, including Burchfield's influential *The English Language* (1985), Greenbaum's *The English Language Today* (1985) and Quirk and Widdowson's *English in the World: Teaching and Learning the Language and Literature* (1985). Each of these in their own way attempted to address issues related to the learning and use of English from a global perspective. Burchfield drew a great deal of attention when he discussed the possible fragmentation of English along the lines earlier seen with Latin:

> The most powerful model of all is the dispersal of speakers of popular forms of Latin in various parts of western Europe and the emergence in the early Middle Ages of languages now known as French, Italian, Spanish, Portuguese, and of subdivision (like Catalan) within these languages, none easily comprehensible to the others... English, when first recorded in the eighth century, was already a fissiparous language. It will continue to divide and subdivide, and to exhibit a thousand different faces in the centuries ahead... The multifarious forms of English spoken within the British Isles and by native speakers abroad will continue to reshape and restyle themselves in the future. And they will become more and more at variance with the emerging Englishes of Europe and of the rest of the world. (1985: 160, 173)

Burchfield's comparison of the dispersal of Latin in the Middle Ages with the position of English in the 1980s provides the starting point for Quirk's (1985) discussion of 'The English language in a global context', in which Quirk argues the case for normativity, declaiming at one point that 'the fashion of undermining belief in standard English had wrought educational damage in the ENL [English as a native language] countries' and that there is no justification for such an attitude to be 'exported' to societies where English has the status of a second or foreign language: 'The relatively narrow range of purposes for which the non-native needs to use English (even in ESL countries) is arguably well catered for by a single monochrome standard form that looks as good on paper as it sounds in speech' (Quirk 1985: 6). By the mid-1980s, then, Quirk had lost some of the linguistic radicalism of his youth, if that indeed was what it was, and seemed anxious to join battle on behalf of both 'Standard English' and 'standards' of English. His 1985 paper also represents something of a rehearsal for his later engagement with Kachru and the forces of 'liberation linguistics' in the pages of *English Today*.

---

[3] See also Randolph Quirk's 1972 volume, *The English Language and Images of Matter*.

Another significant figure in the English studies approach in the 1980s was Tom McArthur, the founding and current editor of *English Today* (from 1985), and the editor of *The Oxford Companion to the English Language* (1992a). McArthur's (1987) paper on 'The English languages' sets out part of his theoretical agenda for the study of World Englishes. As the title of the article suggests, the notion of plural Englishes is foregrounded in the discussion: 'If there are by now "English literatures" [by 1987 a well-established phrase] can the "English languages" be far behind?' (1987: 9). The article later continues, 'various . . . Englishes are developing such institutions as their own dictionaries and grammars', citing the examples of Canadian and Australian English, Tok Pisin and Krio (1987: 10). McArthur presents a model to describe the diversity of World English, essentially in the shape of a rimless cartwheel with 'World Standard English' at the hub:

> Within such a model, we can talk about a more or less 'monolithic' core, a text-linked World Standard negotiated among a variety of more or less established national standards [e.g. British and Irish Standard English, American Standard English, South Asian Standard(izing) English, East Asian Standard(izing) English]. Beyond the minority area of the inter-linked standards, however, are the innumerable non-standard forms – the majority now . . . being unintelligible to one another [e.g. Scottish English, Appalachian English, Indian English, Hong Kong English]. (1987: 10)[4]

Since 1985, *English Today* has had a substantial impact on the discussion and debate about 'English languages' around the world. Issue 41, published in 1995, provides an index of articles in the journal for the years 1985–95. These include articles on 'World English'; 'English in Africa'; 'The Americas' (including the Caribbean and Central America); 'Asia' (East Asia, South Asia, Southeast Asia, Australasia); and 'Europe' (including Britain, identified as 'offshore' Europe, as well as 'mainland' Europe). McArthur's editorship of *The Oxford Companion to the English Language* (1992a) has had a great influence on recent scholarship on World Englishes. The *Companion* explicitly sets out to acknowledge and to accommodate a global perspective on 'varieties' of English, and 'the English languages' (xvii–xxiv). 'In the closing years of the twentieth century, the English language has become a global resource', McArthur asserts. 'As such, it does not owe its existence or the protection of its essence to any one nation or group. Inasmuch

---

[4] In a subsequent article, McArthur (1992d) discusses the whole enterprise of model-making in this field, with reference to the 'biological' models of 'language families' produced by such nineteenth-century German Indo-Europeanists such as August Schleicher; and the 'geopolitical' models of Strevens (1980), McArthur (1987), Görlach (1990) and Kachru (1990, etc.). Such models, McArthur suggests, aim at 'the management of diversity', adding that 'their creators have freely used such terms as "Englishes", "new Englishes" and "World Englishes" in discussing this diversity' (McArthur 1992d: 16–17). Later, he goes on to discuss the question of nomenclature, expressing a preference for his own term, 'English languages' because it 'goes further [than "Englishes"], implying that once what happened to produce the daughters of Germanic has happened again, producing the daughters of a once (more or less) unitarian English' (1992d: 20–1).

as a particular language belongs to any individual or community, English is the possession of every individual and every community that in any way uses it, regardless of what any other individual or community may think or feel about the matter' (xvii). McArthur summarises his thinking on these and other issues in *The English Languages* (1998) and in the recently published *Oxford Guide to World English* (2002).

Another substantial figure in the academic discourse of World Englishes is Manfred Görlach, who has been described recently as 'practically the founder of the study of varieties of English in a world-wide context as a scholarly field' (Schneider 1997a: 3). Görlach's intellectual interests are wide, but it is chiefly as the editor of *English World-Wide* that he has risen to prominence in the field of World Englishes; indeed his work in this field leads Schneider to claim enthusiastically that 'Manfred Görlach was the first to recognize the challenge and importance of these topics as subjects of scholarly study' (1997a: 3–4). Görlach's contribution to this field has been substantial. *English World-Wide* started publication in 1980 under the imprint of Julius Groos Verlag in Heidelberg. In the editorial to the first issue, Görlach mentions that an original suggestion for the title was *Englishes*, but this was discarded because many scholars found such a plural 'unacceptable and unwieldy' (Görlach 1980: 7). Finally a subtitle was added to accommodate the plurality of the object of study – *A Journal of Varieties of English*.

Overall, however, it is probably fair to comment that part of Görlach's own intellectual endeavour has been devoted to the history of English, rather than World Englishes, where his chief contribution has been as an editor, of books, bibliographies and journals. To the extent that he has written in detail about World Englishes, it is chiefly as a theorist (Görlach 1988, 1989, 1995a) and historiographer of lexicography (1990, 1995 a, b). Nevertheless Görlach's work in this field is of immense importance; and it is also worth noting that Görlach himself identifies his work in this area with that of 'English studies', commenting in 1988 that '[a]s a sub-discipline of English Studies, a consideration of English as a world language would provide an ideal opportunity to expand the social, historical and geographical aspects of English Studies – and . . . might well serve to enhance the appeal of a traditional and somewhat ageing discipline' (1988: 37–8). Since Görlach's retirement as general editor of *English World-Wide* in 1998, he has passed the torch to Edgar W. Schneider, who has already carried out extensive work of his own in this field.

Other notable academics in the field of English studies include David Crystal and Sidney Greenbaum. Crystal's early work centred on English studies (e.g. Crystal and Quirk 1964; Crystal 1969, 1975), but throughout the 1970s his interests broadened to include child language acquisition and speech therapy, and by the mid-1980s he was moving away from detailed empirical research and embarking on his present career of academic entrepreneur, encyclopedist, broadcaster and 'populariser' (see p. 32 below). Greenbaum's (1985) volume on *The English Language Today* included contributions on the history of

English, Britain and North America, and a section on 'English in the world context' with papers from Cooper, Görlach and Schröder, Kachru, Lanham and Rickford and Traugott. Greenbaum was also instrumental in setting up corpus linguistics research on international varieties of English, notably the International Corpus of English (ICE) project, which is discussed in the next section.

English corpus linguistics

The history of English corpus linguistics in the last thirty years or so has involved the construction of databases to facilitate computer-based research on the char acteristics of the language used by specific groups of users. In its infancy, corpus linguistics was very much concerned with the construction of 'native-speaker' corpora of language, e.g. the Brown Corpus of American English (compiled by researchers at Brown University in 1964) and the LOB Corpus of British English (devised by researchers at the universities of London, Oslo and Bergen from 1970–8). In subsequent years, other corpora followed, including those for research on language acquisition (e.g. the CHILDES database), as well as a large number of corpora with specific lexicographical functions (e.g. the Cobuild Corpus, the Longman Corpus, etc.) (Kennedy 1998: 19–54). The most important corpus for the study of English worldwide is the International Corpus of English (ICE), which is currently being compiled by fifteen research teams worldwide. This highly ambitious project aims at the development of parallel corpora to enable the comparative study of World Englishes, with particular reference to features at the levels of syntax and lexis. The project was started in 1990 by Sidney Greenbaum at University College London, but after Greenbaum's death in 1996 was led by Charles Meyer at the University of Massachusetts, and then Gerald Nelson of University College London. In many respects, the ICE project might be seen as an extension of Quirk and Greenbaum's earlier work on the Survey of English Usage at University College London, and as a continuation of the UCL English studies tradition. In Asia, the five societies represented by ICE research teams include Hong Kong, India, Malaysia, Singapore and the Philippines, and it is anticipated that at least three teams (Hong Kong, Singapore and the Philippines) will complete their lexical corpora in the next two to three years (Schneider 2000: 121–3).

The sociolinguistic approach

Contemporary sociolinguistics, as it has developed over the last twenty years or so, subsumes a number of different approaches to the study of language and society. These include 'macro' sociolinguistic research (studies of societal multilingualism and language planning that are carried out as part of the sociology of language); 'micro' studies of language variation (linguistically oriented sociolinguistics); and a range of other studies, including anthropological linguistics, language attitudes, pidgin and creole studies and critical linguistics (Trudgill 1978; Bolton 1992). As far as sociolinguistic approaches to World Englishes are concerned, these can be regarded as falling into four types of studies:

- 'the sociology of language' (Fishman *et al.* 1977, 1996);
- studies of the 'linguistic features' of World Englishes (Trudgill and Hannah 1982; Cheshire 1991a, etc.);
- 'socially realistic' studies of World Englishes (Kachru 1992); and
- pidgin and creole studies (Todd 1984).

This procedure of categorisation is by definition reductive, somewhat simplistic and presupposes a synchronic view of 'modern sociolinguistics'. The reality of the sociolinguistic intellectual tradition is a good deal more complex than these categories suggest. Koerner (1995), for example, traces the origins of the sociolinguistic enterprise back through 'several generations of linguistics workers' to the dialect geography of German and Swiss scholars such as Wenker, Wrede and Gilliéron in the late nineteenth century. In the course of his academic career Ferdinard Wrede was to supervise Max Weinreich, the father of Uriel Weinreich, who was to supervise William Labov's doctoral dissertation at Columbia. Raven McDavid was similarly trained by Hans Kurath, who emigrated to America from Austria. Koerner (1995) also traces a genealogy that links Dwight Whitney to Ferdinand de Saussure, Antoine Meillet, Uriel Weinreich and William Labov. Koerner (1995) conceptualises the sources of twentieth-century sociolinguistics as beginning with Wrede (in dialectology), Meillet (in historical linguistics studies) and Max Weinreich (in research on bilingualism and multilingualism). This is, as he points out, only a partial genealogy, as it is focused on the 'linguistic sociolinguistics' of the Labovian tradition, and excludes work on other types of sociolinguistics such as the 'sociology of language', 'anthropological linguistics' and 'the ethnography of speaking'.

The sociology of language and World Englishes

The sociology of language is primarily associated with the work of Joshua Fishman, typically seen as the primary expert in the field, with over 700 publications on this and related areas (Spolsky 1994). During the 1960s and 1970s, a number of other sociolinguists including Charles Ferguson, Einar Haugen, Björn Jernudd and William Stewart also began to investigate areas such as multilingualism, diglossia and language planning using approaches and methodologies associated with the 'sociology of language' approach, and often collaborated with Fishman on joint research and publishing projects (see Fasold 1984).

Fishman has made a number of contributions to the field of World Englishes. Perhaps his primary influence has been at the level of methodology, specifically in investigating 'societal multilingualism', language spread, language maintenance and other 'macrosociolinguistic' phenomena. He uses a range of methods derived from the social sciences, including social survey techniques designed to elicit answers to the question of 'who speaks what language to whom and when?' (Fishman 1965). Fishman began his academic life as a Yiddish scholar, but went on to work extensively on language maintenance and multilingualism in the United States (Fishman 1964, 1968). Later he collated and codified work on the language problems of developing nations (Fishman, Ferguson and Das Gupta 1968), addressed the issues of language and nationalism (Fishman 1972), and language and ethnicity (Fishman 1989), and edited the *International Journal of the Sociology of Language*, which he founded in 1973. According to Spolsky (1994), Fishman's work is 'preeminent for the meticulous analysis of large bodies of data collected in major surveys using the methods of sociology and . . . it has also incorporated the exhaustive elucidation and interpretation of archival materials' (1994: 1266).

During the 1970s, techniques from the sociology of language were also used in the administration and codification of macrosociolinguistic data in the form of 'sociolinguistic surveys' that were carried out (often with funding from the Ford Foundation) in East Africa, West Africa, the Philippines, Jordan and other developing nations (see Ohannessian, Ferguson and Polomé 1975). (Surveys of this kind were not entirely new, however; George Grierson's massive survey of Indian languages took place in the 1890s and the results were published in eleven volumes in 1927.) Language surveys and censuses (and by extension perhaps the 'sociology of language') were thus partly colonial in their epistemological origins, although in the contemporary era such techniques typically have been used in postcolonial situations in the context of national language planning (see Gonzalez and Bautista 1986 on the Philippines; Bacon-Shone and Bolton 1998 on Hong Kong).

The specific relevance of the sociology of language methodology to the description of World Englishes is in the discussion of the background sociohistorical conditions which influence the use of English in postcolonial societies such as India, Singapore or the Philippines. Broadly speaking, most of the descriptions of 'new Englishes' found in the literature (see e.g. Platt and Weber 1980 on English in Singapore and Malaya; numerous entries in McArthur 1992a; Kachru 1983 on Indian English; and Zuengler 1983 on Kenyan English) are preceded or accompanied by details of the historical, sociological and political underpinning of those societies; the 'external history' of these Englishes, as it were. In such cases, sociohistorical information is typically expressed in a discussion of the 'status' and 'functions' of English in the community.

The term *status* here refers to the legal (*de jure*), official, or quasi-official position of a language within a certain society, as, for example, national, sole, joint official (co-official), 'major' or 'minor' and 'second', or 'foreign' language. Other terms may also be used to indicate the comparative status of various languages, including 'language of wider communication', 'regional official language', 'tolerated' language and 'discouraged' language (Bell 1981). The term *functions* refers to the range of uses of a particular language within a community, often involving a dichotomy between the *intranational* functions and *international* functions of a particular language. The intranational functions of English may include its use as a 'lingua franca', and its subsequent use in government, law, education and the mass media. Its international functions include its use as a language of business and commerce, science and technology, international communications and diplomacy.

In addition to the methodological impact of the sociology of language on the study of World Englishes, two books by Fishman and his associates (Fishman, Cooper and Conrad 1977; Fishman, Conrad and Rubal-Lopez 1996) have also delivered specific treatments of 'the spread of English' and 'postimperial English'. These studies were published twenty years apart and the data cited, and commentaries given, suggest a number of developments in the sociopolitical realities of English worldwide. In the late 1970s, the study of World Englishes had just begun; many former anglophone colonies had only recently achieved independence and Fishman's perspective was heavily influenced by his concern to foster vernacular languages. By 1996, the impact of territorial colonialism had been dissolved by the tides of political change, which, Fishman has now suggested, include the increasing globalisation of the world's economy and intellectual life. Little is said directly in either study about the emergence of 'new Englishes', however, although there is some discussion of the indigenisation of English in 'postimperial' settings. Nevertheless, the two studies deserve attention, as they represent important collections of research into a number of issues linked to World Englishes.

In the 1977 volume, after reviewing a wide range of issues linked to the growing spread of English, Fishman makes a number of points: first, he notes the existence of English-speaking 'international' people in the cities of the world, such as foreign technological experts, cosmopolitan local elites, businessmen, students and tourists. At the same time, he notes the concern for maintaining local languages, and the need of many nationalities 'to protect their mother tongues'. He further enters a plea to elaborate a theory of ethnicity, asserting that 'in 3,000 years of social theory . . . no full-fledged sociological theory of ethnicity has been elaborated' (1977: 332), and he urges anglophones to learn more of the world's other languages, traditions and values. His final summation reveals both a sense of threat from English, and the desire to check and discipline the spread of the language. English is still spreading, he concedes, but it is also being checked and is increasingly a co-official language of government, education and even business, where 'protected vernaculars' are used at the middle and lower levels. He concludes that the 'international sociolinguistic balance' rests on three factors: the spread of English; the control of English; and the 'fostering' of vernacular languages (1977: 335).

Almost twenty years later in *Post-Imperial English*, Fishman and his colleagues (Fishman, Conrad and Rubal-Lopez 1996) return to a consideration of some of the same issues. In the first chapter Fishman poses three questions:

- Is English 'still' spreading in the non-English mother-tongue world? (Yes.)
- Is that continued spread in any way directly orchestrated by, fostered by, or exploitatively beneficial to the English mother-tongue world? (Yet to be judged.)
- Are there forces or processes which transcend the English mother-tongue world itself and which also contribute to the continued spread and entrenchment of English in non-English mother-tongue countries? (Yet to be judged.)

Fishman's answers to the second and third questions indicate at least a slight shift away from his earlier position. Noting the existence of multinational corporations from Japan, Germany and the Gulf, he comments that 'the spread of English . . . may have more to do with the growing dominance of the richer countries over the poorer ones (and not merely economically or particularly politically, but also culturally) than with the English mother-tongue countries *per se*' (Fishman 1996a: 4).

In the twenty cases surveyed by Fishman (1996b), five countries are providing elementary education mainly in English or another 'colonial' language (Cameroon, India, Nigeria, Papua New Guinea and Singapore); twelve countries or groups of countries use their own 'major vernaculars' (Cuba, Israel, Uganda, Malaysia, Mexico, Puerto Rico, Quebec, Saudi Arabia, Sudan, Sri Lanka, Tanzania and the European Union); and there are three cases of 'mixed models' (Kenya (with Swahili and English), the Philippines (with Filipino and English) and South Africa (African languages, Afrikaans and English)). In those countries where elementary education is most 'anglified' (e.g. India and Singapore) there is typically a high level of linguistic diversity, and a number of local vernaculars. Fishman also notes that, globally, English has intruded into tertiary level education almost everywhere as an instructional medium (to a greater or lesser extent); the main exceptions being the Sudan, Quebec and the European Union countries (although even here the situation in currently changing). The other seventeen cases break into two categories: those where university education is wholly in English; and those where English is used as a teaching and study medium only in certain faculties or departments. Tertiary education everywhere is thus far more anglified than elementary education, which is, Fishman comments, 'a reflection of the *internal* social stratification and the *external* econotechnical linkage that English so commonly (so omnipresently) both symbolizes and reinforces' (1996b: 625).

Fishman suggests that the status of English in postcolonial societies is related to 'social stratification', although he avoids the use of the term 'neo-colonialism'. Quoting Apple (1986) on 'hegemony', he cites the argument that hegemonic forms are rarely imposed from the outside, but rather more often reintegrated 'within everyday discourse, merely by following our "commonsense needs and desires" ' (1996b: 639). The former British and American colonies that Fishman reviews are, he asserts, 'participating in both trends, in various degrees and with differing priorities' and to characterise the former trend as 'the imperialism of English' is both 'antiquated' and 'erroneous' (1996b: 639).

The linguistic features approach

A complementary method of describing World Englishes focuses on the discussion of linguistic features, through what I characterise here as a 'linguistic features' approach. This requires the linguist to identify and make statements about typical features of language in terms of pronunciation or 'accent' (phonology), vocabulary (lexis), or grammar (morphology and syntax). Typical exponents of this approach are Trudgill and Hannah who describe 'standard varieties' of English in terms of 'differences at the level of phonetics, phonology, grammar and vocabulary' (Trudgill and Hannah [1982] 1994: 3).

In some respects, Trudgill and Hannah's *International English* ([1982] 1994) is an extension of an earlier work by Hughes and Trudgill (1979), entitled *English Accents and Dialects*, which included tape-recordings, transcriptions and a brief linguistic analysis of a range of heavily vernacular British urban dialects, including London, Norwich, Bristol, Pontypridd, Walsall, Bradford, Liverpool, Newcastle, Edinburgh and Belfast. There are, however, a number of differences between *International English* and the earlier volume. First, Trudgill and Hannah ([1982] 1994) use a recorded word-list and reading passage, instead of short snippets of 'authentic speech', as in Hughes and Trudgill (1979). Second, again in contrast to the earlier volume, they focus on varieties of 'standard English' worldwide; in the first edition (1982), these included Australian, New Zealand, South African, Welsh, North American, Scottish, Irish, West Indian, West African and Indian English. The third edition (1994) added an expanded section on creoles, as well as descriptions of Singapore and Philippine English. The amount of linguistic detail covered by individual sections varies greatly; generally speaking there tends to be a rather detailed coverage of phonetics and phonology and somewhat less on grammar and lexis, although this varies, and the section on US English contains a detailed discussion of both grammar and vocabulary. The sections dealing with 'inner-circle' varieties also predominate, with some 100 pages in the latest edition allocated to 'native-speaker' varieties, and 30 devoted to creoles and second-language varieties. The influence of this book around the world has been substantial, both as a model for methodology and also for classroom teaching in sociolinguistics and in courses on World Englishes (Bolton 1983).

Other linguists such as Cheshire have strongly challenged the reliance on a notional standard thus:

> Current descriptions, whether of a non-standard dialect, a 'new' variety or even of a hypothetical international standard variety, are all too often given as lists of assorted departures from southern British standard English or from American standard English, with no attempt at determining the extent to which the local linguistic features function as part of an autonomous system ... In the absence of systematic empirical research, descriptions of different varieties of World English have often been based either on the

writer's personal observations or on the recorded speech of a single person, so that there is no way of seeing how the linguistic features that are said to be characteristic of a given variety of English are governed by social and situational factors. It is impossible, from such descriptions, to distinguish reliably between features that are performance errors and features that are recurrent, 'legitimate' features of a local variety. (Cheshire 1991b: 7)

The above caveat is included in her introduction to her book, *English Around the World* (1991a). Cheshire is at pains to distance herself from earlier descriptions of World Englishes, noting that a rigorous sociolinguistic perspective has much more to offer than other approaches, as 'it can contribute to English-language teaching issues by ensuring that descriptions of world varieties of English have a sounder empirical base than is the case at present' (Cheshire 1991b: 7). Cheshire's collection of case studies is grounded firmly in empirical research. The first seventeen chapters cover Englishes of the inner circle (the UK and USA, Ireland, Canada, New Zealand and Australia); the other twenty-seven, Englishes in the outer circle (South Asia, Southeast Asia and Hong Kong, East Africa, Southern Africa, West Africa, the Caribbean and the Pacific).

A number of these case studies focus on the analysis of sociolinguistic variation and are perhaps more accurately described as 'variation studies' (in the Labovian paradigm) rather than studies of linguistic features *per se*. Some papers attempt to analyse statistical regularities in the linguistic constraints that govern variation, others use qualitative methods and some adopt an eclectic approach. In the case of the outer-circle Englishes, some contributions are primarily 'sociology of language', some are 'variationist', others features-focused and others combine a number of approaches. Cheshire argues, perhaps rather optimistically, that in the case of 'second-language' varieties of English, sociolinguistic analysis can answer the question of where errors stop and where 'legitimate features of a local variety' start – an optimism also reflected in her claim that the chapters she includes are 'all empirical analyses of English which are firmly based on sociolinguistic research that has been carried out in the community in which the language is used' (1991b: 11).

Both approaches have had an influence on the description of World Englishes, although at somewhat different levels of detail. The Trudgill and Hannah approach has served as a model for some linguists when giving a 'broad' description of particular stereotypes of speech in second-language situations. The 'variation studies' approach advocated by Cheshire has been implemented in research aimed at analysing finer linguistic detail. What both researchers share is a focus on levels of linguistic description and a conviction in the centrality of linguistic variation to the study of World Englishes. As is evident from many other studies, however, recently this belief in the centrality of linguistic analysis has often been superseded by an emphasis on other factors, including the sociological and the political.

Braj Kachru and the socially realistic study of World Englishes

Braj Kachru has been very closely associated with the study of new Englishes, or, to use the term that Kachru himself prefers, 'World Englishes'.[5] In his (1992) survey of 'World Englishes: approaches, issues and resources', Kachru summarises the study of World Englishes in terms of eleven related and overlapping issues, identified as:

- 'the spread and stratification of English';
- 'characteristics of the stratification';
- 'interactional contexts of World Englishes';
- 'implications of the spread';
- 'descriptive and prescriptive concerns';
- 'the bilingual's creativity and the literary canon';
- 'multi-canons of English';
- 'the two faces of English: nativisation and Englishisation';
- 'fallacies concerning users and uses';
- 'the power and politics of English'; and
- 'teaching World Englishes'. (1992: 2)

In his discussion of the first issue, Kachru argues in favour of the strength of his model of the spread of English in terms of 'three concentric circles': the inner circle (ENL societies), the outer circle (ESL societies) and the expanding circle (EFL societies), and he also discusses the statistics of English worldwide. In the section on the 'characteristics of the stratification' he discusses the terminology used by researchers to describe the structures of outer-circle Englishes, either as *a lectal range* similar to that found in a creole continuum (e.g. Platt 1977; Platt and Weber 1980), or as a *cline* in English bilingualism (e.g. Kachru 1983).

Kachru's analysis of the 'interactional contexts of World Englishes' acknowledges insights from Halliday (1978, etc.), Labov (1972a, b) and Saville-Troike (1981), which have stimulated work on discourse strategies, speech acts and code-mixing. He explains the linguistic and cultural 'implications of the spread'

---

[5] There seems to be general agreement that the recent study of World Englishes can be dated from the two conferences on English as a world language that took place in 1978, one in April at the East–West Center in Hawaii, and the second in June–July at the University of Illinois at Urbana-Champaign. Braj Kachru played a major role in both conferences (Smith 1981; Kachru 1982). These conferences discussed the sociopolitical contexts of English in the world; the use of English in former anglophone colonies; the processes of 'nativisation' and 'acculturation' in such societies; and the description of varieties of English (Kachru 1992: 1). Throughout the 1980s, other conferences were organised under the auspices of such organisations as IATEFL, TESOL, the Georgetown University Round Table and the East–West Center. By the mid-1980s the term 'World Englishes' was gaining currency (Kachru 1985; Kachru and Smith 1988). The justification for the adoption of this term, Kachru argues, is that: 'The term symbolises the functional and formal variations, divergent sociolinguistic contexts, ranges and varieties of English in creativity, and various types of acculturation in parts of the Western and non-Western world. This concept emphasizes 'WE-ness', and not the dichotomy between *us* and *them* (the native and non-native users)' (1992: 2).

of World Englishes in the outer and expanding circles, while noting that a consideration of 'descriptive and prescriptive concerns' involves an evaluation of the main tenets of theoretical and applied linguistics; an evaluation using the descriptive techniques, methodology and analytical tools of sociolinguistics in the context of the research initiatives of scholars of the outer circle.

The issue of 'the bilingual's creativity and the literary canon' refers to the existence and development of the 'new literatures in English' that have appeared in Africa, Asia and the Caribbean, and the extent to which these 'contact literatures in English' have undergone *nativisation* and *acculturation*. Kachru argues that in South Asia, West Africa and Southeast Asia these literatures are 'both nativised and acculturated', as instanced by the work of the 1986 Nobel Prize winner Wole Soyinka from Nigeria, and the 1988 Neustadt Award winner Raja Rao of India, and he emphasises that the issue of the bilingual's creativity is an important area for linguistic, literary and pedagogical research (Kachru 1986c). The notion of 'multi-canons of English' attempts to accommodate the current sociolinguistic realities of World English and World Englishes, where speakers of a wide range of first languages communicate with one another through English. As a result, Kachru argues, English has become acculturated in many 'un-English' sociolinguistic contexts, in many African and Asian societies where there is no shared Judaeo-Christian or European cultural heritage or shared literary canon, and thus has become 'multi-canonical' (Kachru 1991).

Kachru's concept of 'the two faces of English: nativisation and Englishisation' focuses on the reciprocal effects of language contact: i.e. the effect on English in a localised context ('nativisation'), and the effect on local languages in the same situation ('Englishisation'). English vocabulary is borrowed into local languages around the world (Viereck and Bald 1986; Bhatia and Ritchie 1989); but Englishisation also extends to the level of grammar, as in the adoption of impersonal constructions in Indian languages, or the use of passive constructions with a 'by' equivalent in Korean, both of which have been traced to English (Kachru 1992: 8).

The 'fallacies concerning users and uses' comprise a number of mistaken beliefs, including that English is primarily learnt for its international utility and currency; that it is primarily learnt to communicate with people from inner-circle societies; that the aim of learning English is to adopt a native model of English proficiency; and that 'expatriate' teachers and advisors play a major role in formulating English teaching policies. A consideration of the 'power and politics of English' involves issues related to the ideological, cultural and elitist power of English, associated with 'the immense economic advantage of English to the countries in the Inner Circle, particularly Britain and the United States' (Kachru 1992: 9). On this point Kachru argues that

> [t]he very existence of their power thus provides the Inner Circle with incentives for devising ways to maintain attitudinal and formal control; it is both a psychological and sociopolitical process. And linguistic control

is yet another such strategy, exercised in three ways: by the use of various channels of codification and by controlling these channels; by the attitude towards linguistic innovations [in the Outer Circle]: and by suggesting dichotomies which are sociolinguistically and pragmatically unrealistic. (1992: 9)

On the last issue of 'teaching World Englishes', Kachru argues that this enterprise is particularly intellectually challenging as it relates to three academic areas, those of language, literature and methodology. It is a 'paradigm shift' with wide-reaching implications for English in a postcolonial world order of the kind indicated above. Kachru also points to the increased availability of resources for teaching, noting that many of the key academic books in this area appeared in the early or mid-1980s. Kachru's enthusiasm for the teaching of 'World Englishes' was not shared by everyone. By 1990, Randolph Quirk was becoming increasingly worried by what he termed the 'half-baked quackery' of English teachers preaching the gospel of 'varieties of English', and published a polemical paper taking issue with those he thought to be undermining the importance of Standard English. This involved a challenge to the growing study and teaching of 'varieties', and was to lead him into a celebrated yet decorous debate with Kachru (Quirk 1990; Kachru 1991).

Pidgin and creole studies

In the field of World Englishes there has been periodic discussion about the relationship between the study of English-based pidgins and creoles and the development of new Englishes and World Englishes. That such a relationship exists seems clear; what is frequently in dispute however is its exact nature. As early as the early 1960s, Quirk described pidgins as a 'radical deviant' from English, and 'a different language from English, though closely related, rather than as one of the normal regional variants of English' (Quirk 1962: 16–17). Ten years later he argued that Tok Pisin in Papua New Guinea deserved recognition as 'a newly emerged language' (Quirk 1972: 53).

As the study of World Englishes took off in the 1980s, the specialist journals in the field had to decide on how to deal with pidgin and creole varieties. Görlach (1980), in setting out the editorial policy of *English World-Wide*, discusses the place of pidgin and creole linguistics (PCL) in relation to the studies of varieties. He argues that because of the continuum that exists in many societies linking pidgins and creoles with standard languages, their study 'can therefore with some justification be regarded as being part of English or French or Portuguese studies, as is the study of the respective dialects', citing Krio, Tok Pisin and Sranan as cases in point. He also concedes that 'many will not agree that [. . . this] is sufficient reason to treat these languages this way' (1980: 6). McArthur's *English Today* has adopted a similar editorial policy, with articles by creolists such as Le Page (1986) and Todd (1995), as has Kachru's *World Englishes*, which even devoted a recent issue of the journal to a 'Symposium on English-to-pidgin continua', with articles by Mufwene (1997) on speech continua, Siegel (1997) on pidgin and English in Melanesia, Singler (1997) on Liberia's Englishes and Winford (1997) on Caribbean English creole continua.

Todd's (1984) book on *Modern Englishes: Pidgins and Creoles* was primarily devoted to a discussion of Cameroon pidgin English, Tok Pisin and Caribbean creoles in Britain. Todd claims that in her study of 'modern Englishes' she examines types of English 'which have usually been ignored and often despised' but which 'have facilitated communication among millions of people of all races and many creeds' (1984: 1). She discusses the relationship between pidgins and creoles, on the one hand, and English, on the other, thus:

> If the languages we have studied are to be considered varieties of English, then extensive changes occurred, often within one generation, changes that cannot be captured by traditional linguistic models. If we choose to deny that they are varieties of English and argue that, in spite of their vocabularies, in spite of their word order, and in spite of their syntactic patterning, they are relexifications of African, Asiatic or Pacific languages, we are no nearer a solution that accords with orthodox linguistic theory. Instead we are faced with the problems of how and why languages separated by thousands of miles should be so alike structurally or should behave so similarly when in contact with English. The simple fact is that pidginised Englishes cannot easily be assigned to any family tree. Their vocabulary is certainly English but their lack of morphology makes it impossible to assign them unambiguously to any specific language or group of languages. (1984: 248–9)

In a later paper on pidgin and creole Englishes, Todd comments on the marked variation that is detected in most situations where these are used, asserting that 'in every country whose inhabitants speak an English-based Pidgin or Creole, we find not homogeneity but continuous, multilectal diversity' (1995: 35). In a similar vein, she goes on to note that, in the case of Nigeria:

> The unidealised truth seems to be . . . that for many speakers in Nigeria it is now extremely difficult, if not impossible, to separate Nigerian Pidgin from pidginised Nigerian English or anglicised Nigerian Pidgin. Today, in the spoken medium and in the writings of Aik-Imoukhuede, Oyekunle and Saro-Wiwa, we find not compartmentalised English and Pidgin, not even a continuum from basilectal through mesolectal to acrolectal, but a linguistic amalgam where the interinfluencing is so complete that even articulate linguists are not always certain which varieties they are using or why. (1995: 37)

Todd notes that at a time when pidgins and creoles are an object of interest and study for more linguists than in any previous era, they are also, as never before, influenced by World Englishes: 'It is almost as if scholars are building linguistic reservations to capture and preserve features in speech communities that are disappearing and may soon be as extinct in Pidgins as the accusative case endings now are in the English noun' (1995: 38). She expresses four predictions about the development of these varieties: first, that most English-based pidgins and creoles will continue to merge with World Englishes; second, that closer links between the Atlantic and Pacific pidgins and creoles will be documented from archives; third, that increased efforts will be made to standardise the orthographies of pidgins and creoles (e.g. for the Jamaican and Cameroon creoles, in addition to Tok Pisin and Krio); and finally, that high-calibre creative writers will 'internationalise' some pidginised and creolised Englishes. Todd adds that 'English-based Pidgins and Creoles have the capacity to bridge cultures [. . . and] are a solution to the problems raised by Babel' (1995: 39–40). Todd's professional interest in the study of World Englishes is also attested to by her co-authorship of a 'guide to written and spoken English' entitled *International English Usage* (Todd and Hancock 1986). This handbook is aimed at 'the world community of English speakers' and, for the Asian region, provides brief descriptions of Chinese English, Hong Kong English, Japanese English, Malaysian English, Philippine English and Singapore English.

Cheshire (1991b) also comments on problems in the classification of pidgins, creoles and varieties of English. She notes that although some 'pidgin and creole varieties of English' are clearly 'native speaker varieties' others are learned at school and that '[s]ome pidgins are not termed "English" and although English may have played an important role in their linguistic development it is not clear if they are perceived within the community as "English" ' (1991b: 3). She cites as an example Faraclas (1991) on Nigerian pidgin. Despite the issue of indeterminacy in this context, it seems clear that 'creolistics' overlaps with the study of World Englishes, although even Görlach is ambivalent on this issue. In his 1996 paper, Görlach discusses the existence of 'various forms of broken English', including code-switching, pidgins, creoles, cants and mixed languages. On the case of pidgins and creoles, Görlach asserts that the 'modern Englishes' of Todd (1984) are simply not varieties of English, but are 'independent languages on all counts' (1996: 167). Other situations in areas where English and creoles co-exist, e.g. in the Caribbean, are much more complex. Varieties that are 'marginally English' may increase in number, Görlach concludes, but it seems that 'the problem will remain one of the more messy facts of life' (1996: 171).

The relevance of pidgin and creole studies to the notion of Hong Kong English will be immediately apparent to those familiar with the language history of South China as there are a number of possible linkages to the earlier history of Chinese pidgin English; although it is surprising that the existence of such connections appears to have escaped the notice of most Hong Kong linguists. In fact, as I will demonstrate in later chapters, the origins of 'Chinese English' can be traced back to the early seventeenth century when British mercantile trading ships first reached Macao and Canton (Guangzhou). What much later came to be called 'Chinese Pidgin English [CPE]' (Baker and Mühlhäusler 1990) was at first referred to as 'broken English', 'jargon' and 'Canton English', and various descriptions of this variety were published in the late eighteenth and early nineteenth centuries. One of the earliest analyses of the 'Canton jargon' was authored by the American Samuel Wells Williams (1812–84), one of the most famous sinologists of the nineteenth century, who later went on to become the first Professor of Chinese at Yale University.

Canton jargon or 'Canton English' flourished during the heyday of Canton trade from around 1750 until 1842, at which time British naval and military aggression forced the Qing government to agree to the annexation of Hong Kong island. After 1842, the treaty ports of Amoy (Xiamen), Foochow (Fuzhou), Ningpo (Ningbo) and Shanghai (in addition to Canton) were opened to British ships and Chinese pidgin English spread to these ports. In Hong Kong, linguists typically claim that 'pidgin English has virtually disappeared' (Gibbons 1987: 5), that 'CPE is by now effectively no longer spoken' (Baker and Mühlhäusler 1990: 92), or that it is 'almost extinct' (Shi 1991: 1). Such views may have some truth, but they also tend to obscure the historical links and resonances between varieties of English in southern China such as 'Canton jargon', Chinese pidgin English, China Coast English and contemporary 'Hong Kong English'.

Applied linguistic approaches

Applied linguistic approaches to varieties of World English began in the 1960s with the work of Halliday, MacIntosh and Strevens (1964), who sought to apply insights derived from 'the linguistic sciences' to the new field of applied linguistics, which in Britain and the USA was broadly concerned with theories of language learning, language teaching and language pedagogy. In this early work, Halliday *et al.* discuss the use of varieties of English around the world, noting that 'during the period of colonial rule it seemed totally obvious and immutable that the form of English used by professional people in England was the only conceivable model for use in education overseas' (1964: 292). By the 1960s, they argue, things were very different, and now there was a choice available between American, British, Australian and other regional variants. Thus, they claim (and this has a rather familiar sound) that:

> English is no longer the possession of the British, or even the British and the Americans, but an international language which increasing numbers of people adopt for at least some of their purposes, without thereby denying (at least in intention) the value of their own languages; and this one language, English, exists in an increasingly large number of different varieties ... But the most important development of all is seen in the emergence of varieties of English that are identified with and are specific to particular countries from among the former British colonies. In West Africa, in the West Indies, and in Pakistan and India ... it is no longer accepted by the majority that the English of England, with RP as its accent, are [*sic*] the only possible models of English to be set before the young. (1964: 293–4)

They then go on to discuss the criteria for judging the use of a particular variety as a teaching model, suggesting that there are two major considerations: first, that it is used by a reasonably large number of educated people; and, second, that it is mutually intelligible with other varieties used by educated speakers from other societies. They add that: '[g]iven these constraints, "to speak like an Englishman" is by no means the only or obvious target for the foreign learner' (1964: 296).

The work of Halliday and his associates, and the expression of similar viewpoints in other academic papers, prompted the American Clifford Prator to publish a spirited yet historically misplaced attack on what he called 'The British heresy in TESL' (Prator 1968). This paper is of interest not least because it predates the Kachru–Quirk debate (see above) by some twenty years; but also because some of the issues it raises are still discussed today (see Romaine 1997). Prator's central argument is that 'in a country where English is not spoken natively but is widely used as the medium of instruction, to set up the local variety of English as the ultimate model to be imitated by those learning the language' is 'unjustifiable intellectually and not conducive to the best possible results' (1968: 459). That 'the doctrine of establishing local models for TESL . . . appears to be a natural outgrowth of the much deplored colonial mentality' is, he suggests, plainly seen in former British colonies such as India, Pakistan, Ceylon, Ghana and Nigeria, and is linked to the prolonged use of English as a medium of instruction which moves people to start feeling 'possessive' about the language (1968: 460).

Prator notes that British linguists and teaching specialists, unlike the French and Americans, have accepted and developed this doctrine, as is shown by the kinds of arguments put forward in Halliday, MacIntosh and Strevens (1964), and Le Page (1966).[6] He then queries the notion that, in an ESL ('English as a Second Language') society, English could emerge as one of the indigenous languages of that society. He identifies seven fallacies associated with the British heresy:

- that second-language varieties of English can legitimately be equated with mother-tongue varieties;
- that second-language varieties of English really exist as coherent, homogeneous linguistic systems, describable in the usual way as the speech of an identifiable social group;
- that a few minor concessions in the type of English taught in schools would tend to or suffice to stabilise the language;
- that one level of a language (its phonology) can be allowed to change without entailing corresponding changes at other levels;
- that it would a simple matter to establish a second-language variety of English as an effective instructional model once it had been clearly identified and described;

[6] See also Strevens (1977, 1980, 1985).

- that students would long be content to study English in a situation in which, as a matter of policy, they were denied access to a mother-tongue model; and
- that granting a second-language variety of English official status in a country's schools would lead to its widespread adoption as a mother tongue.

According to Prator these attitudes were definitely a *British* heresy, as American linguists were of like mind in asserting that the only possible model of pronunciation was a 'mother-tongue' one, and that: 'in the eyes of both the French and the Americans, . . . if teachers in many different parts of the world aim at the same stable, well documented model, the general effect of their instruction will be convergent'. Just as there is increasing homogenisation in mother-tongue societies, the forces of 'greater mobility, new media of communication, urbanization, [and] mass education' will also influence second-language varieties (1968: 469–70).

Romaine (1997) provides a point-by-point refutation of Prator's arguments and then turns to a discussion of the ideologies embedded in Prator's paper, with reference to the notion of 'hegemony'. She quotes Gramsci (1985) to the effect that:

> Every time the question of the language surfaces, in one way or another, it means that a series of other problems are coming to the fore: the formation and enlargement of the governing class, the need to establish more intimate and secure relationships between the governing groups and the national-popular mass, in other words to reorganize the cultural hegemony. (Gramsci 1985: 183–4)

The hegemony here is about who controls the language, and who has the right to decide issues of language planning and policies. Romaine compares the Prator debate in the late 1960s to domestic debates in Britain in the late 1980s and early 1990s about the question of 'language standards', the discussions that accompanied the Kingman Report, Cox Report and the development of a national curriculum. Whatever the outcome in Britain, the outcome in Asia, and in other parts of the world where World Englishes are found, has generally meant a defeat for the kinds of viewpoints expressed by Prator in the mid and late 1960s. Since the 1980s, the World Englishes perspective on applied linguistics has been communicated through a number of journals, including *TESOL Quarterly* and *World Englishes*, as well as articles on this specific topic (Kachru 1990; Kachru and Nelson 1996; Brown 2000).

The lexicographical approach

The dimension of lexicography and dictionary compilation is of singular importance in the codification and elaboration of vernacular languages. It was the emergence and development of dictionaries in the sixteenth, seventeenth and eighteenth centuries that fixed and lent authority to 'English' as a national language. The high point of eighteenth-century lexicography was Samuel Johnson's

A Dictionary of the English Language, which was to hold an authoritative position in English letters for a century. In the course of its compilation, Johnson's reflections on the nature of the task shifted a good deal, as the following much-quoted excerpt from the *Preface* reveals:

> Those who have been persuaded to think well of my design, will require that it should fix our language, and put a stop to those alterations which time and chance have hitherto been suffered to make in it without opposition. With this consequence I will confess that I flattered myself for a while; but now begin to fear that I have indulged expectation which neither reason nor experience can justify... may the lexicographer be derided, who being able to produce no example of a nation that has preserved their words and phrases from mutability, shall imagine that his dictionary can embalm his language, and secure it from corruption and decay... (Johnson 1773, cited by Bolton [1966] 1973: 151)

Some 130 years later, Johnson's dictionary began to be replaced by the *Oxford English Dictionary*. The focus of the *OED* was avowedly anglocentric, as its editor, Murray, himself stated in his discussion of 'General explanations' (to the *New English Dictionary on Historical Principles*):

> [T]he English vocabulary contains a nucleus or central mass of many thousand words whose 'Anglicity' is unquestioned; some of them only literary, some of them only colloquial, the great majority at once literary and colloquial, – they are the *Common Words* of the language. But they are linked on every side with other words which are less and less entitled to this appellation, and which pertain ever more and more distinctly to the domain of local dialect, of the slang and cant of 'sets' and classes, of the peculiar technicalities of trades and processes, of the scientific terminology common to all civilized nations, of the actual languages of other lands and peoples. And there is absolutely no defining line in any direction: the circle of the English language has a well-defined centre but no discernible circumference. (Murray 1888, cited in Bolton and Crystal 1969: 60)

The domestic English dictionary tradition as exemplified by Johnson and Murray thus embodied two principles: the potential of dictionaries for 'fixing' and standardising the language (however unrealistic this might turn out to be); and the identification of a 'nucleus' or core of the language (defined according to anglicity). The implementation of that latter principle meant in practice a rather haphazard coverage in the *OED* of the colonial vocabulary used in Britain's far-flung possessions throughout Africa and Asia, a limited coverage of British regional dialect words and a partial inventory of American vocabulary. In an Asian context, however, Yule and Burnell's (1886) *Hobson-Jobson*; Dennys' (1894) *A Descriptive Dictionary of British Malaya*; and Scott's (1896/7) papers on 'The Malay words in English' were used as sources for the first edition of the *OED*, although in a rather patchy fashion (Görlach 1990; Benson 1997). The notion of 'core' versus 'periphery' also led to a pronounced ethnocentrism in British dictionary construction, as Benson (2001) has detailed, with particular reference to the treatment of China and things Chinese in the *Oxford English Dictionary*.

The first dictionaries of World Englishes were arguably glossaries produced in the United States at the beginning of the nineteenth century. These included Pickering (1816), Bartlett (1848), Farmer (1889), Thornton (1912) and Horwill (1935). Noah Webster, by contrast, was concerned to produce a national dictionary, for reasons partly if not wholly political, because '[a]s an independent nation, our honor requires us to have a system of our own, in language as well as government'. Webster further predicted that: '[t]hese causes will produce, in a course of time, a language in North America, as different from the future language of England, as the modern Dutch, Danish and Swedish are from the German, or from one another' (1789: 220–3). His first dictionary appeared early in the nineteenth century (1806), but it was not until 1828 that his major work, *An American Dictionary of the English Language*, was published. In the twentieth century, Webster's was complemented by a number of other works on American English including Craigie and Hulbert (1938–44), Mathews (1951), and a number of dialect dictionaries including Cassidy (1985). Earlier dictionaries of Canadian English include Avis (1967), which has recently been superseded by *The Canadian Oxford Dictionary* (Barber 1999).

Australian lexicography can be traced back to Morris (1898), which was intended as a supplement to the *OED*, and to the list that Lake compiled as a supplement to Webster's (1898) (cited in Görlach 1995b). It is only in recent years that Australia has had its own 'inclusive' national dictionary, *The Macquarie Dictionary*, which was first published in 1981. In 1988, Oxford University Press also published *The Australian National Dictionary*, subtitled *A Dictionary of Australianisms on Historical Principles*. In 1997, the *Dictionary of New Zealand English* appeared, edited by Orsman (1997). South Africa has its own dictionary tradition, starting with Pettman (1913), and continuing to the present with Branford (1976, 1987), and Silva's (1998) *A Dictionary of South African English on Historical Principles*.

India developed its own tradition of glossaries and wordlists, including Whitworth's *An Anglo-Indian Dictionary* (1885) and Yule and Burnell's *Hobson-Jobson: a Glossary of Anglo-Indian Words and Phrases* (1886). Later works have included Rao (1954) and Hawkins (1984), but as yet no fully autonomous national dictionary for India or other South Asian societies has appeared. In West Africa, there have been plans for a number of years to complete a *Dictionary of West African English*, but so far this project remains incomplete (Banjo and Young 1982). For the Caribbean, there are Cassidy and Le Page's *Dictionary of Jamaican English* (1967), and Holm's *Dictionary of Bahamian English* (1982), as well as the recent *Dictionary of Caribbean English Usage* (Allsopp 1996).

Dictionaries are profoundly important for the recognition of World Englishes. As Quirk (1990) has pointed out, it is only when a world variety of English is supported by codification (chiefly expressed through national dictionaries) that one can make a strong claim that such a variety is 'institutionalised'. Perhaps the best example of this in recent times has been the case of Australia where *The*

Macquarie Dictionary has been largely accepted as a 'national dictionary' or, in their own words, as 'Australia's own'. Oxford's *The Australian National Dictionary* is organised on a 'supplementary' basis, unlike the 'inclusive' *Macquarie*, which is intended to stand against the *OED* or *Webster's*. It is also relevant that both dictionaries appeared at a time when Australian society was approaching its bicentennial celebrations and many politicians had begun to advocate the formal political separation from the British crown, and the formation of an independent Australian republic.

By the mid-1990s the editors of *Macquarie* had also become activists for the promotion of World Englishes in Asia. In 1996 and 1997, *Macquarie* helped organise three major conferences in Southeast Asia on the theme *English is an Asian Language. Macquarie's* efforts in this area have a specific lexicographical aim – to play a role in documenting the 'Englishes' of Asia, through the inclusion of Asian English entries and Asian English perspectives, in their dictionaries. The proposed *Macquarie Concise Dictionary: World English in an Asian Context* will include a large number of vocabulary items used in the new Englishes of Southeast Asia, particularly those of Hong Kong, Malaysia, Singapore and the Philippines. Susan Butler, *Macquarie's* publisher, argues that:

> [T]his dictionary will shift attitudes in the region to English. Rather than being seen as an alien language, and a conduit of Western culture, it will be evident that English can also express Asian culture. The flexibility of English, its ability to serve as a vehicle for the expression of local culture, has been one of its great characteristics since it left English shores. (Butler 1997a: 123)

A somewhat different approach to the lexicography of World Englishes is that of Bill Gates' *Encarta Dictionary of World English*, whose publication in 1999 provoked a hail of criticism from a number of quarters, and left one reviewer musing:

> Is this English we are being offered? Or is it the beginning, the beta version, the build 1.0, of an Orwellian newspeak – which may be doubleplusgood in its own way, but nonetheless a language more suited to be uttered over a glass of Victory Gin, while we listen to the crackling Disney telescreen with its news of defeats of other brave new worlds who speak alien tongues, like old English or old German or Yiddish or Masai, and who behave in ways that Mr. Gates and his chums could not countenance? (Winchester 1999: 14)

Popularisers, critical linguists and futurologists

During the 1980s, at the same time as interest in the study of international varieties of English was growing within western universities, a number of popular and popularising accounts of the spread of English were being published in Britain and North America. McCrum, Cran and MacNeil co-authored *The Story of*

English (1986), which accompanied the worldwide broadcast of a nine-part BBC documentary on the history and internationalisation of the English language. Although the series and the book were a popular success in both Europe and North America, they provoked a strong reaction from both linguists intolerant of descriptive inaccuracies, and cultural critics resentful of their perceived triumphalism.

That the charges of triumphalism were justified seems hard to deny. The first part of the television series, 'An English-speaking world', contained such clichés in Robert MacNeil's commentary as 'World War Two was the finest hour for British English'; 'The sun set on the Union Jack, but not on the English language'; and 'English, the language of the skies, is now becoming the language of the seven seas'. The book, largely authored by McCrum, was somewhat more restrained in its commentary but nevertheless found it difficult to avoid hyperbole in places. The style of the book, like much popular academic writing, is journalistic in the sense that a great deal of rather academically complex linguistic research has been condensed if not simplified, footnotes are omitted and references largely consigned to an appendix. The clarity of discussion at times is often impressive but the linguistic chauvinism, if that is what it is, is sometimes intrusive. In the first chapter the authors proclaim that '[t]he rise of English is a remarkable success story . . . English at the end of the twentieth century is more widely scattered, more widely spoken and written, than any other language has ever been. It has become *the* language of the planet, the first truly global language' (McCrum *et al.* 1986: 19).[7] They then proceed to discuss the 'astonishing' statistics of English, citing the numbers of speakers, the richness of its vocabulary and its use in international communications. Their triumphalism was juxtaposed with a brand of 'linguistic liberalism' that also recognised the existence of 'new Englishes':

> The emergence of English as a global phenomenon – as either a first, second or foreign language – has recently inspired the idea . . . that we should talk not of English, but of many Englishes, especially in Third World countries where the use of English is no longer part of the colonial legacy, but the result of decisions made since independence. (1986: 19–20)

[7] McCrum *et al.* are also moved to proclaim the political virtues of the language, when they identify and explain the 'peculiar genius' of English which, they claim, is essentially democratic:

> The arts of speech and literature have been perhaps the special contribution of the English people to European culture, or at least the one for which they are most respected! This, one could speculate, may have something to do with the history of the language. After the Norman invasion, English was neglected and ill-considered by the Latin-writing and French-speaking authorities; so it was unregulated and unimposed upon; from the earliest times it was naturally the language of protest and dissent, the language of the many rather than the few. Its genius was, and still is, essentially democratic. It has given expression to the voice of freedom from Wat Tyler, to Tom Paine, to Thomas Jefferson, to Edmund Burke, to the Chartists, to Abraham Lincoln, to the Suffragettes, to Winston Churchill, to Martin Luther King. It is well equipped to be a world language, to give voice to the aspirations of the Third World as much as the inter-communication of the First World. (1986: 47–8)

To be fair, McCrum *et al.* do at times temper their celebration of English with mention of '[t]he darker, aggressive side of the spread of global English which includes the elimination of linguistic diversity and the attack on deep cultural roots' (1986: 44), as in Quebec. Pidgins and creoles in Black Africa are also mentioned as, we are told, the English language is 'peculiarly susceptible to pidginization' (1986: 45), although they also suggest that 'broken English' is the predominant form of the language in many countries, including Sierra Leone, Uganda, Cameroon, Zambia, Zimbabwe, Bangladesh, the Philippines and Pakistan.

They go on to compare the 1980s vitality of the English language to that of the Elizabethan 'golden age', citing new varieties of 'Spanglish', 'Slanguage' and the multiculturalism of Indianisation and Africanisation that recharges the voltage of innovation. The English language today, they claim, is 'perhaps closer in spirit and self-expression to the Shakespearian extravaganza than at any time since the seventeenth century', adding that, whether spoken or written, 'it offers a medium of almost limitless potential and surprise' (1986: 48).

Chapter 9 deals with the topic of 'The New Englishes', and in this chapter McCrum *et al.* survey the rise of global English and the development of 'new Englishes', commenting on Robert Burchfield's argument that English may break up into mutually unintelligible varieties. McCrum *et al.* partly endorse Burchfield's thesis, claiming that their own observations in the Caribbean, Sierra Leone, India and Singapore support his theory of separate language evolution. In the Caribbean, they relate the existence of creole varieties to the rise of a 'linguistic nationalism' entailing 'the separate development of English', and 'the disintegration of Standard English' in societies such as Jamaica (1986: 309). The authors quote a number of Jamaican academics and writers who regard the rapidly developing, reggae-influenced Jamaican English of the 1980s as a politically distinct language, identified variously as 'Jamaican creole', 'the Jamaican language' and 'nation-language', noting ironically that 'for the mass of the population the idea of a nation-language is a rarefied concept confined to the seminar rooms of the University of the West Indies' (1986: 317). They then discuss the role of English in West Africa, in societies such as Gambia, Ghana, Nigeria and Sierra Leone, where English has an official status in domains such as government, law and education, but where pidgin or creole English is widely used as a *lingua franca*. In Sierra Leone, Krio, a creole based on English, Yoruba and Portuguese elements, is widely used, and its use has been strengthened by its codification through *A Krio–English Dictionary*, the government's promotion of the variety as a national language and the emergence of a local Krio literature (1986: 320–2).

McCrum *et al.* also survey the use of English in India, noting that one estimate of the total number of speakers is around 70 million, which exceeds the total for English speakers in Britain. As in the Caribbean, there is a continuum of spoken English ranging from 'British RP' to street pidgins, and the authors note 'the richness and completeness' of the use of English in India – its use as an official or 'state' language, in education and in such major dailies as *The Times of India* (Bombay); *The Pioneer* (Lucknow); and *The Telegraph* (Calcutta) (1986: 322). Quoting Anthony Burgess, they affirm that Indian English is:

> [a] whole language, complete with the colloquialisms of Calcutta and London, Shakespearian archaisms, bazaar whinings, references to the Hindu pantheon, the jargon of Indian litigation, and shrill Babu irritability all together. It's not pure English, but it's like the English of Shakespeare, Joyce and Kipling – gloriously impure. (1986: 322)

They go on to stress the importance of English in Indian creative writing and literature and argue that Indian English has now developed 'its own literary credibility'. Indian creative writing, novels, poetry and journalism now have an international reputation. Linguistically, there is also interest in compiling a definitive Indian–English dictionary (1986: 332–4). McCrum *et al.* then proceed to discuss the use of English in Singapore, described as:

> the most aggressively self-modernizing nation state in the Pacific, a model for Malaya, Korea, Taiwan and the Philippines . . . [whose] population of about two and a half million people – Chinese, Malay, Indian – is officially encouraged to speak and write English, from the cradle to the grave. (1986: 336)

They also give examples of 'Singlish', the informal spoken variety of Singapore English indigenous to the island-state: words like *shiok* (terrific, beyond description); big *bluff*, man, he! (he's just a show-off); you can *drop* here (you can get out here), etc. (1986: 336). Attitudes to Singapore English, they suggest, are contradictory: on the one hand, it serves as a marker of a proud local identity, on the other it is sometimes the focus of language complaints. In 1978, Lee Kuan Yew, Singapore's elder statesman and then prime minister, described it as 'a very strange Singapore pidgin', and 'a Singapore dialect English which is not ideal . . . which we can improve upon if we concentrate our effort and considerable resources' (McCrum *et al.* 1986: 338). McCrum *et al.* claim that in future 'much more attention will be focused on Singlish as a medium of dissent, a rejection of the formal standards of the past and the voice of a new and distinctive nationalism' (1986: 338). Finally, they speculate that, like Jamaican English, Singlish and other localised forms of Asian English are breaking away from the norms of British English, lending support to Burchfield's thesis that World English is currently mimicking Latin in a process of fragmentation. They conclude:

> English will probably continue to flourish at two quite distinct levels: International Standard (internationally functional) and Local Alternative (locally functional). The former will evolve more or less uniformly throughout the Standard English-using world . . . The latter, the Local Alternative,

will become more and more distinctive and will indeed throw up local literatures, though these are always likely to be overshadowed by the International Standard. (1986: 340)

What is significant about McCrum *et al.*'s discussion of World Englishes is,
alongside its obvious triumphalism and its enthusiasm for world literatures in
English, their explanation of 'new Englishes' in terms of 'linguistic nationalism'.
Such an explanation may work for the creoles of the Caribbean, but does not
function well for African and Asian varieties of English. In these contexts, complex patterns of use and attitude relate to issues of ethnicity and nationalism, as
a review of the literature reveals (see, for example, Gupta 1994 on Singapore;
Sibayan and Gonzalez 1996 on the Philippines; and Pennycook 1994 on Malaysia
and Singapore).

Other popularising works in the 1980s and 1990s were authored by David
Crystal, including *The English Language* (1988), *The Cambridge Encyclopedia of
the English Language* (1995) and *English as a Global Language* (1997), which, as
Crystal explains, was originally prompted by the suggestion of Mauro Mujica,
a leader of the US English campaign lobbying for recognition of English as
the official language of the USA. Its aim was 'to explain to members of his
organization [US English], in a succinct and factual way, and without political
bias, why English has achieved such a worldwide status' (1997: ix). Crystal also
mentions that the report was intended originally for private circulation, but he
later decided to rework and expand it into a book for a wider audience. In spite
of the fact that the suggestion for the study came from Mujica, Crystal claims
that 'this book has not been written according to any political agenda', and that
he was chiefly concerned to present an account of 'the relevant facts and factors'
relating to the description of a 'world language', the place of English, and the
future of English as a global language (1997: x). This slim book is distinguished
by a number of arguments, including his assertion that the 'remarkable growth'
of English is, simply stated, explicable largely in terms of the fact that 'it is a
language which has repeatedly found itself in the right place at the right time'
(1997: 110). In a similar vein, a number of arguments in Crystal's analysis of
the future of 'global English' are reduced to the evocative slogan of 'having your
cake and eating it', a phrase for which Crystal *qua* populariser appears to have a
particular fondness (1997: 138).

Given the triumphalist tone of many such popular works, it is perhaps hardly
surprising that the voices of a 'critical linguistic' approach began to be heard in
the 1990s, and the discourse on World Englishes changed gear dramatically in
1992 with the publication of Robert Phillipson's *Linguistic Imperialism*. At the
centre of Phillipson's theoretical approach on 'linguistic imperialism' are a series
of arguments about the political relations between what Phillipson characterises
as the 'core English-speaking countries' (Britain, the USA, Canada, Australia
and New Zealand) and the 'periphery-English countries' where English either
has the status of a second language (e.g. Nigeria, India, Singapore), or is a foreign

and 'international link language' (e.g. Scandinavia, Japan) (1992: 17). The nature of this relationship, Phillipson argues, is one of structural and systemic inequality, in which the political and economic hegemony of western anglophone powers is established or maintained over scores of developing nations, particularly those formerly colonies of European powers. The political and economic power of such nations in the Third World is, moreover, accompanied by 'English linguistic imperialism', defined by Phillipson in the following terms:

> A working definition of *English linguistic imperialism* is that *the dominance of English is asserted and maintained by the establishment and continuous reconstitution of structural and cultural inequalities between English and other languages*. Here *structural* refers broadly to material properties (for example, institutions, financial allocations) and *cultural* to immaterial or ideological properties (for example, attitudes, pedagogic principles). English linguistic imperialism is one example of *linguicism*, which is defined as 'ideologies, structures, and practices which are used to legitimate, effectuate, and reproduce an unequal division of power and resources (both material and immaterial) between groups which are defined on the basis of language' . . . English linguistic imperialism is seen as a sub-type of linguicism. (1992: 47, original emphasis)

Drawing substantially on Galtung's (1980) analysis, Phillipson enumerates six types of interrelated imperialism: economic, political, military, communicative, cultural and social. Cultural imperialism, defined as 'the sum of processes by which a society is brought into the modern world system and how its dominating stratum is attracted, pressured, forced, and sometimes bribed into shaping social institutions to correspond to, or even promote, the values and structures of the dominating center of the system' (Schiller 1976: 9), includes such subtypes as 'scientific imperialism' and 'linguistic imperialism'. Scientific imperialism is significant because it helps the West maintain a near-monopoly of scientific research at centre universities (which hold those of periphery societies in a relationship of dependency) and forms 'the framework within which the relationship between the core English-speaking countries and periphery-English countries in the ELT (English Language Teaching) field needs to be seen' (Phillipson 1992: 58).

Phillipson also asks who is responsible for the global spread of English in recent decades, and for the 'monolingual and anglocentric' professionalism that has accompanied its teaching worldwide. The 'allies in the international promotion of English' were Britain and the USA, but they, or their political leaders and cultural agencies (such as the British Council and USIS), are only partly responsible. Phillipson claims that the main force has been structural:

> The ELT policy-makers themselves, in Centre and Periphery, in Ministries of Education, universities, curriculum development centres and the like are part of a hegemonic structure. They have shared interests and beliefs, a shared stake in the scientific and educational status quo, a shared

perception of what the central internal constraints are. The structure of academic imperialism has ensured that Centre training and expertise have been disseminated worldwide, with change and innovative professionalism tending to be generated by the Centre. (1992: 305)

Phillipson contends that anglocentric and monolingual professionalism 'almost inevitably' leads to 'a linguicist devaluing of local languages and cultures' (1992: 306). He particularly points to the neglect of African languages in this context, and further argues that in India the power of English 'perverts the efforts of education, diverts funds wastefully, and thwarts the natural multilingual developmental process', noting that '[i]f English linguistic imperialism had not been in operation, other languages would have had much more scope for development in periphery-English countries, and these languages might have followed the course of the languages of many European countries over the past century' (1992: 306). In the final pages, Phillipson restates the objectives of his work:

> The aim of this book has been to try to clarify linguistic imperialism past and present, to unpick some of the relevant strands, and to make some significant connections. It has hopefully shed some light on how the 'white man's burden' became the English native-speaking teacher's burden, and how the role played by ELT is integral to the functioning of the contemporary world order. Linguicism has been evolved as a construct for understanding how language decisions effect unequal resource and power allocation. It seems highly likely that in many neo-colonial contexts linguicism has taken over from racism as an ideology which legitimates an unequal division of power and resources. Linguicism is a neologism which has been applied in the present study to the question of the global dissemination of a language. It has also been elaborated in parallel in minority education studies as a concept for capturing the relationship between the language of the dominant group and dominated (indigenous and immigrant) groups. (1992: 318)

He further suggests that his study demonstrates 'in what way language contributes to certain types of inequality, in the contemporary world as much as in the colonial one' (1992: 318). Phillipson urges the mobilisation of language by changing the structure of such relationships, by studying 'the new forms that linguicism will take in a changing world' while promoting 'linguistic human rights for dominated languages', and by 'alternative aid strategies' in the realm of language education. Finally, Phillipson asks whether ELT can help create 'greater linguistic and social equality', and whether 'a critical ELT' can help fight linguicism (1992: 319).

Pennycook's *The Cultural Politics of English as an International Language* (1994) also deserves consideration because, like Phillipson (1992), the author adopts a specifically political approach in analysing the spread of English throughout the world. Pennycook acknowledges Phillipson's work throughout, endorses his critique of the role of applied linguistics and ELT in 'helping to legitimate the contemporary capitalist order' (1994: 24), and seconds his view that anglophone countries (Britain and America) have promoted English throughout the world 'for economic and political purposes' and 'to protect and promote capitalist interests' (1994: 22). He praises Phillipson for 'helping us to understand how and why the global dominance of English has occurred' (1994: 68), for deconstructing the supposed neutrality of ELT in terms of its task 'to ensure that Third World countries did not leave the capitalist fold or harm those with investments there' (1994: 39), and (no great surprises here) for pointing out that institutions such as the British Council have been 'unabashedly Anglicist' (1994: 146).

While acknowledging the work of Phillipson, Pennycook distances himself from him to a degree, arguing that his own work has a different orientation and that his 'intervention' is located not in language planning but in teaching, where he is concerned to promote a 'critical pedagogy' that would intervene between English and contiguous discourses. His approach is thus at variance with Phillipson's deterministic thesis that sees the spread of English as 'a priori imperialistic, hegemonic, or linguisticist'. Pennycook explains his rejection of determinism with four reasons:

- he is engaged in a struggle against 'all deterministic theses';
- he rejects 'the totalizing tendencies of much critical theory';
- he accepts that there are those 'who have learned and benefited from English'; and
- he is concerned 'to develop some other space for those of us who teach English' (1994: 69).

Since 1994, Pennycook has sought to advance and refine a critical perspective on both World Englishes and applied linguistics throughout a number of his writings, including *English and the Discourses of Colonialism* (1998) and *Critical Applied Linguistics* (2001). Both Phillipson and Pennycook have been influential in establishing the agenda for the critical discussion of World English(es) in the last ten years or so. Related work by others includes Eggington and Wren (1997), Holborow (1999), Ricento (2000), Skutknabb-Kangas (2000) and Tollefson (1995, 2002).

On the futurology front, Graddol's (1997) *The Future of English?* offers a rather different perspective on a number of questions related to the spread of World Englishes, even-handedly rejecting the claim that global English is by definition neo-colonialistic in its orientation, and dismissing Crystal's notion of 'world standard English' in favour of a 'polycentric' future for English standards. Graddol notes that 'English is rarely the main, or direct cause of . . . language loss' (1997: 39). Graddol's approach marks a notable shift away from Phillipson's political and economic determinism, and his analysis appears to move the discussion of 'global English' back into the orbit of liberal-democratic political discussion, although he also warns of the role of English in establishing 'global inequalities' and language shift. At the core of Graddol's reasoning seems to be the belief that a new world order is currently being formed as the global balance of wealth shifts from the West to Asia. Whether this prediction, widely accepted at the beginning of the 1990s, will in fact hold, remains to be seen. Since 1998, a serious economic crisis has hit most Asian economies, including Hong Kong, Indonesia, Japan, Malaysia, the Philippines and Thailand, and the economic future for these societies now seems considerably less secure than it did a decade ago. All of which may serve to emphasise Graddol's repeated assertion that forecasting or prediction is always an inexact science.

Graddol's 'state-of-the-art' report on English also serves to emphasise a second issue: the fact that in the literature one has seen the focus of discussion shift from the centrality of linguistic 'features', via sociolinguistics and the sociology of language, to the overtly political analysis of international relations, postcolonial theory and questions of economic and human geography, with a measure of multi-disciplinary 'globalisation theory' added into the mix. Which again tends to highlight the shift of discourses in this academic arena, away from the 'linguistic' to the 'non-linguistic', away from the description of linguistic features to the cultural and political analysis of the English language in the world.

Current issues

The review of the literature presented above demonstrates just how far the debates and discourses on World Englishes and new Englishes have come since the first identification of this topic in the late 1970s and early 1980s. Within the developing discourses of World Englishes, I earlier identified a number of overlapping and intersecting approaches to the study of this area of linguistics, including the 'English studies' approach, the 'sociolinguistic' approach, the 'applied linguistic' approach, the 'lexicographical' approach, the 'populariser' approach and the 'critical linguistics' approach. What emerges from a study of the academic literature is a picture of a changing discoursal map, marked by a number of paradigm shifts in the last twenty years.

In the late 1970s and early 1980s, linguists such as Richards, Platt, Pride and Trudgill and Hannah were concerned primarily to discuss the 'features' of 'new Englishes' by using a structuralist linguistic methodology and a sociolinguistic commentary. The essence of this approach was the description of linguistic features at the levels of phonetics and phonology (accent), morphology and grammar (syntax), and lexis (vocabulary). It was based partly on the 'English studies' tradition of Quirk, Greenbaum and others, but also on the tradition of urban and rural dialectology familiar to Trudgill and other British and North American sociolinguists. Whatever the precise genealogy of this approach, its emphasis was chiefly on the linguistic description of variation; thus it was a rather small step from the description of *English Accents and Dialects* (Hughes and Trudgill 1979) to *International English* (Trudgill and Hannah 1982), to *English Around the World* (Cheshire 1991a). Similarly, Görlach's work in this period, based on the German 'Anglistik' tradition but incorporating sociolinguistics and pidgin and creole studies (to some degree at least), also retained a core linguistic focus that stressed the centrality of linguistic description.

During the 1980s, Braj Kachru and Larry Smith in North America sought to incorporate the study of World Englishes within a comprehensive global framework of analysis. This remained partly linguistic, particularly the description of World Englishes in the Caribbean, Africa and Asia, but Kachru's analysis went beyond this into a discussion of the sociohistorical, sociopolitical and ideological underpinnings of the discourses of World Englishes. His advocacy of a 'socially-realistic' approach to World Englishes (1992) enabled him to construct a number of interlocking models of World Englishes including the model of the 'three circles of English'; 'norms' in World Englishes; 'variables of intelligibility'; 'bilingual creativity'; 'multi-canons'; and 'power and politics'. Starting with the specific description and analysis of one variety of 'new English', i.e. Indian English, Kachru proceeded in the 1980s to construct an inclusive theory of World Englishes based mainly on a metasociolinguistic conceptualisation and discussion of the object of study. The effects of this rethinking of World Englishes were felt across a range of language studies, including applied linguistics and English language teaching. Kachru's work in this latter area was partly influenced by studies carried out within the 'sociology of language' paradigm, in particular the work of Joshua Fishman and his associates, who from the late 1960s had researched such areas as societal multilingualism, language shift and language maintenance, language and nationalism, and language and race, thus dealing with the sociopolitical underpinnings of sociolinguistics.

The major ideological break in the literature obviously came with the publication of Phillipson's *Linguistic Imperialism* (1992). Up to this point much of the discussion was non-aggressively inclusive, and each of the theorists on the discoursal stage had a largely uncontested space in which to operate: Trudgill on the 'dialects' of World Englishes; Kachru as witness and critic of orientalism and anglicism; and Fishman as the sociological analyst, concerned on ethnolinguistic grounds at the spread of English. Even Quirk played a role in promoting early studies of World Englishes, writing extensively on varieties of English. Kachru and Quirk were co-authors of the introduction to Smith (1981); and the first issue of *World Englishes* under the new editorship of Braj Kachru and Larry Smith was dedicated to Sir Randolph Quirk, 'with professional respect and personal affection' (Kachru and Smith 1985: 212). In addition, most academics writing on this subject until the 1990s were broadly liberal in political orientation.

Phillipson's *Linguistic Imperialism* presented a challenge to what was, by the early 1990s, a recently constituted orthodoxy, for a number of reasons. First, its foundation rests on an ideology derived from Marxist approaches to cultural studies, dependency theory and the conceptualisation of North–South (or 'centre–periphery') relations as those of systematic exploitation and conflict. At the same time, Phillipson and his associates were also able to invoke the notion of 'linguistic human rights' to support their arguments concerning the pernicious consequences of 'English linguistic imperialism', supplementing the claims of

hard-line Marxist ideology with appeals to the more traditionally liberal democratic concerns of human rights. Second, the response from within sociolinguistics and applied linguistics to *Linguistic Imperialism* suggests that Phillipson
succeeded in touching a collective nerve shared by English linguists and sociolinguists working in this field. Even before the publication of Phillipson's book,
Cheshire (1991b), in the introduction to *English Around the World*, expressed her
anxieties about the spread of English thus:

> It is important that amid this understandable interest and enthusiasm we
> do not overlook the more undesirable consequences of the development
> of English as a world language. From a linguistic point of view, for ex-
> ample, the spread of English has all too often been associated with the
> death, or virtual death, of the indigenous languages in those countries to
> which it has been transplanted. English itself is a prime example. From a
> social and political point of view, the spread of English around the world
> was largely the result of exploitation and colonisation, and in many mul-
> tilingual countries English is still the language of an exclusive social elite.
> (1991b: 6)

Nevertheless, at a time when Marxism as a political and economic ideology had
been displaced by capitalism in Eastern Europe and the former Soviet Union,
it is perhaps ironic that Phillipson's book should have won the institutional and
professional support it evidently did. We might then ask: why was it that the
book gained an immediate following, and why was there such a strong response
to Phillipson's ideas?

First, I would suggest the success of Phillipson's treatise may be explained in
part as a reaction against the 'popularisers' of the mid-1980s such as Crystal and
McCrum *et al.* By the late 1980s, partly because of an awareness of issues raised
by cultural studies and the study of the new literatures in English, it had become
increasingly less respectable to indulge in the 'triumphalist' celebration of the
spread of English, and even the rhetoric about the creativity of world literatures
in English was beginning to be challenged. Second, by the early 1990s there was
increasing concern at the plight of minority languages, among sociolinguists in
particular and, in this context, there was a growing belief that English was playing
the role of 'killer language' in many developing societies. Third, there was also
the essential problem of coming to terms with the British (and, to a lesser extent,
American) colonialism which, historically at least, had been responsible for the
original creation of 'outer-circle' varieties of the language in such 'non-native'
contexts as Africa and Asia.

Historically, the impact on the world of 500 years of European colonialism has
been profound, and this is now an issue that many intellectuals in the humanities
and other disciplines are attempting to understand. This task, however, is not
simply one of identifying historical villains, even though colonialism frequently
involved the military and territorial subjugation of non-European populations
and inhuman brutality and violence directed against indigenous cultures in the

Americas, Africa and Asia. Faced with the sheer unpleasantness if not 'horror' of much European colonial violence (Cocker 1998), it is hardly surprising that two typical responses to this have been guilt and outrage.

Currently, within western academia, both responses seem to be finding something like equal expression. In the case of two of the former British settler colonies, the notion that American liberalism (and Australian multiculturalism) is somehow historically based on the brutal genocide of the indigenous populations sits heavily in the stomach of the intellectual community, particularly in the humanities, where identity politics and homespun versions of ethnic nationalism have achieved a respectable liberal cachet over the last twenty years. Such 'local facts' are deeply unpalatable, not least because they challenge our essential comprehension of the world(s) we inhabit. In many instances, what were originally conceived as basically British 'settler colonies' (and until only recently) part of a 'Greater Britain', have reinvented themselves (or are attempting to recreate themselves) as ethnically diverse multicultural nations. Simultaneously, former 'administrative colonies' such as India, Malaysia, Singapore and Hong Kong (i.e. ESL societies) are dealing with various nationalisms, cultural and linguistic, in the postcolonial context.

For western academics like Phillipson and Pennycook, this situation has provided an opportunity to resite the discourses of dependency theory and postcolonial theory from disciplines such as sociology and cultural studies into the discussion of World Englishes. Although this may have already occasioned a reaction from more traditional social theorists in the sociology of language, the injection of this body of theory into the discourse has shifted the balance of debate, as a glance at the journals in sociolinguistics, applied linguistics and even language teaching now testifies. Pennycook's adoption of postcolonial theory, and his redirection of this to linguistics, is particularly interesting although somewhat disingenuous, given that within cultural and literary theory such issues are debated within a fiercely contested intellectual space, with demands on ethnicity and authenticity that may be evaded on the playing-fields of English-language teaching.

Marxist literary theorist Terry Eagleton, for example, takes some postcolonial critics to task for a language characterised by 'portentous obscurantism incongruously remote from the peoples it champions'. He also suggests that some work in the field 'has done little more than reflect the guilty self-loathing of a Western liberalism which would rather, in these hard political times, be absolutely anything but itself' (Eagleton 1996: 206). Perhaps equally relevant for the field of linguistics, however, is Jacoby's (1995) criticism of the interdisciplinary interventions of the postcolonialists which queries: 'Are they serious students of colonial history and culture or do they just pepper their writings with references to Gramsci and hegemony?' (Jacoby 1995:32). All of which is not intended to dismiss postcolonialism entirely, as some work in this area is genuinely inspirational even for the linguist and sociolinguist (see, for example, Young 1990, 1995). But what does seem clear here is that the transfer of postcolonial discourse from its literary provenance to language studies has served to shift the focus away from the 'linguistic' towards the 'non-linguistic', specifically towards a discussion of the politics of language and critical language studies. At its most banal, yesterday's 'expatriate English teacher' becomes today's elocutionist of 'subaltern' voices.

Operating at another level of discourse is Graddol's (1997) survey of *The Future of English*, where it seems that we have Graddol the sociologist wearing the hats of globalist and futurologist. Notwithstanding the general developmental optimism of much of his commentary, Graddol also raises a number of issues (for example, the rapid growth of urban middle classes in Asian societies, the emergence of regional language hierarchies and the polycentrism of English), which relate directly to the language situation in Hong Kong and China. Phillipson's response, set out in the publisher's flyer at the time the book was published, was to describe the report as 'an impressively lucid, impartial and challenging synthesis' which 'demonstrates why reflection on many dimensions of language policy is needed as a counter-balance to misplaced linguistic triumphalism and insularity'. If one pauses to consider the fact that Graddol substantively contradicts Phillipson on many issues of fact – English as a 'killer language'; the conspiracy of western-dominated multinationals, etc. – and ignores him on a range of others, Phillipson's response seems oddly approving. In many ways, it is Phillipson and Graddol who now represent the two sides of current debate: the one alarmist and agitatorial, the other careful, concerned, but cautiously optimistic about the benefits of globalisation.

At the same time, issues related to the politics of colonialism and social class *are* important to the study of language and linguistics, as are other 'political' issues such as gender, modernity and race. Such issues *do* intersect with the study of World Englishes, but what seems important here is the perspective of the scholar and the quality of the analysis. If, as Conrad (1996) suggests, some academics are primarily concerned to make political points in support of conclusions already taken as given, scholarship is bound to be adversely affected. The intersection of linguistics and colonialism is extremely complicated, as indicated by Schwab (1984), Lelyveld (1993), Cohn (1996), Mufwene (2001) and others, and careful research on such issues may lead to unexpected conclusions. In the case of Hong Kong, for example, it is entirely possible to argue that in many respects the creation of 'Cantonese' as a codified language was the work of nineteenth-century missionaries and colonial officials who wrote the first comprehensive dictionaries, grammars and phonologies of what might otherwise have remained a southern Chinese vernacular. Similarly, the expansion and functional elaboration of Cantonese in the period between the 1960s and 1990s was closely connected to government strategies to foster a sense of identity in a refugee community in the aftermath of communist-led civil disturbances (the 1967 'riots'). Far from suppressing Cantonese, as Pennycook has implied (1994: 315), the policy of the Hong Kong government in the late colonial era served, wittingly or otherwise, to encourage its use, even in such 'high' domains as television, radio, the civil service and education (Bolton 2000a: 271). In similar vein, in her recent survey of British colonial language policy, Brutt-Griffler concludes that: 'When Great Britain finally developed an "imperial" policy it was not what advocates of imperial policy had understood by the term, nor what is today called the policy of linguistic imperialism, but rather precisely the opposite. It was a policy of limiting the spread of English to what was minimally necessary to running a colonial empire' (Brutt-Griffler 2002: 105).

Table 1.1 (overleaf) attempts to set out the range of studies currently encountered in the field of World Englishes.

Hong Kong English as a 'new English'

Although the past twenty years have seen the emergence of a large literature on language in Hong Kong, and English in Hong Kong, relatively little research has been published on the 'indigenisation' or 'nativisation' of Hong Kong English. This is surprising given that the term 'Hong Kong English' has long been recognised in the international literature. Munby (1978), Strevens (1980), Todd and Hancock (1986), and McArthur (1987) have all claimed that Hong Kong English has the status of a localised variety of the language. Todd and Hancock (1986), for example, give 'Hong Kong English' its own separate entry in their handbook on international varieties, listing a number of typical features of usage at the levels of phonology, vocabulary and grammar, while McArthur (1987) includes Hong Kong English (along with Singapore English, Malaysian English and Philippines English) in the category of 'East Asian Standard(izing) English'.

As I shall explain in some detail in later chapters, English has a long history of language contact in southern China and Hong Kong but nonetheless local linguists have been reluctant to recognise the autonomy of a localised variety of English. Luke and Richards (1982), for example, state that: 'In Hong Kong . . . English has exonormative rather than endonormative status . . . in that the norm or standard consumed by learners of English is an external one rather than an internal one . . . there is no such thing then as "Hong Kong English". There is neither the societal need nor opportunity for the development of a stable Cantonese variety of spoken English' (1982: 55). This view is repeated by Tay (1991): 'There is no social motivation for the indigenisation of English in Hong Kong. Thus, English in Hong Kong has been considered either a learner's language, a developmental rather than lectal continuum . . . or is described in terms of a cline of bilingualism' (1991: 327). Similarly, Johnson (1994) notes that: 'A Hong Kong variety of English has been mentioned in the international literature . . . and in Hong Kong itself . . . However, the notion has received little support. There is no social or cultural role for English to play among Hong Kong Chinese; it only has a role in their relations with expatriates and the outside world' (1994: 182).

Significant work relating to English in Hong Kong from the 1980s to 1990s includes two books on code-mixing by Gibbons (1987) and Li (1996), one volume on educational linguistics by Lord and Cheng (1987), and a recently published collection of papers on topics in sociolinguistics and applied linguistics,

Table 1.1 *Current approaches to World Englishes (1960s–the present)*

Approach	Exponent(s)	Objective(s)	Timeline
English studies	Quirk (1962, 1972, 1990), Burchfield (1985), Greenbaum (1985), Quirk and Widdowson (1985), McArthur (1992, 1998), Görlach (1991, 1995b, 1998), Schneider (1997b, c), etc.	To describe varieties of English from eclectic, descriptive and historical perspectives. Situated against a tradition of English studies (*Anglistik*), dating from the late 19th century, e.g. the work of Otto Jespersen, Daniel Jones and Henry Sweet.	1960s–present
English corpus linguistics	Greenbaum (1996), Nelson (1996), Meyer (2002), etc.	To provide accurate and detailed linguistic descriptions of World Englishes.	1990–present
Sociolinguistic approaches			
The sociology of language	Fishman (1972), Fishman *et al.* (1977, 1996), etc.	To conduct research on English in relation to such issues as language maintenance/shift and ethnolinguistic identity.	1960s–present
A 'features-based' approach	Trudgill and Hannah (1982), Cheshire (1991), etc.	To describe varieties of English through dialectological and variationist methodologies. Situated against the long tradition of British and European dialectology.	1980s–present

Kachruvian studies	Kachru (1983, 1985, 1986, etc.), Smith (1981, 1987), Lowenberg (1984), Gupta (1994), Bautista (1997), Pakir et al. (1994), etc.	To promote a pluricentric approach to World Englishes, highlighting the 'sociolinguistic realities' and 'bilingual creativity' of outer-circle societies.	1980s–present
Pidgin and creole studies	Reinecke (1937), Todd (1984), Mühlhäusler (1986), Romaine (1988), Holm (1988, 1989), Sebba (1997), etc.	To describe and analyse 'mixed' languages and the dynamics of linguistic hybridisation (beginning with the early work of Hugo Schuchardt 1842–1927).	1930s–present
Applied linguistics	Halliday, MacIntosh and Strevens (1964), Strevens (1977, 1980), Brumfit (1982), Kachru (1982, 1986), etc.	To explore the implications of World Englishes for language learning and teaching.	1960s–present
Lexicography	Webster (1806, 1828) [USA], Yule and Burnell 1886 [India], Butler (1981 [Australia], Allsopp (1996) [Jamaica] Orsman (1997) [New Zealand], etc.	To fulfil a range of objectives, including the expression of a national linguistic identity.	1980s–present [within the World Englishes context]
Popularisers	McCrum et al. (1986), Crystal (1995, 1997), etc.	To interest a mass reading public in issues related to World Englishes.	1980s–present
Critical linguistics	Phillipson (1992), Pennycook (1994, 1998), etc.	To express resistance to the linguistic imperialism and cultural hegemony of English. Derived from Marxian political analysis and/or postcolonial theory.	1990s–present
Linguistic futurology	Graddol (1997), etc.	To predict future trends in the spread of English and English-language teaching (ELT) worldwide.	1997–present

Pennington's (1998a) *Language in Hong Kong at Century's End*. In addition, there is a sizeable body of work dealing with various aspects of the sociolinguistics of multilingualism in Hong Kong, much of which can be classified according to five broad topic areas:

- the status and functions of English in Hong Kong (the sociology of language);
- bilingualism and multilingualism;
- code-mixing;
- language attitude studies; and
- the features of English in Hong Kong.[8]

Many of those working on the 'features' of English in Hong Kong, approach the topic from an error analysis viewpoint. Webster, Ward and Craig (1987) present findings on errors in English 'due to first language interference'; Bunton (1989) is a local Longman guide to 'common English errors'; Boyle and Boyle (1991) is another Longman guide to 'spoken English errors'; Webster and Lam (1991) contains 'further notes on the influence of Cantonese on the English of Hong Kong students'; Potter (1992) is a Longman guide to 'common business English errors'; and Bunton (1994) is yet another local Longman volume on 'social English errors in Hong Kong'.

However, there has been little analysis of 'Hong Kong English' as an autonomous variety of English. An early study was carried out by Tongue and Waters (1978) in a newspaper article entitled 'English, HK-style' published in the *South China Morning Post*, which identified a range of 'local vocabulary', including the use of Cantonese loanwords and Anglo-Indian items, as well as a number of local usages at the grammatical level. Tongue and Waters conclude that '[i]f the use of English in Hongkong increases substantially in the future as some people predict, the categories exemplified in this article will expand too, perhaps to a point where a variety will emerge which may justly be termed Hongkong English. If that happens, the variety will join the growing family of "Englishes"

[8] Work on *the status and functions of English in Hong Kong* includes Gibbons (1982), Luke and Richards (1982), Johnson (1983, 1994), Lord and T'sou (1983), Lord (1987), Bacon-Shone and Bolton (1998), Boyle (1997a, b, d), Hamlett (1997), Pierson-Smith (1997), Evans, Jones, Rusmin and Cheung (1998) and Pierson (1998). Publications on *bilingualism and multilingualism* include Fu (1987), So (1987), Johnson, Shek and Law (1993), Lin (1996), Afendras (1998) and Bacon-Shone and Bolton (1998). Representative work dealing with *code-switching* and *code-mixing* includes Gibbons (1979a, b), Chan and Kwok (1982), Johnson and Lee (1987), Lin (1996), Li (1996, 1998), Boyle (1997c) and Chan (1998). For research on *language attitudes* see Fu (1975), Pierson and Fu (1982), Gibbons (1983), Pierson (1987, 1992), Kwo (1992), Pennington and Yue (1994), Axler, Yang and Stevens (1998), Boyle (1997b), Lin and Detaramani (1998), and Richards (1998). Discussions of *the features of English in Hong Kong* include Tongue and Waters (1978), Platt (1982), Chan and Kwok (1985), Webster, Ward and Craig (1987), Bunton (1989, 1991), Harris (1989), Taylor (1989), Bolton and Kwok (1990), Boyle and Boyle (1991), Webster and Lam (1991), Potter (1992), Benson (1994), Carless (1995), Joseph (1997) and Moody (1997). For a relatively comprehensive bibliography of research on Hong Kong English, see Bolton (2000b).

which constitute the English language as an auxiliary means of communication worldwide' (1978: 2).

Since 1978, despite the general lack of recognition accorded to Hong Kong English, there have been a number of academic books and papers related to the indigenisation of English in the territory. Chan and Kwok (1985) is a study of 'lexical borrowing from Chinese into English'; while Taylor (1989) discusses the use of English in Hong Kong newspapers; Benson (1994) discusses the 'political vocabulary of Hong Kong English'; and Carless (1995) discusses 'politicised expressions' in local newspapers. Joseph (1997) discusses features of syntax explicitly as 'features' of Hong Kong English. He starts with a discussion of the lack of distinction between count noun phrase and mass noun phrase in Hong Kong English, e.g. *British English*, 'a bowl of noodles', versus *Hong Kong English*, 'a bowl of noodle', and then expands into a discussion of the emergence and development of local varieties of language. Joseph's argument is that the appearance of the Romance languages in the late Middle Ages was occasioned by processes very similar to those in progress in Hong Kong English:

> In the context of English in Hong Kong, if history teaches us anything it is that the 'decline' in externally-imposed standards *must* occur if English is to survive in post-colonial Hong Kong... New 'internal' standards must replace them – and that is precisely what has been happening with the emergence of a distinctive form of English. Again, Hong Kong people are not making random errors in English, but regularly occurring patterns largely traceable to the influence of their other principal language. It was by just such a process that the Romance languages came into being, an emergence that was at the same time a crumbling of the standards of Latin measured against the external criterion of Virgil and Cicero, and not a random crumbling, but one connected to the other languages spoken in the former Roman Empire. (1997: 68)

Joseph links the concept of Hong Kong English to the notion of 'identity' in an exploration of a number of the complexities of the local language (and 'languages in contact') situation. It was this issue I set out to explore during the late 1980s when, together with a colleague, I conducted research into the use of a 'Hong Kong English accent' (Bolton and Kwok 1990). We described both segmental and suprasegmental features of the phonology of Hong Kong English, before going on to investigate the reactions of university students to a number of English accents, including RP accents, US accents and Hong Kong accents, through the use of a verbal guise technique. The results of our research indicated that 'Hong Kong English speakers typically share a number of localised features of a Hong Kong accent, although these are subject to a good deal of variation... within the shared norms of Hong Kong bilinguals as a group' (1990: 166). Other results indicated that our respondents 'identified' (Le Page and Tabouret-Keller 1985) with local speakers in a number of ways:

- they could recognise a Hong Kong accent relatively easily;
- they had difficulty in labelling other accents of English; and
- a substantial number of respondents (particularly male students) stated a preference for that accent of English associated with 'Hong Kong bilinguals'. (Bolton and Kwok 1990: 170)

At this point, one might return to the issue of what actually constitutes a 'new English' in a setting like Hong Kong; or, more precisely, given that some local linguists at least recognise the existence of a distinct form of Hong Kong English, what criteria should such a variety satisfy in order to achieve recognition as a legitimate new or World English? As explained above (see pp. 5–6), Llamzon (1983) identifies four essential categories of features: *ecological, historical, sociolinguistic* and *cultural*. I would suggest that Llamzon's checklist of features should be augmented by at least three other sets of features: *linguistic, attitudinal* and *political*.

As far as linguistic features are concerned, the identification of sets of distinctive linguistic items typically associated with a new variety is a central feature of the discussion of such Englishes as Indian English, Malaysian English, Singapore English and Philippine English, as well as other varieties around the world (see Trudgill and Hannah 1982; Cheshire 1991a). At the attitudinal level, one would attempt to gauge the acceptance of the new English within the community. If Hong Kong English is accepted, then by whom – the general public, school teachers, academics, journalists, writers? Is this form of English viewed positively (for example as an expression of local identity) or is it regarded as 'substandard' English (as a collection of errors)? The level of political features potentially refers to a very large matrix of sociological and institutional factors. Has the local variety been recognised by the government, educational institutions or other official (or semi-official) bodies? In Australia, *The Macquarie Dictionary* (1981) and *The Australian National Dictionary* (1988) have both achieved a high degree of official acceptance, partly because they appeared at a time of growing republican sentiment in Australia. The situation in other societies, however, particularly the ESL societies of Asia, is much more ambivalent. In a wider sense, the 'political' would also refer to the history of the community as a former anglophone colony – its autonomy, its governmental and legal institutions, and the use of languages within the educational system.

Butler (1997a) provides another checklist. In her discussion of what makes a variety of World English, she suggests five important criteria:

- 'A standard and recognizable pattern of pronunciation handed down from one generation to another';
- 'Particular words and phrases which spring up usually to express key features of the physical and social environment and which are regarded as peculiar to the variety';
- 'A history – a sense that this variety of English is the way it is because of the history of the language community';

- 'A literature written without apology in that variety of English'; and
- 'Reference works – dictionaries and style guides – which show that people in that language community look to themselves, not some outside authority, to decide what is right and wrong in terms of how they speak and write their English'. (1997a: 106)

It is now possible to make a strong claim that Hong Kong English is well on its way to satisfying at least four of Butler's criteria. First, as far as pronunciation is concerned, it is now well-established, at least in the academic literature, that a distinct local accent exists (see Luke and Richards 1982; Bolton and Kwok 1990; Hung 2000). Second, not only is there a distinct local vocabulary associated with Hong Kong, but this is being recognised within lexicography (see chapter 4). In addition, this local vocabulary has a long historical genealogy in southern China, certainly much longer than has hitherto been recognised. Third, the history of Hong Kong English stretches back in time to the early seventeenth century, when the first British trading ships reached Macao and Canton (see chapter 3). Fourth, like Hong Kong English itself, local Hong Kong Chinese writers in English have had an almost invisible presence in the community, but this too has changed in recent years. Such creative writers now include the novelist Sussy Chako (Xu Xi) and poets such as Louise Ho, Agnes Lam and Leung Ping-kwan. Compared to the Philippines or Singapore, the body of work produced by such local writers is still quite small, but it is nevertheless significant (see chapter 4). On the fifth count, much work still remains to be done in order to promote a positive attitude to a local variety of English through dictionaries and style guides. Whether Hong Kong English will be able to receive the imprimatur of local reference works will depend on a range of factors connected to the sociolinguistic dynamics of the society in a newly postcolonial context (chapter 4). In fact, there is now strong evidence of an increased recognition of Hong Kong English as an autonomous variety on a par with, although different to, other Asian Englishes. A recent issue of the journal *World Englishes* comprises a collection of articles entitled 'Hong Kong English: autonomy and creativity' (Bolton 2000), and an enlarged version of this collection has been published in book form (Bolton 2002).

English in China and Chinese Englishes

One of the key themes of this book is that Hong Kong English has a forgotten past that links it, historically and developmentally, to the beginnings of cultural and linguistic contact between English speakers and Chinese in South China, especially Macao and Canton (Guangzhou). As I will demonstrate in later chapters, this crucially involves a consideration of an early variety of Canton 'jargon' (or 'Canton English'), which later comes to be referred to as 'Chinese pidgin English', and the historical and linguistic links between this earlier variety and contemporary Hong Kong English.

While Hong Kong has no shortage of academic literature dealing with the linguistics of English in Hong Kong society, relatively little has been published (at least in the English-language academic literature) on the sociolinguistics of English in China. In the decades that followed the establishment of the communist government in 1949, research and publications on English in China were greatly limited by the political turmoil of the Cultural Revolution which, during the 1960s and 1970s, devastated many aspects of Chinese life, including education. Even before the Cultural Revolution, the teaching of English in Chinese schools had been supplanted by the teaching of Russian and, by 1957, it was calculated that there were only 850 secondary teachers of English in the whole country. Since the inauguration of the Deng Xiaoping's 'open door' policy (from the late 1970s onwards), a great deal has changed in the People's Republic of China (PRC), including the increased popularity of English learning and teaching. Today, it is estimated that there are some 500,000 teachers of secondary English, and the total number of English speakers in China has been estimated at over 200 million, and rising fast.

One of the first studies to explicitly recognise 'Chinese varieties of English' was that of Cheng (1983), who surveyed the history and use of English in China, as well as examples of the Englishisation of Chinese grammar. At the lexical level, Cheng also identified a range of Chinese 'political English' expressions, such as 'capitalist roader' and 'right deviationist wind' as emblematic examples of distinctive Chinese–English lexis (Cheng 1983: 133). Similar studies from a World Englishes perspective include that of Zhao and Campbell (1995) who present a detailed profile of English in China in the early 1990s, in such domains as education, medicine, media, tourism and science and technology. Tellingly, Zhao and Campbell also challenge the argument that English in China is only 'an instrument of international communication', asserting that such a view is essentially 'an oversimplification of the sociolinguistic reality of Chinese English' (1995: 378).

Other relevant research dealing with the spread of English in contemporary China includes two book-length studies by Dzau (1990) and Ross (1993), as well as a growing number of academic papers on the subject, including Maley (1986), Hao (1988), Pride and Liu (1988), Li (1995), Cortazzi and Jin (1996), Rao (1996), Ng and Tang (1997), Huang (1999), Kang (1999), Wang (1999), Zhang Ailing (2000) and Zhang Jun (2000). One major issue currently under discussion is that of the nativisation of English in the Chinese context, along with debates concerning the appropriacy of various terms including 'China English', 'Chinglish', or 'Chinese English' (Zhang Jun 2000: 55).[9]

Although much of this book is concerned with the archaeology of English in southern China and the historical links between Chinese pidgin English and Hong Kong English, I shall later attempt to connect this discussion with the larger issue of English in the People's Republic of China, where I attempt to make the

---

[9] For a review of these and other issues, see Bolton and Tong (2002).

link between China's forgotten past(s) and forgotten Englishes. The claim that such forgotten pasts exist can be illustrated with reference to a range of sources dealing with the teaching of English in China, including a representative paper by Sun (1996), which claims that '[t]he earliest school offering English courses was set up in 1862', and was known in English as the Imperial Foreign Language Institute (*Jing Shi Tongwen Guan*) (Sun 1996: 36). While it is indeed true that the *Tongwen Guan* played an important role in English-language teaching in the late nineteenth century, the very first schools to teach English were set up in Macao and Hong Kong as early as the 1830s and 1840s. The story of English's forgotten past in South China is set out in chapter 3, but before considering this, we return to the recent past and a discussion of the sociolinguistics of English in Hong Kong in the late British colonial period, in the years from 1980 until 1997.

2 The sociolinguistics of English in late colonial Hong Kong, 1980–1997

Language creates a privileged class and leaves the vast majority frustrated and resentful... If any justice exists in Hong Kong, it exists only for the English-speaking. There is another law for the underprivileged, the non-English speaking.

(Elliot 1971: 23, 32)

The fact is Hongkong English has evolved into an incipient patois, an inevitable process in any colonial setting where the imported tongue cannot avoid absorbing the characteristics of the vernacular, especially one as vibrant as Cantonese.

(*South China Morning Post* 1987b: 28)

In the streets, though, the tempo of American mass culture – from hamburgers to fashion and TV shows – suits Hong Kong's fast-track lifestyle like no other foreign influence. Hong Kong consumers devour anything American.

(*Time* 30 December 1996: 27)

Hong Kong society, 1980–97

The political context

The late British colonial era in Hong Kong was a period of immense and rapidly evolving political and social change for the Hong Kong community, as both its political elite and ordinary citizens were forced to come to grips with the issue of 'reunification' with mainland China and the People's Republic of China (PRC), in addition to coping with numerous changes in the economy and social organisation. At the beginning of this period, Hong Kong was still constitutionally a British Crown Colony, one of the last remaining outposts of a British Empire that had evaporated in the decades following the Second World War. British sovereignty over the 400-square-mile territory rested on a number of nineteenth-century agreements between an imperialistic British government and Qing (Ch'ing) dynasty officials. (Britain had acquired Hong Kong in 1842 during the First Opium War, the Kowloon peninsula in 1860 as a result of the Second Opium War and the New Territories in 1898 as a consequence of European and American pressure on the late Qing dynasty to concede more treaty-port space.)

Both Hong Kong and Kowloon were ceded in perpetuity, but the New Territories were leased to Britain for a period of 99 years. For the post-1949 communist government, such agreements were a source of national humiliation – 'unequal treaties', with no lasting meaning, as 'Hong Kong had always been part of China' (Craddock 1994: 162).

Reunification negotiations with the Chinese government began with the 1979 visit of the British colonial governor, Murray MacLehose (Governor of Hong Kong 1971–82) to Beijing, where he met Deng Xiaoping, who had only recently emerged as the leader of China in the post-Mao era. This began a number of inconclusive diplomatic exchanges about the future of the territory, but negotiations proper did not begin until the visit of the British Prime Minister Margaret Thatcher, now advised by Edward Youde, the new Governor of Hong Kong, to China in September 1982. After two years of negotiations, an agreement entitled 'The Joint Declaration' on the future of Hong Kong was signed in September 1984. The most important provisions in the agreement included the following:

- that Britain would continue to administer Hong Kong until 30 June 1997;
- that thereafter, China would resume sovereignty and Hong Kong would become a Special Administrative Region (SAR) of China 'with a high degree of autonomy';
- that Hong Kong's capitalist system would remain unchanged for fifty years;
- that the legal system would be maintained;
- that Hong Kong people would continue to enjoy those human rights specified by Hong Kong law and international agreements, including the freedom to travel;
- that Hong Kong would have economic and fiscal autonomy, and that the territory would remain a free port;
- that the civil servants would keep their employment and their pensions would be protected;
- that the existing education system would be maintained; and
- that there would be an elected legislature, although the details of this were not stipulated. (Craddock 1994: 208–9)

By this agreement, Britain agreed to transfer both the sovereignty and administration of Hong Kong to the People's Republic of China. In retrospect, this may seem unremarkable or at least inevitable, but at the time there was much initial discussion within the British and Hong Kong governments on resisting this transfer of power. Opinion in Hong Kong, among both the business-political elite and the general public, was greatly alarmed by the negotiations in Beijing. Simon Keswick, then a director of the historically infamous company of Jardine Matheson, is cited in 1982 as stating that 'We must *all* work to stop Communists from taking this place ... At all costs' (Welsh 1993: 506). From 1982 to 1983, Hong Kong financial institutions underwent a major crisis, culminating in a free-fall Hong Kong dollar in September 1983 that left the Hong Kong government 'facing the impending collapse of the entire financial system' (Jao 1985: 364).

The government responded in early October by establishing an exchange 'peg' which fixed the value of the Hong Kong dollar against the US greenback, within a narrow band of variation (the peg system, supported by government funds, continues to the present day). In March 1983, Jardine Matheson, one of the largest British companies or 'hongs' left in the territory, announced that it was transferring its headquarters to Bermuda (*South China Morning Post* 1984a).

In the event, when the Joint Declaration was signed on 26 September 1984, the agreement was greeted with optimism in Hong Kong, and the perennial barometer of the territory's public 'confidence', the Hang Seng Index, registered immediate and substantial gains after two-and-a-half years of turbulent financial anxiety (*South China Morning Post* 1984b). In spite of some disquiet about the full implementation of its provisions, the next five years saw confidence being generally maintained and strengthened. Commercially, this was a period when Deng Xiaoping's 'open door' policy encouraged thousands of Hong Kong businessmen to invest in and to trade with mainland China, while politically it was a period of relative liberalism, at least in terms of the rhetoric relayed to the international community and the people of Hong Kong. The scale of Hong Kong's investment in China was huge – by 1985 Hong Kong had become China's biggest trading partner and by 1988 accounted for between 50 and 70 per cent of all foreign investments in the PRC (Welsh 1993: 520). Hong Kong inhabitants also received reassurances from Beijing that the transfer of sovereignty would be effected according to the principles of 'one country, two systems', and 'Hong Kong people ruling Hong Kong' espoused by Deng Xiaoping and the central government (Craddock 1994: 203).

Hong Kong's confidence in its future was shattered by the Tiananmen Square massacre on 4 June 1989, horrific BBC- and CNN-televised scenes of which were broadcast via the local channels into almost every Hong Kong home. In the days before and after Tiananmen, there were unprecedented and largely spontaneous demonstrations from the Hong Kong public, with estimates of those participating in marches and rallies pitched as high as one million people, in a society with just 1.5 million households. One estimate calculated that 46 per cent of the households on Hong Kong island were represented in just one of the demonstrations that took place at the end of May 1989 (*South China Morning Post* 1989a). Considering the previous political reticence, even 'apathy', of Hong Kong people, the outburst of public feeling was truly remarkable. For an intense period of weeks and months after Tiananmen, Hong Kong people were united, as never before or since, by sympathy for the Beijing demonstrators and disgust at the killings in the Chinese capital. The Hong Kong demonstrations that followed the massacre brought together all sectors of the community:

> Christians and liberals marched shoulder to shoulder with Hong Kong's influential pro-Communist trade union workers. Pro-communist newspapers denounced China's action. Employees at Peking's own Bank of China fixed a banner from their headquarters apologizing for the Chinese

crackdown. Leaders of Chinese enterprises in Hong Kong placed newspaper advertisements condemning the violence. United, unified Hong Kong, Right and Left, Catholic and Communist, all protested against Peking's action. (Rafferty 1991: 9)

Even the pro-communist newspapers expressed their outrage, with the Beijing-funded *Wen Wei Po* proclaiming that the Communist Party leaders were 'murderers' and 'robbers of the people' (Rafferty 1991: 499). Members of the 'expatriate' community (westerners and other foreigners resident in Hong Kong) were similarly shocked by the turn of events, and also participated in various demonstrations, including those urging the British government to provide full British passports to Hong Kong people.

Tiananmen sent the whole community into shock, and resulted in a number of political and social changes in the years that followed. One immediate effect was the immediate worsening of political relations between London and Hong Kong on the one hand and Beijing on the other. Co-operation over key infrastructure projects, including the construction of a new airport at Chek Lap Kok, was severely hindered. Second, there was the question of Britain's responsibility for British passport holders in the territory, as a campaign to raise the issue of the 'right of abode' on the Whitehall agenda gained strength. In 1989, there were an estimated 3.25 million Hong Kong Chinese British passport holders, *without* the right to live in the UK, resident in the territory, out of a total population of some 5.6 million people. On 3 July 1989, a group of anonymous professionals from the advertising industry placed an advertisement in the *South China Morning Post*, appealing to the British government to grant full passports to increased numbers of Hong Kong Chinese British National Overseas (BNO) passport holders (see figure 2.1). The words in the text in the right-hand column read:

> There's no point in being almost British.
> The coins in his pocket bear the impression of the Queen.
> On Saturdays he plays football.
> His school flies the British flag.
> He doesn't think about freedom because he takes it for granted.
> He was raised in the British tradition in a British colony.
> He is one of the millions of people for whom Hong Kong is home.
> And who want to go on living here.
> All they want is some form of insurance for the future.
> And the only form of insurance that will mean anything to them is the
> right of abode in Britain.
> Otherwise being almost British is like being homeless.

In December 1990 the Conservative government, despite initial strong resistance in London and official displeasure from Beijing, announced a plan to issue full British passports to 50,000 selected heads of households including former

Figure 2.1 'There's no point in being almost British', advertisement in *South China Morning Post*, 3 July 1989

government servants, police, business people and others with strong connections with the United Kingdom (*South China Morning Post* 1989b).

Large numbers of other Hong Kong inhabitants decided to emigrate to other destinations. In July 1989, a survey by the Federation of Hong Kong Industries reported that 75 per cent of Hong Kong industrialists were thinking of leaving the territory before 1997 (Rafferty 1991: 499). Some of these later changed their plans and remained in the territory, but many others did decide to leave in the early 1990s. Overall, between 1987 and 1994 a total of 399,273 people quit Hong Kong. The most popular destinations were Canada (57.6 per cent), the USA (23.8 per cent) and Australia (18.6 per cent), followed by New Zealand and the United Kingdom   all English-speaking democracies (Skeldon 1996: 446). The emigrants who left in the early and mid-1990s were 'some of the best educated, well trained, and highly skilled of Hong Kong's population', with a high percentage of college graduates and 'professional, technical, and administrative and managerial workers among them', the vast majority of whom would have claimed at least a working knowledge of English (Skeldon 1994: 31–2). Based on the available figures, it is possible to estimate that at least 10 per cent of the Hong Kong population left Hong Kong in the run-up to 1997, although significant numbers of these would later return having secured overseas passports.

The question of democracy in Hong Kong represented another major political issue for the territory in the years between Tiananmen and 1997. Before 1985, there had been no elections to the Legislative Council ('Legco', Hong Kong's mini-parliament), and all members were either serving civil servants ('Officials') or representatives of the community, often the business community, chosen by the Governor ('Unofficials'). Indirect elections to Legco first took place in 1985, when twelve members were elected through a system of 'functional constituencies' representing the major professions, and twelve were elected by an electoral college. By 1989, there were 26 elected members out of a total of 57. After Edward Youde's premature death from a heart attack in Beijing in 1986, he was succeeded by another sinologist with a Foreign Office pedigree, David Wilson, who held office from 1987 to 1992. Wilson was serving as Governor at the time of the June 1989 massacre, and represented Hong Kong in the difficult months after Tiananmen. He sought to restore confidence in the Hong Kong economy by pressing ahead with the airport, and by initiating other domestic infrastructure projects. He also embarked on a programme of university expansion, which involved the upgrading of polytechnics and colleges and building a new University of Science and Technology. By the late 1990s this ambitious programme had increased the number of universities from two to eight.[1] The Wilson government held elections

---

[1] In the 1980s, there were only two full universities in Hong Kong: the University of Hong Kong, founded in 1911, and the Chinese University of Hong Kong, established in 1963. After 1989, six other universities were established. These included two new universities, the Hong Kong University of Science and Technology and the Open University of Hong Kong, and four upgraded polytechnics and tertiary colleges, City University of Hong Kong, Hong Kong Baptist University, Hong Kong Polytechnic University and Lingnan University.

in September 1991, and this time the total number of seats in the Legco was expanded to 60, of which 18 were directly elected in geographical constituencies, and 21 from functional constituencies. This was the first time in the history of the territory that the majority of seats in Legco were decided through elections (*South China Morning Post* 1991).

Wilson's successor Christopher Patten, who held office from 1992 to 1997, was a political appointee and moderniser who sought to introduce very substantial democratic reforms. In 1994 he announced a package of electoral reforms which was pushed through in spite of strong opposition from the Beijing government. Essentially, these extended the franchise to all eligible voters in Hong Kong's working population of 2.7 million by broadening the definition of 'functional constituencies' to apply to virtually all professions and trades. These reforms followed the letter of the Basic Law, Hong Kong's mini-constitution finalised by Beijing in 1990, but greatly exceeded its spirit by engineering a revised system of virtual universal enfranchisement (Wong 1992). The culmination of Patten's reforms came in the 1995 election, when the Democrats under Martin Lee Chuming and their allies emerged as the dominant group in Legco (Fung and Wong 1995). By that time, however, Beijing had announced that it would no longer countenance a 'through train' approach to political transition, and began to set up its own government-in-waiting in the form of a 'Preliminary Working Committee', described by Beijing officials at the time as a 'second stove'. On 30 June 1997, the colonial Legco was replaced by a new Beijing-appointed 'Provisional Legislative Council', which included most of the members of the previous Legco, with the exception of the Democrats.

Thus, from the early 1980s to the time of the 'handover' on 30 June 1997, the lives of Hong Kong people were beset by one political drama after another, as a series of shifts and changes were constantly reported in the broadcast and print media. In this period, Hong Kong was routinely rated as one of the world's most stressful cities in which to live, along with Beirut and Belfast. Constant change in the political arena, in China as well as Hong Kong, impinged on the lives of ordinary people as a source of both vague and focused anxiety, as thousands of ordinary people coped with issues of adaptation and/or emigration. Ironically, by 'Ninety Seven' the economy was still booming, with record highs in property and the stock market. In the end, the event itself was anticlimactic. Prince Charles came, attended the handover ceremony, and then he and the Pattens sailed out of the harbour on the *Britannia*. It rained.

The economic and social context – an Asian 'economic miracle'

In the late British colonial period, the image of Hong Kong constructed by the Hong Kong Government and propagated by the domestic and international media was that of a serendipitous success story. For much of the 1980s and 1990s a recurrent motif was that of an Asian economic miracle. The government's annual report for 1986 noted an average annual increase in Gross Domestic

Product (GDP) for the previous decade of 8 per cent, and then went on to claim that the territory was the most important financial centre in Asia, the world's third most important banking and financial centre after New York and London, the world's largest exporter of garments, toys, radios and watches, the world's busiest container port and the world's busiest air cargo operation. The same report also cited the Financial Secretary's 1984 assertion that, over the following decade, Hong Kong's per capita GDP 'could with a bit of luck be of the same order as that in the United Kingdom' (Hong Kong Government 1986: 2).

Ten years later that prediction had come true. In 1996 Daniel Fung, the Solicitor-General, was able to report to the Hong Kong Swiss Business Council that 'our per capita GDP now exceeds that of virtually all developing countries, most European nations including the UK itself, and is not far short of that achieved by the world frontrunner, the USA' (Fung 1996: 3). In the same speech, Fung noted that Hong Kong's GDP had risen by 14,000 per cent, from HK$7 billion in the 1960s to HK$1,105 billion in 1996, the equivalent of approximately 20 per cent of China's GDP. In the 1960s per capita GDP stood at US$410; by 1996 it had risen to US$23,000, a figure higher than that of Australia, Canada and Britain. In addition Fung could also assert that:

> Hong Kong is the eighth largest trading community in the world. We have the seventh largest foreign exchange reserves, the eighth largest stock market ... and we are the fifth largest centre for foreign exchange dealing. We have the world's busiest container port having overtaken Rotterdam some years back and the third busiest international airport. We are completing what will be by the time it opens for business in 1998, second only to Heathrow, the busiest airport anywhere in the world. (Fung 1996: 3)

The story of Hong Kong's economic miracle is well documented elsewhere, but its standard components include the relocation of Shanghainese industry and money to Hong Kong in 1949; the UN embargo against China dating from the Korean War; the growth of Hong Kong as a financial centre during the 1970s; and the shift to 'China trade' during the 'open door' era of the 1980s when Hong Kong was to account for almost 60 per cent of total utilised capital investment in the PRC (Allen 1997: 192).

Capitalist rampage

Beneath the glitter and glitz of this success story there is another story, that of the reality of Hong Kong social history and the life of a striving refugee community which provided the labour force for the economic development of Hong Kong from the early 1950s to the 1990s. Hong Kong's alternative history remains largely unwritten, but some indication of its potential thrust may be seen in the following quotation from a paper entitled 'Hong Kong: Britain's Chinese colony', published by the *New Left Review* in 1974:

There are 300,000 hard drug addicts; 80,000 triad gang members; several hundred thousand squatters; sickness and squalor all around. The post boxes are red. It is hot. The policemen wear short trousers. No doubt about it: this must be a British colony. Of the past one would think. No, the time is now. The location: the South China coast. The name: Hong Kong; the 'fragrant harbour', 'pearl of the Orient'. (Halliday 1974: 91)

The colony, Halliday notes, was a place where 'business can go on a permanent rampage, 24 hours a day, 365 days a year' (1974: 94). Halliday's view of Hong Kong reveals 'a reality of exploitation and degradation', where '[u]nder the formal regalia of the Crown this fantastic concentration of wretchedness and cunning has become today's Hong Kong' (1974: 100). Ironically, perhaps, Halliday ends with a plea for an 'immediate end' to colonial rule, thus implying the need for the transfer to Chinese sovereignty at a time when, across the border, the chaos and terror of the Cultural Revolution had still not run its full course.

Population and immigration

Another important part of this story involves the demographics of population and population movement. In 1945 the population was just 600,000, down from an estimated 1.6 million in 1940, while by 1996 the by-census registered an estimated 6.2 million permanent residents. Successive waves of immigration, in the early 1950s and 1960s, led to rapid increases in the numbers of immigrants from the People's Republic of China. Approximately 400,000 mainland Chinese entered Hong Kong in the 1950s, and 120,000 in the 1960s (Siu 1996: 339–40). Until 1980, the Hong Kong government maintained a 'touch-base' policy that permitted illegal immigrants to settle permanently if they were able to reach the 'urban areas' of the colony. This policy ended in 1980, but illegal immigration has continued on a reduced scale until the present day. In addition to the arrival of 'IIs' (illegal immigrants) there has also been a system of legal immigration from the late 1970s onwards. In the 1980s, legal immigrants were arriving in Hong Kong at the rate of 75 a day, and by the mid-1990s this figure had risen to 150. In the 1961 census the population totalled 3.1 million; in the by-census of 1966 it had reached 3.7 million; by the 1971 census, 3.9 million; in the 1981 census 5.2 million; in the 1991 census 5.6; and in the 1996 by-census 6.2 million. The pattern of population growth in the post-war period is illustrated in figure 2.2, which provides an overview of Hong Kong population trends throughout the years of British colonialism.

Another dimension of population movement relates to the attitude of Hong Kong people to the territory as a place of residence or 'home'. Throughout the greater part of the history of the territory, the majority of the population regarded themselves as 'sojourners', or temporary residents, who came to Hong Kong for purposes of work, trade, or migration. There were minimal border controls and people were able to move back and forth into Guangdong province very easily, but home was somewhere else, as Ching (1994) explains:

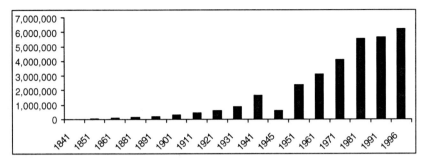

Figure 2.2 The population of Hong Kong, 1841–1996
Sources: Harris (1983: 32), Castells (1986: 16), Hong Kong Government (1996: 12)[2]

Hong Kong had virtually no settled population. True, most of the population was Chinese. This had been the case since the day Captain Charles
Elliot set foot on Hong Kong Island and claimed it for the British Crown.
The small number of indigenous inhabitants, mostly fishermen, were
quickly outnumbered by new arrivals – diplomats, military men and traders
from Britain, Portuguese from Macao, as well as businessmen, legitimate
and otherwise, from Europe and North America. But, most of all, the new
arrivals came from China. Like their Western counterparts, they came to
make their fortune, or merely to find work. Hong Kong offered hope for
young men in a hurry. It offered opportunities that did not exist either
in Europe or in China. But while the young colony attracted people from
the four corners of the world, no one came with the idea of living there
permanently. 'Home' continued to be somewhere else, a village in China
or a county in England . . . For the vast majority of the inhabitants, Hong
Kong simply was not home. (Ching 1994: 4)

The population profile of the community throughout the twentieth century is
presented in table 2.1. As can be seen from the table, from the 1910s to the1930s,
the proportion of residents who were born in the territory fluctuated from around
26–32 per cent of the total. In 1921, for example, only 26.7 per cent reported
Hong Kong as their place of birth; and 69 per cent were born in Guangdong
(Kwangtung) province (of whom 12.8 per cent claimed Sze Yap or 'Si Yi' provenance) and 2.7 per cent were from Chiu Chau (Chaozhou).

It was not until the mid-1960s that a majority of the population could claim
Hong Kong as their place of birth. This also coincided with the emergence of
the term 香港人 *hēung góng yàhn*,[3] i.e. 'Hong Kong person'/'people', and the
beginnings of a distinct Hong Kong identity.

---

[2] Figure 2.2 is based on population estimates from Harris (1983), Castells (1986) and the Hong
Kong Government (1996).
[3] A sizeable number of romanisation systems exist for the transcription of Mandarin Chinese and
Cantonese. Until relatively recently, sinologists and other Chinese scholars used the *Wade–Giles*

Table 2.1 *Population, by place of birth, 1911–91*

Place of birth	Percentage						
	1911	1921	1931	1961	1971	1981	1991
Total	100.0	100.0	100.0	100.0	100.0	100.0	100.0
Hong Kong	31.5	26.7	32.5	47.7	56.4	57.2	59.8
Canton, Macao and adjacent places	–	52.8	41.6	27.0	23.8	20.7	–
Sze Yap	–	12.8	11.9	10.0	7.0	–	–
Chiu Chau	–	2.7	2.3	4.7	4.2	–	–
Elsewhere in Guangdong	–	0.8	6.7	3.9	2.5	13.3	–
Subtotal, Guangdong	61.3	69.1	62.5	45.6	37.5	34.0	–
Coastal provinces and Shanghai	0.5	0.7	0.4	4.1	3.5	–	–
Elsewhere in China	0.4	0.4	1.4	0.8	0.6	5.6	–
China	–	–	–	–	–	–	34.4
Macao	–	–	–	–	–	–	1.2
Other countries	1.8	1.4	2.2	1.8	2.0	3.2	4.6
Unknown	4.6	1.7	1.0	–	–	–	–

Sources: United Nations. Economic and Social Commission for Asia and the Pacific (1974), Hong Kong Government (1981, 1991).

Housing and housing density

The story of Hong Kong's late colonial period was also one of living space. From the late 1940s onwards, the colony had the character of a poor refugee immigrant community struggling for room to breathe in a city that was frequently ranked the world's most crowded. In the 1950s and 1960s refugees and immigrants poured

system from the late nineteenth century and the Chinese Post Office system to transcribe proper names, place names and even examples of speech, especially in Mandarin. In the last thirty years, these systems have largely been replaced by *Pinyin*, the officially endorsed mainland system for the transcription of Putonghua. Thus today 'Ch'ing' as in 'Ch'ing dynasty' is most frequently transcribed as 'Qing', similarly 'Foochow' is now 'Fuzhou', 'Swatow' is now 'Shantou' etc., although 'Hong Kong' has yet to become 'Xianggang', at least within the HKSAR. Throughout this book, wherever early sources are used, the authors' original system of romanisation is usually retained, although this may vary a great deal. In the modern period, linguists in Hong Kong have chiefly used either the 'Yale' system of transcription for Cantonese, or the International Phonetic Alphabet (IPA) system, although recently a newer system devised by the Linguistic Society of Hong Kong (LSHK) has also gained currency. Detailed charts comparing romanisation systems are found in Matthews and Yip (1994: 400–1) and Bauer and Benedict (1997: 471–5). The Yale system is used for transcribing Cantonese throughout various sections of this volume, particularly in chapter 4 and appendix 4, where there is detailed transcription of a number of written Chinese texts. A comparison of correspondences between the Yale and IPA systems is set out in appendix 3, table A3.1, while table A3.2 illustrates the tone-marking conventions used in the Yale system. The Yale system used throughout this book differentiates six tones: *high tone, mid-rising, mid-level, low-level, low-rising* and *low-falling*.

into the territory in successive waves, fighting for a place on the housing ladder that reached from the most primitive forms of dwelling and squatter huts through a hierarchy of public housing – resettlement estates, newer estates, new towns and home ownership schemes – to middle-class private flats and to the luxury apartments of the Mid-Levels, Repulse Bay and Sai Kung.

In 1950, a British writer named Harold Ingrams was commissioned to write an extended report on Hong Kong. In an illuminating section of the book, Ingrams describes the 'appalling' living conditions of the 'vast majority of the people', asserting that '[i]n some ways conditions in this modern and wealthy city of Hong Kong are worse than they were in England in 1840' (Ingrams 1952: 69). Ingrams noted that, at this time, the standard dwelling in Hong Kong was a four-storey tenement, describing life in a typical tenement thus:

> Steep and rickety stairs led to the first floor, where 28 were living in a flat that could have held about six reasonably. There were five or six cubicles along one side and double-tiered bunks on the other. Each cubicle or bunk represents 'home' to one or more people. At the back was a small dark communal kitchen with a tap and bucket for washing, and covered wooden bucket for latrine for all these people... Another steep flight took us to the top floor, where the arrangements were the same and where 32 people lived... Under the one window in the front a boy of about 15 sat on a stool. Before him, laid out on a packing-case top on another stool were exercise books and a book on mathematics. He went to night school, the only school he could get into, and did odd jobs to earn money and was going to be an engineer. (Ingrams 1952: 71)

Later, Ingrams goes on to emphasise that '[t]hese conditions, it must be remembered, are those in which *most* of the working class people of the colony live', and that '[n]ever in my life, in Africa, in Europe, in Arabia, had I seen slums worse than these' (1952: 72). At the same time, he also adds that he had never met slum-dwellers 'who looked so clean and tidy, so cheerful and welcoming', noting that '[t]he Chinese seem able to rise above the drabbest surroundings' (1952: 72).

The housing problems of the early 1950s were exacerbated by continuing waves of immigration from mainland China, with the population growing at the rate of around one million every decade from the 1950s to the 1980s. From 1954 onwards the government embarked on a policy of providing low-cost public housing to rehouse the residents of squatter estates in the territory. By 1982, two million people, approximately 43 per cent of the population, had been housed or rehoused in public housing. This meant that of all capitalist societies, Hong Kong was in second place after Singapore in providing state-subsidised apartments and housing units (Castells 1986: 5). The quality of such units, however, was very low, as 'housing in Hong Kong has been built to the absolute minimum standards which could be tolerated by human beings' (Cuthbert 1985: 143). During the same period, districts of Hong Kong such as Mongkok were frequently cited as the most-densely populated on the planet.

There appears little consensus on the human effects of such overcrowding on Hong Kong people, but Cuthbert comments *inter alia* that 'overcrowding... is directly related to the main indicators of socio-economic class', that 'the poorest people live in the oldest parts of the city, under the most crowded conditions, with the highest residential densities' and that '[t]here are indications that in these areas fertility rates are high, as well as the incidence of mental health problems and crime' (Cuthbert 1985: 136). Even in the better public housing estates and private flats it is common for families of five or six persons to live in small apartments of 400–500 square feet. In many such housing estates, Chinese criminal gangs or 'triads' maintain a strong presence. In addition, activities taken for granted in other societies, such as entertaining guests or taking up hobbies, are severely hindered (Wong 1989: 235). Such high-density living also entails a lack of privacy, creating a range of problems unknown in other societies. For instance, successive reports on the family conditions of University of Hong Kong students in the 1980s showed that the vast majority lacked both a room of their own and a table of their own where they might carry out their studies. In 1985, for example, only 15.8 per cent of Hong Kong University students had their own room and desk at home; 27.6 per cent had no room but did have a desk; and 55.1 per cent had neither a room nor a desk of their own (Hong Kong University 1985: 14).

Social class in Hong Kong

Despite the sizeable disparities of wealth that have characterised Hong Kong society throughout its history, class consciousness has been generally very low. One influential analysis in the 1980s was that of Lau (1982), whose central argument was that immigrant Chinese society in Hong Kong was essentially shaped by three social pressures: a desire for social stability; an emphasis on materialism; and a short-term time horizon. Lau asserted the dominant 'cultural code' in the late colonial era was that of 'utilitarianistic familism', and explains that '[u]tilitarianistic familism can be defined as the normative and behavioural tendency of an individual to place his familial interests above the interests of society and of other individuals in such a manner that the furtherance of his familial interests is the overriding concern' (Lau 1982: 72). In contrast to the organisational force of family obligations, Lau argues that notions of social class were weak and undefined. In his own survey work, only 35.4 per cent of respondents identified themselves as 'working class', and he concluded that 'the fragmented conception of class structure tends to impede the formation, at least in an ideological sense, of two polarised and antagonistic classes, or the possibility of class conflict', and that 'social classes as structural forces in shaping interpersonal relationships and political actions are relatively insignificant in Hong Kong' (Lau 1982: 98).

Other commentators noted the growing importance of a 'new middle class' at this time. Lee suggested that even by the mid-1970s it was possible to recognise the emergence of a new middle class composed of salaried employees in non-manual occupations – ranging from junior clerks and secretarial staff to senior professionals and administrators – which accounted for 36.5 per cent of the population, compared to 51.6 per cent for the working class, and 11.9 per cent for the capitalist class (Lee 1982: 27–8). In his much later survey of the sociological literature, Leung (1996) argues strongly in favour of the notion of the new middle class and its importance for explaining class formation in contemporary Hong Kong society:

> Composed of better-educated and better-paid professionals, administrators, and managers, and lower-level clerical and white-collar workers, the new middle-class can be expected to differ from the class of manual labourers in lifestyle, attitudes, and social aspirations. Furthermore, a substantial portion of the new middle-class were born and raised in Hong Kong, and they do not share the refugee experience and mentality of the older generations. The size of the new middle-class cannot be accurately gauged, but with the society's continuing affluence and the rapid expansion of the economy's tertiary sector, they are judged to make up the majority of the population in the 1980s and early 1990s. Hong Kong has been evolving in the past two decades into a predominantly middle-class society. (Leung 1996: 12)

This social transformation of Hong Kong at the time was accompanied by, if not engineered by, a parallel restructuring of the economy.

The economic transformation of Hong Kong, 1980–97

From 1946 to 1951, Hong Kong functioned primarily as an entrepot for China trade but, with the outbreak of the Korean War and the imposition of a United Nations embargo on trade with China, Hong Kong started its own industries, in particular textiles and garment manufacture. This would not have been possible without the injection of relocated Shanghainese capital and expertise. After trade with China was reopened in 1979, Hong Kong again took on an entrepot role, and its economic base then began to shift from light manufacturing to 'services', including trading, finance and the tourist industry (Ellis 1998: 37). In the 1980s, Hong Kong entrepreneurs moved their factories over the border to southern China where, by the late 1990s, they were employing over 5 million factory workers in the Pearl River delta region. Tsang (1999) reports that Hong Kong's entrepot activity now accounts for more than half of China's overseas trade, that the territory is China's largest 'outside investor' and that, since the early 1980s, there has been a 'structural transformation' of the Hong Kong economy from a manufacturing to a service economy (1999: 31–2).

Evidence for such a claim can be found in macroeconomic statistics. From 1961 to 1996, the share of the manufacturing sector in GDP dropped from around 23.6 per cent to 7.2 per cent, while the number of manufacturing workers fell from 43 per cent of the workforce in 1960 to 12.6 per cent by 1997. Simultaneously, the numbers of those working in service sectors increased sharply, from 14.4 per cent to 43.8 per cent in wholesale, retail, restaurants and hotels; and from 1.6 per cent to 17.9 per cent in the financial and real-estate sector; a process sometimes referred to as 'Manhattanization' (Tsang 1999: 32).[4]

The ongoing transformation of the economy continues to the present. Tsang suggests that recent developments have led to 'a lopsided economic structure', further impacted by the surge in property prices in the years immediately prior to 1997 (1999: 33). Others, such as Ellis (1998), are a good deal more optimistic and argue that 'Hong Kong has become the second most highly developed service economy in the world, after the United States' (1998: 37). Ellis argues that Hong Kong's role as a service centre is best understood in relation to its strategic importance in providing the skills such as finance, design and technology transfer necessary for the development of the territory's hinterland in Guangdong province, which has now become 'Asia's fifth dragon economy' (Ellis 1998: 37–8). In addition, Ellis claims that Hong Kong has an important 'tertius' (or triangulated middleman) role to play between China and, first, western traders, and, second, the overseas Chinese, including the Taiwanese. It does this primarily by re-exporting manufactured goods to and from China, but also through its involvement in offshore trade (e.g. from China to EU countries), which by the late 1990s had netted Hong Kong in the region of US$84 billion. This partly explains the territory's strength as a regional centre for multinational corporations – numbering some 700 compared with 200 in Singapore – and its role as a 'global broker' (Ellis 1998: 40). Ellis also acknowledges 'Hong Kong's highly cosmopolitan population' and its internationalism:

> Apart from the diverse mix of resident nationalities and ethnic groups present, Hong Kong benefits from a citizenry characterized by significant overseas exposure. Around one-third of Hong Kong's university students will be educated abroad in U.S. or Commonwealth institutions. Moreover, if the degree of internationalism is reflected in communications behavior, it is instructive to note that Hong Kong's 6.3 million residents logged a per capita average of 270 minutes of international phone calls in 1995, compared to Singapore's 176 minutes and Japan's 13 minutes. Given these figures, it is not surprising that Hong Kong is Asia's largest teleport, providing international transmissions via a network of 15 commercial satellites. (Ellis 1998: 41)

Whatever the differences between Ellis and Tsang, both agree that the period from the 1980s to 1997 was one of rapid and dramatic change in the economic structure of the territory.

---

[4] A detailed analysis of the transformation of the economy throughout this period is discussed by Leung (1996: 7) and Tsang (1999: 32).

Social welfare and education in Hong Kong

Although Hong Kong's official image in the 1980s and 1990s was that of a *laissez-faire* society where a spirit of 'positive non-interventionism' was a declared policy of the administration, the reality was very different, as the government intervened directly in both housing and social welfare. First, the government was very active in the supervision if not manipulation of land supply and the property market. As Bell explains:

> The Hong Kong government actually derives much of its revenue from land transactions. The territory's land is technically owned by the government, and the government fills its coffers by selling fifty-year leases to developers (the fact that there are no absolute private property rights to land will come as another surprise to boosters of 'Hong Kong-style' libertarianism). (Bell 1998: 16)

From the 1980s until 1997 property prices rose dramatically, and the government was able to benefit from what became the highest property prices in the world. The second major beneficiary of soaring property prices was the local cartel of property developers, with just three real-estate companies dominating the market, and the heads of two of these companies being ranked among the richest men in the world (Bell 1998: 16).

A second major area where government intervention was exercised was in the provision of housing and social welfare. The key era of government involvement here was that of the reformist governor Murray MacLehose, whose period of office ran from 1971 to 1982. MacLehose created the second largest public housing programme in the capitalist world, and oversaw large-scale government intervention in health care, hospitals, transport and education. Such programmes were expanded by succeeding administrations and, from 1991 to 1997, government spending on social services increased at a rate around 10 per cent per year. By the year 1995–6, this accounted for 47 per cent of expenditure, more than Singapore and Taiwan, and a little less than the United Kingdom (Bell 1998: 16).

Education played an enormous part in the social transformation of Hong Kong during this period and, as we shall see later, was an important social variable contributing to patterns of language learning and the spread of English. Before the 1970s, schooling in Hong Kong was generally elitist, and there were also the logistical problems of dealing with vast numbers of refugees. Provision for secondary education was limited, and it was only after the introduction in 1974 and 1978 of educational reforms providing for universal, compulsory and free secondary education that an era of mass education was introduced (Sweeting 1997). In 1989, Governor David Wilson announced the government's intention to expand tertiary education, from around 3 or 4 per cent of the cohort educated at the University of Hong Kong and the Chinese University to around 18 per cent of the cohort in university institutions, and another 7 per cent at other types of colleges. Indeed, as noted above, by the late 1990s, the number of universities had expanded from two to eight.

Over the last twenty-five years, therefore, the expansion of education contributed significantly to the creation of the 'new middle class' discussed above, and also contributed to an increase in equality of opportunity within the society. The proportion of those with either no schooling or only primary education was almost 60 per cent in 1971; by 1991 this figure had dropped to 37.8 per cent. The total for those with secondary education was 33.2 per cent in 1976, which rose to 46 per cent by 1991. For tertiary education, the comparable figures were 4.8 per cent in 1976 compared to 11.3 per cent and rising by 1991 (Leung 1996: 11).[5]

The cultural identity of Hong Kong people – the emergence of hēung góng yàhn

The period of the formation of modern Hong Kong also saw the rise of a distinct cultural identity for 'Hong Kong people' (*hēung góng yàhn*). The emergence and development of this distinct cultural identity began after the 1967 riots which resulted in the majority of the territory's population supporting the colonial government after communist-led groups had set off bombs and carried out killings throughout the summer of that year. The development of a local consciousness was also influenced by the popularity of Cantonese television and films throughout the 1970s and 1980s. Various analyses of this have been put forward by sociologists, anthropologists and historians.

Leung (1996), from the perspective of sociology, suggests that the creation of the modern 'Hong Kong experience' took place throughout the 1970s to the 1990s. In his analysis of the 'moral outlook' of the Hong Kong people, Leung focuses on their materialism and pragmatism and approvingly cites Abbas' comment that 'the only form of political idealism that has a chance [in Hong Kong] is that which can go together with economic self-interest', an attitude that contributes to 'the amoral, utilitarian, and individualist Hong Kong ethos' (Abbas 1992: 5, cited in Leung 1996: 54).

In broad terms, Leung interprets the development of Hong Kong popular culture in terms of 'Chinese tradition and its encounter with Westernization', suggesting that two main strands of influence were, first, the experience of refugees from premodern Guangdong and, second, the reinvention of Shanghai cosmopolitanism in a local context. The first, he argues, found expression in the Cantonese cinema of the period, whereas the Shanghai influence was shown in the popularity of songs in Mandarin Chinese recorded by Shanghai singers. This early phase was followed by a period of Anglo-American influence, the popularity of James Bond and the rock'n'roll of Elvis Presley and the Beatles. The

---

[5] Detailed statistics on changing patterns of education from the 1970s to 1990s are set out here in Leung (1996: 11).

rise of a modern 'indigenous' Cantonese-based culture began in the early 1970s, spawned by television, where local filmmakers became engaged in the making of socially realistic soap operas or 'drama serials', whose popularity continues to the present. Cantonese pop music and feature films, the latter inspired by the success of Bruce Lee, took off in the same period. By the end of the 1980s, the popularity of the Cantonese cinema had reached its high point. Leung reports that, in 1989, only one foreign film (*Indiana Jones*) made the list of the top ten box-office attractions (1996: 67). He explains the rise of popular culture in this period in terms of the expression of a new 'Hong Kong identity', where increasing numbers of local people saw themselves as 'Hongkongese' (or 'Hongkongers'), and comments that:

> while the Hong Kong people have been shedding their colonial cultural baggage, they are also increasingly disposed to regard themselves as distinct from the mainland Chinese. In other words, the rise of the Hong Kong identity is a dual process of dissociation from colonial cultural domination as well as from the social and political life of the mainland. Seen in this light, the articulation of the Hong Kong identity is a cultural and perhaps subconsciously political project – a project which has acquired added significance with the approach of 1997. (Leung 1996: 68)

Leung suggests that in this period Hong Kong people also came to regard main land Chinese as an inferior 'other'. The typical representations of the mainland stereotype ('Ah Chaan' 阿燦) in films and television of this period were variously as country bumpkin, dangerously criminal, or 'authentically Chinese'. Another strand of Leung's analysis registers the scarcity of radical social criticism, and notes the materialistic and utilitarian 'ethos' of money, luxury and materialism in Hong Kong culture (1996: 70).

Evans and Tam (1997), from the perspective of urban anthropology, take issue with sociologists like Leung and Lau Siu-kai who conceive of the 'Hong Kong ethos' in relation to a particular view of 'Chinese culture'. As Evans and Tam point out, 'the discourse on Hong Kong culture among academics often echoes the terms found in tourist brochures: Hong Kong is a place where "East meets West", but where "Chinese tradition" still holds sway' (1997: 4). The origins of this cliché, they point out, were in the colonial past when the fabled meeting in reality meant a 'cultural stand-off' between the Chinese, the colonial officials and more or less everyone else. However inappropriate in contemporary Hong Kong, Evans and Tam note that shards of this discourse remain embedded in the academic and political psyche:

> This colonial history established a powerful discourse of 'East meets West' and the 'modern world meets Chinese tradition'. There was, of course, for a long time a strong 'racial' discourse as well, with the British seeing themselves as representatives of 'civilisation' and Chinese customs as 'barbarian'; while for their part the Chinese held a mirror image of the

gwailou (foreigner). But this discourse has not survived, although academic and political debates in Hong Kong often disturbingly echo these faded sentiments. (Evans and Tam 1997: 5)

In their deconstruction of the 'East meets West' ideological discourse, they make it clear that the recurring opposition between notions of 'western' and 'traditional Chinese/Confucianist' covers a multitude of woolly thoughts and contradictions. Evans and Tam are concerned with the power of stereotypes such as 'westernization' as an unfocused blanket explanation for historical change and modernity. They note that '[m]uch of the debate around Hong Kong identity and culture is dogged by either implicit conceptions of culture, or unclearly defined ones'. In this context, the notion of 'traditional Chinese culture' translates into 'an ideal fantasy past', so that all too often, 'the sociology of Hong Kong has succumbed to a form of idealism in which analysis of the real world is spirited away' (Evans and Tam 1997: 9–10).

Young's (1996) paper on 'Changing identities in Hong Kong' provides a revealing historical perspective on the issues related to 'Chineseness' and the 'Hong Kong identity', that complements that of Evans and Tam. Young notes that the issue of 'Chinese' identity has a long and unresolved history, and notes that, in the Hong Kong context, the expression of the sentiment 'We Chinese' has its own complex history. The point of origin, as in other accounts, is the separation of Hong Kong from mainland China in 1949, and the creation of a refugee community:

> By the end of 1949, those Chinese who had arrived in Hong Kong as refugees, or made a conscious attempt not to return to China instinctively knew that they had chosen to become 'overseas' Chinese. Thus it is not surprising that in the late 40's and early 50's, Hong Kong Chinese were referred to as overseas Chinese by the Taiwan Nationalist regime; local Hong Kong newspapers used the term 'Hong Kong residents', and the designation of a 'Hong Kong person' simply did not exist. (Young 1996: 8)

In the 1950s, Young continues, the Hong Kong Chinese saw themselves as preserving the essence of Chinese culture, because the mainland was dominated by the 'foreign' ideology of Marxist-Leninism, and that 'being Chinese in 50s and 60s Hong Kong meant being Cantonese' (1996: 9). This too was a vague category, because Guangdong was, and is, home to 'numerous dialects, hundreds of counties, and thousands of villages', but Cantonese in Hong Kong was defined against two 'others' – non-Cantonese from the rest of China and *gwailos* from overseas. Young argues that, in colonial Hong Kong, concessions were made to Cantonese culture, and cites the examples of concubinage, legal until the early 1970s, and eating dog-meat, which though illegal still occurs. In recent years, he suggests, there has been a strengthening of Cantonese identity, and '[w]hen a Hong Kong person discusses his Chineseness, that is, "We Chinese", very often what this person really means is "We Cantonese" ' (1996: 11).

Young goes on to explain that the emergence of the label or classification of 'Hong Kong person' appeared only after the 1967 riots, when the majority of Hong Kong residents, appalled at incidents of bombings and murders, consciously chose to support the British colonial regime rather than local communist activists. This meant that 'the [colonial] government ended up winning the sympathies and support of the local population' (1996: 13). Simultaneously, students began to debate the question of identity:

> University students, in endless debates on the question of identity (a new concept in colonial Hong Kong in the late 60's and early 70's), decided that their parents might have been refugees, but that their home was first and foremost Hong Kong, and therefore they must be Hong Kong persons. In short, they were Hong Kong Chinese, different from their compatriots on the Chinese mainland, or in Taiwan. A Hong Kong Chinese was traditional, but he or she also accepted foreign values, and especially Western (although never clearly defined) ways of doing things. Mainland China was seen not only as a separate political entity, but even more significantly, as a totally different cultural-social system from Hong Kong. (Young 1996: 13–4)

After the 1967 riots, the government became more responsive to the needs of the population, introducing new labour regulations, social welfare measures and a public housing programme. Democracy was not yet an issue:

> Caught between colonialism and Communism, and with independence never an option, the fight for democracy seemed meaningless indeed. Ironically, it was only when the majority of Hong Kong people realized that they were being 'handed over' to a Communist regime that democracy gradually became an appeal. (Young 1996: 15)

Young is pessimistic about the survival of a Hong Kong identity, which he sees as being wedded to the future political agenda of the PRC with reference, for example, to Taiwan. His conclusion is that 'the Hong Kong experience has been an unique one in the history of Modern China, and perhaps in the history of the world, and it deserves, and needs to be recorded', but he states that '[a]s for the Hong Kong identity of the Hong Kong person, its survival is not guaranteed' (1996: 18).

The political, economic and social context, 1980–97

The picture that emerges from this review of the contemporary history of Hong Kong is one of rapid and continuous change. At the political level, negotiations concerning the 'return' of Hong Kong sovereignty to the PRC were followed by the 1984 Joint Declaration and, later, the reaction to the events of Tiananmen Square in June 1989. Anxiety about the political future also contributed significantly to emigration throughout the 1990s, leading to a growing diaspora of overseas Hong Kong Chinese in North America and Australia.

At the economic and social levels, a range of specific forces combined to create modern Hong Kong. Economically, these included the transformation of the economy from manufacturing towards financial and service sectors, a transformation that accelerated the growth of a new middle class, who also benefited from the increased wealth of the society. Hong Kong's wealth, measured by GDP figures at least, even surpassed that of the UK in the early years of the 1990s. This same middle class was also able to benefit from the Hong Kong government's increased social welfare provisions, which began in the 1970s and resulted in a huge programme of public housing and the provision of inexpensive medical care through a system of public hospitals. It was also significant in the field of education, as the educational reforms of the 1970s established a system of free compulsory primary and secondary education for all children in the territory. These reforms, together with those in tertiary education, have a direct and major impact on patterns of language learning in the community (see pp. 91–8 below).

At the same time, however, Hong Kong people also had to deal with extremely crowded conditions, with an urban housing density that was among the highest in the world. At the lowest end of the housing scale, Hong Kong still has what the government officially calls 'bed-space apartments', and others refer to as 'cages'. Wood (1997: 38) claims that in the year of the handover, there were up to 10,000 people still living in such 'cages', and describes the five-by-eight-foot cubicle shared by a factory worker and his two sons. Vast differentials of income and personal wealth continue to exist, and a *South China Morning Post* editorial in 1997 reported that Hong Kong had 600,000 people living 'below the poverty line', and went on to note that the rich accounted for 10 per cent of the population but controlled 42 per cent of the wealth of the society, while at the other end of the scale 50 per cent shared 19 per cent (*South China Morning Post* 1997). Even by 1997, the benefits of the 'miracle' economy did not extend to everyone in the society.

Culturally, this same period also saw the emergence of 'Hong Kong people' and a distinct 'Hong Kong identity' as a complex unit of analysis for sociology, anthropology and contemporary history. Writing from the viewpoint of cultural studies, Abbas (1997) notes that 'the Hong Kong Chinese are now culturally and politically quite distinct from mainlanders', and asserts that Hong Kong has been transformed from a *colonial* city to a *global* city (Abbas 1997: 2). Abbas cites King's observation that 'colonial cities can be viewed as the *forerunners* of what the contemporary capitalist world city would eventually become' (King 1990: 38) and adds that 'with the end of imperialism, colonialism could take a global form, and . . . it could decisively abandon the old imperial attitudes and even take on benign characteristics, as in the case of Hong Kong' (Abbas 1997: 3). A related argument thus is 'culture in Hong Kong cannot just be related to "colonialism"; it must be related to this changed and changing space, this colonial space of disappearance, which in many respects does not resemble the old colonialisms at all' (1997: 3). Ultimately, Abbas suggests, the survival of Hong Kong culture will depend on the recognition of the new forms of space – geographical, concrete and cultural – that Hong Kong's recent development as a world city entails:

> One of the most important implications of colonialism in the era of glob-alism is simply that there is no longer a space elsewhere. This means that instead of thinking in terms of displacements, a movement somewhere else, it is important to think in terms of dislocation, which is the transforma-tion of place. Such transformations, even after they have taken place, are often indiscernible and hence challenge recognition. That is why cultural survival is also a matter of changing the forms of attention and seeing the importance of even decadent or degenerate cultural objects. Finally, cul-tural survival will depend on our recognizing that there is today a politics of the indiscernible as much as a politics of the discernible. One has not completely replaced the other, but each acts as the other's silent support. Whether Hong Kong culture as postculture can survive will depend on whether it recognizes a politics of disappearance. (Abbas 1997: 146)

The first part of this chapter has discussed the sociopolitical background to Hong Kong in the late colonial period from 1980 until 1997. The second part will proceed to discuss the role of language within the society, with reference to the sociolinguistics of Chinese and English in the Hong Kong 'speech community'.

The Hong Kong speech community

Within sociolinguistics, the concept of the *speech community* is by no means uncontentious, and the term is defined variously by different sociolinguists (see Hudson 1980: 25–30). Linguists such as Bloomfield and Lyons place the emphasis on a shared language system of some kind, while others such as Labov write of the importance of 'shared norms' rather than a shared language. A similar view is taken by Romaine, who explains the term thus:

> A speech community is not necessarily coextensive with a language com-munity. A speech community is a group of people who do not necessarily share the same language, but share a set of norms and rules for the use of language. The boundaries between speech communities are essentially social rather than linguistic. This means that terms such as 'language' and 'dialect' are, from a linguistic point of view, non-technical notions since there is no objective way to determine when two varieties will be seen by their speakers as sufficiently similar to warrant calling them the 'same' language. (Romaine 1994: 22)

The emphasis here is on the 'norms' and 'rules' for the use of languages, which essentially involve the perceptions, beliefs and attitudes of language users in a particular society. For example, if members of a community regard the use of a number of different languages in a society as a 'norm', they might then include speakers of 'other' languages in their vision of a multilingual speech community.

Alternatively, they may wish to exclude certain ethnic and linguistic groups from their community, and the use of particular languages might be one factor that determines such decisions. The language attitudes of people in a community may then play an important role in determining the characteristics of that society as a speech community. The implications of this for Hong Kong are twofold: first, that if one thinks of the society as a monolingual society, one's perception of the speech community will be that of a Chinese-speaking (and Cantonese-speaking) society. Second, to consider Hong Kong to be a multilingual society involves an attitudinal dimension that recognises and accepts the multilingualism and ethnic diversity of the community.

The view taken here is that Hong Kong is, and historically always has been, a multilingual society, although the specifics of that multilingualism and multi-dialectalism have varied throughout its history. For the purposes of the discussion which follows it may be helpful (though simultaneously reductive) to conceive of the society as comprising three distinct (yet overlapping) types of speech community, that is, the Chinese speech community; the English-speaking speech community; and minority speech communities. In the past, the Chinese and English-speaking communities were typically conceived of as quite separate, but one outstanding feature of the recent linguistic history of Hong Kong is that the numbers of Hong Kong Chinese speakers of English grew rapidly and dramatically in the period of late British colonialism. The history and current dynamics of minority ethnolinguistic groups in the society is under-researched, but it is clear that communities of South Asians, Parsees, Portuguese and Eurasians played a major role in nineteenth-century Hong Kong. Today, groups of Indians, Parsees and Eurasians still exist in the territory, as do Indonesians, Filipinos, Japanese, Malaysians, Nepalis and Thais.

The Hong Kong Chinese speech community

In contemporary Hong Kong, the overwhelming majority of the citizens are ethnically Chinese and are either immigrants from southern China, especially Guangdong and Fujian provinces, or the descendants of those immigrants. Modern Hong Kong has gone through a process of 'dialect-levelling' that has seen the adoption of a localised Hong Kong norm for Cantonese, although that appears to be a relatively recent phenomenon. Some insight into the local language situation at the very beginning of British colonialism is available in the report of the missionary George Smith who visited the early colony in the mid-1840s, and described the language situation there thus:

> Another difficulty, which impresses on Hong Kong a peculiar ineligibil-ity as a Missionary Station, is the great *diversity of dialects* which prevails among its limited population of 19,000 Chinese, and which is necessarily produced by the heterogeneous elements of which it is composed. There are three principal dialects in the island, the speaker of one of which would

be unintelligible to the speaker of another. Under these there are other sub-divisions of the local dialect, more or less distinct, but presenting some features of resemblance. There is the *Hok-ha* [Hakka] dialect, spoken by 3500 settlers from the north-east of the Canton province. The *Pun-te* [Punti, Cantonese], or dialect of the place and neighbourhood, is also subdivided into the *Sin-On* [San-on, Sinan], spoken by the original inhabitants and the settlers from Macao; the *Pwan-yu* [Pun-yue, Panyu], spoken by the settlers from Whampoa; and the *Nan-hoi* [Nam-hoi, Nanhai]. There are also the *Hak-lo* [Hoklo, i.e. Chiu Chau, Fukien] dialect from Fokeen, and some other varieties, each of them spoken by a few hundreds or tens of persons. In such a place, a student of the Chinese language would be placed under great disadvantages. Not only would a Missionary be hindered in his usefulness by the perplexing variety of dialects, but it would be next to impossible for a foreign student of ordinary talent, who had not previously studied the language in some other part, ever to attain a fluent and correct pronunciation of any dialect in Hong Kong. (1847: 511–12)

Smith was visiting Hong Kong in 1845, just three years after the British had established a naval and military base on the island, and was reporting on its suitability as a mission station for the great project of evangelising China. The three major local languages he identifies, *Pun-te* ('Punti' or 'Cantonese'), *Hok-ha* (Hakka) and Hoklo (a term used to refer to varieties of the Fujian/Fukien dialect group), continue to be spoken in Hong Kong today.

Cantonese ('Punti') and other varieties of Chinese. The term *Pun-te* that Smith uses in the above quotation is a transliteration of the Cantonese *bún deih* (本地), meaning 'local', 'native to the country' and, by extension, 'local people'. The spelling was later regularised as 'Punti', a somewhat archaic item of Hong Kong English lexis still used in the Hong Kong law courts to refer to the 'Cantonese' language. In the nineteenth and early twentieth centuries the term *bún deih* was used in distinction to *Hakka* (客家), meaning 'guest family'. This referred to the Hakka or Kejia speakers who, some historians believe, migrated southward from Shanxi province in northern China to the southern provinces in successive waves of migration that began in AD 317. Hakka migrants are claimed to have entered Guangdong between 1127 and 1644 (Moser 1985). The Hoklo of Fujian origin also migrated southwards into Guangdong province, and large numbers of Hokkien (Fukien 福建) people also settled in the far west of Guangdong province and on Hainan Island. Cantonese as a descriptive term for language has a rather recent history, as Faure (1996) explains:

The word 'Cantonese' is a Western word that does not have an exact Chinese equivalent. It was used in the nineteenth century to denote the Cantonese dialect, which in the Ming and the Qing dynasties was referred to Yueyu (the language of the Yue people). But built into the word, obviously, was also a sense of connection with the city of Guangzhou (Canton), where either

Table 2.2 *Chinese dialect groups by region and numbers of speakers*

Dialect group	Approx. number of speakers	Percentage of total
1. *Guanhua* 官話 (or 'Mandarin')	708 million	71.5
2. *Wu* 吳	73 million	7.5
3. *Gan* 贛	31 million	3.2
4. *Xiang* 湘	31 million	3.2
5. *Min* 閩	55 million	5.6
6. *Yue* 粵	40 million	4.0
7. *Kejia* 客家	35 million	3.6

Adapted from Bauer and Benedict (1997: xxxv).

the Xiguan or the Panyu local variant of the dialect might be thought of as its purest form. S. Wells Williams in 1874 and R. H. Mathews in 1931 both used the word to translate 'Guangdong *ren*', the people of Guangdong province. (1996: 37)

The term Cantonese has thus always been ambiguous. On the one hand, it is associated with Guangzhou, and 'Guangzhou speech' (*gwóng jāu wá* 廣州話), the language of the regional capital of Guangdong province, but, on the other, it has also been used as an umbrella term to refer to a wide range of subdialects found throughout Guangdong province (*gwóng dūng wá* 廣東話).

Among Chinese linguists and dialectologists, a preferred term is that of the *Yue* dialects, a group of southern Chinese dialects spoken in parts of Guangdong province, as well as the neighbouring province of Guangxi. This is illustrated in map 2.1, which is taken from Bauer and Benedict (1997).

The map recognises seven major 'dialect families', although each language family also contains a large number of subdialects and local varieties. The seven major Chinese dialect families are set out in table 2.2.

An explanation of the label 'Cantonese' in terms of 'the Chinese dialects spoken in Guangdong province' would be faulty for a number of reasons. As the dialect maps of China and Guangdong show (see appendices 1 and 2), a significant number of other dialects, including *Min* (including Fujian or 'Fukien') and *Kejia* ('Hakka'), are also widely spoken throughout the province. Historically, the picture is further complicated by the fact that this area of southern China was colonised relatively late by Han Chinese settlers from the north.

Moser (1985) claims that Han (central Chinese) military outposts were established in the *Yue* region around 100 BC, but little real colonisation took place until much later. He also states that the earliest *Yue* inhabitants were non-Chinese, who were 'valley-dwelling, rice-raising Tai tribesmen related to existing groups like the Zhuang' (1985: 206). Support for such a claim has come from linguists such as Bauer and Benedict, who have claimed that a number of the colloquial words

Map 2.1 The seven major Chinese dialect families distributed by province
(Bauer and Benedict 1997: xlvi)
*Key to map: (1) Ma = Mandarin, (2) W = Wu, (3) G = Gan, (4) X =
Xiang, (5) K = Kejia, (6) Mi = Min, and (7) Y = Yue.*

still found in the Yue dialects may be the expression of 'an ancient Tai substratum' (Bauer and Benedict 1997: xxxix). Much of the early history of Guangdong
is inaccessible for retrieval, but there seems general agreement that both the
province and the district adjacent to present-day Hong Kong were for many
centuries on the very edges of Han territories. It is further likely that the

original inhabitants of the region were non-Sinitic Austro-Asiatic peoples related to similar ethnic groups in western China and the northern districts of present-day Vietnam, Laos and Thailand. In addition, sea-borne Austronesian migrants from what is now Indonesia may also have settled in the area. According to Balfour (1941), the Punti themselves were relatively recent migrants from North China, who began to arrive in Guangdong province from the Sung dynasty (AD 960) onwards, thus arriving in the area a few hundred years before the Hakkas (who were then dubbed 'foreigners').

In addition to the three groups mentioned by Smith in 1847 (see above), another important ethnic group throughout the early years of Hong Kong were the 'Tanka' boat people. They spoke a variety of Cantonese, but lived aboard boats along the Pearl River estuary and off the coast of the city of Guangzhou (Canton) itself, where they operated the notorious 'flower boats', water-borne bawdy houses servicing the fleets of European and American traders buying tea, silks and spices from Canton. In the early years of the British colony in Hong Kong, the Tankas worked in the harbour on small boats and lighters, and provided a range of maritime services to the British. Balfour (1941) speculates that the Tanka might be descended from early settlers from the East Indies (i.e. present-day Indonesia), claiming that such people were 'the founders of maritime commerce in the Far East', before the arrival of foreign traders from India and Persia around the fourth century AD (1941: 344).

During the Tang dynasty (AD 618–907) northern Chinese settlement in Guangdong province was still rather limited, although significant numbers of Arabs, Indians and Persians had by this time settled at Guangzhou ('Khanfu' in Arabic). Although successive emperors maintained a number of military posts in Guangdong, including one at Panyu, near Guangzhou, large-scale migration of northern Chinese into the area probably did not begin until the Sung dynasty (AD 960–1278). Balfour states that the first major northern clan to settle throughout Guangdong were the Tang family, who had migrated from Honan and were 'the founders of the Punti population' (1941: 446). He also argues that the Punti and Hakka were 'both of the same Northern Chinese stock and belong to successive waves of migration which followed the same route'. Around this time, members of the Tang clan established themselves as major landholders in what later became the New Territories of Hong Kong, and even settled areas of Hong Kong and Lantau island (1941: 446–8). Much later, in the early sixteenth century, Tuen Mun, to the east of Kowloon, became the site of an early trading post for dealing with the Portuguese ships which began to appear in the area. In 1521 a battle between Chinese forces and the Portuguese led to the temporary withdrawal of Portuguese from the area, and it was not until around 1557 that they were able to establish a permanent settlement at Macao. A century or so later, at the beginning of the Qing dynasty, in the years 1662–9, the Manchu government ordered a mass evacuation of all the coastal areas of Guangdong province, in order to deal with the perennial problem of pirates. Most villagers were ordered to move to areas some fifty *li* (approx. 18 miles) from the coast, and at this time many Punti villages in the *San On* (新安) district (of which Hong Kong was a part) were abandoned and resettled by Hakkas. When the British arrived in Hong Kong in 1842, they found that a significant proportion of the 3,000–5,000-strong population (estimates vary) were of Hakka stock (1941: 454–64).

Missionary and colonial studies of Cantonese. The linguistic history of Cantonese over the last 200 years has been complicated by the impact of missionary and colonial studies of Cantonese. When the first Protestant missionary to China, Robert Morrison (1782–1834), reached Canton in 1807, he began learning both the Mandarin and local varieties of the language, and published the first western dictionary of the dialect in 1828, entitled the *Vocabulary of the Canton Dialect.* Throughout the nineteenth century, many missionaries and colonial officials became devotees of the study of Cantonese, producing dictionaries and other guides to the language, including Bridgman (1841), Williams (1856), Eitel (1877) and Ball (1888) (Bolton 2001a). These missionary studies had the effect of granting a good deal of autonomy to the language, at both a spoken and written level, and one of the earliest surviving written documents in Cantonese is the *New Testament in Cantonese*, published in 1873 (Chin 1997: 77). Many of these missionaries and officials were involved in education, and it seems clear that, by the 1870s, the Cantonese dialect was widely used throughout the missionary schools of the period (Bolton 2001b). Indeed, many of the missionaries became convinced that Cantonese was not a dialect but a language with a rich and prestigious history, thus starting a debate among Chinese linguists which continues to the present day. For example, Ball (1888) comments thus on the status of Cantonese:

> An impression appears to have got abroad that Mandarin is the language of China, and that Cantonese and the other languages spoken in China are but dialects of it. The impression is an erroneous one... In fact the Cantonese is more nearly akin to the ancient language of China spoken about 3,000 years ago than the speech of other parts of China. It is more ancient itself than its younger brethren, the other so-called dialects of China... (Ball 1888: xiii)

Ball then proceeds to argue that Cantonese is a *de facto* language with its own 'subordinate dialects' which are 'subdivided into many little divisions spoken in different cities or towns, or groups of cities, towns, and villages where peculiar colloquialisms prevail'. He goes so far as to provide a list of more than twenty subdialects, including the *San Wui* (新會), *Höng Shan* (香山), *Shun Tak* (順德) and *Tung Kwun* (東莞) varieties (Ball 1888: xiv–xv).

It seems that until very recently the study of Cantonese was largely an enterprise undertaken by colonial linguists or overseas Chinese. In the twentieth century, other Cantonese dictionaries have included Cowles (1914), Meyer and Wempe (1947), Huang (1970) and Lau (1977). It was not until the 1980s that mainland scholars began to take a keen interest in the lexicography and phonology of Cantonese. From the mid-1980s until 1997 a significant number of mainland dictionaries and guides to Cantonese were published (see Chen 1998). The debate on the autonomy of Chinese dialects has been discussed in detail elsewhere (DeFrancis 1984; Ramsey 1987; Norman 1988), but it is worth noting that the controversy continues to the present day, and that the introduction to Bauer and Benedict's recent (1997) *Modern Cantonese Phonology* is entitled 'The Cantonese *language*' (my italics).

The rise of modern Cantonese in Hong Kong. The rise of Cantonese in Hong Kong has reflected the creation of 'modern Hong Kong' itself. After the separation of Hong Kong from mainland China in 1949 and 1950, Hong Kong was to go its own way politically, socially and linguistically. As a result of its political separation from the People's Republic of China, Hong Kong avoided the Chinese language reforms of the 1950s which abolished 'full' characters in favour of a simplified writing system and promoted the spoken national language, *Putonghua*. In late colonial Hong Kong, spoken Cantonese was able to spread into many high domains such as the civil service, broadcasting, the business world the professions, in which previously English had held a pre-eminent position. This process was rapidly accelerated after the Chinese language movement of the late 1960s and early 1970s secured recognition for 'Chinese' as a co-official language of the Hong Kong government.

By the 1990s, Cantonese had gained an important position in Hong Kong's language hierarchy. The language was widely used not only in intimate domains such as between family and friends, but also in employment, public life, social activities and even in such official and semi-official domains as the government, civil service and education. It was also the dominant language of Hong Kong popular culture, widely used in television, popular music and films. In many ways, Cantonese can be regarded as *the* language of Hong Kong, as Sin and Roebuck (1996) note:

> In education, Cantonese is used in most primary schools (over 90%) as the medium of instruction, and although the majority of secondary schools (about 90%) claim that English is their medium of instruction, code-mixing of English and Cantonese is prevailing (see *Commission of Education Report No. 6*, Hong Kong Government, 1995). At the tertiary level, the Chinese University of Hong Kong makes a statutory declaration that its 'principal language of instruction shall be Chinese'. . . Chinese, both Cantonese and Putonghua, is also used extensively in the other universities. In religion, church services, whether Catholic or Protestant, are mostly conducted in Cantonese, and Buddhist ceremonies are almost invariably carried out in Cantonese. In mass media, of the 20 or so newspapers, only three are in English. All 50 or so local magazines are in Chinese, except one on news about TV programmes. Although there are English radio and TV channels serving a small proportion of the population, the dominant media language

is Cantonese. In business, while international trade is mostly conducted in English, trade with China is naturally conducted in Chinese. In the government, Chinese has been used as an official language since 1974. Use of Cantonese has been increasing for speeches at the Legislative Council. In the judiciary, the lower courts were permitted to conduct proceedings entirely in Chinese when Chinese became an official language in 1974. (1996: 239)

As far as written norms are concerned, however, the situation in Hong Kong is somewhat more complex. Whereas, after 1949, the educational authorities of the PRC began to promote spoken Putonghua and simplified characters on the mainland, in Hong Kong, they retained the use of the written *baihua* 白話, or 'modern standard Chinese' with full characters. There is also evidence that in Hong Kong, a particularly conservative form of *baihua* has been used. Chin explains this thus:

> The cultural insecurity of an immigrant society where innovation in the Chinese language is not officially validated helped to fossilise the formal usage of Chinese in Hong Kong in its imperial style, whereas the Chinese language on the mainland experienced revolutions both in its written form (i.e. simplified characters) and grammar. For the local people, classical Chinese is old but safe to use. Official documents and even public announcements in Chinese have been written and read in Hong Kong, until now, mostly in the grammar and vocabulary of plain classical Chinese which bears virtually no affiliation to any spoken dialect. (1997: 78–9)

At the same time, however, the influence of the spoken language increased greatly from the 1970s onwards, and a heavily vernacular style of written Cantonese began to be used in a variety of contexts including informal written communications, newspapers, television subtitles, advertising billboards and Hong Kong comic books. According to Chin, the popularity of written Cantonese in the press seemed to be growing rapidly in the 1990s, and newspaper publishers were even supplying Cantonese characters on the internet so that their readers could read their newspapers electronically.

In spite of the growing popularity of 'written Cantonese', however, the use of such a writing system is heavily stigmatised in schools and other official settings. In schools, children are taught from a young age of the existence of a set of correspondences between their spoken language and an acceptable form of Hong Kong-style 'standard written Chinese'. With reference to the written Chinese in Hong Kong, there is a visible system of diglossia in operation, and many 'L' (low) Cantonese grammatical and vocabulary items have corresponding 'H' (high) forms in standard written Chinese. For example, *kéuih* 佢 (third-person-singular pronoun) is the spoken form in Cantonese, as opposed to *tā* 他 in standard written Chinese; with the Cantonese items *ge* 嘅 (genitive marker), *haih* 係 ('to be') and *m̀h* 唔 (negative marker), corresponding to *dīk* 的, *sih* 是 and *bāt* 不. From primary

Table 2.3 *Correspondences between the spoken and written language in Cantonese*

Spoken Cantonese	Standard written Chinese (Hong Kong)	English gloss
dōu 都	yáh 也	also
gó 嗰	náh 那	that
ge 嘅	dīk 的	genitive marker
hái 喺	joih 在	in, at
hóu 好	hán 很	very
haih 係	sih 是	'to be'
kéuih 佢	tā 他	he/she
kéuih deih 佢哋	tā mùhn 他們	they
jó 咗	líuh 了	perfective marker
móuh 冇	muht yáuh 沒有	no
m̀h 唔	bāt 不	not
tùhng màaih 同埋	wóh 和	and

school onwards, Hong Kong Chinese children are taught to differentiate between the spoken language (*háu yúh* 口語) and the 'book language' (*syū mihn yúh* 書面語), and are further instructed that the characters for the spoken language are not acceptable when writing Chinese. They are also taught to read aloud from written texts using the correct 'reading pronunciation' in the 'high' form of Cantonese. This system of diglossia in Cantonese is illustrated in table 2.3, in which the spoken forms of frequently occurring grammatical functors are contrasted with their written forms in standard written Chinese.

Table 2.3 provides only a partial list of the correspondences between such items in the spoken language and the Hong Kong variety of standard written Chinese – a full list would extend to a number of other grammatical functors and scores of vocabulary items. In addition, literacy in written Chinese in Hong Kong does not only involve knowledge of a set of 'conversion rules' from Cantonese speech to written *baihua*, but also some knowledge of classical Chinese norms, the *wenyan* style, as Luke and Nancarrow (1991) explain in their discussion of newspaper texts:

> In essence, the basic ingredients of the language in question are drawn most heavily from modern written Chinese (*baihua wen*), which is in turn based on (spoken) Putonghua. On such a *baihua* base is sprinkled generously and liberally elements from two other sources: Cantonese (Hong Kong style) and Classical Chinese (*wenyan*). The result is a hot-pot with many unique features of its own. It is not simply written *baihua*: in fact it is no longer recognizable to Putonghua speakers and *baihua* users. By the same token its production and comprehension does not presuppose or require knowledge of Putonghua. (1991: 87)

Even though it is possible to write many of the Cantonese items using local or 'dialectal' characters, and these characters are used in some newspaper columns, comic books, advertising and personal letters, the use of a form of written Cantonese is heavily stigmatised in formal domains such as education and serious literature. In spite of negative attitudes to written Cantonese, Mok (1998) found that many of the cartoonists and comic-book authors she interviewed expressed positive attitudes towards a written form of Cantonese language:

> To these creative people, written Cantonese is in no sense a marginalised, or suppressed language. It is more like an aspiring language which is the asset possessed by those people who have been living in Hong Kong over the past twenty years, a period which has seen the rise of the local economy, as well as the birth of a generation who takes pride in identifying themselves as Hong Kong people. (1998: 174)

With the reversion of Hong Kong to Chinese sovereignty, a number of local linguists have expressed anxiety about the future of Cantonese. Bauer and Benedict (1997), for example, suggest that 'it is clear that after China reclaims Hong Kong, it will promote Putonghua in the community as the language of government officers, the air-waves and print media, and the schools' (1997: 433). However, at the time of writing, in spite of government initiatives in various domains, it appears that the vitality of Cantonese is as high as ever. The use of a vernacular written form of the language, 'written Cantonese', provides evidence of this, although a number of commentators have suggested that the use of both the spoken and written language may be curtailed by a more interventionist government language policy at some point in the future.

Minority Chinese languages. The linguistic profile of the Chinese-language community in Hong Kong has been determined largely by the history of migration into Hong Kong from China, and the fact that most migrants have been drawn from Guangdong and Fujian provinces. In 1981, for example, the Hong Kong census indicated that the 'place of origin' ('ancestral home') of 50.3 per cent of the population was Guangzhou, Macao and the neighbouring areas; 16.7 per cent claimed the Siyi (Szeyap) district as their home; Chaozhou (Chiu Chau) accounted for 11.6 per cent; other places in Guangdong for 9.6 per cent; and other places of origin within China for 9.3 per cent (Bauer 1984: 302).

In spite of the strong influence of various forms of Cantonese in Hong Kong, there is still a great deal of linguistic diversity in the community. During the second half of the twentieth century, certain areas of Hong Kong were still associated in the popular imagination with certain ethnolinguistic groups, for example, Hakkas in the northern New Territories, Chiu Chau and Fukien people in the Western district of Hong Kong island and Shanghainese in North Point. Apart from a 'standard' variety of Cantonese and various regional (*hēung háa* 鄉下) dialects of Cantonese, other dialects belonging to the Yue family, e.g. Szeyap, and a number of non-Yue dialects are still used in Hong Kong, including Chiu Chau

Table 2.4 *Chinese dialects in Hong Kong*

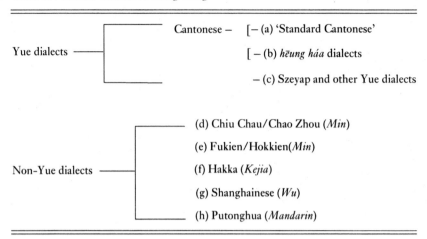

Cantonese –   [– (a) 'Standard Cantonese'

Yue dialects   [– (b) *hēung hάa* dialects

– (c) Szeyap and other Yue dialects

(d) Chiu Chau/Chao Zhou (*Min*)

(e) Fukien/Hokkien(*Min*)

Non-Yue dialects   (f) Hakka (*Kejia*)

(g) Shanghainese (*Wu*)

(h) Putonghua (*Mandarin*)

(Adapted from Bolton and Luke 1999: 39–40)

(Chaozhou), Fukien (Hokkien), Hakka (Kejia), Shanghainese and Putonghua. The major Chinese dialects used in Hong Kong are illustrated in table 2.4.

In the case of the Yue dialects, there appears to be a linguistic continuum with 'standard' Cantonese at one end and broad '*hēung hάa*' dialects at the other, which are distinguished by rural phonological and lexical features. Conversely, speakers from non-Yue backgrounds may speak Cantonese with, for example, a Shanghainese or Fukien accent.

In his study of ethnicity of Hong Kong, Guldin (1997) states that, by the 1970s, Cantonese 'chauvinism' had helped create seven distinct stereotypes of ethnic groups in the community:

- Cantonese people;
- Hakkas ('rural and unsophisticated');
- Chiu Chau people, including Fukien, Hoklos, as well as people from Chaozhou;
- Tankas and other boat people;
- Shanghainese and other northerners (non-southern Chinese);
- 'gwailos' and all kinds of foreigners; and
- overseas Chinese. (1997: 29)

Guldin later goes on to make the points that the linguistic differences between ethnic groups have faded in recent years, and that acculturation to the Cantonese language has accompanied the growth of a 'Hong Kong identity':

> The previous greater salience of the ethnolinguistic level in Hong Kong also seems to have faded somewhat, with a complementary increase at the societal level. Homogenizing factors at work in Hong Kong include a

higher percentage of the population being Hong Kong-born, the continuing acculturative influence of Cantonese both linguistically and socially, and the continuing prosperity of the society as a whole. A richer, more influential, and world-class city has emerged from the refugee entrepot of the 1940s and the second-class manufacturing base of the 1960s, and with it the self-confidence of the Hong Kong population has risen tremendously. The June 4th incident, and the speculation, prospects, and problems surrounding '1997' have all joined to reinforce the feeling of a separate Hong Kong identity, and this has served to decrease the stress on other levels of identity. (1997: 36–7)

Guldin's explanation is broadly correct. What appears to have happened over the last forty years is that dialectal differences between speakers of southern Chinese dialects, Yue and Min, have been levelled with the growth of modern Hong Kong. Knowledge of minority 'home dialects' tends to correlate strongly with age, which is to say that it is mainly the older speakers in Hong Kong families who maintain minority dialects. With universal primary and secondary education, children from minority-language families are socialised through the local schools to acquire 'Hong Kong Cantonese'.

Over the last twenty years or so, this has had a massive impact on the retention of minority languages such as Hakka, Chiu Chau, Fukien and Shanghainese, and in many families there is a classic process of three-generational language shift in progress. Various reports over the past ten years have indicated that knowledge of the Hakka language has greatly diminished, even in the villages of the northern New Territories where it was traditionally spoken. According to Tsui (1999), minority dialects in Hong Kong are now 'heading towards oblivion', partly as a result of government policy (1999: 3). Until the 1960s, Hakka was used in some village schools and for some radio broadcasts. Tsui quotes Lau Chun-fat, a local Hakka specialist on the nature of language shift in the modern Hong Kong period, who explains that 'Hakkas would not want to speak to their children in their own tongue because they wanted to nurture their offspring into urbanised, rich folk' (1999: 3).

On the other hand, there is also evidence that the numbers of non-Cantonese speakers rose in the mid-1990s, in pace with immigration from Fujian province. One 1996 newspaper article reported that, in the three months between February and April of that year, a total of about 1,500 Fujianese (Fukien) people arrived in the territory. Of these, about 86 per cent claimed to speak Putonghua and 21 per cent Cantonese, in addition to their provincial dialect (Lee 1996: 6).

The English-language speech community

For much of the history of colonial Hong Kong, English remained the language of a minority, comprising the British community of colonial administrators, army and navy personnel, the business community and their dependants. It also became a second language for the local Chinese merchant elite, who rose to power towards the end of the nineteenth century. With the annexation of Hong Kong during the First Opium War between Britain and China in 1842, and the development of the 'treaty-port' system, English began to spread through education, notably through the various mission schools that were established. Early mission schools in Hong Kong included St Paul's College (1851), Diocesan Girls' School (1860), Diocesan Boys' School (1869) and St Joseph's (1876), although there was one prestigious government institution, the Central School (1862), which later became Queen's College. Such schools played a significant role in the linguistic history of Hong Kong as a British colony, in educating a compradore class of merchants who played a key role in Sino-European and Sino-American trade, as well as in the promotion of modernity in late nineteenth-century China (Smith 1985).

As we saw above, the establishment of the early system of mission schools did not mean that the study of Chinese was neglected entirely. Western missionaries who arrived in China from the beginning of the nineteenth century onwards encountered a richly literate culture that, as in the case of India, spoke for an advanced civilisation with its own strong literary and philosophical tradition. Many of the largely Protestant educators who set up the first missionary schools in Hong Kong had a profoundly orientalist interest not only in the Mandarin language but also the dialects of South China, notably Cantonese, Hakka and Fukien. Consequently, Chinese language and literature were taught alongside English at most mission schools, creating a category of school referred to as 'Anglo-Chinese', a term which survives until today. In Anglo-Chinese schools, English was used as a teaching medium and as the printed medium for most textbooks, although Chinese language and literature was also accorded an important place on the timetable. Education became effectively segregated from the beginning of the twentieth century, when a system of separate schools was established catering for Chinese children from elite backgrounds, on the one hand, and children from 'expatriate' backgrounds on the other.

The University of Hong Kong was established in 1911, and although this increased the demand for English-medium education, large numbers of Chinese-medium schools were established in the 1920s and 1930s (So 1992). Nevertheless, the colonial educational system remained heavily elitist until the 1970s, and English-medium secondary education was associated with privilege and social class. In the late nineteenth and early twentieth centuries, there existed a huge social gap between Europeans and Chinese in Hong Kong, although this was as much a factor relating to social class as anything else:

> Few Europeans spoke any Chinese dialect; few were scholars, with a schol-arly interest in Chinese society, culture, and civilization; nearly all carried with them to Hong Kong class notions derived from their own very class-conscious society. Most were ethnocentric; but the concept of ethnocen-tricity does not explain entirely European attitudes and behaviour toward the Chinese population. The factor of class must be taken as crucial: the

British often treated the lower classes in Britain as badly as they at times treated Chinese in Hong Kong. Most contacts with Chinese at this period were with servants of various types, chair and rickshaw coolies, Chinese in menial or service occupations. Attitudes to Chinese were, then, close to middle-class attitudes to servants in Britain, for servants in that country were perceived as members of another race – dank, incomprehensible, illiterate troglodytes. (Lethbridge 1978: 167)

Even in the 1920s, the British community was very small, numbering, in 1921, only about 4,000 people, compared with a total population of some 625,000. Many of the employees of British firms in Hong Kong lasted for only one 'tour' of six years before being moved on to another posting. Much of the Chinese community was also composed of sojourners, and at that time under 20 per cent of the Chinese population of Hong Kong and Kowloon had been born in the territory. Border controls were minimal and there was unrestricted traffic across the border, with around 8,000 people shuttling to and fro each day in the late 1930s. A large population of Tanka boat people lived on sampans and junks at Aberdeen, Shaukeiwan and Stanley.

Racial discrimination against Chinese took a number of forms in the interwar years. Many managerial positions in Hong Kong businesses or 'hongs' were reserved for Europeans. The government only began to appoint Chinese to the Executive Council (the Governor's advisory cabinet) in 1926. In 1935 the acting colonial secretary is quoted as stating that 'Government has fully and frankly accepted the policy of replacing, wherever possible, European by Asiatic', but it was not until after 1945 that this policy began to take effect. Members of the Chinese elite were also excluded from living on Victoria Peak or joining the Hong Kong Club. In the colony, contact between most Europeans and Chinese was limited to that with lower-level staff in employment, or with shopkeepers and domestic servants, with whom they communicated in a form of pidginised English. The Chinese elite also were numerically small, and '[t]here was then virtually no Chinese middle class with whom they [Europeans] could work on equal terms, while the few rich Chinese kept very much to themselves and the Chinese visible on the streets were mainly of the coolie class' (Gillingham 1983: 15).

After the end of the Second World War, some forms of colonial social apartheid continued into the 1950s and 1960s. Ingrams, visiting Hong Kong in 1950 under the sponsorship of the Colonial Office, noted that the Chinese were no longer excluded from the Peak, but that considerations of class and race were still strong, and that 'Hong Kong is still very much a place of racial divisions and social cliques', but added the qualification that:

However unfortunate they are, cliques are common in many colonies and, human nature being what it is, they can probably never be entirely ironed out. If we allow that, we can understand the more easily the far more important lack of contact between the races. There are obviously more contacts of this kind in Hong Kong than there are in many other colonies, because facility of contact depends first of all on comparability of 'civilisation' and the Chinese are the most civilised (from a European standard) of any race inhabiting colonial territories. Another thing that makes for ease of contact is the number of Chinese who are westernized. (Ingrams 1952: 116)

Having said this, Ingrams then proceeds to note a number of factors hindering contact between the races, including 'difficulty of language', 'prejudice', the limited resources of Europeans in reciprocating the lavish hospitality of wealthy Chinese, and the awkwardness of contact between the English and the middle-class Chinese, which was partly attributable to 'the insularity of the English family'. Ingrams makes a plea for increased contact, as '[c]ontacts like this bring something rich in intimacy and friendship' (1952: 117).

Twenty years later, a former missionary turned social activist in the territory, Elsie Elliot, expressed a far more jaundiced view of the colonial establishment in Hong Kong, paying particular attention to the part that language played in maintaining social injustice. In a 1971 Quaker-supported publication entitled *The Avarice, Bureaucracy and Corruption of Hong Kong*, Elliot presented a damning indictment of the linguistic imperialism of the colonial legal system, noting that:

> more than 98% of the people of Hong Kong are expected to understand laws written in a foreign language. I never understood why in some countries there are revolutions over language, until I saw the problems created by language in Hong Kong. Of those who know English, probably only 5% can be called truly conversant with the language. This is one reason why colonialism is always a sin, and all colonies come to a bloody end. Language creates a privileged class and leaves the vast majority frustrated and resentful... If any justice exists in Hong Kong, it exists only for the English-speaking. There is another law for the underprivileged, the non-English speaking. (1971: 23, 32)

Elliot was writing at the beginning of the decade that was to see a number of reformist measures, including substantial government intervention in education. During the 1970s, access to public education increased dramatically, and this was to have a major impact on the learning of languages and the subsequent degree of multilingualism in Hong Kong society. In the 1960s, typically only the privileged were able to provide their children with a complete secondary education and, as far as English was concerned, a system of *elitist bilingualism* dominated education (Bratt-Paulston 1980: 2). In Hong Kong, children progressed from an elite (or 'famous') primary school to an elite secondary school and then to either the Chinese University of Hong Kong or the University of Hong Kong. By the 1980s, the rich had started sending their children overseas for higher education but, locally, from the 1970s onwards, basic educational reforms meant that every child had the opportunity to gain an education, and increasing numbers of children from poorer backgrounds were able to go to university. Thus the earlier system

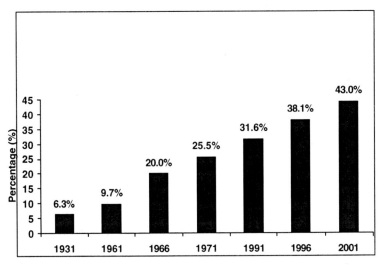

Figure 2.3 Census results for knowledge of English in Hong Kong, 1931–2001

began to shift towards a system of *mass* (or *folk*) *bilingualism* which, in spite of its great imperfections, gave a large proportion of children the opportunity to acquire at least some English in 'Anglo-Chinese' secondary schools, where English textbooks were used.

The proportion of students going to university increased from around 2–4 per cent at the beginning of the 1980s to something like 17 per cent by 1996 (with an additional 8 per cent going overseas for university education). In 1989, the government upgraded a number of post-secondary colleges and financed the establishment of a new university of science and technology so that, by the late 1990s, there were eight local universities, compared with two at the beginning of the 1980s. In all of these institutions, with the possible exception of the Chinese University of Hong Kong, English is predominantly used as the language of lectures and textbooks. The educational reforms of the 1970s and 1980s have contributed more than any other factor to the spread of English within modern Hong Kong society. This is supported by the census figures for the period, which indicate a rise in the proportion of the population claiming a knowledge of English from 9.7 per cent in 1961 to 43 per cent in 2001 (see figure 2.3).[6]

The identity of the 'English-speaking community' by the end of this period raises a number of questions. What criteria do we use to define such a community? Are we referring only to 'first-language' or 'mother-tongue' speakers of the language? Who qualifies as a member of such a community, and how are the

---

[6] The 2001 census indicates that 43 per cent of the Hong Kong population now claim to be able to speak English. Of these, 3.2 per cent claim English as a 'usual' language, and 39.8 per cent claim to speak English as 'another' language (Hong Kong Government 2001: 38–9).

boundaries between such a community and other communities to be drawn? For much of the history of the colony, the answers to these questions might have been self-evident, as this community would have comprised British, Americans and others for whom English was a 'first language' or 'mother tongue'. Knowledge of English as a second language would have been highly restricted among 'ethnic Chinese'. Racial and social barriers would have served as extra-linguistic isoglosses that marked the boundaries of such a group. By the late 1990s, however, many such boundaries would have broken down. Within the territory, greater numbers of Hong Kong Chinese than ever before now claimed a knowledge of English. In addition, many thousands of those who had emigrated to Canada and other destinations in the 1980s began to return to Hong Kong, as did large numbers of young people who had been sent abroad for their education in the same period. English began to function as a second language or even 'second first language' among a number of ethnolinguistic minority groups in Hong Kong.

Minority speech communities

In North America and Britain in recent years, there has been increasing attention paid to the position of minority ethnolinguistic groups. In Britain, for example, a recent report in *The Times* claims that 'London is the most linguistically diverse city on earth', and that 307 languages were spoken by schoolchildren attending the city's schools, with Cantonese in eleventh place (Charter 2000: 8).

In Hong Kong, discourses of 'East versus West' and 'Chinese versus English' have tended to obscure the position of ethnic minorities in the society. Such minorities fall into two groups: first, recent immigrants from mainland China, who face a variety of language problems depending on their place of origin and educational background and, second, 'minority speech communities' of non-Chinese background, many of whom have a long history in Hong Kong society. Getting clear information on the numbers and characteristics of minority groups in Hong Kong is by no means easy as the government only occasionally releases figures on the ethnic background of such groups. At the time of writing, the last official government statistics on such minority groups were released in April 1996, and are set out here as table 2.5.

There are other problems in estimating the totals for various ethnic groups in Hong Kong. In addition to the relatively small numbers of American, British, Canadian and Australian citizens listed above, there are also many thousands of Hong Kong people holding passports for such countries who are not counted. It is also unclear to what extent the figures for Indonesians and Malaysians are accounted for by passport holders for these countries who are, in fact, of ethnic Chinese descent. At the same time, there are also significant numbers of other groups not listed, including Nepalis and Pakistanis. Other even smaller groups are also absent, such as the Parsees (originally from Persia), who have a very long history in South China and Hong Kong. A number of these groups trace their origins in the colony to the beginnings of British colonialism. Parsee traders were

Table 2.5 *Minority groups in Hong Kong*

Country	Number of people	Approx. percentage
Philippines	139,300	2.3
USA	36,000	0.6
UK	34,500	0.5
Canada	29,000	0.5
Indonesia	25,900	0.5
Thailand	25,100	0.5
Japan	24,200	0.3
Australia	21,100	0.3
India	21,000	0.3
Malaysia	13,900	0.2

Source: *South China Morning Post*, 8 April 1996.

active in the opium trade in Guangzhou before coming to Hong Kong, where they continued to trade but also engaged in philanthropy. The founding of the University of Hong Kong in 1911 was made possible by the donation of funds by H. N. Mody, 'a Parsi gentleman', memorialised by the university's foundation stone. Members of the early Indian community included traders but also Sikh soldiers and policemen, and today Sikhs and Pakistanis are still employed as security guards and watchmen. In addition, there is a large Nepali population, composed of ex-Gurkas and their families.

Unlike many European and North American societies, there is no specific legislation prohibiting racial discrimination in Hong Kong, and many of these smaller groups feel discriminated against in certain ways. One recent report by Gidumal (1998) noted that groups such as Indians and Filipinos regularly faced discrimination and prejudice, and even Japanese often encounter a discriminatory pricing system, with a special 'Japanese rate' for certain goods and services. Sometimes there may be a linguistic dimension to this, because some members of minority groups may be excluded from certain jobs through the requirement for a 'native English speaker' in employment advertisements, while other positions may require Chinese-language qualifications. In the local education system, it has been suggested that not enough attention is paid to creating an awareness of racial and ethnic diversity in Hong Kong society, with one recent study suggesting that more attention should be paid to 'multicultural' issues:

> While English is taught as a culturally-neutral communicative tool, the Chinese subjects (Chinese Language, Chinese Literature and Chinese History) tend towards cultural indoctrination. It is of course highly desirable that students learn to appreciate their own culture, but it is essential that at the same time they are encouraged to be critical of it. The typical presentation of Chinese culture and history through the Chinese subjects

gives an impression of China as a monolithic, culturally uniform entity, glossing over the enormous regional, cultural and historical variety which characterize Chinese civilization and the modern Chinese state. Hong Kong's own cultural and historical legacy, and the Cantonese language and literary tradition are undervalued. In addition, the diversity which continues to characterise Hong Kong society, with its long-established English-speaking and Indian communities, is also given little recognition across the school curriculum. (Human Rights Monitor 1999)

Such minority groups in Hong Kong also form their own speech communities in the sense that many of them have a shared language other than Cantonese. For example, most Filipinos speak the Tagalog-based national language, Filipino, but they may also speak another regional variety such as Ilocano, or Cebuano. Indonesians and Malays typically speak Bahasa Indonesia and Bahasa Malaysia, which are actually rather similar, but may also speak varieties of Chinese if they have an ethnic Chinese background. The Japanese speak Japanese, the Thais Tai and Lao, and the Indians usually speak Hindi and/or another Indian language. The citizens of the USA, UK and Australia would usually speak their own national variety of English. In addition, there are also biracial people, or 'Eurasians' of a mixed ethnic parentage, who are often bilingual in English and Cantonese. At the same time, however, all these minority groups would be linked to the wider Hong Kong speech community in various ways, both non-linguistic and linguistic. In fact, many such Hong Kong residents are often surprisingly proficient in spoken Cantonese, while others may only use English or other languages.

To return to the issue of the Hong Kong 'speech community', a number of inferences and conclusions suggest themselves based on the above discussion:

- The Chinese speech community in Hong Kong has always displayed a good deal of variation although, with the social and cultural formation of modern Hong Kong in the second half of the twentieth century, there has been a concerted move towards dialect-levelling and the creation and maintenance of a Hong Kong norm for spoken Cantonese.
- In the same period there was a notable spread in the knowledge of English in the community, so that by the late 1990s it might be argued that the vast majority of the English-speaking community in Hong Kong were Hong Kong Chinese who spoke English as a second language.
- Among the non-Chinese minorities of Hong Kong there is much greater linguistic and ethnic diversity than has previously been recognised.
- Hong Kong is not a monolingual community (if indeed such a community exists anywhere), but is a multilingual speech community with its own specific characteristics.

Whether one regards the speech community as an all-encompassing whole or as differentiated into smaller subgroups may depend on the task at hand, the purposes of the analysis and the aims of the investigator. To suggest that, as so many have done in the past, there exist merely two speech communities in Hong Kong ('Chinese' versus 'expatriate') would be a gross simplification. Recently, a celebrated Hong Kong Chinese legislator, Christine Loh, attempted to promote a more inclusive approach to multilingualism and multiculturalism in Hong Kong, by arguing that 'the Hong Kong mix' of races and languages is an asset that should be more widely recognised, and advocating a policy of multiculturalism on behalf of the Citizen's Party of Hong Kong (Loh 1999: 16).

Sociolinguistic issues in Hong Kong, 1980–97

During the period of late British colonialism, issues related to language and society in Hong Kong were not simply the object of academic study for professional linguists and educationalists, but matters of general concern if not anxiety, and widely discussed by the mass media and the public at large. In 1981, the Hong Kong Government invited a panel of overseas 'experts' from Australia, Germany, the UK and the USA to carry out a review of the education system in the territory. The subsequent report came to be known as *The Llewellyn Report* (Hong Kong Government 1982). It noted that the expansion of education in the previous thirty years had been rapid and far-reaching, and that the 'push for expansion' was related to economic priorities and the 'need for a qualified labour force to fuel the economy' (Hong Kong Government 1982: 111). The report identified five critical areas that deserved policy attention in education.

The first of these was the need for 'the establishment of a comprehensive language policy for the education system which does not neglect the current emphasis being placed in English in schools'. At the same time, the authors of the report stated that they favoured 'a shift towards the universal use of the mother tongue in the former years accompanied by formal teaching of English as a first foreign language'. This, they argued, would lead to 'genuine bilingualism in the senior secondary years'. The other four priorities identified were teacher training, curriculum and examination development, the expansion of university-level education and the increased capability for educational research and educational policy making (Hong Kong Government 1982: 112–13).

One significant measure of the reactions to *The Llewellyn Report*, and the general level of interest in issues of language, was the publication in June 1983 of four articles with the arresting title of 'The Language Bomb', co-authored by two local linguists, Robert Lord and Benjamin T'sou (later reprinted in book form as Lord and T'sou 1985). Despite the dramatic title, for the most part the articles comprised a carefully argued discussion of a number of local language issues, including the role of English in education; the use of the role of Chinese, including Putonghua; the use of English in the domain of law, and the need for translation; and the need for careful, but flexible, language planning. Lord and T'sou argued that it was necessary to retain English as a teaching medium for Hong Kong children 'at some stage in their education', but made a number of other recommendations including:

- increased attention to the teaching of Chinese, 'especially modern standard Chinese and Putonghua';
- the promotion of a policy of 'bilingual education' as the basis for all decision-making on issues of language and education; and
- the training and employment of specialist translators in government, education and law. (Lord and T'sou 1985)

Possibly the most contentious statements on language were in the third article, in which T'sou discussed the characteristics of individual language behaviour and bilingualism in Hong Kong. T'sou suggested that the local population's preference for Cantonese films might be explained by 'language fatigue', noting that Hong Kong was 'the last hub of recalcitrant dialect and sub-ethnic culture within the larger Chinese society'. He then went on to argue that the rapid expansion of the education system had led to the cultural and linguistic impoverishment of local students, producing 'semilingual' cultural eunuchs:

> The end result of the educational system, based on complaints and opinion commonly expressed, is very often a product which can be generally described as a 'cultural eunuch' – someone who knows what things could or might be like in cultural terms but who is not able to take part. This product is brought about by the encrustation of a light veneer of Western culture, glimpsed through exposure to the English language in schools and the media, on to a less than wholesome body of Chinese values and culture... the prevalent semilingualism in the case of our cultural eunuchs requires attention even now if Hongkong is to remain a viable social entity in the next century. (T'sou 1985: 17–19)

Throughout the 1980s and 1990s, matters of language policy and language planning were of recurrent interest to both the government and the general public. After the publication of *The Llewellyn Report*, an Institute of Language in Education was set up by the government, and a series of Education Commission reports on a wide range of issues, including language, were issued at various times during the 1980s and 1990s. By the early 1990s, the government was becoming more interventionist in its language policies and was encouraging secondary schools to adopt Chinese as the medium of instruction. At the same time, the government was campaigning against the use of 'code-switching' and 'code-mixing' in schools, arguing that 'the use of mixed-code in schools should be reduced in favour of the clear and consistent use in each class of Chinese or English in respect of teaching, textbooks and examinations' (Hong Kong Education Commission 1994: 20).

Not surprisingly, linguists at local universities were also involved in debates about language at this time. Some were also drawn into the public debates concerning such questions, and their views were regularly solicited in the print media and on television. During the same period, hundreds of specialist articles on language and language education were published both locally and in international journals. Bruce's (1996) bibliography of 'Language in Hong Kong education and society' groups publications on language in Hong Kong into a number of topic categories. Those studies primarily concerned with sociolinguistics (i.e. the study of language and society) in Hong Kong are categorized in Bruce's study according to the following topic areas:

- language attitudes and policies (35.2 per cent of 'sociolinguistic' studies);
- Chinese languages in Hong Kong and South China (24.8 per cent);
- bilingualism and multilingualism (16.7 per cent);
- 'Hong Kong English' (11.6 per cent);
- language alternation, i.e. code-switching and code-mixing (9 per cent); and
- language standards (2.7 per cent).

These figures show that a majority of sociolinguistics articles in this period were concerned either with language attitudes and policies (including the medium of instruction issues) or with issues relating to societal bilingualism and multilingualism.

Language planning in Hong Kong – official language policies

From the late 1960s to the late 1990s, the colonial government failed to formulate a clear language policy for the community, a failure often excused by the government as 'non-interventionism', but described by others as political 'vacillation' (Branegan 1991: 27). It was not until 1974 that Chinese was recognised as a co-official language in the territory. During the period of British colonial rule, the English language had the status of the official language of government, the official language of law, and was *de facto* the more widely used medium of secondary and university education, but the *Official Languages Ordinance* of 1974 established that Chinese and English would thenceforth 'enjoy equality of use'. A decade or so later, after the negotiations between Beijing and London determined the arrangements for the 1997 handover, the position of Chinese was further strengthened by the publication of *The Basic Law of the Hong Kong Special Administrative Region*, Article 9 of which stated that: 'In addition to the Chinese language, English may also be used as an official language by the executive authorities, legislative and judicial organs of the Hong Kong Administrative Region' (Chinese Government 1992: 7).

In 1995, the Hong Kong Government announced that its new language policy would be 'to develop a civil service which is "biliterate" in English and Chinese and "trilingual" in English, Cantonese and Putonghua' (Lau 1995: 19), an official policy statement which is still in force. In the years immediately prior to the July 1997 handover, an increasing proportion of Cantonese was used in Legislative Council speeches, and since July 1997 the Provisional Legislative Council has mainly used Cantonese to conduct its proceedings. Since the early 1990s the government has been trying to establish training courses in Putonghua for Hong Kong civil servants but, at present, Cantonese, rather than Putonghua, is still the dominant variety. Similar changes have taken place in the legal system in Hong Kong and, from 1986 onwards, the 'Bilingual Laws Project' has resulted in a large proportion of the written laws of Hong Kong being translated into Chinese. From the late 1980s to the mid-1990s, amendments to the *Official Languages Ordinance* extended the use of spoken Chinese into the higher courts. In December 1995, the first civil High Court case was heard in Putonghua and, in August 1997, the first criminal case was conducted in Cantonese in the High Court (Cheung 1997; Wei 2000).

Many local linguists have been less concerned about a conflict between English and Chinese than the tension between Cantonese and Putonghua. The use of Cantonese in Hong Kong is obviously out of step with the language policies of the PRC, which specifically promote Putonghua, together with the written correlate of simplified Chinese characters instead of the 'full characters' used in Hong Kong and Taiwan. Cantonese may be a mere 'regional dialect' in the PRC, but Hong Kong is the Cantonese-speaking capital of the world. Sin and Roebuck comment that, given the wide use of the language in education, religion, the print and broadcast media, and government, 'the status of Cantonese is much higher than is normally thought and cannot be simply brushed aside as the "vernacular" ' (Sin and Roebuck 1996: 252).

The PRC's official language policy is essentially opposed to the use of 'regional dialects' such as Cantonese, Fukien and Shanghainese in government, education and other official domains of use. Language planning in the PRC since the revolution has been presented in the form of a national 'language reform policy' (Cheng and Pasierbsky 1988: 1279–81), which attempts to tackle four main issues: illiteracy, the development and promotion of a standard national language, the promotion of simplified Chinese characters and the promotion of the romanised alphabetic writing system, 'Pinyin', for certain specialist purposes. A *China Daily* newspaper report on language policy in 1992 emphasised the standardisation of language, especially in its written form, noting that: 'The State Council demanded that all departments and local governments support the work of the committee by assuming leadership in the standardization of the language and Chinese characters' (*China Daily*, 26 September 1992: 1). Evidently Hong Kong's language planning diverges from that of the PRC in a number of important respects. With regard to the PRC's push to standardise written characters, it should be noted that, in Hong Kong the use of 'written Cantonese' is popular in advertising, newspapers and comic books, and a number of local linguists have expressed concern about the future 'autonomy' of Cantonese (Bauer and Benedict 1997; Chin 1997). A recent article in the *Straits Times* of Singapore announced that the Chinese government was introducing a new law from 2001 to 'standardise language use across the nation, including preventing encroachment by the country's many dialects' (*Straits Times*, 17 November 2000). The article went on to report that the new law is intended to prescribe the mandatory use of Putonghua and standardised written characters in the civil service, law, education, films, television and other forms of communication, such as advertising, noting that this new legislation was intended to halt 'the intrusion of foreign words and the misuse of the Chinese language' from Hong Kong into mainland China.

The 'medium of instruction' issue

The policy vacuum that existed before 1997 can be seen most clearly within education, although, in fact, the British colonial administration attempted as early as the mid-1970s to introduce a policy of vernacular language education. In 1973, the government published a 'Green Paper', or policy proposal, in favour of using Chinese as the teaching medium in the lower forms of all secondary schools, explaining its thinking thus:

> The medium of instruction bears significantly upon the quality of education offered at post-primary level. Pupils coming from primary schools where they have been taught in the medium of Cantonese have a grievous burden put on them when required to absorb new subjects through the medium of English. We recommend that Chinese become the usual language of instruction in the lower forms of secondary schools, and that English should be studied as the second language. (Cited in Gibbons 1982: 117)

The publication of the Green Paper aroused strong opposition from parents and schools, and the government backed down on these early plans to promote Chinese as a teaching medium. Finally, in the White Paper of 1974, it settled for a *laissez-faire* approach, allowing individual school principals to decide the teaching medium in their schools. It is significant that this policy shift occurred at just that point in time when the educational system of modern Hong Kong was being created. It thus appears that the initial instinct of the colonial government was to opt for Chinese-medium instruction which, for the vast majority of schools, would have meant Cantonese.

Ironically, therefore, the promotion of Cantonese was a feature of colonial language policy in the territory, just as the use of regional Chinese dialects in religion and education had been a tenet of missionary language policy throughout the nineteenth century. The promotion of 'mother-tongue' education in contemporary Hong Kong can thus be seen as both missionary and colonial; the PRC has never had a policy of promoting the 'mother tongue' as a teaching medium. In nineteenth-century China, classical Chinese was used as the language of the educated or 'Mandarin' class; after the foundation of the Chinese Republic in 1911 a new form of standard written Chinese, *baihua*, was adopted. When the communist government came to power in 1949, the standard written language was further amended through the use of simplified characters and a form of the spoken language, *Putonghua*, was promoted as a national and official language for use in government and education. Despite this historical irony, many

of those working in education from the 1970s have been concerned to promote
the use of Cantonese for a range of sound educational reasons, including the
practical necessity of teaching lower-ability groups for whom English is a major
obstacle to learning, as well as the desire for greater social equality (Kwok 1982:
40–3; Pun 1997: 95–6).

The government's failure to implement a strong policy in favour of *either*
Chinese- *or* English-medium instruction in the mid-1970s was perhaps symptomatic of its dilemma. To follow its instinct and implement Chinese-medium
education would have incurred the displeasure of the majority of local parents and
schools, but to adopt a vigorous policy of promoting English would have meant
that the government ran the risk of accusations of linguistic and cultural imperialism. By contrast, in Singapore, Lee Kwan Yew, bolstered by the authenticity
of his role as the nation's postcolonial leader, had few qualms about the promotion of English as the official language of administration, business and education
(McCrum *et al.* 1986). The result of this 'vacillation' in Hong Kong government
policy led to the continued increase in the proportion of 'Anglo-Chinese' schools,
secondary schools that advertised themselves as English-medium institutions. In
practice, however, few of these schools provided a total immersion in an English-
based education system, and by the late 1980s and early 1990s, the 'English-
medium' system in place could be described as a 'continuum' (Johnson 1994:
187). At one end of the scale were prestigious secondary schools which prided
themselves on teaching every subject (apart from Chinese studies) through the
medium of English, while at the other end of the scale were the lowest-rank
schools which used Cantonese for teaching almost all subjects, even though the
majority of textbooks were in English and students took English-medium examinations. In between these two extremes were the majority, using both spoken
Cantonese and English (together with English textbooks) in a 'mixed mode'
practice of teaching. Among other things, this resulted in the extensive use of
code-switching and code-mixing among the younger generations of students
(Johnson 1994: 188).

Throughout the 1980s and 1990s, the government tried in various ways to
encourage Chinese-medium education, including offering incentives for secondary school principals to adopt Chinese as a teaching medium. Given the
strong parental demand for English-medium schools, however, these measures
had little effect. In 1994, for example, the statistics showed that over 90 per
cent of all secondary schools were at least nominally English-medium (Johnson
1994). Shortly before the handover, the colonial Hong Kong government sud-
denly formulated a coercive strengthening of policy and, on 22 March 1997, it
announced that in future approximately only 100 secondary schools (some 22 per
cent of the total of 460) would be allowed to use English as a teaching medium
and that punitive measures (e.g. a maximum fine of $25,000 and two years in
jail) might be used against school principals who did not follow the instructions
of the government (Kwok 1997). The figure of 100 was amended to 114 after
predictable protests from schools and parents, but at present the policy remains

one of providing 'firm guidance' for secondary schools, and of encouraging the use of Cantonese as a teaching medium.

Why the colonial government in its last few months should have chosen to break with its *laissez-faire* past so dramatically remains something of a mystery. What seems clear however is that the announcement of this policy was a decision of the colonial government *not*, as has been the subsequent perception, the decision of the first Beijing-appointed Chief Executive, Mr Tung, Chee-hwa, and his advisors. There are a number of possible explanations of the policy change. The government may finally have accepted the arguments of those local educationalists who despaired of the inefficiency of the previous system, particularly with reference to the education of lower-ability children. Alternatively, some government members may have believed that by promoting an education system based largely on Cantonese they would be supporting a local Cantonese-speaking community faced with a takeover by northern Chinese communists. Supporting Cantonese, therefore, would also mean supporting a local Hong Kong identity, and the 'high degree of autonomy' promised by the Draft Agreement of 1984.

Since the announcement of this policy there has been a great deal of government rhetoric in support of 'mother-tongue' teaching, but it is by no means clear that it will continue unaltered into the future. Recent reports in the newspapers suggest that the government is split on the issue of language policy. For example, the Secretary for Education and Manpower was recently quoted as reaffirming his belief in the government's 'mother-tongue' policy (Chan 1999: 2), but a report one week later cited the head of a government-appointed working group on the medium of instruction as stating that senior secondary students 'should have freedom to choose which language to be taught in if the schools believed they had teachers capable of using English to teach' (Cheung 1999: 4). A newly appointed Director of Education was also reported as calling for a 'radical overhaul' of the education system, adding that the government was 'keeping an open mind' on the teaching medium issue (Moy 1998: 1). To many in Hong Kong, it seems that the government is again undecided on the issue of a clear language policy for education, all of which moved the *South China Morning Post* to publish this editorial on the topic, which noted the apparent confusion in current official thinking:

> Contradictory findings follow one another with bewildering speed ... Even as one government-sponsored working group recommends that secondary schools teaching in Cantonese should be allowed to choose which language to use as a medium of instruction at senior level, fears are being voiced that the government could be planning to make all SAR schools switch to mother-tongue teaching ... It will cause great dismay among the public if the remaining 114 schools teaching in English are made to change. An international city with cyber-world aspirations needs schools that teach in the language of business and modern science. (*South China Morning Post*, 22 November 1999: 16)

Whatever happens in the next few years, it would be surprising if Hong Kong jettisoned English entirely as a medium of school instruction. Despite the government's reassurances, many parents remain unconvinced that the language can be effectively taught if its status is relegated to that of a 'foreign' language. The government is also under pressure to maintain and improve the 'standard' of English from a business community anxious that Hong Kong's economic prosperity, and its status as a centre for international business (already dented by the post-1997 Asian economic crisis), will be further eroded in comparison with its regional rival Singapore, or its rapidly developing mainland competitor, Shanghai.

There is also an important class dimension to all this, as many Hong Kong parents feel that their children's access to English is being restricted by these new policy measures and that, as in other societies, 'the requirement for children to have education in the mother tongue can lead to an apartheid situation which may be socially divisive and/or oppressive' (Gupta 1995: 1). If the new policy continues in its present form, many parents worry that the English-medium schools will become largely the preserve of children of parents from middle- or upper-middle-class backgrounds, who are most adept at steering their children through the competitive system of kindergarten and primary school necessary to gain entry to the more prestigious English-medium schools. Some parents opt to send their children to 'international schools' based in Hong Kong. Since the 1960s, the British-oriented English Schools Foundation (ESF) has catered mainly to British and 'expatriate' children but, by the late 1990s, 70 per cent of its 10,600 pupils at secondary and primary level were from Chinese backgrounds. The chairman of the ESF was recently quoted as asserting that 'the word expatriate is now outdated', and that large numbers of Canadians and other 'returnees' from overseas countries were joining the schools (Wan 2000b).

In addition, many of the high-ranking civil servants and educationalists who are responsible for formulating language policies often choose to educate their own children overseas, typically at private schools and universities in Australia, North America and Britain (Postiglione 1998). The issue of language and social class in Hong Kong is one of a number of sociolinguistic issues that have been under-researched up till now, as Lee (1998) indicates. Other issues of importance include questions relating to multilingualism and multiculturalism, immigrant education, with specific relevance to immigrants from mainland China, and the problem of 'language standards', a discourse applied even-handedly to 'falling' standards of Chinese and English. All these have been influenced greatly by the rapid and dramatic political, economic and social changes that have occurred in the HKSAR (Hong Kong Special Administrative Region) over the last few decades (see pp. 50–71 above).

Linguistically, the effects of bilingualism and multilingualism have been studied most frequently in such areas of language contact as linguistic borrowing, code-switching and code-mixing and the description of English in Hong Kong, and it is now time to look at these areas in more detail.

Languages in contact – linguistic borrowing, code-switching and Hong Kong English

From 1980 through to the end of the 1990s, a number of studies concerned with various mechanisms of language contact were published, including work on linguistic borrowing from English into Hong Kong Chinese and from Chinese into English, as well as a series of studies of code-switching and code-mixing in such domains as secondary education, university and the print and broadcast media.

Linguistic borrowing

In 1982, Chan and Kwok published a study of lexical borrowing from English into Chinese in the Hong Kong context, followed by a 1985 account of lexical borrowing from Chinese into English (Chan and Kwok 1982, 1985). More recently, others who have researched this topic include Benson (1993, 1994, 2000), Carless (1995), and Moody (1996).

Lexical borrowing from English into Chinese. At the core of Chan and Kwok's (1982) study is a list of 358 Cantonese words borrowed directly from English as 'phonetic loans'. The authors argue that, of these 358 Cantonese words, 330 have been 'fully integrated' into Hong Kong Chinese, in the sense that they can be represented in writing by the use of locally acceptable Chinese characters. The other 28 words lack Chinese characters, and are often represented in writing by using an empty 'mouth radical' (口), or by the insertion of an English word. The table 2.6 illustrates their description of linguistic borrowing from English into Cantonese.

Chan and Kwok explain the motivation for phonetic borrowings in terms of five sociological forces:

* convenience in need-filling;
* precision in expression, and avoidance of ambiguity;
* bilingualism;
* the desire for novelty; and
* the stylistic possibilities of loanwords.

They go on to explain that the process of lexical borrowing involves a number of linguistic changes affecting the borrowed items. At the phonological level, they suggest that 'certain general tendencies may be observed' including processes of substitution (e.g. where /r/ is replaced by /l/ as in the loan /tse lei/車梨, for English *cherry*, or /tʃ/ is replaced by /dz/ in /dzi si/芝士 for *cheese*); creation of disyllabic words ending in /si/ for monosyllabic English words ending in /s/ or a cluster containing /s/ (e.g. /bɑː si/巴士 from *bus*, and /wai si/威士 and /dɔː si/多士 from *waste* and *toast*); the reduction of consonant clusters (e.g. /si dɔ be lei/士多啤梨 for *strawberry*, /baːk laːn dei/白蘭地 for *brandy*); the adoption of

Table 2.6 *Phonetic loans from English into Hong Kong Cantonese*

English word	IPA transcription of the spoken Cantonese word	Chinese characters where available
amen	ɑ:mɑ:ŋ	亞孟
angel	ŋɔn kei ji	安琪兒
baby	bi bi / bi (dzai)	啤啤/啤仔
ball	bɔ	波
cartoon	kɑ: tuŋ	卡通
cash	kɛ sy	—
daddy	dɛ di	爹哋
darling	dɑ: liŋ	打玲
friend	fɛn	—
fail	fei lou	肥佬
film	fei lam	菲林
guitar	git tɑ:	結他
hamburger	hɔŋ bou (bɑ:u)	漢堡(飽)
HI-FI	hɑ:i fɑ:i	—
I.Q.	ɑ:i kwiu	—
jam	dzim	占
lemon	liŋ muŋ	檸檬
margin	mɑ: dzin	孖展
M.C.	ɛm si	—
number	lam bɑ:	冧巴
order	ɔ dɑ:	柯打
party	pɑ: ti	派對
quart	gwat	骨
report	pɔt	—
romance	lɔŋ mɑ:n si	浪漫史
salad	sɑ: lœt	沙律
sandwich	sɑ:m man dzi	三文治
tart	tɑ:t	撻
taxi	dik si	的士
vitamin	wai tɑ: miŋ	維他命
whiskey	wai si gei	威士忌

(Adapted from Chan and Kwok 1982: 87–125)

syllable-timed patterns of stress in words like /dze lei/啫喱 and /fɑ: san/花臣 for *jelly* and *fashion*; and the tendency to create disyllabic loans from monosyllabic source items (e.g. /fɑ:t lɔŋ/法郎 from *franc*, and /ma: hɑ:k/馬克 from *mark*) (1982: 34–6).

Graphologically, loans may be written in a number of different ways. First, they may be written using Chinese characters already in existence, for instance, as in the case of 威士忌 *whisky* and 士巴拿 *spanner*. Second, if there are no existing characters appropriate to transcribe new loans, new characters may be created for the purpose, often using the mouth radical 口, to indicate that the 'new' word 'sounds like' the character, as in the word for *coffee* 咖啡, composed of the mouth radical 口, and the characters indicating the sounds /gɑ:/ 加 and /fei/ 非 (37–8). Grammatically, Chan and Kwok state that the majority of phonetic loans in their list belong to the wordclass of nouns, although there are significant numbers of adjectives such as /fit/, /sɔfu/ and /sɔ/ (English *fit, soft* and *sore*), which in Cantonese assume the grammatical function of a stative verb. A small number of verbs have also been borrowed, notably /bui gɔt/杯葛 for *boycott*, /sœt/恤 for *set* (in the context /sœt fɑ:t/恤髮 *to set hair* or to have one's hair styled), and /pɑ: si/ and /fei lou/ from *pass* and *fail*, in the educational context. If words become established loans, they may then in turn form 'hybrids'. For example, /siu bɑ:/ 小巴 *small bus* or *small van* is derived from /bɑ: si/巴士, and /gau bɑ:/九巴 ('Kow-bus') is an abbreviation of *Kowloon Motor Bus Company* (39–42). At the semantic level, Chan and Kwok claim that there may be a narrowing of meaning when an English loanword is used in Cantonese, and provide a number of examples to support this argument, including the restricted use of /lɑ:ŋ/ to describe a *round* or circular movement (44).

They also suggest that lexical borrowing into Cantonese typically involves 'four stages of integration'. First, there are those words usually written in English (especially address terms such as 'Sir') whose usage is restricted to colloquial, informal discourse, as well as the letters of the English alphabet which are used for a variety of purposes, and occur in abbreviations such as *BB, CID, DJ, MC* and *TV* (53–8). Second, there are loans that have widely accepted Chinese characters used for informal writing in popular newspapers in Hong Kong, e.g. /fɔ sou/科蘇 for *floorshow*, /lɑːi san/拉臣 for *licence*, /au sai/歐西 for *outside* and /sa: dzin/沙展 for *sergeant* (58–60). The third stage comprises loans whose spoken forms are used on formal occasions, in news broadcasts and government speeches, and whose written forms also occur in more formal writing such as newspaper reports and official publications. Examples include /bɑ: si/巴士 for *bus*, /ɔ sik/柯式 for *offset* as in 'offset printing', /pou si kɑ:t/甫士咭 for *postcard* and /dik si/的士 for *taxi*. Also in this category are the numerous words describing various food items imported from the West, including /dzi si/芝士 for *cheese*, /kuk kei/曲奇 for *cookie*, /bɑ:n gik/班戟 for *pancake*, /sai lɑ:ŋ/西冷 for *sirloin*, and /si dɔ bɛ lei/士多啤梨 for *strawberry* (60–2). The fourth category of loan-words refers to those words which have 'gained acceptance in standard Chinese' and whose characters have been 'largely standardised', to the extend that they are now found in standard dictionaries. Examples of words in this category include as /bɑ: lœy mou/芭蕾舞 *ballet* (dance), /bɛ dzau/啤酒 *beer* (liquor), /hœŋ ban/香檳 *champagne*, /gɑ: fɛ/咖啡 *coffee*, /gɑ: lœn/加侖 *gallon*, /hɑ:k/克 *gram*, /ŋɑ: pin/鴉片 *opium*, /bɔŋ/磅 *pound*, /lœy dɑ:t/雷達 *radar*, /lɔi fuk tsœŋ/來福槍 *rifle* (gun), and /tɑ:n hɑ:k/坦克 *tank* (62–3).

Bauer and Benedict's (1997) study of Cantonese phonology also includes a number of lists of phonetic loans from English into Cantonese, and they are able to identify a much larger number of items. Building on Chan and Kwok's earlier research, they identify a total of 450 words as directly borrowed from English, of which around 180 are 'characterless' words or 'chorphans'. These chorphans do not have a corresponding Chinese character and are written in their lists either with mouth radicals, or by using English orthography (as in the case of 'BBQ', 'DJ', 'MTR', etc.).

Lexical borrowing from Chinese into English. In a 1985 study that was intended as a continuation of their earlier work, Chan and Kwok published a study of lexical borrowing from Chinese into English. This time they focused on phonetic borrowings from Cantonese and Mandarin into the English language and, at the core of their study, they included a list of phonetic loans, predominantly from Cantonese, into English:

> *Bohea, Cathay, char, Chin, chin chin, China, Ching Ming, chopsuey, chow fan, chow mein, chow (chow-chow), choy sum, Chung Yeung, Confucius, congou, cumshaw, dimsum, ding how, fan-tan, fanqui (fankwei), fen, feng shui (fung shui), fo, foki, foo yong (fu yung), galingale, ginseng, give face, gung ho, gweilo, Hakka, Han, hoey, hong, hyson, I-Ching, kaifong, kaito, kaolin, ketchup, kowtow, kuk, kumquat (cumquat), kung fu, kung hei fat choy, Kuomintang, Kuoyu, Kwan-yin, kylin, laisee, lama, lap sap, li, loquat, lychee, mafoo, mahjong (mahjong), Manchu, Mao, maotai, Middle Kingdom (Central Kingdom), Nankeen, oolong, pakpai, pak-choi, Pekingese, Pekoe, petuntse (petuntze), Pinyin, pipa, Putonghua, Renminbi, samfoo, sampan, samshu, Shanghai, Shantung, sharpei (sharpi), shih tzu, souchong, soy, tai chi (chuan), tai tai, taipan, Taiping, Tanka, tao, tea, Tin Hau, tofu, tong, tung, tycoon, typhoon, wok, wonton, yin, yang, yuan, yum cha, yum sing,* and *Zen.* (Chan and Kwok 1985 : 225–83)

Other processes of word-formation they mention include 'using native resources' (i.e. coining words, or semantically modifying the use of existing words); the addition of the prefix *Chinese*; and the use of 'loan translations' or 'calques'. In the first category, they identify *coinages* or semantically modified items such as *dough sticks, pyjamas* and *concubines.* Examples of *Chinese*-prefixed terms include *Chinese banjo, Chinese boxing, Chinese cabbage* and *Chinese chopper,* whereas loan translations are grouped according to such headings as 'food', 'crime' and 'politics and society'. These include *bird's nest, hairy crabs, lotus seeds, shark's fin, winter melon* (food items); *Big Circle Gang, chasing the dragon, grass sandal, triad, snake boat, snake-head, white paper fan* (crime and the underworld); *face, gweilo, iron rice bowl, sweeping graves, the Cultural Revolution, the Gang of Four* (politics and society).

Benson (1994) focuses on a discussion of the political vocabulary that became prominent in Hong Kong newspaper reports in the run-up to the 1997 change in sovereignty. The terms he discusses include *convergence, the transition, the handover, the takeover, continuity, the Legislative Council* (or *Legco*), *the sandwich class, pro-democracy, pro-China, local, expatriate, illegal immigrant(s), illegal immigration, the four little dragons, the second stove* and *second kitchen*. In a similar analysis, Carless (1995) identifies such items as *black hand, one country, two systems, second stove, three-legged stool, through train* and *warlords*.

Code-switching and code-mixing

During the 1980s, a number of Hong Kong sociolinguists and applied linguists also began to study phenomena related to 'code-switching' and 'code-mixing'. Essentially, these studies were concerned with language alternation in a variety of domains in Hong Kong, including education, broadcasting and the written media. One of the first studies of this type was carried out in secondary schools in Hong Kong, by Johnson (1983). Johnson's research was conducted in five secondary schools in Hong Kong, ranging from the prestigious to less prestigious. Johnson recorded teachers using English as a teaching medium for a wide range of subjects including economics, geography, history, mathematics, science and social science. He found that there was a significant degree of variability in the frequency of code-switching among teachers but, overall, there was a large quantity of switching in use. He identified 2,489 switches in 44 lessons, which averaged out to one switch in every 18 seconds of talking-time. Code-switching in Johnson's study was used for a variety of teaching strategies including class management, elicitation, presentation and explanation.

In the conclusion to his study, Johnson noted that it revealed 'an enormous range of language behaviours' among teachers, and suggested that future policy decisions might accept such diversity and grant teachers the flexibility to establish modes of instruction suitable for the tasks they faced. He went on to express doubts about the implementation of a North American 'immersion' model of education where languages are rigorously separated, stating that he is unconvinced 'that there is anything intrinsically wrong with code-switching in bilingual classrooms' (1983: 282). In a later paper, Johnson and Lee report that, given the choice between different modes of teacher talk, a majority of secondary students opted for a 'bilingual mode' (51 per cent), compared to only Cantonese (46 per cent), or only English (3 per cent). Broadly speaking, their conclusion was that a bilingual teaching mode was 'effective' and 'adapted to the abilities, needs, and aspirations of the full range of pupils entering Anglo-Chinese secondary schools' (Johnson and Lee 1987: 107, 113).

Gibbon's (1979a, b, 1987) studies of code-mixing in Hong Kong focused on the use of a code-mixed variety of Chinese and English used by students at the University of Hong Kong, which Gibbons referred to as 'u-gay-wa' or 'mix'. According to Gibbons the variety of 'mix' spoken by students had 'three contributory elements': Cantonese 'which dominates at the phonological, lexical, syntactic, morphological and semantic levels'; a large element of borrowing from English; and an 'idiosyncratic element' of its own (Gibbons 1979b: 34–5). In this study, Gibbons further suggested that there was an important social-psychological dimension to the use of 'mix' among Hong Kong students. While there was a high degree of stigmatisation against Cantonese-speaking Hong Kong Chinese using English in conversation, there were also strongly negative attitudes to the use of 'mix', in spite of the high frequency, if not popularity, of this variety among the group of students in question. Gibbons sought to explain this apparent discrepancy through a study of covert attitudes using a 'matched guise' study of reactions to varieties of recorded speech (i.e. Cantonese, English and 'mix'). He found that first, 'mix' covertly attracts a degree of the status associated with English and, second, that the use of 'mix' is a strategy of neutrality, allowing speakers to appear neither 'totally westernised' nor 'uncompromisingly Chinese' (Gibbons 1987: 120–1).

Later studies by Yau (1993), Li (1996) and Lee (1996) indicate that code-switching and code-mixing had, by the 1990s, spread throughout a large number of domains other than education. Yau's study focused on the occurrence of code-mixing in a range of written materials including Chinese textbooks in subjects such as economics, commerce, computer studies, geography and world history; magazines dealing with audio-equipment, business, decoration and computers; and popular entertainment books including books on astrology, business administration and soft pornography. Yau explained the frequency of mixing in the written media by reference to a number of factors including the dominance of English textbooks in schools, the lack of standardisation in translation, the gap between the writing systems of Hong Kong and the PRC, and the 'sheer volume of new products and new ideas as well as the speed with which they have been introduced to Hong Kong' (Yau 1993: 31–2). Li's (1996) study analysed data from 3,000 news clippings taken from the quality and popular Chinese press. Li argued that a number of reasons contributed to the code-mixing in the print media in Hong Kong, including the factors of 'availability and specificity', semantic explicitness, 'linguistic creativity' and the 'principle of economy' (Li 1996: 83–109). Li's examples of code-mixed words that are more specific than the Chinese equivalents include such items as *bar code*, *bar hopping*, *charisma*, *information highway*, *junk food*, *politically correct*, *scenario*, *synergy effect*, *virtual reality* and *workshop* (1996: 85). Lee's (1996) study analysed patterns of code-mixing and code-switching in the speech of disc jockeys presenting music on Chinese-language radio stations.

English in Hong Kong and 'Hong Kong English'

As noted in chapter 1, during the 1980s and 1990s, there was a growing interest in the identification and description of new varieties of English in the Caribbean, West and East Africa and many parts of Asia, including India, Malaysia, Singapore and the Philippines. In the case of Hong Kong, the notion of a localised variety of English received much more attention internationally than locally. For example, by the 1980s, the term 'Hong Kong English' had been discussed by a considerable number of international academics, including Munby (1978), Strevens (1980), Todd and Hancock (1986) and McArthur (1987), who all claimed that Hong Kong English has the status of a localised variety of the language. Todd and Hancock (1986), for example, give 'Hong Kong English' its own separate entry in their handbook on international varieties and list a number of typical features of usage at the levels of phonology, vocabulary and grammar. McArthur (1987) includes Hong Kong English, along with Singapore English, Malaysian English and Philippines English, in the category of 'East Asian Standard(izing) English'.

Within Hong Kong, however, the notion of 'Hong Kong English' received a much less favourable treatment from local commentators than that accorded it by international academics. Indeed, most descriptive studies of English in Hong Kong during the 1980s approached the issue from an 'error analysis' perspective, tending to associate the term with deviations from the norm of 'standard British English', and treating it as evidence of the flawed competence of Hong Kong Chinese language users and proof of 'falling standards' of English.

As early as the 1970s, a number of articles appeared detailing the weaknesses and shortcomings of Hong Kong students in learning English. Kwok and Chan's (1972) discussion of the language proficiency of Hong Kong is largely anecdotal, but they tend to characterise the language abilities of their students in terms of subtractive rather than additive attributes. At the core of their argument is the fact that their students experience difficulty in gaining a thorough command of both Chinese and English, asserting that '[i]t is difficult enough for the Hong Kong Chinese to learn standard written Chinese, but much of his time and effort is used to learn English'. As a result, they argue, '[t]he additional burden contributes to poor standards in both languages' (Kwok and Chan 1972: 77–8). Similarly, in a later paper they discuss the difficulties of students in mastering the elements of a creative writing course, noting that as English was acquired largely in the classroom 'native fluency is rarely achieved' and that their creative writers 'have to face the problem of writing about their own culture in an alien language' (Kwok and Chan 1975: 38).

Around the same time, Hunter (1974) reported that there was much discussion about 'the poor standard of English spoken and written in Hong Kong by non-native speakers', and suggested that the problem could be seen as symptomatic of the gulf between the Chinese-speaking and English-speaking communities (1974: 15). The use of 'bad English' could thus be seen as 'a successful compromise between the twin necessities of communicating with another community and of remaining an acceptable member of one's own' and a way of 'informing one's interlocutor that one is not trying to become accepted by his community' (1974: 17). Hunter also suggested that:

> Hong Kong English may have its own norms of correctness derived from the interaction of Cantonese and English spoken by native Cantonese speakers and from the social, cultural and psychological forces which bear on the acquisition of English in this particular context. The low 'ceiling' of English in Hong Kong may result from an unconscious awareness of these norms. (1974: 17)

Given a strongly normative attitude to English among local educators, it is perhaps unsurprising that the majority of studies of local English approached the topic from an 'error analysis' viewpoint.[7]

Until the 1990s, there were only a few attempts to describe 'Hong Kong English' as an autonomous variety of English. One early study was that of Tongue and Waters (1978), which gave an account of certain usages typical of a local style of Hong Kong English including items at the level of both vocabulary and grammar. Distinctive vocabulary items currently in use included: colonial words and phrases also found in other former Asian British colonies, such as *chop, congee, praya, compradore, nullah, coolie, tiffin, griffin* and *shroff*; Americanisms such as *apartment, car-port, elevator, gas, cookie, drugstore, movies, mail, candies, cotton candy* and *block*; Cantonese loanwords borrowed into English speech, including (in Tongue and Waters' transcription) items such as *dim sum, lai chee, lungan, wantan, fantan, foki, hong, kaifong, laisee, mafoo, fa wong, chow faan, fung soyee (or sui), min toi, cumshaw, taipan, tai tai, lap sap, kwailo, yum sing, yum cha, tin fong, ching cha, mau tai, ma chai*; and the use of 'loan translations' from Chinese, e.g. *lucky money, yellow colour, Hongkong side* and *cheap sale* (Tongue and Waters 1978).

At the grammatical level, Tongue and Waters discuss a number of local usages that are typical of local speakers, many of which, they claim, are found in other Asian societies. They group these into a number of categories, including: *the use of 'redundant items'* (e.g. 'They were discussing *about* politics all night', 'He stressed *on* the importance of punctuality', 'Please return *back* the file when you've read the memo', 'Are you seeking *for* an apartment?', 'Although he was ill, *but* he insisted on addressing the meeting'); *choice or omission of preposition* (e.g. 'We'd like to put up a play', 'This is where I get down', 'May we avail ourselves the opportunity of providing you with this service'); *pluralisation of nouns which have no plural* (e.g. 'We have excellent furnitures of all kinds for sale', similarly, 'underwears', 'headgears' and 'equipments'); *use of singular instead of plural* (e.g. 'Beware of pilferer', 'Public relation office', 'Beware of pedestrian', 'Business hour 8-3', 'Office hour 9-4' and 'Enquiry'); and *the use of 'isn't it' as an all-purpose question-tag*. The authors conclude that:

> If the use of English in Hongkong increases substantially in the future as some people predict, the categories exemplified in this article will expand too, perhaps to a point where a variety will emerge which may justly be termed Hongkong English. If that happens, the variety will join the growing family of 'Englishes' which constitute the English language as an auxiliary means of communication worldwide. (Tongue and Waters 1978: 2)

As noted in chapter 1, since 1978, despite the general lack of recognition accorded to Hong Kong English, there have been a limited number of studies

---

[7] See, for example, Webster, Ward and Craig (1987), Bunton (1989, 1991), Boyle and Boyle (1991), Webster and Lam (1991) and Potter (1992).

related to the indigenisation of English in the society. These include Chan and Kwok (1985), Taylor (1989), Benson (1994) and Carless (1995) on various aspects of lexicography and Joseph (1997) on syntax. Bolton and Kwok (1990) argued that the question of Hong Kong English was directly linked to issues of identity, citing Le Page's thesis that 'people create their linguistic system . . . so as to resemble those of the groups with which from time to time they wish to identify' (Le Page 1986: 23). Bolton and Kwok then suggest that many Hong Kong speakers of English model their speech forms, consciously or unconsciously, on the speech of educated bilinguals. They further note that, in a 1983 sociolinguistic survey of languages, 74.8 per cent of the sample described their way of life as 'Hong Kong', compared with 23.6 per cent for 'Chinese'. A similar response was noted for personal identity, with 40.5 per cent of the population claiming to be 'Hong Kong citizens', 29.7 per cent 'Hong Kong Chinese' and 20.2 per cent 'Chinese' (Bolton and Kwok 1990: 166).

Others who have also argued in favour of the recognition of Hong Kong English as a local variety or new variety of English have included Pennington (1995), who asserts that 'the form of English spoken in Hong Kong is a unique combination of Cantonese phonology and morphology, English phonology and morphology, and possibly new phonological rules and morphological combinations which "neutralize" . . . the difference between the two source codes' (1995: 7). Pennington also argues that the 'primary vehicle' for intranational linguistic creativity in Hong Kong is mixed-code Cantonese English, and 'that there are definitely different varieties and norms for English in Hong Kong and that the English of Hong Kong Cantonese speakers may represent what has been termed, in contrast to the "Old Englishes", a "New English"' (1995: 15–16). However, during this period, the issue of Hong Kong English as a new English was not only a question of sociolinguistic research and evaluation, but was also the focus of various ideologies in the community.

Ideologies of language

One of the themes of this chapter is that the discussion of sociolinguistic issues in the territory has been influenced greatly by the rapid and dramatic political, economic and social changes that have occurred in the HKSAR over the last few decades. As in many other societies experiencing rapid change, the discussion of language issues is accompanied by its own ideologies and myths. I am using the terms 'ideology' and 'myth' here to refer generally to the cluster of beliefs, emotions and opinions that surround issues of language. It must be noted that such ideologies and myths may have a basis in sociolinguistic reality but, crucially, that the ideologies that underpin many sociolinguistic commentaries are often covert or obscured. As Cameron (1990) points out, the task of 'demythologizing' sociolinguistic commentaries involves 'essentially . . . making explicit the hidden assumptions which underlie linguists' models, showing that they are historical constructs . . . and subjecting them to critical scrutiny' (1990: 79–80). Three of the most powerful myths in the sociolinguistic description of Hong Kong in recent years have been what one might dub the 'falling standards myth', the 'monolingualism myth' and the 'invisibility myth'.

The falling standards myth

The myth of falling standards has had a remarkably lively existence in the past few decades in Hong Kong. As we saw above, the discourse on 'low' standards of English was strong as early as the 1970s, even at the University of Hong Kong. And, again as noted above, by the early 1980s some academics were describing their students as 'cultural eunuchs' who were 'semilingual' in English and Chinese (see, for example, T'sou 1985).

Other academics joined the chorus of lament. Gibbons (1984) claimed that 'after about 800 hours given over to English in the primary school curriculum, most pupils enter secondary school with no more than the most rudimentary competence in English and some without even this' (1984: 65). He also cites Lord's (1974) assessment of the linguistic proficiency of local students:

> For the majority of students entering the University of Hong Kong English is not a viable means of communication at all. About a fifth of them cannot make themselves understood in English, and their comprehension of spoken English is poor in the extreme. Few students can write English which is not bizarre. (Lord 1974, cited in Gibbons 1984: 66)

Gibbons' explanation of low levels of attainment among Hong Kong schoolchildren was based on a framework of analysis derived from Schumann's (1978) model of 'social distance' and 'acculturation' within a discourse of 'Chinese' versus 'westerners'. Gibbons also argued that 'the students in elite schools in Hong Kong appear to achieve a much higher standard of English than their age peers in non–elite schools' (1984: 69). Ultimately, Gibbons asserted that the prospects for English learning in Hong Kong 'are not particularly good', because of a 'resistance to acculturation', a 'lack of integrative motivation' and 'very limited opportunity for direct social contact with English native speakers' (Gibbons 1984: 72).

The debate concerning 'low' or 'falling' standards of English has run from the mid-1980s to the present, although it probably reached a peak in the late 1980s, when a *South China Morning Post* editorial declared that '[t]he decline in the standard of spoken and written English in recent decades is obvious and measurable, and efforts by the Government and the tertiary education institutions have been insufficient to stop the slide' (*South China Morning Post* 1989c: 18). The debate was not confined to academics, but was rehearsed and expressed in the broadcast media and the local press, with editorials on language policy, feature articles, news reports and letters to the editor regularly appearing in the *South China Morning Post*. Many of the arguments also turned on the choice of language for schools between English, Cantonese and Putonghua but, as Lin (1997) notes, one of the strongest arguments in favour of English was economic, expressed through an identification of English with business, trade and prosperity. One 1986 editorial in the *South China Morning Post* made the case for English thus:

> English is pre-eminently the language of international trade, which is, and for the foreseeable future will remain, Hongkong's *raison d'être*. There are indications that the territory's role in world commerce, far from diminishing as 1997 approaches, will increase in importance. Southeast and East Asia is widely seen as the growth area of the future and we are ideally placed to take advantage of this. Hongkong, as a stable and sophisticated oasis, is the obvious choice of any overseas company wishing to participate in the boom years ahead. The widespread use of English is an obvious added attraction. (*South China Morning Post* 1986a: 10)

A second editorial appeared in the same newspaper some two months later expressing concern about the possible effects on business and finance of the promotion of Cantonese:

> It is honourable for the people of Hongkong to feel a sense of 'nationalism' as we move towards 1997 and the change of sovereignty which will again make the territory part of China . . . Cantonese is and should always be the mother tongue of Hongkong. There is no dispute in this. But it is a fact of life that Hongkong has grown to become a world leader in trade and finance on the back of and assisted by the English language . . . It cannot be disputed that the international language in trade and commerce and a plethora of other interactions is English. And so it should be in Hongkong. (*South China Morning Post* 1987a: 8)

The reference to nationalism in the editorial also pointed to another strand in this debate, which was overtly political. In fact, some months earlier, the *Post* had published another editorial in response to a warning from a Chinese Education Ministry official (Mr Yang Xun) that the promotion of Cantonese as the teaching medium ran against the grain of mainland policy and would be 'a step backward for Hongkong'. The *Post*'s response in those pre-Tiananmen days was to endorse such concerns:

> Mr Yang has made an important point. We would recommend a fresh look at the subject. Putonghua and English are the languages which Hongkong should be stressing. English has, because of its adaptability, subtlety and richness, plus historical accident, become the language of international contact. Hongkong's status as a centre of world trade must be maintained, and our children must learn English to prepare them for the role they will one day assume. Putonghua is the official language of the nation to which Hongkong will be irrevocably joined after 1997. Our children will also become citizens of China, and should speak the language of their compatriots as well as English. (*South China Morning Post* 1986b: 16)

The political was to take a number of other forms in the language debates of the era. One news report even suggested that many schoolchildren were beginning to lose the motivation to study English because there was 'a different political atmosphere with Hongkong coming under Chinese rule' (Lau 1986: 4). Ten years later, the politics of English took a new turn when significant numbers of the Chinese business and political elite started to 'drop' the use of English first names in favour of their Chinese given names. One prominent civil servant explained his decision by saying 'I do not have a Christian name, because I am not and have never been a Christian', adding that 'I have always been an atheist and the name "Brian" is, in fact, a product of colonialism' (*South China Morning Post* 1996: 11).

From an empirical perspective, very little hard research was conducted on the issue of 'falling' language standards during these years, and what was done was inconclusive at best. King (1987) reported on the results of the Hong Kong Examinations Authority's (HKEA) English language examination for the years 1984 and 1986. After analysing a substantial number of statistics relating to 15,000 students, his conclusion was that there was no 'convincing evidence to suggest that the English standard of the best students coming through the Hongkong system has deteriorated in recent years' (King 1987: 17). However, he went on to add that '[i]t is clear that the whole of the secondary system is being seriously affected by the presence of large numbers of students whose English language standards are quite inadequate to cope with an education in the medium of English' (1987: 17), which suggested that the root cause of such perceptions was the rapid expansion of the educational system. Johnson and Cheung researched levels of reading literacy in the mid-1990s as part of the International Association for the Evaluation of Educational Achievement (IEA) World Literacy Project. Their results showed good levels of attainment in Chinese-language reading proficiency, but relatively poor levels of proficiency in English literacy, although the research report suggests that this result might be influenced by the quality of schools as much as the choice of language, as '[g]ood schools produce good results in both Chinese and English and poor schools are equally consistent in producing poor results' (Johnson and Cheung 1995: 10).

As has been shown in many other societies, ideologies about 'falling standards' are often related to other factors, including social class divisions. Romaine (1994) suggests that '[s]tandards of language use and standard languages are essentially arbitrary conventions which can be learned only by going to school', and that '[t]his is precisely why they are so effective in maintaining barriers between groups' (1994: 202). She also points out that such debates have existed in Britain since the fifteenth century, and continue to the present day, even at Oxford University. In the Hong Kong context, one plausible inference with reference to these 'language standards' debates is that, in large part, they were a reaction to the rapid and unprecedented expansion of education, as well as the pace of political and social change in the society at large. These ideologies continued to be voiced until the 1997 handover (Boyle 1997d), and notions of a 'decline' in English still persist. However, if there was ever a 'golden age' of English in the colonial period, it was arguably during the 1950s and 1960s and was particularly associated with Edmund Blunden's tenure as Professor of English at the University of Hong Kong (1953–64). Blunden's students were drawn from a very narrow section of the population and went on to take up high positions in the worlds of business and civil service. In the 1960s, such alumni could perhaps claim a 'superiority' through their command of English, as they would have represented the apex of an English-speaking elite, in a society where, according to the 1961 census report, only 9.7 per cent of the population claimed to know English. By the 1980s, with the rapid spread of varying proficiencies in English through the newly expanded education system, these graduates could no longer argue that few other people had a command of this language. They could, however, and did argue that standards had 'fallen', thus contributing to a peculiar variety of neo-colonial nostalgia.

The monolingual myth

The 'myth of monolingualism' is persistent in many communities where the sociolinguist sees diversity, variation and multilingualism. It may be true that 'in England they speak English', but they also speak many other languages as well. A recent survey on the languages of London schools reported that 307 languages were spoken by the city's schoolchildren, with Cantonese listed in eleventh place. The degree of multilingualism in Hong Kong, among bilingual and trilingual Chinese, as well as among various linguistic minority groups may be less dramatic, but it does exist. Throughout the 1980s and early 1990s, however, many Hong Kong linguists seemed reluctant to recognise the particular forms that multilingualism takes in Hong Kong, choosing instead to emphasize the dominance of Cantonese in the local community.

Thus Fu comments that 'Ninety-eight percent of the population speaks Chinese at home' and that 'English continues to remain more a foreign language than a second language to most people' (1987: 28); Yu and Atkinson state that 'Hong Kong [is] a British colony where 98% of the population are Cantonese-speaking Chinese' (1988b: 307); Yau describes the speech community as 'a virtually monolingual Chinese society' (1989: 179); So affirms that 'Hong Kong is an essentially monolingual Cantonese-speaking community' (1992: 79); and Yau claims that 'Hong Kong is basically a monoethnic society' (1993: 25). Few would deny the vitality of Cantonese but, at the same time, the notions of linguistic homogeneity and ethnic purity hardly match the daily experience of life in a community that has so relatively recently morphed from a *wah kiu* ('overseas Chinese') refugee community into a vibrant Chinese metropolis. Chako (1995) describes its flavour thus:

> As a child in Hong Kong, I spoke English with a British-Indonesian-Cantonese accent, and never really knew what my 'mother tongue' was. Today, many Hong Kong Chinese children also find themselves in

confusion about their native language. They speak fluent English with a Filipino accent, acquired by daily proximity to their maid, or they rattle on in Canadian English, the fallout of their parents' pre-1997 pursuit of a passport... My minibus driver in Kowloon Tong exhibits an admirable command of Tagalog, and is besieged by a flock of willing tutor-passengers who want to know when he's moving to Manila... Whether we're talking language (who put the 'putong' in putonghua anyway?) culture (Confucius or Cantopop?) or political ideology (hands up, all you capitalist communists), Hong Kong Chinese can hardly claim to have a clear-cut 'Chinese' identity. (1995: 30)

Recently the view of Hong Kong as a 'monolingual' and 'monoethnic' society has been strongly challenged by a number of Hong Kong sociolinguists, including Afendras (1998), Bacon-Shone and Bolton (1998) and Patri and Pennington (1998). Bacon-Shone and Bolton, working from a variety of census and language survey data, point out that empirical results indicate that knowledge of English in the general population expanded greatly during the 1980s and 1990s.[8] For example the total number of respondents claiming to speak English 'quite well', 'well' and 'very well' rose from 6.6 per cent in 1983 to 33.7 per cent in 1993; conversely the numbers of those stating that they did not speak 'at all' dropped from 33.1 per cent in 1983 to 17.4 per cent in 1993 (Bacon-Shone and Bolton 1998: 76). These results were supported by the official by-census carried out in 1996, where 3.1 per cent of the population claimed to speak English as 'a usual language/dialect', but another 34.9 per cent reported speaking English as 'another language/dialect' (giving a total of 38 per cent of all those claiming to know English) (see note 6 above). By 2001, this figure had risen to a total of 43 per cent. The dramatic change in the linguistic profile of the society in this time may be related to a number of factors, but it seems certain that the extension of education through the primary and secondary reforms of the 1970s and the university reforms of the late 1980s and early 1990s have played a major role in the spread of English throughout the community. The change in patterns of multilingualism can be seen in figures 2.4 and 2.5.

The number of respondents claiming to know English 'quite well' increased remarkably over this ten-year period, from 4.7 per cent in 1983 to 26.6 per cent in 1993. Similarly, the totals for 'well' and 'very well' rose from 1.8 per cent to 7.1 per cent, and the total of those saying that they knew no English at all dropped from 33.1 per cent to 17.4 per cent (Bacon-Shone and Bolton 1998).

[8] The background to the 1983 and 1993 surveys is discussed extensively in Bacon-Shone and Bolton (1998). While being aware of the shortcomings of the survey method and language censuses I believe that the results that we gained from these two surveys were relatively reliable. In the 1983 survey, I and my co-researcher Kang Kwong Luke benefited from the considerable expertise of the Census and Statistics Department of the Hong Kong Government (Bolton and Luke 1999). In the 1993 survey, the questionnaires were administered by telephone by the Social Sciences Research Centre (SSRC) at the University of Hong Kong, who have conducted hundreds of similar surveys for many institutions including the Hong Kong Government.

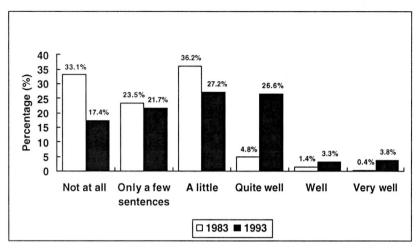

Figure 2.4 Language surveys and knowledge of English, 1983–93

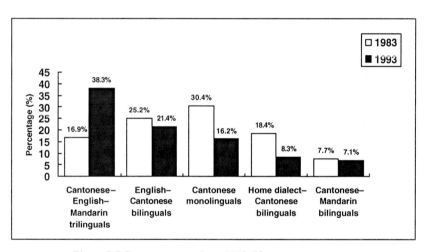

Figure 2.5 Language groupings, 1983–93

At the written level, English also plays an important role in formal communications of all kinds, in government, the legal domain, in university textbooks
and teaching materials, and as a professional language of business and technical
communications in the territory. In the 1993 survey conducted by Bacon-Shone
and Bolton, 54.7 per cent of those that wrote notes, memos, etc. at work normally used English, and 59.2 per cent of those who read written materials at
work read materials written in English. The pre-eminent language of newspapers and print media is Chinese, and in the popular dailies, a localised variety
of 'written Cantonese' is also used for informal styles of newspaper reporting.

The dominance of Chinese in the print media is evidenced by the numbers of Chinese-language newspapers, which number more than thirty, compared with two main English-language dailies, the *South China Morning Post* and the *Hong Kong iMail* (Chan 2000: 325).

In the 1998 study, Bacon-Shone and I point out that English and Cantonese have an increasingly complex relationship in many domains in Hong Kong, including in government, law, education and business. In this context, our 1993 survey results indicated that 'English has also intruded into the private domain of Hong Kong families in unexpected ways', and we were able to cite results which reported that:

- 56 per cent of the population had an English name, with 43 per cent claiming to use that name 'all of the time', and 30 per cent having an English name on their ID cards;
- 53 per cent used English to write out the words on a cheque;
- 57 per cent had close relatives in an English-speaking country;
- 30 per cent either had a close relative who was planning to emigrate to an English-speaking community, or were planning themselves to emigrate; and
- the vast majority reported hearing a good deal of code-mixing (English words in Cantonese speech) in various domains: at home, 45 per cent; among friends, 75 per cent; at school, 90 per cent; at work, 79 per cent; and in public, 83 per cent. (Bacon-Shone and Bolton 1998: 84–5)

Since the early 1990s, there has also been a strong trend among Hong Kong university students, who now all have access to computers either from within their institutions or at home, to use the internet to 'chat' informally to each other through e-mail and ICQ program. In this, they often use a 'mixed' form of written English and Chinese, with Cantonese vocabulary items and conversational particles 'romanised' into a linguistic matrix of written Hong Kong English (see chapter 4, pp. 218–20 below).

In the same study, we also reported that bilingualism was not confined to Cantonese and English, but that a substantial number of respondents also claimed a knowledge of Putonghua (1.1 per cent as a usual language, 25.3 per cent as 'another language' in the 1996 census). In order to carry out a more detailed statistical analysis of the 1993 survey results, Bacon-Shone employed a statistical procedure called CHAID (Kass 1980) which helped identify those underlying demographic variables related to claimed ability in English. In this procedure, a range of possible explanatory variables were considered including *district, sex, place of birth, ancestral home, education, age, occupation* and *now studying*. These variables were considered in relation to ratings of 'ability in English' as set out in figure 2.4 above, where there are six levels of response ranging from 'not at all' to 'very well'.

The results of this procedure were that the most important independent variables were rank-ordered in the following order of importance: (i) *place of birth*, (ii) *education*, (iiia) *age* and (iiib) *now studying* (variables *age* and *now studying* are of equal rank). *Place of birth* distinguished primarily between those born in Hong Kong (around 60 per cent of the population) and those born in mainland China (35.6 per cent), with other countries accounting for 4.6 per cent. In broad terms, therefore, the implications of this for the general population were that if you had been born in Hong Kong, had received a university education, were aged between 12 and 29, and were currently studying, it was highly probable that you would have a high proficiency in English, regardless of other demographic factors. Conversely, if you had been born in mainland China, had a low level of education, were of an older age-group, and were not studying, it was almost certain that you knew no English. The 'demographic' of the Hong Kong monolingual Cantonese-speaker was thus hardly a role model for Hong Kong's aspiring classes.

A converse inference was simply that by the 1990s knowledge of English had become the marker of a general middle-class (new middle-class) identity for Hong Kong Chinese. In this study, according to the empirical evidence, it seemed clear that Hong Kong could hardly be described as 'an essentially monolingual Cantonese-speaking society'. Bacon-Shone and I duly concluded that Hong Kong could be more accurately described as 'a multilingual society, where speakers of the majority language, Cantonese, and speakers of minority "dialects" of Chinese also tend to report increasing degrees of fluency in both English and Putonghua (Mandarin)' (Bacon-Shone and Bolton 1998: 85).

The extent of reported multilingualism can be seen quite clearly in figure 2.5, which is based on a statistical technique that was used to divide the samples for the 1983 and 1993 surveys according to language repertoires. Using this technique, we were able to group individuals into a number of mutually exclusive categories: 'Cantonese monolinguals', 'Home dialect–Cantonese bilinguals', 'English–Cantonese bilinguals', 'Cantonese–English–Mandarin trilinguals' and 'Cantonese–Mandarin bilinguals'.

Figure 2.5 shows that any claims made about monolingualism in Hong Kong would need to be carefully qualified. It is true that in 1983 the single largest group *were* Cantonese monolinguals, but these speakers accounted for only 30.4 per cent of the population. By 1993, as we can see, the balance had shifted dramatically, with Cantonese–English–Mandarin trilinguals accounting for 38.3 per cent of the population, and the figure for 'Cantonese monolinguals' dropping to a mere 16.2 per cent.

Other patterns of multilingualism in Hong Kong are related to the presence of a number of non-Chinese minorities in the community, who often speak Cantonese and English as well as minority languages. The history of such groups in the society is under-researched, but such communities as the South Asians, Parsees, Portuguese and Eurasians played a major role in nineteenth-century Hong Kong. Today, significant numbers of Indians, Parsees and Eurasians still live in the territory, as do Indonesians, Filipinos, Japanese, Malaysians, Nepalis, Pakistanis and Thais. Of these, by far the largest group is that of Filipinos, predominantly Filipina domestic helpers or 'amahs', whose the numbers rose from 72,000 in

1991 to approximately 170,000 in 1999. Not only do such workers make a major contribution to the Hong Kong economy in enabling many middle-class couples with children to both hold full-time employment, but research suggests that they also make a linguistic contribution to the society in providing an opportunity for the children of such families to gain an early facility in spoken English. Afendras (1998) notes that 'Hong Kong's "guest" domestic workers may be emerging as the main caregivers and, at the same time, as live-in English tutors for middle-class children', and that 'Filipinas . . . may be making a contribution to the ecology of English far greater than has hitherto been recognized' (1998: 136–7).

The invisibility myth

The apparent reluctance of earlier studies to consider the multilingual character of Hong Kong society has been matched by a similar attitude to the existence of Hong Kong English as an autonomous variety. For example, Luke and Richards claim that 'In Hong Kong . . . the norm or standard consumed by learners of English is an external one rather than an internal one . . . there is no such thing then as "Hong Kong English"' (1982: 55), a judgement echoed by Tay, who asserts that '[t]here is no social motivation for the indigenisation of English in Hong Kong' and that 'English in Hong Kong has been considered either a learner's language, a developmental rather than lectal continuum . . . or is described in terms of a cline of bilingualism' (1991: 327). Johnson also endorses this view, and comments that the notion of a Hong Kong variety of English has so far gained 'little support', as '[t]here is no social or cultural role for English to play among Hong Kong Chinese; it only has a role in their relations with expatriates and the outside world' (1994: 182).

As indicated above, however, such views present only a partial picture. In chapter 4, I re-examine such previous judgements in the light of the recent profound social and political changes in the territory. From a sociopolitical perspective, one obvious motivation for now so doing is the passing of British colonial rule. Whatever the future of the Hong Kong Special Administrative Region which came into being in July 1997, it is now simply a historical fact that Hong Kong is no longer a colony of Great Britain. Given the experience of other Asian societies, it is unavoidable that Hong Kong's postcolonial development will impact greatly on its sociolinguistic dynamics. A second reason for reconsidering the role of English (as well as its 'visibility') at this time is that the essential conditions necessary for the emergence of such a variety may be already present in the community.

The sociolinguistics of English in Hong Kong – summary and conclusions

In this chapter I have attempted to discuss in some detail the characteristics of Hong Kong society from a sociology of language perspective. For the most part,

I have confined the discussion to the last seventeen years of British colonial rule but, where relevant, I have moved outside this time frame in order to provide a clearer picture of the historical, social and linguistic backgrounds to a discussion of the dynamics of English in Hong Kong.

Hong Kong is an extraordinary society that has experienced extraordinary changes in a relatively short period of time. Immediately after the Second World War, the population of Hong Kong exploded as a result of continuous waves of immigration from Guangdong province and other parts of China, with its population almost quadrupling between 1945 and 1951. Since then, its population has continued to increase at an average rate of one million people per decade, to 3.1 million in 1961, 4.1 million in 1971, 5.6 million in 1991 and a projected 7 million total in the year 2001 (Cheung 2000). In the late 1940s, the transfer of Shanghainese industrial expertise and capital helped set up the labour-intensive low-cost industries, such as textiles, garments and plastics, that became the major employers in the period up to the mid-1970s. These Shanghai émigrés brought with them a cosmopolitanism and cultural capital that found expression in the film industry, music, food and entertainment in 1950s Hong Kong. The Shanghainese were soon outnumbered by huge numbers of refugee immigrants from southern China, many of whom came from small towns and premodern agricultural communities in the Pearl River delta and Guangdong province. These immigrants provided the labour force for the low-cost industries of the 1950s and 1960s, and were initially housed in extreme conditions of discomfort and overcrowding.

After the riots and social disturbances of 1966 and 1967, Hong Kong underwent another period of rapid change. In the 1970s, MacLehose's reformist administration began to provide a greatly expanded range of social services, including public housing, health care, public transport and education. The equivalent of the British 1870 Education Act (providing for elementary education for all) took effect in Hong Kong in 1974, and the equivalent of the British 1944 Education Act (providing secondary education) went into effect in 1978. Judged by the usual economic indicators, Hong Kong society became rich extremely quickly in the period of its modern formation, with the per capita GDP rising from US$410 in the 1960s to US$23,000 by 1996, although great disparities of wealth continue to exist. The territory's separation from mainland China meant that Hong Kong also began to develop its own cultural identity. By 1971, a majority of the population (some 56 per cent), could claim to be 'Hong Kong-born', and by 1991 this proportion had risen to almost 60 per cent. By the early 1980s, it was clear that Hong Kong people (a term that first appeared after the 1967 riots) were no longer 'sojourners', but 'Hong Kong people', *hēung góng yàhn*, with their own distinctive culture in film, television, music, print media and much else.[9]

---

[9] Since 1997, a number of competing and often contradictory trends have emerged in the sociolinguistics of Hong Kong society. Official language policies promoting the increased use of the 'mother tongue' have been accompanied by a range of anxieties concerning both the future status of

The period from the 1960s to the 1990s also witnessed the rise of the modern Hong Kong Cantonese language, thus contributing to the specific characteristics of the 'speech community' in the territory. Immigrants and their children from the different dialect areas of Guangdong and Fujian province quickly adapted their speech to meet the norms of urban metropolitan Cantonese in the territory. The use of indigenous dialects, such as Hakka, began to decline rapidly at this time. After the riots and disturbances of the 1960s, language rights and the recognition of Chinese as an official language became a focus of intellectual radicalism in the early 1970s, which led in turn to the recognition of 'Chinese' as

Cantonese and the continued use of English within the HKSAR. The blurring of linguistic concerns with political worries also seems to be a recurrent theme in such discussions. For example, Ng (2001) recently penned a scathing assessment of government policies (entitled 'Cosmopolitanism at risk') in which she equated recent linguistic trends with a growing ethnic nationalism:

> A few years ago, the streets of Central teemed with people of every race and colour. Now, the crowd is almost uniformly Chinese and local. Bilingualism used to be the rule in street signs and public notices, now they often are in Chinese only. Although the media has always consisted of more Chinese than English, now a non-Chinese speaker might stay unaware of even major news ... In the Legislative Council, English speeches are given little coverage. Subtly but certainly, non-Chinese-speaking people find the Chinese speakers around them less prepared to make allowance for their disability. Their areas of activity and awareness have diminished. Barristers who have no Chinese more frequently find themselves out of work. Patriotism and nationalism are the prerequisite for political advancement. Only Chinese food is politically correct for official functions. The best people swear by Chinese medicine. The only jarring note is that most senior civil servants (all of whom are Chinese) send their children to Britain and the US to be educated. (Ng 2001: 16)

Ng goes on to equate such trends with the increasing sinicisation of Hong Kong, as well as concerns about the continued autonomy of the HKSAR, culturally and politically, noting that 'The SAR Government is to move towards greater concentration of power in the hands of a few senior officials, and power is to be exercised personally and directly, in imitation of Beijing' (Ng 2001: 16). Ng's measured yet pessimistic conclusion is that:

> The determination to cleanse Hong Kong of its colonial past and its multiculturalism, and strive for a stronger and purer Chinese identity will do Hong Kong no good. Nor does Hong Kong's situation require such fundamental ethnic cleansing, even if pervasive economic hardship is making people seem stuck in pessimism. Hong Kong's fundamental institutions and values are sound. They have made Hong Kong prosperous. China's recent success is a story of how the leadership succeeded in steering the nation away from old habits into a modern society – such as Hong Kong ... To marginalise what is non-Chinese will not make the SAR a jewel of the ascending China. It will only strip Hong Kong of its cosmopolitan nature and expose its raw centre as no more than second-rate and provincial. (2001: 16)

Such concerns accurately reflect the current mood of postcolonial Hong Kong (in late 2002). The most salient change in the community since the handover has been a major economic crisis that hit the HKSAR in early 1998 and has continued to the present. In this period, the value of many apartments has been halved, and unemployment levels have gone to 7 per cent and rising. The government is currently running a sizeable budget deficit, and has responded by cutting civil service salaries, which have been matched by similar cuts in the business sector. On the political front, the HKSAR government is now introducing 'anti-subversion' legislation (Article 23), which many fear is designed to further limit political and press freedom in the society.

a co-official language of government and law in 1974. Nevertheless, the demands of parents in the mid-1970s ensured that English was retained as a language of textbooks and at least at a nominal level of instruction in the vast majority of secondary schools. The use of Cantonese in this period also began to expand into many so-called 'high' domains of use, including government, the law courts and broadcasting. The fact that English occupied the space of a *de jure* official language in the territory allowed Cantonese to elaborate its functions in Hong Kong in ways that were denied to 'dialects' in Guangzhou and other parts of mainland China, where official policy forcefully promoted the national language, Putonghua.

The pre-eminence of Cantonese in the 1970s and 1980s helped foster among academics and others the ideology of Hong Kong as a 'monolingual', 'monoethnic' and 'monocultural' society. The fact that this ideology was at odds with the early history of the society, as well as its contemporary development, seems to have weighed little against the force of such belief. By the 1990s, however, it became clear that Hong Kong's linguistic profile was changing, and this was reflected in the results of language censuses and surveys for this period (Bacon-Shone and Bolton 1998). The numbers of those claiming a reasonable command of English rose from 6.6 per cent in 1983 to around 33.7 in 1993. By 1996, a total of 25.3 per cent of the population also claimed a knowledge of Putonghua, either as a usual language (1.1 per cent) or as another language (24.2 per cent). Multilingualism was not only confined to these languages, as there are also minority groups of Chinese dialect speakers, as well as Filipinos, Indonesians, Thais, Japanese, Indians, Malaysians, Parsees and others resident in the territory.

After the Joint Declaration of 1984 had decided Hong Kong's political future, English became problematised in a range of language debates in academic circles and the media. The 'falling standards' debate became a focus of commercial, political and ethnic anxieties. Against this political backdrop, there seemed to be little space for a recognition of 'Hong Kong English'. In other Asian societies such as India, Singapore and the Philippines, there was a growing awareness and occasional pride in a local variety of English, as well as a local literature written in that variety. Among the general Hong Kong population, however, there was a tendency to regard Hong Kong English as, if not non-existent, 'bad' and 'incompetent' English (Harris 1989: 40). Among linguists, this attitude took different forms, as it was mediated by a more sophisticated and professional approach that described the English proficiency profile of local speakers in terms of concepts such as 'error analysis', 'approximative systems', 'interference', 'transfer', 'communicative strategies' and 'interlanguage'. Identifiable language contact phenomena included 'code-mixing', 'code-switching', 'language alternation' and 'mixed-code', and linguists strove to describe and analyse the linguistics of language contact from a professionally modern perspective. In spite of the anxieties about 'falling standards' and 'monolingualism', knowledge of English in the community continued to spread, as did what at least appeared to be a localised variety of the language; which drew the interest of journalists if not academics. A 1987 *South China Morning Post* editorial noted:

> The fact is Hongkong English has evolved into an incipient *patois*, an inevitable process in any colonial setting where the imported tongue cannot avoid absorbing the characteristic of the vernacular, especially one as vibrant as Cantonese. (*South China Morning Post* 1987b: 28)

In the 1990s, the numbers of English speakers increased, particularly among the younger age groups. One result of the popularity of emigration to North America in the late 1980s was that by the mid and late 1990s, large numbers of Hong Kong residents had been educated abroad. A *Time* magazine article of 1996 noted that, with the exception of Filipino domestics, the 34,000 resident Americans then constituted the largest foreign community, outnumbering the 27,000 British. The authors went on to argue that Hong Kong's style was becoming rapidly Americanised:

> In the streets . . . the tempo of American mass culture – from hamburgers to fashion and TV shows – suits Hong Kong's fast-track lifestyle like no other foreign influence. Hong Kong consumers devour anything American. Disney's new stores push everything from T shirts to gold Mickey Mouse earrings. American retailers such as Timberland, Esprit and Toys 'R' Us have sprouted in American-style malls – which are catching on in a society that had always preferred the small, mom-and-pop store. Cricket is out; basketball is in, overtaking soccer as the preferred sport among teenagers. The National Basketball Association runs a nine-person office in Hong Kong. On television, the Cantonese version of the NBA's 'Inside Stuff' attracts 56 per cent of the young male Chinese audience. (Elliot and Strasser 1996: 28)

The same article then discussed Chief Executive Designate Tung Chee-hwa's intention to 'revamp' Hong Kong's education system along US lines in order to promote high-tech industries, and that four out of six university vice-chancellors polled had American passports. The prediction that Hong Kong universities would move towards an American unit-credit system has proved substantially correct, and this change now has been made at most tertiary institutions in the territory.

At the same time, around and after the 1997 handover, there was a rapid growth in the use of personal computers and the internet at all Hong Kong universities, and most schools. Hong Kong students have become remarkably computer literate in a very short space of time, and much computer communication (particularly website use on the internet) is conducted in English, including e-mails and ICQ online chat. Whether all this is evidence of increasing 'Americanisation' remains to be seen. Hong Kong's culture, like its language, has a strong hybrid quality. But if the photograph of the young schoolboy in a traditionally British school blazer was emblematic of Hong Kong people in the weeks after Tiananmen (p. 54 above), by 1997 it was almost certain that the same boy had swapped his blazer for a baseball jacket and his school cap for a Nike hat.

Amongst linguists, the discussion of sociolinguistic issues in the 1980s and 1990s was conducted in the language of modern linguistics, and the metalanguage of what Phillipson calls 'ELT professionalism' (Phillipson 1992: 13). Very few linguists apparently realised that the issues being debated had a resonance with the arguments concerning language contact and contact languages that had been made in the South China context for at least 200 years. Many of those engaged in the analysis of Hong Kong's linguistic 'problems' in the late colonial period also seemed largely unaware of now forgotten discourses on language from earlier stages of contact between southern Chinese people and British, Americans and Europeans in the region. One exception to this was Pennington (1998c) who discussed the linkage between nineteenth century Chinese pidgin English and the hybridised and code-mixed Cantonese of the 1990s, and suggested that, in contemporary Hong Kong:

> In the new breed of Hong Kong Chinese, the mediation of languages and cultures is an internal one that takes place inside individual speakers as they interact within the home speech community. Through this community-internal mediation process, the younger generation of Hong Kong Chinese are creating hybrid identities from a mixed pool of linguistic and cultural resources. (1998c: 28)

Somewhat earlier, my own thinking on these issues had led me to research the archives on the history of language contact in southern China with particular reference to the early descriptions of 'Canton jargon', 'Canton English' and Chinese pidgin English. In chapter 3, I discuss these findings in an investigation of the 'archaeology' of English in China.

3 The archaeology of 'Chinese Englishes', 1637–1949

The people there gave us a certaine Drinke called Chaa, which is only water with
a kind of herbe boyled in itt. It must bee Drancke warmed and is accompted
wholesome.   (Mundy 1637, in Temple 1919: 191)

Sing-chong used to think that we had, like them, a mandarin dialect and a vulgar
tongue, the latter being that called pigeon.   (Fisher 1863: 98)

'Pidgin' has ceased to be used in intercourse with educated Chinese – it is, in
fact, highly insulting to employ it . . . it appears likely that 'pidgin', as a business
language, will soon be extinct. Its place is being rapidly taken by English which,
though often incorrect, is still definitely English.   (Cannon 1936: 138)

Prologue – the Portuguese in Asia and China

Around the year 1500, the European world changed, as the old certainties of the
medieval world were shaken by the scientific advances in astronomy, nautical engineering, ship-building and navigation which culminated in Columbus' voyage
to North America in 1492. Europe started to come to terms with a 'global' view of
world geography, a process that would involve European powers in world trade,
military conquest and imperialism. Over the next 400 years, mercantilism became
a conduit for European capitalism, Christianity and colonisation throughout the
Americas, Africa and Asia. This change in consciousness involved a shift away
from classical scientific thought and the dogmas of the Roman Catholic church
towards a practical science and secular geography based on the actual experiences of the European explorers and seafarers. Between the mid-fifteenth and
mid-seventeenth centuries, the icons of this altered world view were the charts,
maps and globes of a Renaissance geography based on the technologies of ship
design and navigation and the direct, hazardous experience of sea voyages to
previously unreachable areas of the world.

The argument has been made that the immense expansion of geographical
knowledge during this period helped lay the foundations of European modernity
and science. O'Sullivan (1984) suggests that 'the voyages of discovery were in

a way large-scale experiments, proving or disproving the Renaissance concepts inherited from the ancient world' (1984: 3). Many of the late fifteenth-century explorers were consciously aware of being engaged in a historical enterprise called 'discovery', and in their accounts of their voyages they were anxious to dissociate themselves from the earlier mythic and fanciful accounts of Marco Polo and Sir John Mandeville, whose *Travels* included descriptions of headless men and women and other freakish phenomena. The actual dynamics of European explorations and trade are, however, keenly debated among historians. Frank (1998), for example, has challenged Eurocentric histories that have linked European expansionism to 'rise of the West' discourses, arguing that the economies of Asia were 'far more "advanced"' than those of Europe until at least 1800 (1998: 5). He argues that it was only through their access to relatively cheap gold and silver in their American colonies that Europeans were able to wrest control of an Asian-based system of global trade in the nineteenth century (1998: 353).

Linguistically, however, this period witnessed the rise of European vernacular languages, including English, French, Italian, Portuguese and Spanish. As Haugen notes, '[t]he close connection of grammar and politics is shown in the fact that the first Spanish grammar appeared in 1492 and was dedicated to Queen Isabella; it was intended to be a companion of the Empire, the author wrote, and should spread Spanish along with the rule of the Spaniards' (1966: 260). The rise of the vernaculars was also linked to sixteenth-century print capitalism. Before 1500, 77 per cent of the books printed in Europe were in Latin, after 1575 a majority were in the vernacular and, by 1640, only a small number were being published in Latin (Anderson 1983: 18). European vernaculars, therefore, were increasingly used to record the voyages of discovery, as well as the new geographical knowledge that such voyages produced, '[t]hus the laicization of scientific culture followed as Latin, the language of the cleric, was abandoned in favour of Portuguese in order to make the natural history of the New World and the heroic feats of the nation available to a wider public' (Livingstone 1992: 59). By the late sixteenth century, travel literature of this kind was also established in England through the writings of Richard Hakluyt and Walter Ralegh.

The first European power to establish trading settlements in Asia was Portugal, who erected a fort at Cochin in India in 1503, took Goa in 1510 and defeated the Muslims at Malacca in 1511. From the 1540s onwards the Portuguese based in Malacca began to trade with the overseas Chinese, chiefly from Canton (Guangdong) and Fukien (Fujian), who had settled overseas in Luzon (in the Philippines), Borneo, Timor, Indo-China and other settlements in the East Indies. Portuguese ships began regular visits to the island of Liampo (Ningbo) off the Chekiang (Zhejiang) coast opposite the Chusan (Zhousan) islands. Liampo, a 'collection of matshed huts', became the first European settlement in China, and the Portuguese 'squatters on the China coast' (Coates 1978: 13–14). Chinese silks and porcelain bought at Liampo were shipped by the Portuguese to Japan in exchange for silver, which was reinvested in similar shipments to Malacca. According to Coates, after 1549, the Portuguese were forced to relocate first from

Liampo to Sanchuang (Sancian) then to Lampakkau (Langbaiao), both islands in the Pearl River estuary. In the early 1550s, the Portuguese traders moved from Lampakkau to the narrow peninsula of Macao, and by 1560 had managed to establish themselves there with the unofficial permission of the Chinese authorities (Wade 2001). This gave the Portuguese an important role in sea trade with China: the Chinese themselves had been forbidden to trade abroad; the Arabs had lost control of their traditional sea routes to the Portuguese; the Japanese were forbidden to enter Chinese ports; Spain had only a marginal presence in Asia; and no other western maritime nations, such as the Dutch and English, had as yet gained entry to the Asian trade (Coates 1978).

A triangular Asian trade with Malacca and Japan led to Macao's prosperity. Pepper and other spices from the Moluccas, cotton and muslin from India, birds' nests from Siam (Thailand), and a variety of other goods from Europe including metalware and clocks were shipped from Malacca to Macao and then traded in the China market. Much-desired Chinese silks, along with firearms, Persian carpets, cotton and other goods were shipped from Macao to Japan. In Nagasaki the Portuguese received silver for their cargoes, which could be reinvested in Canton. This was an immensely profitable trade; and the merchants of Macao prospered accordingly. Chinese initially were forbidden to stay in Macao overnight, but gradually Chinese tradesmen, craftsmen and boatbuilders began to occupy the basements of the city's houses, where their presence was tolerated by the authorities. Coates' description of Macao's 'days of greatness' from the 1550s to 1640s lyrically depicts 'a city of adventurers enjoying a rich life'. For Coates, the Macao Portuguese were orientalised aristocrats: '[b]old and superstitious, hospitable and remarkably tolerant of outsiders who came in peace, kind to each other, with a strong sense of being one community, they conducted this trade and worshipped in their churches, with their golden-skinned Malacca wives and sun-blackened African slaves, their entire lives the unique, exotic fruit of the grafting of West on East' (Coates 1978: 37–40).[1]

The successful traders of Macao began to build churches and colleges, including St Paul's University College, which was run by Jesuits and acquired full status in 1594 – one of the first western universities in Asia. St Paul's is also credited with founding the first western library of Chinese books, including writings on China in both European languages and Chinese. From the 1560s onwards Portuguese books on Macao began to appear, including a *Portuguese–Chinese Dictionary* from the 1580s, widely attributed to Matteo Ricci and Michele Ruggieri (Barreto 1997). It was Matteo Ricci who led the Jesuit mission to China in the late sixteenth century. He began studying the Chinese language and literature in 1582, reached Beijing in 1601 and stayed there until his death in 1610. Matteo Ricci's diaries, published in

---

[1] The accuracy in detail of Coates' vivid, almost literary, narrative of Macao cited here has been questioned by professional historians. Some of the complexities of historical research on the early Portuguese settlements in South China are discussed by Chin (2001) and Wade (2001).

Latin in 1615 and then translated into other European languages, were 'widely read and popular' from the beginning of the seventeenth century (Mackerras 1989: 31). Ricci described Chinese scholarship in mathematics, astronomy, medicine, the role of Confucian classics in Chinese culture, the education system and the practice of official examinations. He was impressed by many aspects of Chinese society including its size, prosperity and abundance, arguing that the Chinese were a peaceful people, and that 'neither the King nor his people even think of waging a war of aggression ... In this respect they are much different from the people of Europe' (Gallagher 1942: 55, cited by Mackerras 1989: 33). Other Jesuits translated Confucius or, like Louis Daniel Le Comte, similarly recorded highly favourable views of Chinese government and law in their memoirs.

The Jesuits were the first western linguists in China, and the *Portuguese–Chinese Dictionary* was followed by a number of other influential writings on the Chinese language, as well as dictionaries. Matteo Ricci and his colleagues devised a scheme for the phonetic transcription of Chinese using the Latin alphabet, thereby helping to establish a tradition of 'alphabetisation' or 'romanisation' among both western and Chinese linguists that has continued to the present. In 1626, Nicolas Trigault, a French Jesuit, published his dictionary of Chinese, entitled *Aids to Listening and Reading for the Western Scholar*, which again sought to alphabetise written Chinese characters. Trigault assisted in the publication of Ricci's diaries, which also contained a commentary on the characteristics of the Chinese language (Tong 2000). The Jesuit influence in China was felt most strongly for some 120 years, until the death of Kangxi (1654–1722), who had become Emperor in 1661. Du Halde anthologised Jesuit writings in his four-volume *General History of China* (1738–41), which had a major influence on European intellectuals including Leibniz, who is said to have believed that China and Europe were the two greatest civilisations in the world, and Voltaire, who admired the Chinese system of government, in which '[t]he educated mandarins were the fathers of cities and provinces, and the king that of the empire' (Mackerras 1989: 38).

Much earlier, however, many other popular writings on China had appeared, including *The Travels of Marco Polo* (c. 1300), and Mendoza's *History of the Great and Mighty Kingdom of China* (1585). These works were well known, which meant that China was no *terra incognita* for the first British travellers to the country, at least in terms of text. Peter Mundy, who wrote an early travel account of southern China in 1637, was probably familiar with a range of early missionary and travel writing on China and, in his diary, he refers to Samuel Purchas' *Purchas His Pilgrimes*, a massive compendium of travel writings first published in London in 1613 (Temple 1919: 316).

The Weddell expedition and Peter Mundy in China (1637)

The very first British in China left few records of their presence, but a small number of British travellers may have visited Macao in the period 1580–1620

(Coates 1978). The first contact between British traders and the Chinese that we have an extensive record of occurred in 1637, when an expedition of four ships under the command of Captain John Weddell arrived in Macao and Canton (Guangzhou). A narrative of this encounter was recorded in the diaries of an English mercantile trader, Peter Mundy, whose writings, published as *The Travels of Peter Mundy*, are a fascinating memoir of early contact between the British, the Macao Portuguese and the Chinese. Peter Mundy was a factor (or licensed trader) for 'Courteen's Association', an early rival to the East India Company, and his diaries were published in edited form by Richard C. Temple in five volumes from 1907–36. Volume III, part I, contains an account of some 160 pages on Macao and China (Temple 1919). Mundy's account of Weddell's expedition operates on at least two levels, first as a narrative of events, material and diplomatic, and second, as an early form of European travel literature, providing what is evidently the first written description of British reactions to things Macanese, Chinese and the otherness of China.[2]

Mundy records a litany of errors, misunderstandings and misjudgements as Weddell's fleet blunders menacingly around Macao and southern China, apparently terrifying the Macanese–Portuguese and Canton authorities alike. The Macanese and Chinese responses to the arrival of the British merchantmen varied from the ambivalent to the overtly hostile. The four ships under Weddell's command stayed in southern China from 27 June 1637 until 28 December of the same year, when they were summarily thrown out of Macao, 'expelled in all hast, in a Manner perforce, outt of the Citty and Country, even by Fire and sword as one May well say' (Temple 1919: 301). In the intervening six months the British sailors and traders on board these ships had participated in and witnessed a round of confusion, mayhem and murder that involved all three parties, the British, the 'Portugalls' and the 'Chinois'.

Weddell's small fleet of four ships, the *Dragon, Sunne, Catherine* and *Planter*, and two pinnaces, the *Anne* and *Discovery*, left England on 14 April 1636 with letters of authorisation from King Charles I. They arrived in Portuguese Goa on 7 October the same year, to find their opportunities of free trade limited by the Portuguese authorities. Weddell left Goa on 7 January 1637 and established British factories in the East Indies (Indonesia) at Bhatkal, Cochin and Achin, sailing from there via Malacca to the Pearl River off Macao, where he arrived on 27 June (Morse 1926). The Portuguese in South Asia and East Asia were currently at war with the Dutch, and the British were also perceived as a threat. Portuguese trade with China was restricted to Macao, with only occasional visits to Canton, and the Portuguese were worried that the arrival of British merchantmen would disrupt or displace their trading monopoly in the region. According to Morse,

---

[2] It is probable, however, that regular contacts between British and Chinese sailors and traders began somewhat earlier as a result of early East Company voyages to Bantam (in present-day Indonesia) from 1602, and the establishment of an East India Company factory at Hirado from 1613 to 1623 (Farrington 2002).

Map 3.1 Macao and Canton in the seventeenth century
Source: Cameron (1970: 241). This map shows the geography of the Pearl River estuary during the seventeenth and eighteenth centuries, although British settlements at Hong Kong and Kowloon did not exist until after 1842 and 1860.

this meant that 'the [Portuguese] Governor, from the very first day, adopted every available means to prevent these English interlopers from securing any trade' (Morse 1926: 17–18).

Following the governor's instructions, Weddell's fleet first anchored off Macao at Taipa, while a fleet of six Portuguese ships prepared for their departure to Japan. Towards the end of July, Weddell began to lose patience with his Portuguese hosts, who were stalling on the issue of trade, and set sail towards Canton. On 1 August Weddell's ships were intercepted and halted at Chuenpi (Chuanbi) by a fleet of forty Chinese junks. Weddell ignored Chinese requests to go no farther and continued to Anunghoi (in the Bocca Tigris), where he anchored on 8 August. On 12 August the Chinese forts at Anunghoi opened fire on the *Dragon*'s barge, and Weddell responded by moving his four merchantmen closer to the Anunghoi forts. When the Chinese opened fire, Weddell responded with his superior firepower – the first recorded acts of violence between British and Chinese. The British guns devastated the fort, and its occupants took flight:

> Some of our shotte soe lighted and Frighted them thatt within ½ howre there ran outt att the gale Neare a score of them along the strand, and soe gotte beehind a point... Our boates well Manned were sent ashoare; butt by the tyme they were gotten halffe way; there came Forth off the Fort aboutt a Dozen More, butt None of any quality thatt wee could perceave. (Mundy 1637, in Temple 1919: 197)

Weddell's men entered the abandoned fort to find 'potts, pannes, stooles, etts. rubbish' and 'aboutt 44 smalle Drakes [cannon] of Near 4 or 5 hundred waightt each', which they took back to their ships ('Whatt Booty') (Temple 1919: 197). In spite of the fusillades of cannon-fire from both sides, no casualties were recorded at the fort, but then Weddell decided that the best means of defence was attack. The next day they captured a Chinese junk, took the captain and his son hostage and put English sailors aboard so that the junk could be used to surprise other Chinese boats. What appear to be the first Chinese fatalities are recorded somewhat casually in the description of 'Thomas Robinson's skirmish with the country folk' in a passage which describes the actions of a shore-party in one of the villages along the Pearl River, near the Anunghoi fort:

> Thomas Robinson's skirmish with the country folk[3]
> All provisions of refreshinge growinge scarce in the Shipps and sicke men much necessitated, Thomas Robinson went on shoare with the barge and a whitt flagg to certaine villages to procure what he might, beinge accompanied only with 7 musketters, and haveinge passed about a Myle upp in the Country, made their his Station in an open porch of one of their Idoll Temples, untill the people had brought in henns, hoggs, etc., for which, whilest the mony was payinge, he descried about 350 Chinesses, armed with swords, bucklers, launces, etc., makeinge towards them; and beinge approached very neare, they began to rayse a confused shoute after the manner of the Irish hubbub. Wherupon he called to his Company instantly to handle their musketts and to be carefull that they were not cutt off from the passage to the waterside to which they now approched, but were resolutly and undauntedly put to retreate by ours, whoe, discharginge 3 att once and then retyringe whilest the others came upp, held them play in a fayre manner without any dammadge (though they lost some), till they had recovered the waterside, where beinge arryved, they found a supply of about 60 small

---

[3] Temple's sources include not only Mundy's diary but also a number of other documents concerning Weddell's 1637 voyage, including Public Record Office manuscripts; the 'Continuation of the voyage of Weddell's fleet' text from the *Marine Records*, vol. LXIII; Captain John Weddell's own account of the expedition (*O.C.* 1662); the 'Courteen Papers'; the 'Hague Transcripts' (with records from Dutch sources); and the 'Lisbon Transcripts' (from Portuguese sources) (Temple 1919: viii–ix). This text is from the *Marine Records*.

shott sent from the Shipps, invited by the discharginge of their musketts in this occasion. With these, beinge reinforced, they marched upp againe and recovered what they had formerly paid for and were constrained to leave behind. Yett offred they noe violence to people or howses. (Temple 1919: 202)

The key words in this paragraph seem to be 'though they lost some'. This seems to mean that although the British sailors suffered no 'dammadge', i.e. casualties, 'they' (the Chinese 'country folk') lost some men as a result of British musket fire. The mention of 'the Irish hubbub' is also significant, as it appears to be the appearance of the Chinese 'other' as the presumably Irish 'familiar' which moves ship's officer Robinson to order his men to shoulder muskets and commence firing. When reinforcements arrive the shore party recover their purchases and the record notes that they 'offred noe [more] violence to people or howses'; which was presumably evidence of British 'fair play' reasserting itself under difficult circumstances.

Over the next few months Weddell and the other traders ignored the warnings of the Portuguese and tried, using the services of a number of unreliable translators or linguists, to establish direct trade links with Canton (Guangzhou). A number of battles and skirmishes ensued along the Pearl River, and the traders sent by Weddell to Canton were taken hostage by the authorities. Eventually Weddell and the others were forced to appeal to the Portuguese for help in negotiating a settlement with the Chinese, who by now regarded the British as a particularly dangerous breed of sea-pirates. Weddell's fleet finally departed Macao on 28 December, in disgrace.

Peter Mundy's diary

Mundy's journal can be read as early travel writing, in which he provides a series of descriptions of the people – Portuguese, Japanese and Chinese – their social customs, their appearance, their dress and their food. Mundy was highly impressed with the evident riches and opulence of Macao during its 'golden epoch', describing the settlement from the sea as 'a pretty prospecte somewhatt resembling Goa, although not soe bigge' (Temple 1919: 164). He also notes that the Macanese men were all from Portugal, whereas their wives were usually Asian, adding that 'this place affoards very Many ritche Men, cladde after the Portugall Manner' (Temple 1919: 269), before providing a description of the women, noting the similarity with the Portuguese wives in Goa, which he had visited on the journey east:

Their women like to those at Goa in Sherazees [shawls] or lunghees [petti-coats], one over their head and the other aboutt their Middle Downe to the Feete, on which they ware low Chappines [cork-soled shoes]. This is the ordinary habitt of the weomen of Macao. Only the better sort are carried in hand Chaires like the Sidans att London, all close covered, off which

> there are very Costly and ritche brought From Japan. Butt when they goe
> withoutt itt, the Mistris is hardly knowne from the Maide or slave wenche
> by outtward appearance, all close covered over, butt that their Sherazzees
> are Finer. (Temple 1919: 269–70)

He goes on to add that indoors the women 'wear over all a Certaine large wide
sleeved vest called Japan kamaones or kerimaones beecause it is the ordinary
garment worne by Japanese, there being Many Dainty ones brought From thence
off Died silke and of others are Costly Made here by the Chinois off Ritche
embroidery off coulloured silk and golde' (Temple 1919: 270). He also notes the
presence of 'Japoneses' (Japanese) living in Macao, and his description of them
includes mention of their use of what appears to be an early form of paper tissues:

> Some Few Japoneses wee saw in this Citty: most of them Christians...
> They blow their Noses with a certaine soft and tough kind off paper which
> they carry aboutt them in small peeces, which having used, they Fling away
> as a Fillthy thing, keeping handkercheifes off lynnen to wype their Faces
> and hands. (Temple 1919: 294–5)

Mundy was impressed at the hospitality he and the others from Weddell's fleet
received in the city. Two days after the fleet arrived, Mundy was a member of
Weddell's group when he called on the captain-general of Macao, Domingos da
Camara de Noronha, at Government House, bearing letters from King Charles
I and the Viceroy of Goa. During this visit, they were taken round the Church
and College of St Paul by the Jesuit Fathers. Mundy records a description of
these buildings, starting with a description of the Collegiate Church of Madre de
Deos: 'the rooffe of the church aperteyning to the Collidge (called Saint Paules)
is of the fairest Arche that yett I ever saw to my remembrance, of excellent
worcke manshippe, Don by the Chinois, Carved in wood, curiously guilt and
painted with exquisite collours, as vermillion, azure, etts.' (Temple 1919: 163).
Although Protestant, Mundy also praises the missionary endeavours of the Jesuits
or 'Paulists', noting that they 'Neither spare Cost nor labour, Dilligence Nor
Daunger to attaine their purpose' (Temple 1919: 164). He was also a keen observer
of things Chinese during these months, and his journal provides a description
of the customs of the Chinese in Macao and the Pearl River delta, including a
specific appendix, where he declared that in spite of the travails of their stay 'yett
will I adde 2 or 3 lynes in Commendation of this soe great, Ritche and Famous
a kingdome, For as Much as I saw and heard, with somwhatt off their language,
numbers, etts. particularities' (Temple 1919: 301).

Mundy's impressions of China are largely favourable. He likes the climate,
and discusses the absence of sickness amongst the men, and the 'healthy aire'
of the place. 'Chinas excellencies' include 'Antiquity, largenesse, Ritchenesse,
healthynesse, Plentiffullnesse. For Arts and manner off governmentt I thinck
noe Kingdome in the world Comparable to it. Considered alltogether' (Temple
1919: 303). Whether this impression was based entirely on his own first-hand

observations, considering the fact that his view of China had been so restricted, seems doubtful. It is perhaps more likely that Mundy had already read widely on China through missionary and other accounts, and also that he was affected by the prevailing opinion in Europe that China was a great civilisation (a view that would alter radically by the early nineteenth century). As a trader, Mundy also devotes a sizeable section of his appendix to a description of trading 'commodities', most of which he claimed were 'very ritche, rare, good and Cheape'. Chief among these were 'Gold' and 'Raw silke'. Another commodity was 'China Porcelane', which Mundy mentions is 'the best in the world'. Other goods include powdered sugar ('very good, smelling like roses'), 'muske', 'Greene ginger' and 'Conserves off severall sorts very good and Cheape' (Temple 1919: 304).

Mundy's account gives an overwhelming impression of a country of wealth, abundance and, at a culinary level, an Eldorado of taste sensations. He records his first taste of 'Leicheea' (lichees): 'as bigge as a Wallnutt, ruddy browne and Crusty, the skynne like to thatt of the Raspis [raspberry] or Mulberry, butt hard, which Doath easily and cleanly come offe, having within a Cleare white (somwhatt) hard palpy substance, in tast like to those Muscadine grapes thatt are in Spaine ... It is said they are proper only to this Kingdome of China, And to speake my owne Mynde, it is the prettiest and pleasauntest Fruit thatt ever I saw or tasted' (Temple 1919: 162). He also notes the sale of snakes and dogs for the table, but perhaps the most significant entry is the section which describes his introduction to tea (or 'chaa' as he calls it), which is the first written account from an Englishman in China of the drink that would dominate trade in the coming two centuries, involve British merchants in opium smuggling and lead to the eventual annexation of the island of Hong Kong in 1842.

> Chaa, what it is.
> The people there gave us a certaine Drinke called Chaa, which is only water with a kind of herbe boyled in itt. It must bee Drancke warmed and is accompted wholesome. (Temple 1919: 191)

In the same village where he drinks tea, Mundy is also invited to the 'Pagode' or temple, where, after witnessing a fortune-telling ceremony, he is given food and a pair of chopsticks: 'Then broughtt they us some henne cutt in smalle peeces and Fresh porcke Don in like Manner, giving us Choppsticks to eatt our Meat, butt wee knew not how to use them, soe imployed our Fingers'; which is washed down with 'warme Rack [or 'arak, spirits] outt of a straunge bottle' (Temple 1919: 194).

Also included in the appendix is an account of the 'Coynes and Waightts used at Macao in China', with a listing of a system of coinage based on the *tay* ('tael'), *massa* ('mace'), *cundoreene* ('candareen') and *casse* ('cash'). Thus, the system based on 'decimation' yielded the following values: one *tay* equalled ten *massaes*, one *massa* equalled ten *cundoroneis* and one *cundoreene* ten *casse*. The *casse* (or 'cashe') is described as 'a Copper Coyne with China characters', whereas the other coins are 'paying outt their gold and silver by waightt, cutting itt outt in smalle peeces'

(Temple 1919: 309–10). Mundy also mentions the use of the 'abacus', although he does not give it a name, commenting that '[m]ost China Men can write and cast uppe accompts which they Doe [by] pen, as allsoe by an Invention with beades in stead of Counters, and Deciphered when I come to speake of their Numbers' (Temple 1919: 312). Mundy comments on a range of other things Chinese, including boats and shipping, religion, housing, attire, gambling and marital customs.

The linguistics of Peter Mundy

The linguistic interest of Peter Mundy's diary can be seen at a number of levels. As with later travellers, traders, missionaries and colonial officials, one central problem was that of communicating with the Chinese officials and traders at Macao and Canton. Weddell had, however, managed to gain the services of an interpreter, so that when he attempted to force his way into the mouth of the 'river of Cantan', he was able to negotiate with 'dyvers Manderyns' through interpreters on both sides using Portuguese for negotiation (Temple 1919: 186). Mundy provides a description of their interpreters:

> Our Interpreters, who they were.
> The aforesaid interpreter was a Chincheo, runaway From the Portugalls att our beeing att Macao, who spake a little bad language. There is another Named Antonio, A Capher Eathiopian Abissin, or Curled head, thatt came to and Froe aboutt Messages as interpreter, little better then the other, runawaie allsoe From the Portugalls to the Chinois, it beeing an ordinary Matter For slaves on some Discontent or other to run away From their Masters; and beeing among the Chinois they are saffe, who make use of their service. (Temple 1919: 192)

What is not spelt out here, in fact, is how Weddell acquired the services of these two interpreters. As both were runaways from the Portuguese at Macao, we can assume that the Chinese mandarins provided them. The first was a Chincheo, i.e. someone from Fukien province, and the second was, in Temple's gloss, 'a negro slave answering to the name of Antonio' (1919: 192). A third linguist, 'Pablo Noretti', apparently a Chinese Christian from Macao, presents himself, and it is largely his interpretation and brokering with the Chinese that precipitates the disastrous course of events that follows. It is only when the Portuguese arrange for Father Roboredo to assist them that the British can begin to extricate themselves from the very serious difficulties they face. Again, we can infer, translation would have been the key. Roboredo, perhaps, or the other Jesuits in Macao, certainly, would then have been able to supply accurate interpreters and translators, both to negotiate verbally with the Chinese and to translate key documents. What was obvious from all this was that a command of Portuguese was crucial, and that the British traders' ignorance of the Chinese language severely handicapped them in their attempted dealings with the Chinese. As many of their successors in China trade at Macao and Canton were later to discover, and to complain, British traders frequently were left completely reliant on the services of their interpreters or 'linguists'.

Mundy was no mean linguist himself. When he joined the East India Company in 1627, it was noted by the Court of Directors that he 'hath in some good measure gayned the French, Spanish, and Italian tongues' (Temple 1907: lii). Boxer further attests to the fact that Peter Mundy 'had a good working knowledge of both Spanish and Portuguese' (Boxer 1968: 123), which would have been necessary given the importance of the latter language as an international maritime *lingua franca*.

Mundy's English

The sections of Mundy's *Travels* on Macao and China were written only twenty-six years after the publication of the Authorised or King James version of the Bible, which first appeared in 1611. By the early seventeenth century, English had begun to emerge as a literary language, although many scholarly and scientific works continued to be published in Latin. During the sixteenth century English had become a 'self-conscious language' (Millward 1996: 227–8), and throughout the century there were debates about the purity of the language and the rival merits of using existing English forms or creating new English words as alternatives to French and Latin loans. Thousands of Latin loans were adopted into the language, including such now-familiar items as *expect*, *industrial* and *scheme*, which were originally regarded as 'inkhorn terms' (Millward 1996: 231). Spelling also attracted a good deal of discussion at this time, and a number of proposals in favour of spelling reforms were put forward, including those of Cheke (1569), Smith (1568) and Bullokar (1580) (cited in Millward 1996: 232). The first monolingual dictionaries of English date from the early seventeenth century: in 1604 Robert Cawdrey published *A Table Alphabeticall*, which included 2,500 'hard usuall words', and provided definitions for these (Millward 1996: 236). A number of other dictionaries followed, including Bullokar's *An English Expositor* (1616), Cockeram's *English Dictionarie* (1623), Blount's *Glossographia* (1656), Philipps' *New World of Words or a General English Dictionary* (1678) and Kersey's *A New English Dictionary* (1702). Later, Bailey's *An Universal Etymological English Dictionary* (1721) became a standard reference work until its replacement by Johnson's *A Dictionary of the English Language* (1755).

Grammar was not forgotten, with publications including Bullokar's *Bref Grammar* (1586), Gill's *Logonomic Anglica* (1621) and Wallis' *Grammatica Linguae Anglicanae* (1653), the last two being published in Latin. During the latter half of the sixteenth century the speech of the London area was already being privileged in some treatises on the language. Puttenham (1589) in *The Arte of Englishe Poesie* states that the English of the North 'is not so Courtly nor so currant as our Southerne English is, no more is the far Westerne mans speach' and praises 'the usuall speach of the Court, and that of London and the shires lying about London within lx myles, and not much above' (cited by Millward 1996: 249).

At a phonological level, the most important changes affecting the pronunciation of English at this time were those related to the processes associated with what is generally referred to as the 'Great Vowel Shift'. This series of phonological changes began in the late Middle English (ME) period and was largely complete in educated varieties of English by the end of the eighteenth century. The Middle English long vowels took on 'higher position' pronunciations, and Middle English high vowels became diphthongs. From a historical perspective, the Early Modern English (EME) period is regarded as an era when the phoneme system of Present-day English (PdE) was coalescing, but there was still a great deal of variation, both within educated varieties and throughout the many dialects of Britain. In simple terms, it has been described by Nist as sounding similar to the 'Anglo-Irish brogue or the British dialects of present-day Somersetshire or Dorsetshire' (Nist 1966: 241).

At an orthographical level, a degree of standardisation had been adopted by printers, but there was still a great deal of variation in spellings and this was particularly true of the personal writing of individual authors. Freeborn (1992) notes a number of features of spellings *circa* 1600, including the use of a redundant <e> (sometimes corresponding to an earlier /ə/, sometimes following a final <o>), and the interchangeability of <i> and <y> for the vowel /i/, both of which occur frequently throughout the Mundy texts. One also sees the use of <y> instead of <i> in such words as <arryved, fayre, mynde, rayse, swymming, tyme, wyde> and the use of 'double vowels', perhaps indicating vowel length (Görlach 1991), as in <bee, hee, mee, wee>. Conversely, consonants are often doubled, particularly in final position, thus <aboutt, att, broughtt, mightt, thatt>. In addition, a number of French-influenced spellings can be found, including <bataille>, <coullor> and <sodaine>, reflecting the massive influence of French and Latin borrowings by this time.

Morphologically, Mundy's English displays a number of features typical of Early Modern English. Noun plurals are consistently marked by -s, and there are few 'irregular' plural forms. The use of the possessive apostrophe occurs, as in *the King of Spaine's Dominion*, although the apostrophe is omitted in the expressions *gods will* and *Gods providence*. One also finds the use of the genitive phrase in a number of instances, including '2 of the Clocke in the Morning'. PdE pronominal forms occur throughout, including *he* (predominantly spelt *hee*), *him* and *his*; *wee*, *our* and *ours*; *you* and *your*; and *they*, *them* and *their*; and there are no occurrences in the texts of *thou* or *thee*. Relative pronouns also tend to follow PdE norms, and include *that*, *which*, *who* and *whomsoever*. Verb morphology is more complex, where the ME system of strong versus weak verbs is giving way to a system of 'regular' versus 'irregular' forms (Millward 1996: 271). Examples of irregular forms in the texts that distinguish themselves from British PdE include past *drave*, *spake* and *ware* ('wore'), and past participle *gotten*, while we also find the use of *lighted*, for PdE *lit*, and *frighted* for PdE *frightened*.

Third-person-singular indicative forms include both *-s* and *-eth* forms, with examples of the latter including *eateth, knoweth, standeth* and *taketh*.

Syntactically, the word order generally conforms to the SVO pattern of PdE, but there are instances, after introductory adverbials, where a VSO pattern is found, as in 'Yet offerd they no violence to people or houses', or 'Now beegan wee to Mistrust the Dealing of Nurette and to Fear the saffety off our Merchants att Cantan'. The word order in negative constructions is also sometimes marked, as in 'Itt beeing Not now tyme to looke on'. Within the verb phrase, one can notice the lack of the progressive-passive combination in 'whilest the mony was payinge'. In the noun phrase, there is also the use of the reduplicative subject pronoun, as in 'The *Dragon* shee cutt both her Cables...'.

Perhaps the most distinctive development during this period was the vast increase in the English lexicon, which borrowed vocabulary not only from Latin and Greek, but also from other European languages such as French, Italian, Spanish, Portuguese, Dutch and German. In addition to loans from European languages, there was also the introduction of loanwords from Amerindian and Asian languages, a phenomenon explained by Millward in terms of the discovery of 'a New World' in North America, and by reference to the British successfully vieing 'with the Portuguese, French and Dutch for control of the Indian subcontinent' in Asia (1996: 287).

Mundy's Portuguese

Furber notes that, 'when the English, Dutch, Danes, and French arrived in the East Indies [which included India and all points east], Portuguese had long since developed a "Creole" form in which discussions between Europeans and Asians were carried on', and that this was 'the "lingua franca" of commerce from the Red Sea to Canton' (1976: 298). Even after the East India Company had established itself in India throughout the seventeenth century, Portuguese continued to be necessary, and was, in the words of one sea-captain and trader 'the Language most Europeans learn first to qualify them for a general converse with one another as well as with the different Inhabitants of India' (Hamilton 1727, cited by Furber 1976: 298). Every European trading factory employed Portuguese–Indian interpreters (or 'linguas').

Mundy's record of his stay in Macao and China contains a large number of Portuguese words, or Indo-Malay and Indo-Chinese words 'filtered' through Portuguese. Some words were directly derived from Portuguese, including *Canton* (from *Cantao*), *muster* (from *mostra*, 'pattern' or 'sample'), and *quitasoll(e)* (from *quita sol* 'bar sun'). Others were of a 'hybridised' form, and seem to be drawn from the varieties of 'Indo-Portuguese' that were spoken throughout the Portuguese settlements in India, Malacca and the East Indies. His diary also includes a large number of such items of 'mixed' Indo-Portuguese provenance, including various forms of the words *bamboo, cash, catty, chop, junk, pagoda, putchock, rattan, tea* and *typhoon*.

The major authority on the etymology of such items is still Yule and Burnell's (1886) monumental work, *Hobson-Jobson: a Glossary of Anglo-Indian Colloquial Words and Phrases*. Many of their entries attest to the importance of Portuguese in filtering vocabulary items from all those societies with whom the Portuguese had contact in the early colonial period. Thus, *bamboo*, although of 'exceedingly obscure origin' is said to be borrowed through Portuguese from the Canarese word *banwu*, the Konkani *manbu*, the Javanese *bambu*, the Malay *samambu* or, possibly, in the form *bambu* or *mambu*, from Persian or Arab traders. *Cash* may be from the Tamil *kasu*, but was widely used by the Portuguese, in the form *caixa*, to refer to the small coinage used throughout the Malay Islands, especially by the Chinese. The word *catty* (a measure of weight equal to approx. 625 grams) is derived from *kātī* or *kati* in Malay–Javanese. *Chop* (originally a permit to conduct trade, leave port, etc.) is said to be derived from the 'Hindustani' *chhāp*; *junk* from the Javanese and Malay *jong* and *ajong*, 'a ship or large vessel'; *pagoda*, possibly from the Portuguese *pagão*, 'a pagan'; *dagaba* from Ceylon, Sanskrit *bhagavat*, or the Persian *butkadah*. *Putchock* (a fragrant root used in the manufacture of incense) is possibly derived from the Malay *puchok*; *rattan* is from the Malay *rotan*.

Many contemporary accounts of the history of English underestimate the extent of lexical borrowing from Portuguese during the early seventeenth century. Millward, for example, lists only eight English items derived from the Portuguese experience in the 'Far East and New World' during this period: *albacore, betel, cashew, mango, pagoda, tank, tapioca* and *yam*. In addition, she lists five other 'native' Portuguese loanwords: *auto-da-fé, palaver, molasses, albino* and *dodo*, and further notes fifteen items of colonial Spanish borrowed into English: *alpaca, avocado, cannibal, canoe, chili, cigar, coyote, hammock, iguana, llama, maize, papaya, potato, puma, tomato* (1996: 286).

Yule and Burnell (1886) make a much stronger claim about the influence of Portuguese on Anglo-Indian English, noting that:

> The conquests and long occupation of the Portuguese, who by the year 1540 had established themselves in all the chief ports of India and the East, have, as might have been expected, bequeathed a large number of expressions to the European nations who have followed, and in great part superseded them ... The natives in contact with the Portuguese learned a bastard variety of the language of the latter, which became the *lingua franca* of intercourse, not only between European and native, but occasionally between Europeans of different nationalities. This Indo-Portuguese dialect continued to serve such purposes down to a late period in the last century, and has in some localities survived down nearly to our own day ... The foundation of this *lingua franca* was the Portuguese of the beginning of the 16th century; but it must have soon degenerated, for by the beginning of the last century it had lost nearly all traces of inflexion. (1886: xviii)

Yule and Burnell suggest that a number of distinct sets of Portuguese and Portuguese-based words were still in general use in South and Southeast Asia in the late nineteenth century, including:

(i) *generally used 'Anglo-Indian colloquialisms'*: *almyra* ('wardrobe, chest of drawers' from Port. **almario**), *aya* (or 'ayah' a 'native lady's maid or nurse-maid', from Portuguese **aia**), *cameez* ('a shirt' from Port. **camisa**), *caste* ('breed, race, kind' from Portuguese **casta** or **caste**), *cobra* (the poisonous hooded snake from Port. **cobra de capello**), *goglet* ('a waterbottle, usually earthenware' from Port. **gorgoleta**), *gram* ('grain' or horse-feed in India from Portuguese **grão**), *mistry* or *maistry* ('a foreman', 'a master workman' from Port. **mestre**) and *mosquito* (from the Port. and Spanish diminutive of **mosqua**, 'a fly'));

(ii) *items specific to the South of India*, including *fogass* ('a cake baked in embers' from the Portuguese **focaça**), *margosa* ('the nīm tree' of India and Ceylon, from Port. **amargosa**), *pial* ('a raised platform' from Port. **poyo** and **poyal**), *picotta(h)* ('an ancient machine for raising water', from Port., **picota**, a ship's pump) and *rolong* ('fine wheat flour' or 'semolina', from Port. **rolão**, or **ralão**));

(iii) *items from Bombay*, such as *batel* (a 'sort of boat', from Port. **batell**), *brab* (a 'wild' palm, from Port. **brava**, 'wild'), *foras* ('lands reclaimed from the sea' at Bombay, from Port. **foro**, 'quit-rent'), *oart* (in western India, 'a coco-nut garden', from Port. **orta** or **horta**), *vellard* (a 'causeway' in Bombay, from Port. **vallado**, 'embankment'));

(iv) *items associated with China*, such as *comprador* (a 'house-steward' or 'butler', from Port. **comprador**, purchaser), *joss* (explained by Yule and Burnell as 'pidgin' language for 'God', from Port. **Deos**) and *linguist* ('interpreter', from Port. **lingua**));

(v) *other terms*, such as *bandeja(h)* (a 'tray' or 'salver' for presents, from Port. **bandeja**), *castees* ('children born in India of Portuguese parents', Port. **castiço**), *covid* ('the name of a measure', as of cloth, from Port. **covado**), *cuspadore* (a spitoon, from Port. **cuspadeira**), *Gentoo* ('a gentile' or 'heathen' applied to Hindus in contrast with the 'Moors', from Port. **Gentio**), *kittysol* (an 'umbrella' from Port. **quita-sol**, 'bar sun') and *Moor* (a 'Mohammedan', and particularly 'a Mohammedan inhabitant of India' from Port. **Mouros**); and

(vi) *other Asian words 'which bear the mark of having come to us through the Portuguese'* including: *areca* ('betel-nut' from Malayālam, *aḍakka*, through Port. **areca, arecha, arequa**), *avadavat* (a type of 'cage-bird' in India, brought to Europe from 'Guzerrat', the name of which is 'Ahmadabad'), *batta* ('difference in exchange of money or weight', from Canarese, *bhatta*, Port. **bate, bata**), *benzoin* ('a kind of incense', possibly from Arabic, through Port. **beijoim, beijuim**), *betel* (from Malayālam, through Port. **betre** and **betle**), *cassanar* ('priest of the Syrian church of

Malabar', through Malayālam, *kattanār*, Port. **caçcaneira**), *catamaran* ('a raft formed of three or four logs lashed together', from Tamil, *kattu*, 'binding' and *maram*, 'wood'), *chop* (a 'permit', 'seal', or 'stamp', from Hindustani, *chhāp*, Port. **chapa** or **chapo**), *coir* ('coconut fibre' from Malayālam), *congee* ('rice gruel' from Tamil *kanjī*, 'boilings') and *copra (h)* ('dried coco-nut', from Malayālam, *koppara*). (See Yule and Burnell 1886: xviii–xix)

A later authority on loanwords in English, Serjeantson (1935), includes a list of 43 loans from Portuguese, which are dated according to the approximate time of their entry into English:

> *marmalade* (1480), *reis* (1555), *milreis* (1589), *padre* (1584), *flamingo* (1565), *coco* (1579), *molasses* (1582), *sargasso* (1598), *madeira* (1585), *yam* (1588), *buffalo* (1588), *palanquin* (1588), *typhoo* (1588), *mandarin* (1589), *bayadère* (1598), *areca* (1599), *port* (1691), *peccary* (1613), *macaw* (1668), *grouper* (1697), *macaque* (1698), *ginny* (1620), *assagai* (1625), *dodo* (1628), *pintado* (1602), *caste, cast* (1613), *emu* (1613), *comprador* (1615), *tank* (1616), *pagoda* (1634), *lorcha* (1653), *palmyra* (1698), *goglet* (1698), *moidore* (1711), *senhor* (1795), *pareira* (1715), *palaver* (1735), *joss* (1711), *verandah* (1711), *cangue* (1727), *ayah* (1780), *margosa* (1813), *massage* (1876).

In 1997, *The Oxford Dictionary of Foreign Words and Phrases* provided a list of 54 Portuguese words in English for the period from the sixteenth to twentieth century, and of these some 37 are said to have come into use before the end of the nineteenth century, including 34 not mentioned either by Serjeantson or Yule and Burnell: *amok, banyan* (sixteenth century); *aldea, copaiba, fidalgo, ipecacuanha, maraca* (seventeenth century); *auto-da-fé, commando, cuspidor, elephanta, piranha* (eighteenth century); *amah, bucellas, carioca, fazenda, fazendeiro, feijão, garimpeiro, guarana, lingua geral, samba, senhora, senhorita, serra, sertão, vigia, vindaloo, vinho, vinho branco, vinho tinto* (nineteenth century) (Speake 1997: 508). There is an obvious and substantial discrepancy between these lists: Millward has a total of 28 Portuguese and Spanish borrowings for the Early Modern English period, Serjeantson lists 43, while Yule and Burnell's introduction cites 71. This gives only a partial indication of the impact of Portuguese in Asia, and scrutiny of the individual entries in *Hobson-Jobson* reveals a stratum of Portuguese that runs through scores of 'Anglo-Indian' and other Asian English words.

Mundy's 'Asian English'

Linguistically, Mundy's diary can be seen as an example not only of Early Modern English, but also as perhaps one of the first examples of texts inscribed with the vocabulary of a form of early Asian English, certainly in the context of China. But the language of Mundy's journal is notable not so much for examples of early pidgin, but much more for examples of early 'Asian English(es)', particularly at the level of vocabulary. The point here is simply this: what have been referred to since the early 1980s as the 'new Englishes' of Asia may not be new at all, but have a forgotten history that stretches back to the very first contact between English speakers and the indigenous populations of Asia. In the case of China, Mundy's diary is very significant, for in it we can find clues to the later development of the English language along the South China coast, in Canton, Macao and Hong Kong. In addition, the influence of Portuguese on English in Asia also relates to the issue of 'relexification' in pidgin and creole studies, an issue that is discussed later in this chapter.

Table 3.1 provides a list of some 88 words and expressions that occur in the sections of Mundy's *Travels* which record his stay in Macao and can be seen as representative of an early Asian-English vocabulary. Even in this short glossary, I would argue that it is possible to see the influence of Portuguese in a substantial number of items. In addition to the 27 items which appear to be derived directly from either Portuguese or Spanish, Portuguese would have also provided a filter for most of the other Asian items derived from such source languages as Arabic, Cantonese and Malay–Javanese, and would thus have influenced the vast majority of the other words in the list.

A number of points can be made about table 3.1. First, although many of these words appear foreign to the contemporary reader, a number would also be familiar (spelling difficulties aside), for example, *bambooes*, *chaa*, *chacculatte*, *chopstickes* and *hurracanes*. Second, Mundy's journals provide an important source of early attestations for such items. The *OED* has *char* listed from 1919 (compared with *Hobson-Jobson*'s 1616), *chocolate* from 1604 and *furacanes* for 'hurricane' from 1555. But Mundy's references to *chopstickes* and *kimaones* predate both the *OED* and Yule and Burnell. The appearance of the word *chopstickes* here also seems to bely the *OED*'s etymology, which states that 'In Chinese and in "pigeon-English" *chop* means "quick"; "quick sticks" would be a kind of equivalent of the Chinese name, *k'wâi-tsze*, i.e. "nimble boys", "nimble ones"', as this explanation relies on the existence of a pidgin variety of Chinese English that historically had not yet come into existence by 1637. In fact, an alternative explanation is suggested by another entry for *chopstick* in the *OED*, which explains the term thus: 'The cross-stick (of iron wire, whale-bone, etc.) attached to a deep-sea fishing-line a short distance from the sinker, from which the short lines bearing the hooks are hung', with attestations from 1615. The obvious inference here is that the term *chopstick* before 1637 was used as a nautical term to refer to a particular type of stick used aboard ship, and that resemblance of this stick to the Chinese sticks used for eating allowed for the semantic extension of the nautical term.

Second, a number of these items would *not* today be familiar to users of English in the 'inner circle', but would be familiar to users of English in 'outer circle' societies throughout Asia. For example, *cattees* (sing. 'catty'), *choppe* ('chop', i.e. 'seal' or 'stamp') and *tay* ('tael') are still used by English speakers and the English-language press in Hong Kong, and *catty* and *chop* are also used in Malaysia and Singapore (see chapter 5). A third point relates to the classification of these items

Table 3.1 *Early Asian English (Mundy 1637)*

Word in Mundy	English gloss[a]	Earliest citation in *Hobson-Jobson*	Earliest citation in *OED*	Source language(s)
Albricias	a reward	–	–	Sp.
Adarga	a leather jerkin	–	–	Port.
Aguos	a seed, or 'grain'	–	–	Port.
Bamboo	bamboo	(1563) mambu	(1563) mambu	Sund., Jav., or Can.
Barsa	a six-foot cask	–	–	Port.
Beeombo	a Japanese screen	–	–	Jap., Port.
Cajanes	palm leaves	(1673) cajans	–	Ma., Jav.
Cantan	Canton	(1516) Cantão	(1860) Canton	Port., Ar.
Cape Merchantt	a cape-merchant, chief merchant	–	(1613) Cape-Merchant	It., Eng.
Caphila	a caravan	(1552) Cafilas	(1594) caffylen (pl.)	Port.
Capher	a black person	(1300) K'fir	(1700) Kafrs	Ar.
Cargazone	a cargo	–	(1657) cargo	Port.
Casa Blanca	a district of Macao	–	–	Port.
Casca grossa	a 'pommelo', a tropical fruit	(1661) Pumpelmoos	(1858) pomelo	Port.
Casse	a cash, coin of low value	(1510) cas	(1598) caixa	San., Port.
Cattee	a unit of weight	(1554) Cate	(1555) cathyls	Ma., Jav.
Cauchinchina	a region of southern Vietnam	(1516) Concam china	(1853) Cochin-China	Ann., Port.
Cavallero	a cavalier	–	(1470) Caualero	Sp., Port.
Chaa	tea	(1616) chaw	(1919) char	Cant.
Chacculatte	chocolate	–	(1604) Chocolate	Mex.
Chacwan	Shakwan, an island in the Canton River	–	–	Cant.
Chadjan	*Cham-jan*, assistant military governor	–	–	Cant.
Chamblett	'camlet', a cloth made of wool and silk	–	(1400) chamlyt	Fr.
Champin	*Tsungping*, a high-ranking Chinese maritime official	–	–	Cant.
Champa	a region of Indo-China	(640) Mah 'champ'	–	San.

Word in Mundy	English gloss	Earliest citation in *Hobson-Jobson*	Earliest citation in *OED*	Source language(s)
Chappines	woman's cork-soled shoes	–	(1577) Choppines	Sp., Port.
China Porcelane	Chinaware	(1350) China-ware	(1634) Cheney ware	Eng.
China roote	the root of a plant (*Smilax China*)	(1563) Root [. . .] of china	(1587) China root	Eng.
Chincheo	a port in Fujian province, a Fujian person	(1517) Chincheo	–	Fuk.
Chinois	a Chinese person	–	(1577) Chinishe (1613) Chinois	Fr.
Choa	a sea-going junk	–	–	Cant.
Choppe	a 'chop' or permit	(1534) chapa	(1614) Chop	H.
Chopstickes	chopsticks	(1711) Chopsticks	(1699) Chopsticks	Eng.
Coiveall	capital, in the financial sense	–	(1709) Capital Stock	Fr., Lat.
Cundoreene	candareen	(1554) cumduryns	(1554) cumduryns	Ma.
Dachein	'dotchin' or 'steelyard'	(1554) Dachem	(1696) Dotchin	Cant.
Enseada de Andres Feo	Tong-ku harbour	–	–	Port.
Enseada de Don Juan	Taipa anchorage	–	–	Port.
Falankee	a European	(930) Afranjah	(1634) Frangee	Ar., Per.
Firmean	letters patent, permit	(1561) Firmao	(1616) Firma	Per.
Fumaone	a village in the Canton estuary	–	–	Ch., Port.
Grogram	a fabric of silk, mohair and wool	–	(1562) grograyn	Fr.
Hurracane	a hurricane	–	(1555) furacanes	Sp., Port.
Hitow	a Chinese maritime official	–	–	Cant.
Isla Verde	Green Island, off Macao	–	–	Port.
Island of Castro	an island off Macao	–	–	Port.
Jounck	a type of ship, a 'junk'	(1300) Junks	(1555) *Giunche*	Jav., It., Port.
Jurabasse	an interpreter	(1603) Jurabassa	–	M-J

(*cont.*)

Table 3.1 (*cont.*)

Word in Mundy	English gloss	Earliest citation in *Hobson-Jobson*	Earliest citation in *OED*	Source language(s)
Keby	a broker, from the Port. *queve*	–	–	Port.
Killicks	a heavy stone used for an anchor	–	–	–
Kimaone	a *kimono*, a form of Japanese dress	–	(1886) kimono	Jap., Port.
Lanteea	a cargo-boat	(1540) Lanteeas	(1697) Lanch	Sp., Port.
Leicheea	lichee	(1588) Lechias		Cant.
Lunghee	a petticoat or loincloth, 'lungi'	–	(1634) lung	Per.
Macao	Macao	(1567) Machao	(1778) Macao	Cant., Port.
Maceta	a flower pot	–	–	Sp.
Manchooa	a *manchua*, a cargo-boat	(1512) manchuas		Ma., Port.
Mandareene	a Chinese official, a 'mandarin'	(400) mantrins	(1589) Mandeline	H., San., Port.
Massa	mace	(1539) mazes	(1588) Mases	Jav., Ma.
Mestizo	mixed-race male	(1546) mestiços	(1588) Mestizo	Sp.
Mestizninhes	mixed-race females	(1799) Mesticia	(1582) Mestisa	Sp.
Monton de Trigo	Mount Trego, Montanha Island	–	–	Port.
Moores	people of Arab descent	(1752) Moorish	(1390) More	Gr., Port.
Muscodd	a bag of musk	(390) muscus	(1398) muske	Lat.
Muster	a sample	(1444) amostras	(1578) moster	Port.
Pagode	a pagoda	(1516) pagodes	(1634) Pagotha	Per., San., Port.
Paquin	Peking (Beijing)	(1520) Pequij	(1783) Pekin	Ch.
Peeco	a measure of weight, *picul*	(1554) pico	(1588) pyco	M-J
Portugall	a Portuguese person	–	(1662) Portuges	Port., Eng.
Puchuc	a fragrant root used for joss sticks	(1516) puchô	(1588) Puchio	Ma.
Quan Moan	*Kwan mun*, customs officer	–	–	Cant.
Quitasoll	an umbrella or 'parasol'	(1588) quitasoles	(1588) quitasoles	Port.
Quittaoo	an island in the Canton estuary	–	–	Ch., Port.

Word in Mundy	English gloss	Earliest citation in *Hobson-Jobson*	Earliest citation in *OED*	Source language(s)
Rack	a strong alcoholic drink, from dates or grain	(1420) arak	(1516) huraca	Ar.
Rattan	rattan (cane)	(1511) rótas	(1681) rattans	Ma.
Rialls	a silver coin	–	(1611) Real, Reall	Sp.
Sarsenette	a type of soft silk	–	(1463) sarsenet	A-F
Sattin	satin	(1350) Zaitūn	(1366) satyne	Lat.
Sea grashoppers	a type of fish	–	–	Eng.
Sherazzee	a shawl	–	–	Per., Port.
Somars	a small ship	–	–	Port.
Taccassy	a rank of Chinese judge	–	–	Cant.
Taffatie	light silk, or a mixture of silk and wool, 'taffeta'	(1726) Taffat	(1386) Taffata	Per.
Tuffaon	a typhoon	(1540) Tufan	(1588) touffon	Ar.
Tay	a unit of weight, a tael	(1540) taels	(1598) Tael	Ma., Port.
Tayffoo (island)	'Tiger Island' in the Canton River	–	–	Cant.
Tonpuan	*T'ung-p'an*, a high-ranking Chinese official	–		Cant.
Tunkee	a region of North Vietnam, 'Tongking'	–	(1697) Tonquinese	Ch.

Key to source languages:
A-F = Anglo-French, Ann. = Annamite, Ar. = Arabic, Can. = Canarese, Cant. = Cantonese, Ch. = Chinese, Eng. = English, Fr. = French, Fuk. = Fukien, H. = Hindustani, It. = Italian, Jap. = Japanese, Jav. = Javanese, Lat. = Latin, Ma. = Malay, Mex. = Mexican, M-J = Malay-Javanese, Per. = Persian, Port. = Portuguese, San. = Sanskrit, Sp. = Spanish, Sund. = Sundanese

[a] The glosses in this table, particularly those of place names, are drawn mainly from Temple (1919).

in terms of semantic field, or area of human activity. Given the nature of early maritime and mercantile contact between British traders and Asian communities, most of the 89 words can be assigned to lists in the following categories: (i) *trade and commerce*, (ii) *place names*, (iii) *weights, measures and coinage*, (iv) *ranks and titles*, (v) *peoples and races*, (vi) *ships and shipping*, (vii) *food and drink* and (viii) *flora*. The most numerous items are those referring to trade and commerce, place names, weights, measures and coinage, and ranks and titles.

Fourth, for many of these items there is a great variation in spelling. For example, *Chinois* is also rendered as 'Chinaman', 'Chinesas' (masculine and feminine forms respectively), 'Chineses', 'Chinessees' and 'Chinesses'; *Jounckes* ('junks') is also spelt 'Joncks', 'Junckes' and 'Juncks'. Given the great diversity of spelling in Early Middle English this is perhaps to be expected, but it serves at least to emphasise the observation that, at a time when the English language in Britain was only partly standardised in terms of its orthography, there was an early new English that was emerging in Asia. This was being created through the direct experience, observation and record-keeping of early travellers, and this 'old, new English' of seventeenth-century Asia has bequeathed a lexical legacy which survives in today's Asian Englishes. The Malay (or Malay–Javanese) element in this early Asian English would have been significant, as Malay was used as a *lingua franca* in Southeast Asia for some time before the Europeans arrived, and the first East India Company publication of 1603 (A *True and Large Discourse of the Voyage . . . to the East Indies*) contains a list of some fifty common phrases in 'Malies speech, such is used in the Indies'. This short glossary was later supplemented by a 1614 pamphlet entitled *Dialogues in the English and Malaiane Languages* (see Farrington 2002).

Many of these words, of course, did not survive, and disappeared very rapidly from usage; for example, the ranks and titles of Chinese officials change throughout the Qing (Ch'ing) dynasty, Republican China (1911–49) and the post-1949 era of the People's Republic of China. New words and expressions take their place at every stage, a number of which have found their way into 'Chinese English', 'Hong Kong English' and even other varieties of English. The same applies to place names.

Mundy on the Chinese and Japanese languages, and Chinese English

In addition to his commentary on China, Macao and the Macanese, Mundy also discusses some of the characteristics of both the Chinese and Japanese languages. He bases his description of Chinese language on the accounts that he was able to gain from a 'Merchant' who had been taken hostage during the fighting in the Pearl River estuary. He describes the Chinese writing system, noting how '[t]he China writing beeginning From the rightt hand toward the lefft, and their lynes from the topped', and the use of brushes and ink: '[t]hey all write with pencills and blacke and Red Incke made into Dry past which they Distemper with water when they will use itt'. He also comments on the difficulty of Chinese, noting that 'there are said to bee many thousands of these Characters and soe various, yett a Man May much sooner and easier expresse his Minde with our 24 letters' (Temple 1919: 315). The Chinese characters copied down by Mundy are not reproduced in Temple, although they are found in the original manuscript lodged in the Bodleian Library (see figure 3.1).

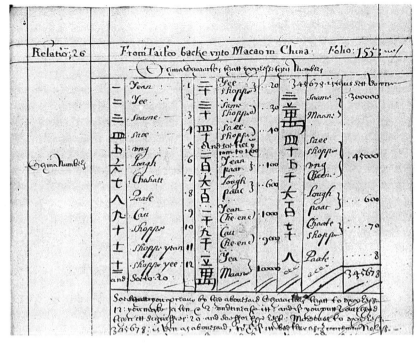

Figure 3.1 Mundy's Chinese

Earlier in the manuscript, Mundy gives an account of 'the salutation of a Chinois', which he identifies as 'Touzzee', which corresponds to dō jeh 多謝, or 'thank you' in contemporary Cantonese. He then goes on to provide a small number of common words and phrases in the Japanese language (or 'Japonian language'), together with a list of Japanese numerals.

He also comments on the Chinese pronunciation of English words, noting that Chinese speakers pronounce 'very well' as 'vely wen' and Peter Mundy as 'Pe-tang Mun-ty'. In what is probably the first diagnosis of the pronunciation difficulties faced by Chinese speakers of English, Mundy comments that 'it seemes thatt P, L and D are hard to bee Found att the end off their words, especially R, sildome used and hard to bee pronounced by them, allthough it is sometymes by some thatt live among the Portugall att Macao' (Temple 1919: 313).

Mundy in Macao – postscript

The initial contact between British mercantile traders and both the Macao Portuguese and the Chinese foreshadowed the pattern of contact that was to develop over the next 200 years. Weddell's attempts to open trade in Canton were clumsy and aggressive and alerted the Canton authorities to the attentions of a new breed of aggressive 'redhaired barbarian' knocking at the gates of the Middle Kingdom. By the time they left, the British had disgraced themselves with their Portuguese hosts, and when Peter Mundy called on Captain-General Noronha, on Boxing Day to bid farewell, he was virtually thrown out of Government House. Captain-General Noronha was particularly enraged that the British fleet, against the Portuguese wishes, had offered passage to a number of rich Portuguese wanting to leave Macao. That night, some of the captain-general's men went to Weddell's house in Macao 'all armed with swords, bucklers, gunnes and lighted Matches to thrust us outt of the towne att thatt Instant' (Temple 1919: 318). Weddell and his men thus 'finally departed in all humility, having been eased out jointly by the Chinese and Portuguese; but Weddell's voyage had established the thenceforth unchanging Chinese view that, of all barbarian intruders, the English were the most violent and dangerous' (Coates 1978: 58).

The development of British trade at Canton, 1644–1839

It took the East India Company a further 100 years to establish regular trade at Canton. The first East India Company ship to reach Macao, the *Hinde*, had done so in 1644, but found the Portuguese enclave 'destitute of all sorts of commodities; there not being to be bought in the City, either Silks raw or wrought, or Chinaroot... nor indeed anything but chinaware...' (cited in Morse 1926: 32).

China trade at this time was, unsurprisingly, greatly affected by the Chinese view of westerners. From the sixteenth to the early nineteenth century, the western merchants who reached China in their trading ships were classified as 'barbarians', and were regarded by the officials of the Chinese empire as no better than the barbarous tribes of Central Asia, or the *Miao-tzu* and *Lo-lo* peoples of China's southwest. The various 'countries of the Western ocean' were frequently confused in imperial documents. One general term for foreigners, first applied to the Portuguese, was *fo-lang-chi* (佛郎機), a term borrowed during the Crusades from Arab traders, who called the Europeans in the Near East 'franks' (Fairbank 1953: 10). In Mundy's diary, this appears as 'Falankee' (see above), as *firinghee* in *Hobson-Jobson*, and still survives in the word *farang* in Thai English, with cognates in a host of Mediterranean, Middle-Eastern and Asian languages (including Arabic, Greek, Hebrew, Tamil, etc.).

In Chinese eyes, the Dutch and the British were interchangeable, and the term 'redhaired barbarians (or foreigners)' or 'hung-mao-fan' (*hùhng mòuh fāan*, in Yale transcription) was used to refer to both. According to an imperial 'compendium' published in the 1750s, perhaps the most notable characteristic of Europeans is their appearance, as 'their flesh is dazzling white, and their noses are lofty'. The outstanding feature of the compendium, according to Fairbank (1953: 10), was the 'utter and indiscriminate confusion' of the peoples of such countries as

England, France, Sweden, Japan, Holland, Russia, Cambodia, the Philippines, Java, Malacca and Sumatra.

From 1709 the East India Company was consolidated as 'the United Company of Merchants of English Trading to the East Indies', and the tea trade flourished. In 1717 the two ships that were sent from London were instructed to load 'tea as much as the ship can conveniently stow' (Morse 1926: 158). In 1725, imports totalled an estimated 250,000 pounds; by 1805 this figure had risen to some 24 million pounds per year. From around 1757, the Chinese government decreed that it was forbidden to trade with foreigners in all ports in China except Canton, which then consolidated its position as the key location for sino-western commerce. From the early eighteenth century, the East India Company supercargoes had begun to act together as a 'council' in their dealings with Chinese officials. At the same time, a number of the most important Chinese merchants of Canton set up their own collective body, the 'Co-hong', which soon constituted a local trading monopoly who alone would retain the major rights of dealing with the redhaired barbarians. In 1720, the Co-hong published a thirteen-article charter that established guidelines for the conduct of the Canton trade from then until the first Opium War with Britain in 1839. The charter required all foreigners at Canton to deal through the 'merchant guild' or Co-hong. Goods such as teas and silks could only be purchased through Co-hong members, although other items such as fans and tea sets could be purchased from local merchants. The Co-hong's aim was 'control of the pattern of trade and the costs charged for engaging in trade in South China. The merchant guild's members served as intermediaries who helped the government keep watch over and control the Western barbarians' (Rubinstein 1996: 24).

The 'Canton system' evolved over the next fifty years or so and, if nothing else, its growth indicated that the Chinese authorities now recognised the need for a system that would accommodate both 'the Chinese government's wish to keep the West at arm's length and the desire of several influential merchants to carry on a large-scale trade with Westerners' (Rubinstein 1996: 25). The system as it developed had the following characteristics: western merchantmen were permitted to trade in only one port, Canton, and only through the members of the Co-hong. The British and other westerners were confined to Canton, and even there they were restricted as to where and how they could live. The Co-hong merchants rented out the factories (large warehouses with offices and accommodation attached) to the westerners, who were permitted to live in Canton for the duration of the trading season each year, from August to March. At the end of the season, the westerners would either return to Europe or the United States or move to Macao at the mouth of the Pearl River.

By the beginning of the nineteenth century, three English-speaking groups were involved in the Canton trade. First, there were the traders of the East India Company, now the largest, richest and most powerful trading corporation in the world, in many ways the first modern 'transnational' corporation. Second, there were the so-called 'country traders', who plied the local sea routes between India, the East Indies and China. At the end of the eighteenth century these country traders were receiving increased backing from East India 'houses of agency', which had their main offices in London and Edinburgh, such as Fairlie Bonham, Rikards MacIntosh and Fletcher Alexander (Rubinstein 1996: 33). Financed by such companies, the Canton country traders, who by the 1820s and 1830s included Magniac & Company, Thomas Dent & Company and Jardine & Matheson's, grew in wealth and power. The country traders were heavily involved in trading two products from India which had elicited strong demand from China, Indian cotton and Indian opium. The third group were the Americans, who began trading at Canton in 1784 and who soon became Britain's main trading rival in southern China, not least in the highly profitable opium trade (Rubinstein 1996: 35–6).

It was this period between 1720 and 1839 that saw the origins of what later came to be called 'pidgin English' or 'Chinese pidgin English'. (The term 'pidgin English' was not however used until the mid-nineteenth century, and in this period, reference was usually made to the 'broken English', 'jargon', or 'mixed dialect' used at Canton.)

Early accounts of the Canton jargon, 1747–1800

As we saw above, the Co-hong supervised the trade of the British and other European merchants (or 'factors') in Canton, and this system was to last until the First Opium War or First Anglo-Chinese War of 1839–42. One way in which they did this was to provide their own interpreters or 'linguists' for the European traders, who translated chiefly through the 'jargons' of 'broken Portuguese' and 'broken English'. One of the earliest references to broken English in South China is in the memoirs of Commodore George Anson, a British naval captain who visited Canton in 1742 and 1743 and published his memoirs in 1748 (Walter and Robins [1748] 1974). In his account of the numerous difficulties in conducting trade in South China, Anson complains of the shortage of adequate interpreters, noting that: 'we imprudently choose... to carry on the vast transactions of the port of *Canton*, either by the ridiculous jargon of broken *English*, which some few of the *Chinese* have learnt, or by the suspected interpretation of the Linguists of other Nations' (Walter and Robins 1748: 361).

Anson goes on to provide one of the earliest attestations for Chinese pidgin English and, recounting the story of yet another British–Chinese altercation over money, quotes a Chinese linguist's explanation of his own dishonesty, saying that: 'he had no other excuse to make than the strong bias of his Nation to dishonesty, replying, in his broken jargon, *Chinese man very great rogue truly, but have fashion, no can help*' (Walter and Robins 1748: 335).

Noble's *A Voyage to the East Indies in 1747 and 1748* comments on both the sexual and linguistic contacts between British sailors and the Canton Chinese.

He describes the adventures of two ship's officers in the company of a local pimp, who importunes: '*Carei grandi hola, pickenini hola?*' ('Would you like an older whore, or a younger one?') (Noble 1762: 240). Later, Noble further describes this broken dialect as a 'a mixture of European languages . . . mostly, as we formerly hinted, of English and Portuguese, together with some words of their own' (1762: 262–3). In 1793, after approximately a century of trade on the South China coast, the first official diplomatic mission, the 'Macartney Embassy', was sent from Britain to China. The embassy's aim was to open 'modern diplomatic relations' between the newly industrialised Britain and the 'Middle Kingdom' of China, with the related objectives of securing the right to extend trade (out of the confines of Macao and Canton) into many other locations, and permission to establish a diplomatic mission in Peking. The embassy was an almost total disaster. Lord Macartney was granted only a very brief audience with the Emperor at the Summer Palace, and summarily dismissed. Not one of the requests presented at the Imperial Court was granted and the embassy returned to Britain with an understandable sense of failure: 'The Embassy had been very well treated, but it cannot be said to have done any good: the only impression it made on the Chinese, it was said, that England was a tributary state' (Couling 1917: 320).

Perhaps the most amusing of the many accounts of the embassy was that provided by Macartney's manservant, Anderson, who sold his story to a London publisher, who helped ghost-write the memoir. In an appendix to the book, Anderson provides a glossary of Chinese, transcribed into a form of 'romanisation' or alphabetic writing, and English. Many of the seventy-odd items he cites are still decipherable as Cantonese or Mandarin words, but he also presents the following as examples of 'Chinese':

Chinchin	To supplicate *or* pray
Chop-chop	To make haste
Chow-chow	Victuals *or* meat
Ickoochop	Very best
Josh	God *or* Deity
Lobb, Lobb	Joining *or* coition

What is significant here is that most of these items are later listed by pidgin and creole scholars as examples of 'Chinese pidgin English', including *josh* (or 'joss'), derived from Portuguese *deos*, or *chinchin*, *chop-chop* and *chow-chow*, arguably from Chinese, as well as the word *ickoochop* of hybrid Sino-Indian origin (equivalent to the later anglicised equivalent 'first chop'). By this time *hab*, from English 'have' was a pidgin item, and *lobb*, by analogy, is likely to be derived from 'love', selected, one presumes, in preference to more vulgar alternatives. The Pearl River between Macao and Canton was home to a Lob Lob creek, where Tanka 'flower boat' girls and their waterborne pimps plied their trade with lonely mariners (Hickey 1769).

Missionary linguistics and Canton jargon

The British and American Protestant missionaries who came to southern China at the beginning of the nineteenth century sought to replace the profane *lobb* of the lonely sailor by the sacred mission of evangelising China. Once in China, however, their spiritual ambitions were later blurred by those of secular achievement, in the service of trade, government service and academic works, particularly those related to the study of Chinese language and linguistics. Such orientalist missionary scholars provided the basis of nineteenth-century missionary sinology.

Between 1807 and the early 1830s, British and American Protestant missionaries reached Canton and Macao. These included Robert Morrison, sent to China by the London Missionary Society and who first arrived in Canton in 1807, and the Americans Elijah Coleman Bridgman and Samuel Wells Williams, both of whom worked on the influential *Chinese Repository*, the first English-language journal on Chinese studies published in China.[4] In addition to the *Repository*, Morrison, Bridgman and Wells Williams produced an impressive body of linguistic and sinological work. Morrison's publications included *A Grammar of the Chinese Language* (1815), *A Dictionary of the Chinese Language* (1815–23), a translation of the Bible into Chinese (1823) and the *Vocabulary of the Canton Dialect* (1828) (Bolton 2001a). Bridgman published a number of works in Chinese, including a history of the United States of America, religious texts and a learner's guide to Cantonese entitled the *Chinese Chrestomathy in the Canton Dialect* (1841). Wells Williams also published a number of dictionaries and guides to Chinese, including *A Syllabic Dictionary of the Chinese Language* (1874), but he is best remembered for his monumental two-volume work *The Middle Kingdom* ([1848] 1895), through which he became the best-known American sinologist of the nineteenth century (Hutton 2001).

In 1836 and 1837, Wells Williams published two articles on Chinese pidgin English in the *Chinese Repository*. For Wells Williams and other missionaries, the use of the Canton jargon was directly caused by the restrictions imposed by the imperial government on the 'intercommunication' of 'natives' and 'foreigners'. He notes that:

> Hundreds of Chinese now acquire enough of the jargon spoken to do business, while hardly a foreigner ever devotes an hour to learn the language of the Chinese. The effect of an intercourse so circumscribed can never be

---

[4] The *Chinese Repository* was established in Macao by the American Protestant missionary Elijah Coleman Bridgman, assisted by the young Samuel Wells Williams. The *Chinese Repository* began publication in May 1832, and continued printing until December 1851. Throughout these years, the *Repository* attracted a large number of contributors including missionaries and colonial officials such as Caleb Cushing, John Bowring, John Francis Davis, Peter Parker and Thomas Francis Wade. The vast majority of the articles in the early years, however, were authored by Bridgman, Wells Williams, Robert Morrison, John Robert Morrison and Karl Gützlaff. The second largest group of contributors to the journal were merchants and traders like Robert Inglis, Robert Thom and Charles W. King. The *Repository* published a wide range of articles on many aspects of life in China, including geography, government, history, language, literature, trade and commerce (Malcolm 1973).

otherwise than to keep the two parties totally separated from each other in all those offices of kindness, sympathy, regard, and friendship, which result from a knowledge of each other's feelings and wants. (1836: 429)

Wells Williams suggests that the absence of westerners proficient in Chinese is a major cause of 'much of the indifference and suspicion of the Chinese exhibited towards foreigners' and, in this context, notes some of the difficulties attached to learning the Chinese language, including the lack of elementary books, grammars and vocabularies; the task of memorising the characters; and the law 'denouncing as traitors all those natives who dare to teach the language of the "central flowery nation" to outside barbarians' (1836: 430). In addition, there is the easy accessibility of the mixed 'dialect':

[T]he foreigner on landing hears a dialect spoken, which with an entire disregard of all rules of orthography and syntax, he can soon 'pick up', which is sufficiently extensive for commercial intercourse with the Chinese. With this jargon he soon becomes well acquainted, and in a short time looks upon the acquisition of the language as a useless as well almost impracticable undertaking. Indeed, of so long standing is the gibberish spoken here, that few ever think of paying any attention to the Chinese. (Williams 1836: 430)

Wells Williams further reports on the situation at Macao, where the dialect is 'a medley of Portuguese and Chinese', but notes that at Canton, Whampoa and Lintin, 'English is the only medium of conversation between foreigners and Chinese' (1836: 431). The inducement for the Chinese to learn the dialect is the interest in trade, a 'master passion in the heart of a Chinese'; although it would be a mistake to believe that they can understand foreigners speaking to each other in 'good' English, 'for that is nearly as unintelligible to them, as Chinese is to the foreigner' (1836: 431). Faced with a shortage of teachers, most Chinese learners 'pick up' the language where they can.

Wells Williams provides a short linguistic analysis of the features of the dialect, commenting, however inexactly, that the Canton dialect 'is destitute of the consonants *b*, *v*, *d*, *r* and *st*', for which 'in writing the sounds of the English words, the native uses *p*, *t*, *l* and *sz*; and in pronouncing, comes as near the sound he hears as possible' (Williams 1836: 432) He also notes the use of manuscript books which use Chinese characters to record the English pronunciation of words, describing their use as 'very common':

Not only the names of articles but idioms, phrases, and rules of etymology, are sometimes found in them, thus making a partial grammar. A few examples from the book now before us will show how correctly English words can be written in Chinese. In pronunciation, the true sound of course is more nearly attained. Those which follow are the numbers are far as twenty; the sounds of the Canton dialect being the rule of pronunciation: 'wun, too, te-le, faw, fi, sik-she, sum-wun, oot, ni, teng, lum-wun, te-lup, ta-teng, faw-teng, fi-teng, sik-she-teng, sum-wun-teng, oot-teng, ni-teng, tune-te'. (1836: 432)

Other examples of English words transcribed through characters include *chay-she-mun* 'chess men'; *sze-kay-le-sze* 'scales'; *sze-taw* 'stove'; *che-na-wi-le* 'January'; *aw-kuh-she* 'August'; *wi-sze-wun* 'west wind'; *e-too* 'earth'; and *pe-fu-law* 'buffalo'. Wells Williams also notes the use of the suffix '-ee' in words like 'catchee'. He states that the key vocabulary of Canton English is 'not great' (including approximately fifty items), but adds that 'the prevalence of the Chinese idiom, and the confusion consequent upon it to an English ear, together with the bad pronunciation of the words, render this jargon one of the most singular modes of communication that can anywhere be found' (1836: 433).

The second article similarly discusses two 'manuscript vocabularies' (transcribed in Chinese characters) circulating in Canton at the time, one for Portuguese, the other for English. Wells Williams was particularly incensed at the second of these, entitled *Hungmaou mae mae tung yung kwei hwa*, which he translates as 'those words of the devilish language of red-bristled people commonly used in buying and selling':

> Against the title of the second vocabulary we have a strong objection. It is another instance of the studied contempt this people endeavor to throw upon everything foreign; and cannot be too strongly reprobated. In several places, things and occupations are stigmatized by the epithet of *devilish*, and that without the least necessity. Nothing of this kind is to be discovered in the Portuguese and Chinese collection, where the term *foreign* is used. This continual endeavor to degrade the English in the eyes of their countrymen appears to run through all classes of the Chinese; and we were rather surprised that any one should have condescended to prepare a vocabulary of a 'devilish language'. (1837: 278)

He notes that the vocabulary comprises sixteen pages, with under 400 words listed according to four headings, 'numbers', 'men and things', 'words used in conversation' and 'eatables', and he provides a short list of examples, illustrating through orthographic eye-dialect the approximate values of the Chinese characters used to indicate pronunciation. Thus 'tael' is pronounced *te*, 'jacket' *tik-ka*, 'alike' *a-loo-sum* ('all the same'), 'to sell' *say-lum* ('sell 'em'), 'commonly' *so-so*, 'to exchange' *cheen-che* ('change'), 'to want' *kah-le* (from the Portuguese *querer*), 'tailor' *tay-le-mun* ('tailor man'), 'cook' *kok-mun*, 'an account' *kan-ta* (Portuguese *conta*), 'a husband' *hah-sze-mun*, 'a wife' *wi-foo*, 'a beggar' *kum-sha-mun* or *kum-shaw-man* ('cumshaw man'), 'unclean' *tah-te* (or 'dirty'), 'to call' *kah-lum* (or 'call 'em'), 'the earth' *kaw-lang* (or 'ground'), 'distant' *lang-wi* (or 'long way'), 'please' *chin-chin*, 'to set', *sheet-tum* (or 'sit down'), 'great' *kah-lan-te* (from the Portuguese *grande*), 'leisure' *hap-teem* (or 'have time'), 'whither' *kwut-yu-ko* (or 'what you go?'), 'to enter' *ko-yeen-si* (or 'go inside'), 'occupied' *hap-pe-chun* (or 'have pidgeon' or 'have business'), 'presently come' *tik-lik-ke-kum* (or 'directly come'), 'not understand' *no-sha-pe* (Portuguese *não saber*, or 'not know'), 'orange' *loo-lan-che* (Portuguese *laranja*) and 'gentlemen's sons' *meet-che-mun*, or 'midshipman' (1837: 278–9).

Wells Williams reserves particular scorn for the local linguists or interpreters:

> None of these 'linguists' can read the simplest document in English; nor
> can more than two or three of them understand two Englishmen in their
> common conversation. Persons in England might suppose that a Chinese
> would be glad to receive instruction, and qualify himself for his profession;
> but we know that not one of these linguists ever comes to a foreigner for
> aid, or ever thinks of taking any lessons in the English language. They pick
> up their words in conversation and from vocabularies and native teachers.
> (1837: 279)[5]

The 'present barbarous jargon', he argues, would best be improved by producing
a chrestomathy (i.e. a learner's manual) and a dictionary, which would do much
to promote 'a better mutual good will'. At the same time, he urges the westerner
to learn Chinese, as: 'The man . . . who learns the language, even to this limited
extent, will truly save himself from many impositions; and, not unfrequently, will
command respect, and secure influence, far beyond what he could do without
such knowledge. In this case, as in all others, he would find that knowledge is
power' (1837: 279).

The missionary response to Canton 'jargon' was to see it as a barrier set up by
the Mandarin officials against the evangelisation and enlightenment of China. In
1833, in the introduction to the second volume of the Chinese Repository, Elijah
Bridgman argued that language was important on two counts. First, there was
the desirability of spreading a knowledge of the English language because, as in
India, 'by acquiring a knowledge of the English tongue, the native youth will be
introduced into a new world. He will live and move in a new atmosphere. He will
be acted upon by new influences. He will see and feel a thousand new relations'
(Bridgman 1833: 2). Second, there was the need for western missionaries to learn
Chinese, as

> Such knowledge will give the foreigner power and influence with the
> Chinese, and over them too – a power which will be both harmless and
> beneficial to all. It is of little use to come in contact with the Chinese unless
> we can communicate freely with them – interrogate them, and be interro-
> gated; hear them argue for, and defend their high superiority; and in turn,
> let them hear the opposite statements . . . It is impossible that forms, and

---

[5] Wells Williams' scathing assessment of the linguists at Canton is challenged by recent historians,
in particular, by the work of Van Dyke (2001), whose considered assessment, based on detailed
and careful research, is that 'if the great expansion in the volume of the trade from 1700 to 1842
is any indication of their success, then we would have to say that the linguists, on the whole, did a
remarkable job keeping the system operating as smoothly as possible'. The linguists 'were on the
front lines the entire time struggling with the languages and the idioms; balancing the cultural and
political differences between the foreigners and the Chinese and between the foreigners themselves;
moderating the tensions at every level of the operation; balancing the financial and time constraints
of all the officials and traders; and guiding the trade along as best they could' (Van Dyke 2001:
371–2).

usages, and claims founded in error and falsehood, can stand against the *force of truth*. (1833: 4–5, original emphasis)

Morrison's 1834 glossary of Canton jargon

In addition to Wells Williams' accounts of Canton jargon, there is a glossary provided by John Robert Morrison (the son of Robert Morrison) in a manual of China trade, published in Canton, sold at the 'No. 4 Danish Hong' and entitled *A Chinese Commercial Guide consisting of A Collection of Details Respecting Foreign Trade in China* (Morrison 1834). This short glossary is set out below:

Glossary of words and phrases peculiar to the jargon spoken at Canton (Morrison 1834)

Can do?	Will it do? Also used, through mistake, for 'how d'ye do?'
Catchee	To get, to bring, to find, &c.; also to become, as 'this thing hab *catchee* cold', for 'this has become cold'.
Chinchin	from Chinese *tsing*, to request, and *tsing ah*, a salutation. To ask, to thank, to salute, & c. Chinchin joss, to worship the gods.
Chop	from Malay *chapa*, a seal or stamp, any thing sealed or stamped; hence government edicts, licenses, &c., also stamped or printed documents. Again, a *thing* licensed, as a *chop-boat*; also a *place* able to give licenses, as a *chop-house*, i.e. a custom-house.
Chop	is also used as synonymous with 'quality', as *first chop* or *No.1 chop*, for 'best quality'.
Chop-boat	is a kind of cargo boat, also used, when fitted up, as a travelling boat for foreigners.
Chop-chop	quick, fast, as *too muchy chop-chop*, for 'very quick'.
Chop-sticks	the well known sticks of wood or ivory used by the Chinese in eating.
Chow-chow	mixed, miscellaneous; the mixed meats of the Chinese; hence, food of any kind; to eat food.
Chunam	to paste, to glue together; to whitewash.
Conshuns	price, for conscientious, a reasonable price.
Consoo	from *kung so*, a public place of meeting; applied by foreigners only to the hong merchants' hall of assembly.
Counta	an account current, to count.
Cow-cow	to be noisy and angry, to scold; an uproar.
Cumsha	probably from Fuhkeen *kum-seäh*, 'I will thank you', – or from Canton *kum sha*, 'a sand of gold', – denotes a gift, a present. Certain charges on vessels, which were originally presents, are so called. This word, and the phrase 'can do?' are the first expressions learned by the Chinese and are in universal use in Canton.

Country	is used to denote a province, a district, or even a village.
Dollar-boat	is the name of a boat, employed as a passage boat between Canton and Whampoa, for which the lowest fare is $4.
Face	appearance in society, reputation, credit; to *lose face* denotes to fall into discredit.
Fan-kwei	foreign devil, a contemptuous designation applied to foreigners.
Fashion	manner, mode of doing a thing, habit or practice.
Fast-boat	a kind of boat nearly corresponding, in its objects and use, to our post chaises
Hong	a factory, a place of commercial business, a commercial establishment. *Hong merchants* are by the Chinese called 'foreign hongs', there being also silk hongs, tea hongs, &c.
Joss	from Port. *deos*, a god; joss-house, an idol temple; *joss pidgeon*, religious services; the phrase is also used to denote the work of providence, or otherwise fate, as 'he die, hab joss pidgeon', – it was his fate to die.
Junk	name applied by foreigners to the large Chinese vessels.
Lingoo	a linguist, [. . .].
Mahcheen	a merchant, named adopted by the 'outside merchants', or shop-men.
Makee	is often considered a necessary prefix to a verb, as 'you makee see this side', for 'look here'.
Mandarin	from Port. *mandar*, to send; a commissioned officer, any one in the employ of government, of whatever rank. The *mandarin dialect* is the general language of the empire, which must be understood by all official persons. Mandarin is often used as an adjective, having then a laudatory or superlative signification.
Maskee	never mind, leave it alone, it is of no consequence.
Muster	a sample, a pattern, a specimen.
Nex' day or tomorrow nex' day	the day after tomorrow.
Ol'o custom	old custom, usage; this expression is an excuse for every fault.
Pay	to give, to deliver to, as 'pay that chit for him', give him that chit, or note.
Piece	a numerical particle, as 'one piece man' for 'a man'.
Pidgeon	or pidginess, a corruption of the English word business, denotes also a matter, a thing. 'That no makee good pidgeon', – the thing is ill done.
Plum cash	prime cost.
Posa	for purser, an assistant in commercial house.

Quisi	bad, inferior, low vulgar, indecent.
Sabbee	from Port. *saber*, to know. 'My no sabbee' i.e. I do not know him.
Savee	cleverness.
Side or si'	a position, situation, place, as outsi', topsi', downsi'; which si' denotes where, whence.
Smug' pidgeon,	smuggling'
Take care for	to patronise; 'chinchin you take care for my', I beg you to patronise me, – be my customer.
Tanka boats	from *tan ka*, egg house, are small boats, the residences of the boat-people, also used as ferry-boats.
Two muchy	very much, very many, very, extremely.
Wantchee	to want.
Welly few	very few, very little. (Morrison 1834: 1–2)

This jargon is to all intents the same variety described by Wells Williams, and by 1857 the term 'Canton English' is also used to describe the type of language spoken at Guangzhou (Anon. 1857). The term 'pidgin English' does not emerge as a label of description until much later, around 1859, but twentieth-century scholars of pidgin English later based their descriptions of early forms of pidgin English on the data gleaned from accounts of travellers such as Anson (1748), Noble (1762), Hickey (1769) and Anderson (1795), and the writings of later 'sojourners' such as Wells Williams (1836, 1837). It is also worth noting that a number of the items in the 1834 list above are still heard at times in Hong Kong English speech, including *can do, chop, chop-chop, hong, joss, nex' day, piece, quisi, side* and *welly few*. To understand the emergence of Chinese pidgin English at this time, however, it is necessary not only to have access to *attestations* of use, but also to consider the *contexts* of its use.

Chinese pidgin English – the contexts of use

Canton (Guangzhou)

The main centre for the development of Chinese pidgin English between the 1720s and the 1830s was Canton (Guangzhou) which, as we have seen, was the only port in China open for foreign trade. No foreign women were allowed to stay in Canton, and the foreign traders were restricted to a particular area of the western district of the city, just outside the city walls, that fronted on to the Pearl River and came to be known as the 'thirteen factories'. By the early nineteenth century, these factories included the New English factory belonging to the East India Company, the American factory and the Danish, Dutch, French, Spanish and Swedish factories (Downs 1997). The term 'factory', derived from the Portuguese *feitoria*, had a quite specific meaning in this context, referring to the living quarters, offices and warehouse of a merchant company, and could generally be glossed as the equivalent of a 'trading station'.

At the height of the Canton trade (1800–39) the population of traders resident in the factories was quite small. In 1837, for example, it was recorded that there were only 307 foreign residents in Canton: 158 English, 62 Parsees, 44 Americans, 28 Portuguese, 4 Indians, 3 Dutch, 2 Swiss, 2 Prussians, 2 Germans, 1 Danish and 1 French (*Chinese Repository* 1837). These residents would have been served by a large number of Chinese staff, including cooks, watchmen, livestock-tenders, coolies and personal servants. Each factory also employed a number of professional staff including the house comprador, who was in charge of the purchase of all provisions and equipment for the factory.

All trade within the factories was regulated by the Chinese customs superintendent (the 'Hoppo'), and the Co-hong. The Chinese 'linguists', who spoke pidgin, were appointed by the Hoppo to serve as linguistic and administrative intermediaries between the foreign traders and the Co-hong, and between the foreign traders and the Hoppo. Many of the Co-hong merchants also communicated in pidgin with the foreign residents in Canton, and apparently became rather friendly with their foreign counterparts. At this time, Chinese pidgin English in Canton would have been used first, between English-speaking foreign traders and the Chinese merchants of the Co-hong and their staff; second, to local employees including the comprador and his subordinates; third, to personal servants within the factory; fourth, with local shopkeepers and tradesmen; and fifth, as a means of communicating with the Tanka girls aboard the 'flower boats' on the Pearl River.

For the local population, the context for the wider acquisition and use of pidgin would have been in the interaction between Chinese pilots, sailors, merchants and workmen who supplied goods and services to foreign ships. The 'provisions trade' was particularly important and Van Dyke (2000) reports that, by the 1830s, compradors were supplying goods to over 180 ships per year. Each European 'company' ship carried a crew of 100–150 men, and the 'country ships' (active in the opium trade between India and Canton) carried crews varying from a dozen to a hundred. During the season, these ships would converge on Canton, usually from November onwards, crowding the Whampoa anchorage and the river. Although the sailors would have been restricted to Whampoa for much of their stay, it was common practice to allow the ships' crews shore leave in the days before sailing, so large numbers of sailors regularly visited 'Hog Lane', a street located in the factories district, to test the grog and buy quantities of 'curios' such as fans, figurines, scarfs, shawls, silks and small paintings.

Macao

The situation at Macao was somewhat different. After foreign trade was restricted to Canton, Macao developed as a base for the East India Company and the other European companies, where they could build their summer houses and, later, where their families could reside. After 1784, the British and other Europeans were joined by the Americans, as well as other country traders active in the opium trade. The Anglo-American community grew rapidly from the end of the eighteenth century through the early decades of the nineteenth century, but the European population remained quite small. Da Silva (1998) reports that in 1830 there were 4,628 foreigners, including 2,149 white females, 1,202 white males, 779 female slaves, 350 male slaves and 148 people belonging to other ethnic groups. Nevertheless, the presence of British and American women provided a social life impossible at Canton. Downs describes the scene at Macao in these years thus:

> In the years before the treaties, Anglo-American social life in China attained its fullest development at Macao, where traders of both nationalities periodically retired. The genteel, decaying Portuguese colony became the Ascot, the Monte Carlo, the Riviera, and even the home of tired traders after a busy tea season at the factories. At Macao dwelt the wives and families, as did the mistresses and the occasional ladies who brightened the hours of relaxation between the strenuous sessions at Canton. (Downs 1997: 49)

Macao would not have had the huge periodical influx of ships that occurred in Canton. In fact, by the early 1800s, most of the company ships would have by-passed Macao, pausing there only to pick up pilots on their way upriver. But Macao attracted large numbers of Americans and other 'country traders' engaged in the opium trade, and this would have had a significant effect on patterns of language use within the enclave.

Linguistically, the situation at Macao was quite complex. By the end of the eighteenth century, the settlement's population had become increasingly 'hybrid', and 'a native population of Macanese – a mixture of European Portuguese, Portuguese Asians, and Chinese – had emerged' (Porter 1996: 77). In addition to the figures cited for foreigners listed above, da Silva also estimates the Chinese population at around 45,000 citizens (1998: 49). Within the community, varieties of Chinese, Portuguese, Portuguese creole (or *patoá*) and English would have been spoken, but it is likely that by now Portuguese or Portuguese creole as a trading *lingua franca* would have been losing ground to English, or at least English in its pidgin variety.

In sum, therefore, the contexts of use for English 'pidgin' at Macao in the 1820s and 1830s would have been similar to those in Canton: first, as a commercial language used by Europeans with Chinese traders and merchants; second, as a language used with local shopkeepers and tradesmen; and third, as a language used with domestic staff in family residences. In addition, it may have been growing in importance as a nautical language used aboard the country ships that were increasingly using Macao as a base for opium smuggling in the years before the First Opium War.

Pidgin English and Chinese Englishes, 1751–1949

Treaty-port days

After the Treaty of Nanking (Nanjing) at the close of the first Anglo-Chinese War of 1839–42, the five 'treaty ports' of Canton (Guangzhou), Amoy (Xiamen), Foochow (Fuzhou), Ningpo (Ningbo) and Shanghai were opened to Britain and other western powers. Canton jargon, or 'Canton English', spread north and, by the 1870s, it was reported that the 'uncouth and ridiculous jargon' was 'the almost exclusive medium of communication between natives and foreigners at the open ports' (Nevius 1872: 204). It was even suggested that 'the Chinese themselves are, to an extent, adopting this language . . . owing to the fact that men of different provinces cannot understand each other's dialect' (Simpson 1873: 45).

One important reason for the spread of Canton English was the expansion of China trade and the comprador system from Canton and Hong Kong northwards in the wake of the Second Opium War. According to Hao (1970), some knowledge of English was a requirement for the position of comprador, as 'through his expertise in pidgin English and his knowledge of the West, he became a middleman between East and West, not only economically but also socially, politically, and culturally' (1970: 180). After the ratification of the Treaty of Tientsin (Tianjin) in 1862, numerous other 'ports' (and inland enclaves) were opened to western missionaries, merchants and colonial officials. By the turn of the century, over forty Chinese cities had been opened to western powers, and a system of treaty-port 'semi-colonialism' had been established in China. Map 3.2 indicates a number of the most important western settlements in China.[6]

In spite of the spread of its use to the northern ports, pidgin English continued to attract disapproval and condemnation, particularly from those from outside China, being variously described as 'vile jargon', 'a grotesque gibberish' and 'revolting . . . baby talk'.[7] Nevertheless, as Shaw observes, pidgin had a certain utility in the foreign community:

> Pidgin is spoken not only by the English residents in communicating with their servants and employees, but also by the merchants and visitors to China of all other nations. The Dutch captains who voyage to Hong Kong from Batavia with little knowledge of our pure vernacular, are often excellent hands at Pidgin. The French and Germans make use of it with few exceptions, and learn it on arrival quite as a distinct study. (1897: 553–4)

By the early twentieth century, however, there was greatly increased access to educated varieties of English through mission schools and other sources, and some Chinese speakers of English developed a distaste for pidgin. For example,

---

[6] Map 3.2 is based on information from Bickers (1999) and Elder (1999).
[7] Yule and Burnell ([1886] 1969: 709) describe pidgin as a 'vile jargon'. Gill (1880) uses the term 'a grotesque gibberish' and Bird (1883) describes it as 'revolting . . . baby talk' (the latter two sources are cited by Reinecke 1937: 785).

Map 3.2 China's treaty ports and other centres of foreign trade, 1842–1916 (with approximate dates of their opening to the West)

Green (1934) notes that 'hundreds of mission schools have for years past been turning out thousands of Chinese who speak English at least as well as most non-English peoples; even among servants there are those who really resent being addressed in pidgin' (1934: 331). In the 1930s, Cannon describes the situation in Hong Kong thus:

> 'Pidgin' has ceased to be used in intercourse with educated Chinese – it is, in fact, highly insulting to employ it. On the other hand, 'pidgin' seems to have filtered down to the working class, intelligent members of which

have realised that, without some means of talking to and understanding European supervisors, they have little chance of becoming foremen and gang-leaders. At Hong Kong chair-coolies and ricksha pullers are beginning to learn a few odd words. As regards the future, it appears likely that 'pidgin', as a business language, will soon be extinct. Its place is being rapidly taken by English which, though often incorrect, is still definitely English. (1936: 138)

By 1944, Hall was writing about the 'decline' of pidgin English, which he claimed had begun in the 1890s. After the end of the Second World War, and the formation of the PRC in 1949, conditions in the treaty ports in mainland China changed drastically. According to some accounts, pidgin English continued to be spoken in Hong Kong during the 1950s and 1960s among tradespeople and servants, but most contemporary writers claim that Chinese pidgin English no longer exists, even in Hong Kong. As noted above, linguists have relied largely on the accounts of western travellers, China traders, missionaries and others in identifying the data necessary for their studies of Chinese pidgin English, and such data have then formed the basis of their analysis.

The linguistic analysis of Chinese pidgin English

Although there were one or two early attempts to provide an analysis of Chinese pidgin English, notably Dennys (1870, 1878), little systematic work on the description and analysis on this variety of pidgin was done before the 1930s and 1940s. Reinecke (1937) and Hall (1944) both carried out pioneering studies in this area, and it was Hall who first coined the term 'Chinese Pidgin English' (CPE).

Hall's (1944) article proved to be particularly influential in the field of pidgin studies, and his analysis of CPE has subsequently been quoted by a number of linguists working in this field. Hall provides a great deal of fine-detailed analysis, particularly at the levels of phonology and syntax, although there are a number of problems. One very obvious issue is his sources. Essentially Hall's data consist of a number of eighteenth-century sentences and nineteenth-century texts, supplemented by the collection of a number of spoken texts in the form of 'orally dictated material' from five British and American informants, who were apparently missionaries, teachers or colonial officials. The subsequent linguistic analysis appears too heavily influenced by the characteristics of the informants, which raises the obvious issue of why Hall chose to interview only British and American informants and to base his phonemic description of CPE on their speech.[8] For a range of reasons, it would have surely been more logical

---

[8] Hall's analysis of CPE appears to be skewed by the characteristics of his informants. For example, at the phonological level, the CPE accent is frequently transcribed as a rhotic accent. This rhoticity appears to have been extended from American and British speakers to Chinese speakers of CPE, as when the cook inquires of her mistress: *misī, hwatajm čaw dinər?* ('Missee what time chow dinner?') (Hall 1944: 107).

to describe the type of pidgin English spoken by Chinese informants. Nevertheless, Hall's paper essentially represents one of the first modern analyses of CPE and has influenced the work of later linguists, including Baker (1987), Baker and Mühlhäusler (1990) and Shi (1991).

Recent studies of Chinese pidgin English

Baker (1987) considers CPE with reference to both its internal development and its possible influence on other varieties of Pacific pidgins, and provides a meticulous analysis of CPE, based on the analysis of more than sixty texts dating from 1793 to 1944. Shi's (1991) article 'The linguistic features of Chinese pidgin English' relies heavily on Hall's analysis but appears to contain a number of errors concerning lexis that tend to mar its effectiveness. Baker and Mühlhäusler's (1990) work in this area is detailed and rigorous.

Baker and Mühlhäusler consolidate and extend Baker's earlier work, and offer a more detailed linguistic analysis of selected features of CPE. This paper is the most comprehensive and thorough study of CPE ever published in the academic literature. Their linguistic analysis begins with a discussion of CPE phonology, based largely on nineteenth-century sources. At the level of the consonant system, Baker and Mühlhäusler compare Cantonese phonology with that of CPE, highlighting the following features:

(i)   the fact that Cantonese has five pairs of aspirated and non-aspirated plosive contrasts: [pʰ] [p], [tʰ] [t], [cʰ] [c], [kʰ] [k], [kʰw] [kw], of which only the non-aspirated, unreleased [p], [t] and [k] occur in syllable final-position; and that in CPE, words ending in a plosive are often represented with a final [i], as in *sendee, makee*, etc.;

(ii)   Cantonese has only three fricatives, [f] [s] and [h]; *v* is usually represented as *b* or *p*, e.g. *hap* (1747) and *hab* (1804) 'have'; [θ] and [ð] are written as *t* and *d*, e.g. *ting* and *dat*; and *z* as *j* or *g*, e.g. *squigi* (from 'squeeze') and *pigeon* from 'business';

(iii)   the lack of contrast in CPE between [s] and [ʃ] as suggested by the spellings *joss* and *josh*;

(iv)   the representations in CPE of English words with a final *f* with the addition of a final vowel corresponding to [o] or [u], e.g. *thiefo, wifo, wifoo*, etc.;

(v)   in the case of the Cantonese nasals, [m], [n] and [ŋ] may occur finally, but lateral [l] does not; and English words with a final [ɫ] are written in CPE with the addition of *o, a* or *um*, e.g. as in *hola* 'whore', *lillo* 'little', *callum* 'call';

(vi)   *r* is typically represented by [l] in CPE, as in *lice* 'rice', etc.; and

(vii)   as consonant clusters do not occur in Cantonese, there are some examples in their data where CCV(C) is altered to CVCV(C), e.g. *sitop* 'stop' and *sileek* 'silk'.

They comment that there is little phonological evidence of a reduced vowel system in CPE, compared to 'standard English' but, overall, their judgement is that 'the phonology of CPE is heavily but unsystematically influenced by Cantonese' (1990: 98).

Lexically, they argue that CPE's vocabulary is 'overwhelmingly English-derived', and that before 1800 there were very few Chinese borrowings, e.g. the exclamation *hi-yah, cumshaw* 'gift, bribe', *chin chin* 'worship, greeting', *hoppo* 'senior customs officer', *sampan* 'kind of boat', *typan* 'supercargo', *samshu* 'liquor' and *fanquei* 'European' (literally, 'foreign devil'). Most of these words are 'found in (non-pidgin) English texts describing visits to Canton in this period and were thus probably in regular use among the East India Company's employees' (1990: 99). Chinese-derived items from the nineteenth century include *fukki* 'friend', *swan pan* 'abacus' and *man* 'slowly'. They also note the distinctive use of *pay* and *tim(e)*, where 'pay' is used with the sense of 'give', perhaps influenced by the Cantonese *béi* ('give'); and 'time' is perhaps influenced by Cantonese *dím* ('time'), but come to the conclusion that '[t]he Cantonese contribution to the lexical forms of CPE as a whole is nevertheless rather small' (1990: 99). Portuguese-derived words include *ladroon* 'thief', *joss* 'god; idol', *comprador* 'agent, servant', *mandarin*,[9] *savvy, carei, grandi, pickenini, secure* 'guarantee' and *(oc)casion* 'reason' from Port. *ocasião* 'reason'. There are also words of Indian origin, such as *chop*, *bauhru* or *bobbery*, 'uproar' or 'trouble', and *cash* 'small coin', although these, they concede, may also be regarded as derived from Portuguese. The word *tepoy* (from Hindi *tipāsē*), they suggest, is Anglo-Indian (1990: 99–100).

Baker and Mühlhäusler focus their morphological and syntactical discussion on eight features of CPE, including five where Shi (1986) identified Cantonese substrate influence. On a point-by-point basis they challenge Shi's identification of substratum influences, and refer to other pidgins such as Tok Pisin in order to demonstrate that forms such as 'topic chain' constructions, the occurrence of *man* as the second element in many compounds, e.g. *soldier man*, and the use of interrogatives like *what for* 'why', *what thing* 'what', etc., occur in a number of different pidgins. They do concede that forms such as *what fashion* 'how', *so fashion* 'thus, in this way' and *how fashion*, may be calques derived from Cantonese *dím yéung* ('how manner') and *gám yéung* (lit. 'thus manner'), and that the classifier *piece* is calqued from Cantonese.

Baker and Mühlhäusler place particular emphasis on the differences between eighteenth- and nineteenth-century CPE forms of the copula. Their analysis indicates that the eighteenth-century copula was usually *have* (*hab, hap*), but its use declined markedly after 1831. Zero-copula occurred at all times, but was a majority form only in the period 1831–70. The use of *hab* and *belong* as copula appears to be unique to CPE, although in the nineteenth century *hab* was slowly replaced by *got* and *habgot*, as it developed a specialist use as the completive

---

[9] According to Yule and Burnell, *mandarin* is possibly derived from the Hindustani *mantri* 'a counsellor, a Minister of State' ([1886] 1974: 550).

marker. Following Baker (1987), they also discuss the CPE pronoun system, again noting the process whereby, after 1800, *I*, *me* and *my* all occur as the subject pronoun and *me* and *my* as the non-subject pronoun, before *my* ultimately gains ascendancy in all positions. They note that CPE data are drawn in virtually all cases from exchanges between two people only, but that it is possible for English plural pronouns to occur, as in an attestation from 1811, where two Chinese officials inform a foreigner that *we takey petition before he know you come city* (Lindsay, 1840: 290, cited by Baker & Mühlhäusler 1990: 104). They consider the hypothesis that CPE took the form it did through the relexification (i.e. the 'replacement of the lexicon') of an earlier Portuguese-based form of speech, but reserve judgement on this issue.

Baker and Mühlhäusler move on to discuss the implications of their findings for pidgin and creole linguistics, asserting that '[t]he recent history of pidgin and creole studies have moved from an assumption that they represented a uniform phenomenon to the recognition of the existence of an increasingly larger number of structurally and socially different types', including jargons, stable pidgins and expanded pidgins (1990: 107). They argue that a crucial factor in establishing and maintaining the stability of CPE was the written vocabularies used by Chinese learners of the language:

> A final factor which appears to be unique to CPE is its mode of transmission which was not exclusively through face-to-face interaction of adults as with other pidgins, but also involved, from at least the 1830s (and perhaps much earlier) the use of printed chapbooks as primers, for self-study or as a 'textbook' for use with a teacher . . . it seems increasingly probable that the chapbooks influenced the form of lexical items. (Baker and Mühlhäusler 1990: 109)

Baker and Mühlhäusler emphasise that a detailed analysis of historical factors is necessary to gain a complete picture of the developmental characteristic of CPE. On the issue of Cantonese substratum influence in CPE, they argue that:

- there is evidence of 'non-systematic' Cantonese influence in phonology throughout all phases of CPE;
- there are *no* CPE syntactic structures of unambiguous origin;
- there are only a few words of Cantonese origin, most dating from the eighteenth century; and
- there are a few calques from Cantonese in CPE, which appear after 1830.

They add that the period 1830–40 was the era of increased substrate influence and pidgin expansion, mainly because of the increasing numbers of westerners at Canton, and the parallel increase in contact between such traders and local merchants and servants. They also highlight the influence of various vocabularies, glossaries and chapbooks, suggesting that these 'probably played a major role in both the propagation and stabilisation of CPE, an unprecedented event for any pidgin or creole language' (1990: 112).

Glossaries and chapbooks – Chinese-language sources for pidgin English in China

As noted above, Baker and Mühlhäusler (1990) make much of the impact of glossaries, vocabularies or 'chapbooks' in contributing to the formation and stabilisation of CPE as a distinct variety of speech. Shi also notes that '[t]he practice of learning CPE from a phrasebook played an important role not only in the development of the pidgin during the 18th and early 19th century, but also in the quick spread of CPE from Canton to other Treaty Cities in the middle of the 19th century' (1993: 463), while Baker and Mühlhäusler refer to the use of such chapbooks as 'unique' to CPE (1990: 109). My own view is that Shi and Baker and Mühlhäusler may tend to both under- and overestimate the impact of such vocabularies on the spread of English and pidgin English in China.

First, I suggest, they underestimate the very long tradition of transcribing foreign languages that already existed in China long before the arrival of westerners. Second, Baker and Mühlhäusler perhaps overestimate the impact of such written glossaries in 'fixing' the pronunciation of English sounds, in terms of precisely defined Chinese equivalents based on the selection of particular Chinese characters. A related implication is that the practice of notating English sounds through the use of Chinese characters was unique to the development of CPE in China, and is unparalleled in other areas of linguistic contact. This is patently not the case, as even in contemporary Hong Kong Cantonese-speaking students in local primary and secondary schools routinely use Chinese characters as an *aide memoire* to transcribe the sounds of English words in the margins of their textbooks (Radio Television Hong Kong 1997).

In fact, the practice of using written Chinese to transcribe the sounds of foreign languages has a long and complicated history. Historical records show that the first official institution to study foreign languages was established in China in 1276, and was called the Office of Interpreters 會通館 (*Huitong Guan*). An Office of Translators 四夷館 (*Siyi Guan*) was later set up in 1407. Both these organisations were active in preparing glossaries of 'Chinese-barbarian-translated-languages' 華夷譯語 (*Huayi Yiyu*) for Asian languages, particularly the languages of those societies that bordered on, and paid tribute to, the Middle Kingdom – Mongolian, Tibetan Sanskrit, Persian and Siamese. The first glossary may have been a Mongol–Chinese vocabulary, compiled in 1382, and later vocabularies included those for Japanese, Korean and Malay, typically utilising Chinese characters to indicate the pronunciation of each of the foreign languages (Wild 1943).

In 1748 these two institutions were amalgamated under the name of the 會通四夷館 *Huitong Siyi Guan*, and these glossaries were updated and re-edited. When Fuchs visited the Palace Museum in Peking in 1931, he came across a collection of ninety-eight volumes of these *Huayi Yiyu* and reported that, in addition to the transcription of nine Tibetan dialects, fifteen dialects of southwest China, Siamese, Burmese, Liukiu and Sulu, there were also vocabularies of English, French, German, Italian, Latin and Portuguese (Fuchs 1931). He estimated that the volumes for European languages were published around the year 1748, and commented that the English vocabulary 'consists of only two volumes the English of which is written by a man, apparently a Chinese, who had not mastered the language and who made frequent mistakes' (1931: 92). What is significant about these glossaries is the way in which words are presented: first the word from the foreign language is set out, then it is translated into its written Chinese character equivalent and this is followed by the use of other Chinese characters to give an approximate phonemic representation of the foreign word's sound. Thus the use of Chinese characters to transcribe the sounds of foreign languages has had a long history in Chinese philology, and could not be a feature of linguistic description and notation peculiar to the representation of the 'Canton jargon'.[10]

In addition, the evidence cited by Fuchs for the existence of *Huayi Yiyu* for European languages at this time is in itself remarkable, particularly in the case of English, as this has received little attention in the academic literature. Portuguese–Chinese dictionaries date from the late sixteenth century, but it was not until the middle of the eighteenth century that Chinese-language glossaries of Portuguese came into being. The vocabulary mentioned by Fuchs is one example from this period, and another important glossary was included in a work printed in South China in 1751, generally referred to as *The Monograph of Macao*.

The Monograph of Macao (1751)

In 1751 two Chinese officials in southern China, Yin Kuan Jen and Chang Ju Lin, wrote an official study or 'gazette' of Macao called the 澳門記略 *Aomen Jilüe*, usually translated as *The Monograph of Macao*. This book contains two volumes, divided into three sections, the first of which describes the geography of Macao and gives details of the tide and winds around the enclave. The second section gives a history of the Chinese official contact with the Portuguese from the sixteenth to the eighteenth century. The third section describes the layout of the city and the appearance and customs of the Portuguese and slave populations, and contains a Chinese–Portuguese glossary, comprising 395 words and expressions. The book also features a number of illustrations, including one of a 'Portuguese gentleman' in Macao (see figure 3.2 below).

The vocabulary is laid out in a similar fashion to the *Huayi Yiyu* glossaries, although it differs from these earlier works by omitting a written form of the Portuguese language. Instead, there is a system of entries, where usually between one and three Chinese characters are set out as headword entries, indicating the meaning of a particular item. Every entry is then followed by a combination of characters, which, if read aloud in Cantonese (and occasionally in Mandarin), indicates the approximate pronunciation of the equivalent Portuguese word or expression. For example, the first word in the list is the Chinese character for the

---

[10] I am very grateful to Dr Geoff Wade of the Centre for Asian Studies at the University of Hong Kong for drawing my attention to these early glossaries.

Figure 3.2 The engraving of a Portuguese man from *The Monograph of Macao* (1751)

word 'sky'; this is followed by two other Chinese characters, whose pronunciation in Cantonese, *sīu ǹgh*, approximates to the 'reconstructed Portuguese' equivalent *céu*. The second headword on the list is the Chinese character for 'sun', followed by two characters whose pronunciation in spoken Cantonese, *sō lòuh*, approximates to the Portuguese *sol*; and so on, through the other 395 words in the list.

The Monograph of Macao is well known to historians and has been discussed widely for the insights that it offers into eighteenth-century life in Macao, but the vocabulary has only been studied by linguists in the last fifty years, since its first translation into Portuguese (Gomes 1950). Bawden (1954) followed this with a detailed transcription of the glossary and careful analysis of both the Chinese and Portuguese items that occur in the list. According to Bawden, the list is particularly noteworthy because the 'Portuguese' items represented by the list are tokens of the dialect of 'Indo-Portuguese' that was spoken at Macao at that time. Bawden claims that he can recognise and 'translate' 370 of the 395 words in the list into his 'reconstructed' Portuguese, that is, the Indo-Portuguese variety thought to be spoken in Macao at this time. These are grouped into five categories: (i) 'heaven and earth', (ii) 'men and things', (iii) 'clothing and food', (iv) 'implements and numbers' and (v) 'commonly used words'.

For scholars such as Bawden (1954) and Thompson (1959), this 1751 glossary is chiefly of value for the information that it provides about the development of the Macanese dialect, which by the twentieth century was referred to as Macao *patoá*, or *Macaista*, and by now has all but disappeared from use. In the context of pidgin studies, however, *The Monograph of Macao* is an immensely valuable document, as it provides direct evidence of the kind of Chinese–Portuguese glossaries that were circulating in Macao and Canton and in use at least up until the 1830s. It is also interesting to note a number of items included in the glossary of 'Early Asian English' from Mundy's *Travels* in table 3.1 above are also found in the *Monograph* list, i.e. *bambú* (bamboo), *caixa* (casse), *camelão* (Chamblett), *Casa Branco* (Casa Blanca), *condorim* (Cundoreene), *dachém* (Dachein), *fachi* (Chopstickes), *Ilha Verde* (Isla Verde), *jamboa* (Casca grossa), *jurubaça* (Jurabasse), *Mandarim* (Mandareene), *rota* (rattan) and *tael* (Tay).

A major issue with specific reference to pidgin studies is 'relexification'. As we saw above, Baker and Mühlhäusler (1990) are sceptical of the notion that Chinese pidgin English was relexified from pidgin Portuguese. They concede that opportunities for relexification, however, did occur in the early nineteenth century, when many British, American and European traders settled in Macao; the Chinese they employed may have had some knowledge of pidgin Portuguese. They also suggest that some relexification may have also occurred through the use of the printed vocabularies or 'chapbooks' that were circulated in Canton and Macao. In this context they again quote Wells Williams, who suggests that the author of the English vocabulary was one and the same as that of the Portuguese vocabulary, surmising that the anonymous lexicographer 'knew much less of English than he did of Portuguese' (1837: 239).

My argument here is that the wordlist from *The Monograph of Macao* represents at least one important 'missing link' in this chain of connections, as it does provide a written transcription of the Indo-Portuguese dialect as spoken in Macao around 1751, and may have influenced the earliest Chinese–English chapbooks that were published in South China at this time. Whether or not the evidence of relexification it affords is sufficiently compelling for pidgin scholars such as Baker and Mühlhäusler to revise their account of the development of CPE remains to be seen.

The Common Foreign Language of the Redhaired People (c. 1835)

The chapbook entitled *The Common Foreign Language of the Redhaired People* 紅毛通用番話 (*Hùhngmòuh tūngyuhng fāanwáa*)[11] was published in Canton around the year 1835, and is probably the same, or very similar, to the pamphlet that Wells Williams (1837), Hunter (1882) and Leland (1876) refer to in their discussions of pidgin English (although the title varies somewhat in their published accounts). In Wells Williams (1837), the title of the glossary is given as 紅毛買賣通用鬼話 *Hung-maou mae mae tung yung kwei hwa*,[12] which translates broadly as 'The Redhaired People's Buying and Selling Usual Ghost Language'. Williams is particularly averse to the epithet 'ghost', which he translates as 'devilish'. In spite of this difference, the contents of the glossary seem very similar. Williams states that '[t]he English vocabulary consists of only sixteen pages, containing less than 400 words' (1837: 278), which is quite close in description to the *Hung maou tung yang fan hwa* (*Hùhngmòuh tūngyuhng fāanwáa*) referred to by Baker and Mühlhäusler (1990). This, I believe, is identical to the *Redhaired* glossary reproduced in appendix 4 to this book, which contains sixteen pages and 372 headings or headwords.

Leland (1876) mentions a similar glossary in his introduction, when discussing 'native vocabularies published for the benefit of compradores and servants', where he mentions 'a little volume of twelve or fifteen pages... entitled "A Vocabulary of Words in Use among the Red-Haired People"' (1876: 4). In his memoir on his life in Canton in the 1820s and 1830s, Hunter also provides a detailed description of such a pamphlet:

> In the Canton book-shops near the Factories was sold a small pamphlet, called 'Devils' Talk'. On the cover was a drawing of a foreigner in the dress of the middle of the last century – three-cornered hat, coat with buckles, lace sleeves, and in his hand a cane. I have now one of these pamphlets before me. It commences thus, 'Yun', and under it is its 'barbarian' definition, expressed in another Chinese word whose *sound* is 'man'. After many examples of this kind come words of two syllables – thus, 'kum-yat', with their foreign meaning expressed by two other Chinese characters pronounced 'to-teay' to-day – and so on to sentences, for which the construction of the language is peculiarly adapted. This pamphlet, costing a penny or two, was continually in the hands of servants, coolies, and shopkeepers. The author was a Chinaman, whose ingenuity should immortalise him. I have often

---

[11] The transcription of pronunciation is given here in the Yale (Cantonese) equivalent. In pinyin this would be *Hongmao tongyung faanhua*.

[12] The pinyin equivalent would be *Hongmao maimai tongyong guihua*.

wondered who the man was who first reduced the 'out-landish tongue' to a current language. Red candles should be burnt on altars erected to his memory, and oblations of tea poured out before his image, placed among the wooden gods which in temples surround the shrine of a deified man of letters. (1882: 38–9)

Hunter's description of his pamphlet indicates a striking similarity to the *Redhaired* glossary in appendix 4. In both cases, the cover of the pamphlet seems to be a direct copy of the engraving of 'a Portuguese gentleman at Macao' that had appeared some eighty years earlier in *The Monograph of Macao*, as shown in figures 3.2 and 3.3 below.

There are a number of other similarities between the *Monograph* and *Redhaired*, including style of presentation. The *Redhaired* vocabulary is set out in four sections: (i) 'numbers used in business'; (ii) 'common expressions referring to people and things'; (iii) 'everyday language'; and (iv) 'food and miscellaneous'. A comparison of the *Monograph*'s 395 headings with the 372 headings of *Redhaired* reveals that 95 of the headings (as specified by a Chinese character or combination of characters) are shared, including:

> *areca nut, banana, black, boat, buy, cat, cent, chair, chestnut, cold, come, curtain, dead, die, dog, dove, drink, early, eat, eight, elder brother, emperor, far, father, fish, five, foot, four, goat, good people, ground, hat, have, hot, human beings, ink, inside, jaggery, knife, lemon, mandarin, milk, money, moon, mother, night, nine, north, not have, oil, old people, one, one hundred, one thousand.*

In addition, there are sixteen pairs of items which are partly related to each other, which is to say that the meanings of the pairs of words in the two lists are synonymous, or closely related. In a majority of instances, the word has been transcribed in the second list using an alternative or synonymous character, as in the listings for: *bed, cash, cook, coolie, customs house, food, go, husband's father, mat, son, speak, table, tea leaves, thin, trousers, vegetables* and *you.*

There is no doubt that the *Redhaired* vocabulary represents an important piece in the jigsaw that is the history of pidgin English in southern China. Indeed, as far as I am aware, with the exception of the English glossary mentioned by Fuchs (1931) discussed above, this is the earliest Chinese glossary of the English language in existence. The considerable overlap between the two lists provides some evidence of relexification from Portuguese into English. In addition, there are a significant number of Portuguese words in the *Redhaired* list, which lends support to the notion that pidgin English in the early nineteenth century was still significantly influenced by Portuguese. Words of obvious Portuguese origin in the list include *covado, carei, conta, comprador* and *padre*. There are some words of mixed Indo-Portuguese provenance, such as the measure and currency words, *catty, cash, candareen, mace, tael* and *picul*, which have their origin in Malay languages but may have been 'filtered' through Portuguese.

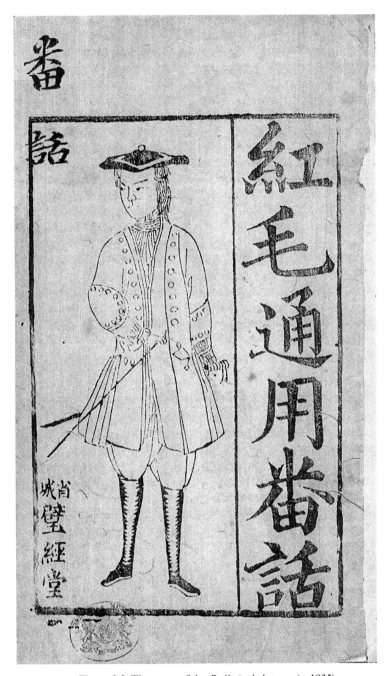

Figure 3.3 The cover of the *Redhaired* glossary (c. 1835)

What is also remarkable about the list is that a number of the items appear to be neither English nor Portuguese. The English translations of the headings are, respectively, 'small orange', 'duck', 'ham', 'butter' and 'pipe'; and the Yale transcriptions of the Chinese characters indicating their English/pidgin pronunciation are *(ng)ā a bei sīn, (ng)ā ng gaa, sing gā a, sih mā a yíh* and *bēi bah*. After some consideration, I decided that these in fact indicate the Swedish words, *apelsin* 'orange', *anka* 'duck', *skinka* 'ham', *smö* 'butter' and *pipa* 'pipe'. This inference is partly supported by the linguistic resemblance of these items to Swedish words, but also by the journal of a Swedish pastor, Olof Toreen, who visited Canton in 1751. Toreen comments that the Canton Chinese 'generally converse with the *Swedes* in broken *English*; and sometimes in broken *Portuguese, French* and *Dutch*: and some of them speak a few words of *Swedish*' (1771: 237–8). The speculation that these entries are Swedish or Danish recently received support from a historian of the Canton trade who reports having seen Swedish and Danish used in lists of ships' provisions otherwise written in English (Van Dyke March 2000, personal communication). The *Redhaired* glossary is reproduced in appendix 4, together with a transcription and translation of the pamphlet.[13]

The *Redhaired* glossary was no doubt significant at the time, but later many other vocabularies were also compiled, possibly the most influential of which was a work entitled *The Chinese and English Instructor* which appeared after the Second Opium War in 1862, was published at Canton and circulated in Hong Kong, and, almost certainly, throughout the treaty ports.

The Chinese and English Instructor (1862)

The Chinese and English Instructor is the English title of a remarkable book by a Chinese linguist, comprador and businessman, who identifies himself on the title page as 'Tong Ting-kü'. The Chinese title 英语集全 is romanised as *Ying Ü Tsap Ts'ün* ('English words collected complete'). Selby and Selby (1997) were the first to identify this work as 'the major source' on Chinese pidgin English, which indeed it does appear to be (and more).

The *Instructor* is a very substantial and sophisticated guide to English. Whereas *Redhaired* consisted of only sixteen rather badly printed pages with 395 words, the *Instructor* runs to a total of 524 pages in six volumes, and includes approximately 9,500 headwords in the form of lines of dialogue. It is, in other words, a substantial Chinese–English, English–Chinese dictionary, arranged for the most part according to topics and situations. In his preface, Tong states that his work is written 'chiefly to suit the Canton people who have transactions, or are connected, with foreigners'. He explains the organisation of the entries thus:

---

[13] I wish to thank Stephen Selby of the HKSAR Government for his generous advice on decoding a number of items in this glossary, as well as Nara Barreto (Macao), Alan Baxter (University of Macao), James K. Chin (University of Hong Kong), Cedric Lee (Chinese University of Hong Kong) Isabel Morais (Macao), Paul Van Dyke (Macao) and Michelle Woo (University of Hong Kong) for their valuable help. All errors, of course, are my own.

The words are first given in Chinese; then, the pronunciation of such words, written in English [i.e. romanisation]; then the meaning of those words in the English language; and lastly, the pronunciation of the English words written in Chinese, so that the book is not only useful for Chinese to learn English, but at the same time it will enable foreigners to learn Chinese. (1862: preface, written in English by Tong himself)

Tong also mentions that the words are arranged under 'different headings', and the opening section of the first volume provides an index, a summary of which is presented below in order to convey some idea of the impressive scope of this work.

The index of *The Chinese and English Instructor*

Vol. 1

On Astronomy	1–3
On Geography	4–12
On times and season	13–20
On Ranks and Titles	21–44
On the Body	45–51
On Edifice, Building &c	52–61
On Musical instruments	62–64
On Armament	65–68

Vol. 2

On Ships and Appendages	1–15
On Carriages &c	16–17
On Impliments, Furniture &c	18–29
On Books, Stationery, Forms &c	30–36
On Agricultural Impliments &c	37–46
On Works	47–48
On Wearing Apparels & Ornaments	49–57
On Food, Wine, Tea &c	58–69
On Plants, Fruits, Flowers &c	70–87

Vol. 3

On the Animal kingdom	1–17
On Stone and Jade	18–20
On Minerals; Coins &c	21–26
On Tariff of Imports	27–45
On Tariff of Exports	46–62
On Dutyfree and Contraband Goods	63–65
On Sundry goods	66–68
On Opium, Tobacco &c	69–70
On Lacquered & Ivoryware &c	71–75
On Piece goods	76–81

Selby and Selby explain that 'the phonetic transcription into Chinese characters of the English is rigorous and very effective', as the author uses a transcription that employs 'three levels of refinement':

> First, where the standard Cantonese pronunciation of a Chinese syllable is close enough to the corresponding English syllable, the character is used. Where no suitable character is available, an *ersatz* syllable is created using the 'mouth' radical and *fan-qie* method, according to the prevailing

convention for reproducing colloquial Cantonese words which are not normally written down. Finally, for English sounds with no corresponding Chinese sound, diacritics are placed alongside the Chinese characters, based on the methods employed by Qian Long in his Manchu dictionaries of the Chinese minority languages. (1997: 124–5)

An additional feature of the *Instructor* is that for a subset of entries, mainly dialogues, the Chinese reader is given instruction on how to read these both in 'English' and in *fāanwáa* (i.e. 'foreigner language', a term broadly corresponding to 'pidgin'). At a phonological level, the Selbys infer that there was a good deal of variation:

it was not pronounced in a consistent way by Chinese and English speakers, nor was it pronounced consistently among the Chinese themselves. When first learned by Chinese, words would be pronounced as their individual Chinese characters. As the speaker got more experience of speaking to foreigners, he would mould his pronunciation closer to the English, as far as he was able. (1997: 126)

They proceed to note that 'there was no contrast in Pidgin (as he spoke it) between aspirated and unaspirated consonants, even though such contrasts exist in both Chinese and English'. Consequently, the word 'price' is transcribed with characters indicating both *pou-laai-si* and *bou-laai-si* (1997: 126).

At the level of vocabulary, the Selbys argue that 'a very small base of common words filled a wealth of meanings', and that 'at the earliest stage there was a core of words derived not directly from English but from a variety of Portuguese, Malay and English' and that to these was added 'a gradually more extensive vocabulary' (1997: 129). Such words, they suggest, may have included *bi-jin* (pidgin), *kam-sha* (cumshaw), *de-lam* (tellum), *se-lam* (sellum), *bui-lam* (boilum), *si-bui-lam* (spoilum), *gi-lam* (killum), *go-lam* (callum), *ma-si-gi* (maskee) and *gou-dang* (godown). Syntactically, much of the patterning corresponds to Chinese, although there are instances where the word order corresponds to English, as in the handling of time and place. The conventional Chinese order of words is: time, place, action. In pidgin, however, an English-like structure is adopted in sentences such as *mai go si hi dou-ma-la*, 'I shall go and see him tomorrow' (1997: 128).

One striking feature of the *Instructor* is the use of detailed vocabulary lists relating to various topics of general and specialist interest, at a time when China had been forcibly opened to the West. Tong was one of the very first Chinese educated in English and, at this point in his career, appears to be filling the role of cultural and linguistic middleman, at a time when he himself was striving to cope with and learn from the new fields of knowledge that contact with westerners entailed. Tong, the lexicographer, also had a command of 'alphabeticisation' or 'romanisation', which he used to present new words and new worlds to his readers. For example, in the second section of volume 1, he provides a list of countries, together with their romanised names, including the following: Africa, *Ah feeli ka*; America, *Fah ki kwok*; Arabia, *Ah la pak kwok*; Australia, *Sun kum san*; Japan, *Yat poon kwok*; Lisbon, *Sai yeong kwok king sing*; London, *Ying kwok king sing*; Mongol, *Mung koo*; Prussia, *Pak tau kwok*; Russia, *Ngo lo see kwok*; San Francisco, *K'au kum san tai fow*; Siam, *Chim lo kwok*; Singapore, *San chau fu*; Spain, *Tai lu sung kwok*; Sweden, *Sui teen kwok*; and Turkey, *Thoo ye ki kwok*.

Taken as a whole, it would be logical to argue that the primary function of *The Chinese and English Instructor* is as a manual, combining both a dictionary and collection of texts (or chrestomathy) for the teaching of English. The great majority of the work is devoted to the representation of 'English' in its fuller form, not *fāanwáa* or 'pidgin'. The majority of *fāanwáa* texts are included in volume 6 of the work, in those sections devoted to dialogues of various kinds, and the Selbys' suggestion that these texts were afterthoughts and squeezed onto the page, regardless of whether there was enough space, appears very plausible. Nevertheless, the written *fāanwáa* texts in the *Instructor* are probably the largest single source for Chinese pidgin English available to any Pidgin and Creole scholar.

I would also argue that the *Instructor* served not only as a dictionary, or chrestomathy, but also as a handbook on compradore modernity, with lessons on China trade, the vocabularies of trading items, currencies, weights and measures, and financial exchange. This was a modernity shaped by a range of disparate influences associated with the western presence in China in the mid-nineteenth century, including capitalism, colonialism, orientalism, religion and linguistic negotiation; all the elements of what historians have recently come to refer to as 'colonial modernity'. These elements also combine in the personal story of the author of the *Instructor*, 'Tong Ting-kü' or Tong King-sing 唐景星 (1832–92), as he was perhaps better known.[14] Reproduced as figure 3.4 is the only known photograph of Tong King-sing, from Liu (1982).

According to Liu (1982), at the time he wrote the *Instructor*, the thirty-year-old Tong was working as 'a roving salesman' for Jardines on board steamboats travelling to the Yangtze ports. Later, after he started work as compradore, he

---

[14] Tong King-sing was one of three brothers who were educated at the Morrison Education Society School, established in Macao and Hong Kong in the late 1830s and early 1840s. According to Smith (1971), the three brothers were Tong Mow-chee (1828–97, T'ang Mao-chih, also known as T'ang T'ing-chih and A-chick), Tong King-sing (1832–92, T'ang Chaing-hsing, also known as T'ang T'ing-shu and Tong Ying Akü) and T'ang T'ing-keng (also known as Tong Ying-sing and Afu, who was born in 1845). Tong King-sing served as interpreter in the Hong Kong Magistrate's Court from December 1851 until January 1856. Two years later, Tong King-sing moved to Shanghai, where he worked as clerk and interpreter at the Imperial Maritime Customs from 1858–61. He then started work with Jardine Matheson, and from 1863–73 he served as Jardine's Shanghai comprador. In 1873 he resigned in order to become the manager of the China Merchants' Steam Navigation Company, a shipping business sponsored by the Chinese government (Liu 1982). He later founded the Kaiping coal mines in northern China, which he managed until his death in 1892. See Smith (1971, 1985) and Liu (1982) for fuller accounts of his life.

Figure 3.4 Tong King-sing – 'China's first modern entrepreneur'

was described by William Keswick, the Jardine *taipan*, as 'the man who knows English so well' (cited in Liu 1982: 106). Liu also includes an example of Tong's penmanship from his time at Jardines, at a point when Tong was seeking to have some of his personal debts to the company reduced:

> To replace myself in the proper footing I have worked hard indeed. When-
> ever I have a few minutes to spare I always work for my native friends who
> all make me as their representative in business connecting with Foreign

houses. To watch their interest I have been requested by them to accept a directorship in the Union S.N. Co. and the North China Steam [*sic*] Co. . . . I have been always aiming at something which I can feel proud to offer to your firm, but have not yet succeeded and I have every hope that something will soon be under my command. You may rest sure that so long as I have the honor to be in your service I will do my best in looking after the interest of your house and I can say that ever since I entered the service I might have a little error in my judgment, but I never have robbed or squeezed you in the slightest degree as most of Chinese servants do. Having received a thorough Anglo-Chinese education I consider squeezing the Employer is a sinful & mean act. (Tong King-sing 1868, cited in Liu 1982: 104)

Tong King-sing later went on to make an outstanding career as an independent businessman investing in steamships and mining. Liu argues that he was 'perhaps the most notable personage with a comprador background in modern Chinese history', dubbing him 'China's first modern entrepreneur' (1982: 104). He was also one of the very first students to learn English at a missionary school in Hong Kong, the Morrison Education Society School, which was established by John Robert Morrison in memory of his father.

It is interesting to note that, in the extract of the letter above, there are clearly two items of an early lexicon of Chinese English, i.e. *squeeze* 'cheat, or extort', and *Anglo-Chinese* in the sense of 'connected with British interests in China'. By this time, another emergent variety of English was that of a specific lexicon of Chinese English, or 'Anglo-Chinese' or 'China Coast' English, both terms which were used to refer to hybridised varieties of English in China at this time.[15]

'China Coast' English

By the mid-1860s, knowledge of English was being spread throughout the treaty ports by compradores and linguistic middlemen like Tong. At the same time, the first mission schools had started up in Hong Kong, Canton (Guangzhou), Amoy (Xiamen), Shanghai and Ningpo (Ningbo). After the Second Opium War, missionary education would spread rapidly throughout many areas of China, giving increasing numbers of students the opportunity to gain some knowledge of English, a knowledge associated with the changing world of late Qing China, in which the technological advances of western societies were now intruding

---

[15] Tong's *Instructor* was followed by other volumes on similar principles for the teaching of English to Chinese people. These include Stedman and Lee's (1888) *Chinese-English Phrase Book in the Canton Dialect* (aimed at Chinese immigrants in the United States), Mok's (1904) *English Made Easy* (published in Hong Kong) and Kwong's (1923) *An English and Chinese Dictionary* (simultaneously published in Hong Kong, Shanghai, Singapore and San Francisco).

rapidly. Knowledge of the western world and English as *the* western language became a hallmark of modernity, Chinese capitalism and social and political change.

At the same time, increasing numbers of western traders, missionaries and colonial officials were coming into contact with many different aspects of Chinese life. In the same way that anglophone settlers in other parts of the world had to come to terms with new flora and fauna, peoples, cultures and foods, westerners began to adopt a vocabulary that reflected the reality of life around them in treaty-port China. This resulted in a number of glossaries of 'Things Chinese', written by various authors and ranging from the academic (Giles 1886) to the encyclopaedic (Ball 1903) to the 'humorous' (Leland 1876; Hill 1920). All these works demonstrated an obvious overlap between notions of a 'pidgin English' and a 'China Coast' or 'Anglo-Chinese' vocabulary (Munn 2001). Between 1834 and 1920, there were at least seven glossaries of pidgin English and/or 'Anglo-Chinese' vocabulary published.[16]

In table 3.2 a selection of 'China Coast' vocabulary is set out in tabular form, with the fourth column indicating the source of the citations. Three sets of items have been deliberately omitted from the table for reasons of economy: first, commonly occurring pidgin items (particularly frequent in Leland 1876; Barrère and Leland 1889; and Hill 1920); second, place names; and third, encyclopaedic references to contemporary Anglo-Chinese history. The omitted pidgin items include such relatively common expressions as *boilum*, *bymby*, *can do*, *catchee*, *cutee*, *foolo*, *litee*, *look-see*, *makee*, *more better*, *muchee*, *no can do*, *topside*, etc.

It should also be noted that there is an obvious overlap, if not confusion, between the categorisation of what was 'pidgin' and what was 'Anglo-Chinese' or 'China Coast' vocabulary. Leland's and Hill's books give the subject a 'comic' treatment, but Giles' (1886) work was influential in academic circles, and he is cited in both *Hobson-Jobson* and the *OED*. It was also the case that Leland's and Hill's works were not simply about 'pidgin English', they were about something else as well, what linguists would today call 'languages in contact', 'contact linguistics' and the associated processes of 'code-mixing' and 'lexical borrowing'. In the wider context of Asian Englishes, the list below provides an illustration of how categories such as 'Anglo-Indian' and 'Anglo-Chinese' overlapped in the treaty ports of China. A substantial number of items listed are of Anglo-Indian provenance, e.g. *chit*, *chop*, *congee*, *coolie*, *curry*, *custard apple*, *dhoby*, *mandarin*, *mango*, *monsoon*, *nullah*, *paddy*, *shroff* and *tiffin*. Other words and expressions are Malay and Indo-Portuguese, phonetic borrowings from Chinese or loan translations or 'calques'.

Table 3.2 demonstrates that, by the late nineteenth century, a new contact vocabulary of Chinese English had come into being. In a sense this was to be

---

[16] These glossaries are: Morrison (1834), Leland (1876), Giles (1886), Yule and Burnell ([1886] 1969), Barrère and Leland (1889), Ball (1903) and Hill (1920).

Table 3.2 *'China Coast' vocabulary, 1834–1920*

Item	English gloss	Source language(s)	Citations
agar-agar	a variety of sea-weed	Malay	L, G, YB, B, H
ai yah!	an exclamation of surprise	Cantonese	L
almari	a closet, cupboard	Portuguese	G, YB, BL
amah	a wet-nurse	Portuguese	L, G, YB, BL, B, H
bamboo oysters	a type of oyster, farmed through the arrangement of bamboo poles placed in water	English	G, H
bêche-de-mer (bicho-da-mar)	a type of sea-slug used in Chinese cuisine	French, Portuguese	G, YB, B, H
betel	the leaf of a plant chewed in India and China	Portuguese	G, YB, B, H
bird's-nest	the edible nests of swallows, used in soup	calque from Chinese	G, YB, B, H
black-haired race	a name for the Chinese people	calque from Chinese	G, B, H
bobbery	a disturbance or row	Hindustani	L, G, YB, BL, H
bohea	a type of black tea	Chinese	G, YB, B
Bombay duck	a type of dried fish	Anglo-Indian	G, YB, BL
bonze	a Buddhist priest	Japanese	G, YB
brinjal (bringal)	an aubergine	Sanskrit, Portuguese	G, YB, H
bungalow	a house, originally in Bengal	Hindustani	G, YB, H
campoi	a type of tea	Cantonese	G, YB
candareen	a weight equivalent to one hundredth of a tael (approx 0.38 grammes)	Malay	L, G, YB, B, H
cangue	a wooden yoke worn by criminals	French, Portuguese	L, G, B, H
cash	a copper coin of low value	Sanskrit, Tamil, Portuguese	L, G, YB, B, H
catty	a weight equivalent to 16 taels (625 grammes)	Malay	L, G, YB, B, H
celestial empire	a name for China	calque from Chinese	G, B, H
char	tea	Cantonese	G, YB
charpoy	a bedstead	Persian, Hindustani	G, YB, BL
chee-chee	a derogatory term for Eurasians	Anglo-Indian	G, YB

Item	English gloss	Source language(s)	Citations
chit	a letter, note or IOU	Hindustani	G, YB, BL, H
chop	a seal or stamp	Hindustani	M, L, G, YB, BL, H
chunam	a type of cement or plaster	Sanskrit, Tamil	M, G, YB, B, H
cloisonné	a type of decorative enamel used in ceramics	French	G, H
Co-hong	the federation of Chinese merchants at Canton before 1839	Chinese	
compound	a walled enclosure for the offices and houses of foreigners	Malay, Portuguese	G, H
comprador(e)	a local agent for foreign traders	Portuguese	L, G, YB, BL, H
Confucius	the renowned philosopher who lived from 551–479 BC	Chinese, Latin	G, B, H
congee	rice gruel or rice porridge	Tamil	G, YB, BL, B, H
congou	a type of tea	Chinese	G, YB, B
consoo (house)	the building at Canton housing the Co-hong merchants	Cantonese	M, L, G, YB, BL
coolie	a labourer or workman	Gujarati, Tamil	L, G, YB, B, H
covid	a measure of varying length, sometimes referred to as the 'Chinese foot'	Portuguese	G, YB
cumshaw (cumsha)	a gift or bribe	Chinese, pidgin	L, G, YB, BL, H
curry	a spicy dish or sauce	Tamil	L, G, YB, BL
custard apple	a variety of fruit, the *Anona reticulata*	English	G, YB, B
dhoby	a washerman	Sanskrit, Hindustani	G, YB, BL
Dragon-boat Festival	a Chinese festival	calque	G, B
fa wong	a gardener	Cantonese	H
face	appearance, reputation, status	Calque	M, L

(*cont.*)

Table 3.2 (*cont.*)

Item	English gloss	Source language(s)	Citations
factory	a trading establishment	Portuguese	G, YB, H
fan-kwei (fanqui)	a derogatory term for westerners	Cantonese	M, L, G, YB, BL, H
fantan	a gambling game	Cantonese	G, B, H
feng-shui (fungshui)	a system of geomancy	Cantonese	L, G, B, H
gingall (ginjal)	a type of heavy musket	Hindustani	G, YB, B, H
ginseng	a medicinal root	Chinese	G, YB, B, H
godown	a warehouse	Malay	L, G, YB, B, H
gong	a bronze disc struck for musical effect	Malay	G, YB, B
grass character	a style of written Chinese	Calque from Chinese	G, H
grass-cloth	a type of linen	Calque from Chinese	G, YB, H
griffin	1. a westerner newly arrived in Asia 2. a new horse on the racetrack	English	L, G, YB, BL, H
Hakkas	a distinct ethnic group in southern China	Cantonese	G, B, H
hampalang	all in all, everything	Cantonese	G, H
Han	the dominant ethnic group in China	Chinese	G, H
hong-boat	a type of small boat	English	G, YB
hoppo (hoopo)	the superintendent of customs at Canton	Cantonese	G, YB, BL
hyson	a variety of tea	Chinese	G, YB, B
jinricksha (rickshaw)	a man-drawn cart	Japanese	L, G, YB, BL, B, H
joss	1. Chinese gods 2. the Christian god	Portuguese	L, G, BL, H
joss-house man	a western missionary	Pidgin	L, G, BL, H
junk	a type of sailing-boat	Javanese, Portuguese	M, G, YB, H
kaifong	a neighbourhood of a town	Cantonese	G, B
kao-liang	a variety of cereal or 'tall millet'	Chinese	G, H
kumquat (cumquat)	a small orange	Cantonese	L, G, YB, B, H
kung he(i)	an expression of congratulations	Cantonese	L, B

Item	English gloss	Source language(s)	Citations
lakh (lac)	one hundred thousand	Sanskrit, Hindustani	G, YB, H
lally-lung (laliloong)	a thief or criminal	Portuguese, Pidgin	L, G, BL, H
lama	a Buddhist priest	Tibetan	G, YB
larn-pidgin	an apprentice, *lit.* 'learn business'	Pidgin	L, G, BL, H
lascar	a South Asian sailor	Persian, Portuguese	G, YB, BL
linguist (lingoo)	an interpreter	Portuguese	M, G, YB
literati, the	the scholarly class in Imperial China	Latin, English	G, B, H
loquat	a variety of orange	Cantonese	L, G, YB, B
lorcha	a type of sailing boat in South China	Portuguese	G, YB, H
lowdah	a captain of a Chinese junk	Cantonese	L, G, H
mace	a weight equivalent to one tenth of a tael (approx. 3.8 grammes)	Malay	L, G, YB, B, H
mafoo	a groom or stable hand	Cantonese	L, G, BL, H
mahcheen	a merchant	Chinese	G, B
Manchu	an inhabitant of Manchuria, whose leaders ruled China in the Qing dynasty	English, pidgin	L, BL
maskee	an expression equivalent to 'never mind!' 'that doesn't matter'	Portuguese, pidgin	M, L, G, YB, BL, H
matshed	a structure made from matting	English	B
Middle Kingdom	a name for China	Calque	G, B, H
monsoon	seasonal winds and rains	Arabic, Portuguese	G, YB, B, H
nankeen	a type of cotton cloth originally from Nanking	Chinese	G, YB, B, H
nullah	an open watercourse or sewer	Hindustani	G, YB
number one	of the best quality	Pidgin	L, H
oolong	a type of tea	Chinese	G, YB

(cont.)

Table 3.2 (*cont.*)

Item	English gloss	Source language(s)	Citations
paddy	rice in the husk or in the field	Sanskrit, Malay	G, YB, B, H
pagoda	a temple	Persian, Sanskrit, Portuguese	G, YB, B, H
pailow (pailou)	an ornamental gateway or arch	Chinese	G, YB, H
pidgin (pigeon)	a business, occupation	Pidgin	M, L, G, YB, B, H
piece (piecee)	a classifier e.g. 'one piece man'	Pidgin	M, L, YB, H
piece-goods	varieties of cloth and textiles	English	YB
pigtail	a plait or 'queue' of hair worn by men during the Qing dynasty	English	G, YB
puckerow, to	to seize, or misappropriate	Hindustani	G, YB
pukka (pakka)	permanent, correct or real	Hindustani	L, G, YB, BL
punkah	a large ceiling fan	Hindustani	L, G, YB, B, H
punti	1. local 2. Cantonese ethnicity and language	Cantonese	G
putchuck (putchock)	a fragrant root used for joss sticks	Malay	G, YB, H
rattan	a type of cane from a palm tree	Malay	G, YB, B
rice-Christians	Chinese Christian converts motivated by material gain	English	G, H
sampan	a small boat	Cantonese	L, G, YB, B, H
samshoo	a type of rice wine	Chinese	L, G, YB, H
savvy (sabe)	to know	Portuguese	M, L, G, YB, H
sepoy	a South Asian soldier	Persian, Portuguese	G, YB
side (si')	in a position or place, e.g. 'downside'	Pidgin	M, L, BL, H
sing-song	theatrical or similar entertainment	Pidgin	L, G
sola topee	a pith helmet worn for protection against the sun	Hindustani, Portuguese	G, YB, BL, H
soy (soya)	a plant used for beans and sauce	Chinese, Japanese	G, YB, B, H

Item	English gloss	Source language(s)	Citations
squeeze	a commission or bribe	English	L, G, YB, B, H
sycee	a type of silver	Chinese	L, G, YB, B, H
swanpan	an abacus	Chinese	G
tael	a weight equivalent to one sixteenth of a catty (approx. 38 grammes)	Malay, Portuguese	L, G, YB, B, H
taipan	the head of a trading house in South China	Cantonese	L, G, BL, H
tai-tai	the wife of a Chinese official	Chinese	G, H
tao-t'ai	a provincial officer during the Qing dynasty	Chinese	L, G, B, H
taoism	a system of philosophy and religion	Chinese	G, B
teapoy	a three-legged table	Anglo-Indian	G, YB, B
tiffin	lunch	English, Anglo-Indian	L, G, YB, BL, H
topaz (topas)	1. Someone of mixed Portuguese–Asian descent 2. a bathroom attendant	(poss.)Hindustani, Tamil	G, YB
triad	a Chinese secret society	English	G, B
twankay	a type of tea	Chinese	G, YB
tycoon	a wealthy businessman	Chinese, Japanese	G
typhoon (tyfoon)	a violent storm	Arabic	G, YB, BL, B, H
whanghee	a cane stick	Chinese	G, YB
yamun (yamen)	the official residence of a Chinese mandarin	Chinese	L, G, BL, B, H
yin and yang	the two fundamental forces of the universe, feminine and masculine	Chinese	G, B
yuloh	to row a boat	Shanghainese	L, G, H

Key to citations:
L = (Leland 1876); G = (Giles 1886); YB = (Yule and Burnell 1886); B = (Ball 1903); H = (Hill 1920); BL = (Barrère and Leland 1889); and M = (Morrison 1834)

expected. Many of the items listed here as 'China Coast' English later occur in lists of 'Hong Kong English', and are still in frequent use in Hong Kong. A number of these words have also passed into British, American and other Englishes.

In many other parts of the world where British colonies were established – North America, the Caribbean, South Africa, Australia, New Zealand and India – new lexicons were created in order to cope with the communicative needs of the new environment. This same process also occurred in treaty-port China, less obviously perhaps than in India and other parts of South Asia, but occur it did. At the same time, however, the notion of 'pidgin English' was being actively promoted in Britain and the United States in the conscious attempt to create a racially derogative stereotype of the Chinese in the minds of the western public.

Pidgin English and the representation of China in the West

Pidgin English represented the Chinese character to the West, particularly in Britain and the United States, through the periodical and popular press. A viciously racist example of this is the doggerel accompaniment to a *Punch* cartoon which appeared in 1858 (during the Second Opium War) (see figure 3.5). The line-drawn cartoon has a willow-pattern background and shows a Chinese mandarin striding forth, a curved sword in his right hand and a parasol in his left, his elongated queue in the hands of a costumed pageboy marching in step behind. The verse above the cartoon is entitled 'A Chanson for Canton'.

The political jingoism promoting the British cause for free trade ('not COBDEN himself can take off the ban / By humanity laid on JOHN CHINAMAN'), and the crassly offensive stereotyping of the Chinese character ('rogue', 'brute', 'cruel', 'stubborn', 'nasty', 'sly', 'coward') is accompanied by a pidgin couplet in the second stanza: 'Sing lie-tea, my sly JOHN CHINAMAN, No fightee, my coward JOHN CHINAMAN'. From the 1860s, similar treatments of pidgin, though not usually so directly obnoxious, began to appear in the comic supplements to treaty-port newspapers, and a collection of such verses formed the core of what was to be the most famous nineteenth-century source book on pidgin English, *Pidgin-English Sing-Song*, authored by Charles Godfrey Leland (1876). Leland was an American popular writer, journalist and slang lexicographer, who by the 1870s had settled in London. His *Pidgin-English Sing-Song* had a dual function. First, it served as phrasebook for westerners interested in learning the *lingo*, as the author explains: 'for those who expect to meet with Chinese, either in the East or California, this little book will perhaps be useful, as qualifying them to converse in Pidgin' (1876: 8). Second, it was also intended to reach the market for popular literature, where Leland already had a niche as a comic writer on German-Americans.

Leland never visited the Far East or China, but wrote *Pidgin-English Sing-Song* while he was in London, although he acknowledges the help of two celebrated sinologists, Robert Kennaway Douglas and Herbert Allen Giles. The book comprises some twenty-two 'Ballads', and twelve 'Stories' written in Leland's version

A CHANSON FOR CANTON.

JOHN CHINAMAN a rogue is born,
The laws of truth he holds in scorn;
About as great a brute as can
Encumber the Earth is JOHN CHINAMAN.
   Sing YEH, my cruel JOHN CHINAMAN,
   Sing Yeo, my stubborn JOHN CHINAMAN;
   Not COBDEN himself can take off the ban
   By humanity laid on JOHN CHINAMAN.

With their little pig-eyes and their large pig-tails,
And their diet of rats, dogs, slugs, and snails,
All seems to be game in the frying-pan
Of that nasty feeder, JOHN CHINAMAN.
   Sing lie-tea, my sly JOHN CHINAMAN,
   No fightee, my coward JOHN CHINAMAN:
   JOHN BULL has a chance—let him, if he can,
   Somewhat open the eyes of JOHN CHINAMAN.

Figure 3.5 A Chanson for Canton (*Punch*, 10 April 1858)
Source: Dawson 1967: 133.

of pidgin. In addition, at the end of the volume there is a list of 'Pidgin-English vocabulary', supplemented by a list of 'Pidgin-English names' comprising personal
and street names, chiefly from Hong Kong. Other pidgin English phrase books
were published in the treaty ports, notably Airey's *Pidgin English Tails* (1906) and
Hill's (1920) *Broken China*, but none achieved the popularity of *Pidgin-English
Sing-Song*. Leland was evidently very proud of his role as a pidgin scholar as,
in 1891, he wrote to his niece about his participation in the Oriental Congress
where:

> I was referred to in the Congress as being 'beyond question at the *very head*
> of Pidgin English learning and literature'. There's a proud position for a
> man! Yes – I am the Shakespeare and Milton and Grimm and Heine and
> Everybody Else of that language. When pidgin English shall become...
> the common language of the world, then I shall be a great man! (Pennel
> 1906: 349)

Reading Leland's verses, however, reveals a crude racism not too distant from
the *Punch* verses of 1858, as illustrated by an excerpt from the ditty 'Ping-
Wing':

> PING-WING he pie-man son,
> He velly worst chilo allo Can-ton,
> He steal he mother picklum mice,
> An thlowee cat in bilin' rice.
> Hab chow-chow up, an' 'Now,' talk he,
> 'My wonda' where he meeow cat be?'
> . . .
> Ping-Wing see gentleum wailo – go
> He scleamee, 'Hai yah – fan-kwei lo!'
> All-same you savvy in Chinese,
> 'One foleign devil lookee see!'
> But gentleum t'hat pidgin know,
> He catchee Ping and floggum so,
> T'hat allo-way flom that day, maskee
> He velly good littee Chinee.
> (Leland 1876: 29–30)

Leland's 'rhymes and stories' were penned not only during an era of unequalled
western expansion into China through the treaty-port system, but also during
a period of mounting sinophobia in the United States. By the 1870s, the US
government was already taking initiatives to exclude Chinese immigrants from
settling in the country, and the 1882 Exclusion Act was to remain in effect until
1943 (Lee 1996). Leland's book contributed to an anti-Chinese discourse that
was spread across all classes of society in both the United States and Britain.
By the turn of the century in Britain, cheap Chinese labour was seen as a threat
to the British working class, at a time when a few Chinese immigrants were

attempting to establish themselves as laundry-owners or laundry-workers. Lee reports that in 1906, at least one Liverpool newspaper carried a report on the Chinese consumption of cats and reflects that even in the British cultural imagery of the 1990s, 'the trope of the cat-eating Oriental is as popular as ever' (Lee 1996: 232).

In this context, it again seems ironic that, despite his flawed scholarship and obvious racism, contemporary pidgin scholars indicate that 'Leland probably did more than anyone else to draw attention to the existence of CPE' (Tryon, Mühlhäusler & Baker 1996: 486).

Linguistic theory, pidgins and creoles

Nineteenth-century linguistics was dominated by the 'comparative' method associated with such German linguists as Bopp, Grimm and Schleicher. These linguists concentrated on the careful analysis of linguistic data, with particular reference to the sound patterns or 'sound laws' of languages in the Indo-European language family. They also sought to establish genetic relationships between languages and the links between living languages and extinct parent or 'proto-' languages, which might then be reconstructed on the basis of linguistic evidence. By the end of the nineteenth century, comparative linguists were confident that they would be able to provide a classification of the world's languages and to construct genealogical trees of all the world's language families. Tree diagrams of the kind drawn by August Schleicher (1821–68) provided iconic representations of the genetic and kinship relationships that existed between languages, contributing to his *Stammbaum* theory of languages (Bolton 2000c).

The early nineteenth century saw missionary work on Caribbean creoles, Indo-Portuguese in Sri Lanka and a range of other mixed languages and jargons, but it was not until the 1880s that such varieties attracted the notice of serious linguists schooled in the German tradition. The foremost of these was the German-born Hugo Schuchardt, who never ventured to the tropics but developed his intense interest in language-mixing through a massive correspondence with missionaries, colonial administrators and others living in societies where pidgins and creoles were spoken. Schuchardt published over forty articles on pidgins and creoles between 1880 and 1914, and is regarded by some as 'the father of creole studies' (Holm 1988: 29). Schuchardt and his contemporary, Johannes Schmidt, developed the notion of a 'wave theory' (*Wellentheorie*) as an alternative to Schleicher's tree model of language families. Languages like pidgins and creoles presented a number of problems for comparative linguists, not least among which was the challenge that such contact languages posed to the family-tree model of language relationships. The question was, 'Where is there a place in the conventional tree for languages originating from two very different parts of the world which somehow combine to form a "mixed language"?' (Sebba 1997: 34). A second issue related to the speed of language change; pidgins and creoles could appear and evolve very rapidly, contrary to the principle of gradual change derived from the 'uniformitarianism' of nineteenth-century geology.

The study of pidgins and creole languages has grown into a distinct branch of linguistics over the past thirty or so years, but many of the ideas debated within this field have their provenance in much earlier discussions of language variation. One basic distinction is that between *pidgins* and *creoles*. A typical linguistic definition is that '[a] *pidgin* is a simple, spoken language which evolves to permit communication between people who do not share a mother tongue', in contrast to *creoles*, which are 'the mother tongues of groups of speakers'. A second distinction is that 'a pidgin tends to be learnt in conjunction with one or more mother tongues', and 'a creole tends to be the sole mother tongue of its speakers' (Todd and Hancock 1986: 351–2). There were many theoretical discussions in the 1960s and 1970s on the *monogenesis/polygenesis* dichotomy. The monogenetic explanation was simply that 'many of the world's pidgins and creoles could be traced to a common origin, the Portuguese pidgin that arose in the fifteenth century in Africa... that was eventually relexified (or translated word for word) into the pidgins of other European lexical bases that gave rise to the modern creoles' (Holm 1988: 46). The polygenetic view is that 'pidgins and creoles arose independently... but developed in parallel ways because they used common linguistic material (from Indo-European and West African languages in particular) and were formed in similar physical and social conditions' (Romaine 1988: 92).

Another biologically related term widely used in the discussion of pidgin, creoles and mixed languages is *hybridisation*. Whinnom (1971) argues that 'not only is there no other wholly satisfactory term for the phenomenon of language-mixing, but, *mutatis mutandis*, the biological and linguistic processes of hybridization are closely comparable if not mechanically identical' (1971: 91).

He further distinguishes between 'primary', 'secondary' and 'tertiary' hybridisation. For biologists, he argues, primary hybridisation equates with 'fragmentation'. Secondary hybridisation is 'the inter-breeding of distinct species', which in linguistics is matched by such processes as 'naïve' foreign-language learning and bilingualism (1971: 91–2), but tertiary hybridisation refers to the use of a pidgin *lingua franca* by speakers who do not share a common first language. It is language-specific and has no biological analogue (1971: 105). In the context of World Englishes, McArthur uses the term 'hybridisation' to refer to a wide range of language contact phenomena, including code-switching and code-mixing, as well as the use of 'Anglo-hybrids' such as Frenglish, Russlish and Chinglish (1998: 14, 45).

Linguistics and hybridisation

In recent years, scholars in literary and cultural studies have been attracted by the notions of hybridisation and hybridity discussed in the writings of Mikhail Bakhtin. Bakhtin's notion of 'double voicedness' associated with hybridisation, 'a mixture of two social languages within the limits of a single utterance, an encounter, within the arena of an utterance, between two different linguistic consciousnesses, separated from one another by an epoch, by social differentiation, or by some other factor' (1981: 358), has been frequently invoked in the discussion of the cadences and creolisation of new literatures in English.

In linguistics, the term 'hybrid' may have a specific meaning with reference to lexical (or 'vocabulary') borrowing, but the notion of hybridisation seems not to extend to any wider, precisely articulated theory of language contact. Nor does it seem that the term is now considered an important item of metalanguage for those working in the field of pidgin and creole studies. A reading of contemporary accounts of pidgins and creoles reveals a relatively low level of agreement on theoretical and discursive frameworks. At the level of description, other issues include the mechanisms of *depidginisation* and *decreolisation*, the processes by which mixed languages are influenced by, and approximate towards, 'standard languages' in speech communities where both varieties are present. A number of controversies in the field still focus on the nineteenth-century theories of 'monogenetic' versus 'polygenetic' explanations, seemingly unaware of the power such terms had in nineteenth-century debates on the racial classification of human beings, and the role of such concepts in the development of race theory. Elsewhere, I have argued in some detail that, in the Chinese context, fear of racial mixing and racial miscegenation was located at the heart of the treaty-port response to pidgin, which might help explain why such varieties were often vilified as 'bastardised jargons' (Bolton 2000c: 47).

Many descriptive linguists see their main task as the systematic, if not scientific, description of language, and consider 'lay' opinions (i.e. views uninformed by linguistics as a discipline) to be biased and inaccurate. Kale, for example, asserts that 'pidgins and creoles are, linguistically speaking, languages with equal status to other languages and not merely broken forms or second-rate varieties of some other language', and that 'it would appear to be the layperson's knowledge about the supposed limitations of pidgins which has perpetuated the unfortunate and inaccurate belief that these languages are simple and unsystematic forms of some other language' (1990: 107).

It seems again ironic, that, in the case of 'Chinese pidgin English', pidgin scholars have relied almost exclusively on the jottings and memoirs of laypersons such as sailors, merchants, missionaries, diplomats and journalists to provide them with their primary data.

Depidginisation and the spread of English in China and Hong Kong

From the late nineteenth century onwards, in Hong Kong, as well as in the other parts of China, the key factor in shifting the acquisition and use of English from a pidgin form towards a more 'standard' variety of English was access to instruction, and access to schools where English was taught. With access to the

English of the classroom, the process of depidginisation could then occur. As early as 1870, Dennys wrote that this process was underway, and notes '[n]umbers of Chinese, indeed, thanks to emigration to the United States, and the increased facilities available in the British Government schools at Hong-kong, now learn to talk English with fluency and correctness' (Dennys 1870: 119); and by 1934 Green comments that 'hundreds of mission schools have for years past been turning out thousands of Chinese who speak English at least as well as most non-English peoples' (Green 1934: 331).

One important agency for the teaching of English in China between the late 1830s and 1949 was Protestant missionary education, but the practice of English teaching in missionary schools and colleges was by no means uncontested. In spite of the virtual colonisation of treaty ports by western powers, led by Britain and America, there was no direct equivalent to the 'Anglicist' policy promoted by Macaulay's (1835) Minute on Indian Education. The approach of missionaries and colonial officials was often much less anglicist than orientalist, albeit a brand of orientalism with distinctly evangelical characteristics. Many missionaries were active in the field of dialect studies and lexicography, and Protestant missionaries also energetically promoted the romanising (or 'alphabetising') of biblical, religious and educational texts. Between 1890 and 1904, 133,870 extracts or complete Bibles were published in romanisation, while only 2 per cent of religious materials were printed in Mandarin (DeFrancis 1950: 23). Such missionary fondness for dialects was promoted partly by a distrust of Mandarin as an analogue of Papist Latin, and partly by the very practical need to communicate directly with their often uneducated constituency.

Some of the first missionary schools were established in Hong Kong, notably the Morrison Education Society School (opened at Macao in 1839) and the Anglo-Chinese College (which moved to Hong Kong from Malacca in 1843). Other schools, established by American and British missionaries, followed at Ningbo (1851), Shanghai (1851) and Dengzhou (1866) and, by 1877, there were twenty such schools teaching some 231 students (Deng 1997: 32). In the early years of the twentieth century, the numbers of Protestant missionary schools multiplied; by 1911, there were more than 3,000 operating in China, catering to an estimated 139,000 pupils (Deng 1997: 32). From around 1890, there was also a great expansion in higher education at university level, and around sixteen Protestant and Catholic colleges and universities were established and run by western missionaries in the period 1890–1949 (see pp. 231–3).

In the missionary schools, the curriculum typically consisted of both Chinese and 'western' subjects, and the Chinese Classics often occupied a central position, as most missionaries believed their pupils needed to gain proficiency in their own language and literature. English was taught in a substantial number of schools, though its use as a teaching medium was the subject of fierce debate. The Presbyterian Calvin W. Mateer, a founder of Shantung (Shandong) (Cheeloo) University, believed that education should serve the aim of providing a native ministry, that all instruction should be given in Chinese and that this should be done through the medium of the Chinese dialects:

> I believe in colloquial literature, as the kind of literature of the Christian work in China. Who believe the gospel we preach? Who fill all churches? The unlearned and the poor. Let us not ignore the providence of God in this matter. Let us adapt our Bibles, our books, and religious literature generally, to the class of people he gives us. If colloquial language is good enough to preach the Gospel, it is good enough to write it also. (Mateer 1878: 222)

In spite of the opposition of Mateer and others, English continued to gain ground in many missionary schools, as its use was linked to the teaching of scientific subjects. Even so, strong opposition to the widespread use of English continued into the following century:

> The protagonists maintained that many Chinese wish to learn English and that if a missionary did not teach it they would get it elsewhere under non-Christian auspices... The opponents contended that few pupils remained in school long enough to acquire sufficient English to enable them to read it well... and that most of those seeking it desired it only as a means of obtaining employment in the customs service, in minor government positions, and in foreign business houses. (Latourette 1929: 443)

A missionary like Tenney (1889), who advocated a role for English in the teaching of science, was also concerned to emphasise a continued place for Chinese, arguing that '[b]oth should be recognized as part of the same great movement, the awakening of China' (Tenney 1889: 470). Nevertheless, many missionary schools responded to parental demands for English, and thus provided an educational access to English, at least in the treaty ports throughout China. Missionary secondary and college education would survive on the mainland until the founding of the People's Republic in 1949, after which many missionary organisations retreated to Hong Kong.

In Hong Kong, a system of elite government and missionary schools slowly developed over the second half of the nineteenth century, although most of these schools provided instruction in Chinese as well as English. In nineteenth-century Hong Kong, an English-language education could pave the way for a position as interpreter, compradore, lawyer, doctor, or government advisor. English-medium schooling was also given increased encouragement through the establishment of the University of Hong Kong in 1911. At the opening of the university the then-governor of Hong Kong, Sir Frederick Lugard, discussed the importance of English in education. Just as Latin had once been the language of learning in Europe, there might be a similar role for English in China. Claiming that '[t]he vast populations of China speak no common language, nor is the Chinese written language well adapted as a vehicle of Western knowledge', Lugard suggested that:

> If then for a period China should find it necessary, as the nations of the West did, to use an alien tongue as a common medium for new thoughts and expressions, I should imagine that no language would be more suitable than English, which already in a 'pidgin' form constitutes a medium for the exchange of ideas between merchants of the North and South. If 'pidgin' English has served as a medium for commerce why should not King's English serve as medium for Western education? (Lugard 1908, cited in Mellor 1992: 72)

It was hoped that the university would serve the mainland, and its original aims included training doctors and engineers to serve in China, as well as providing arts graduates for the Chinese civil service. The fall of the Manchu government in 1911, however, led to a succession of political disturbances which culminated in virtual civil war in Canton (Guangdong) province in the 1920s, and prevented the implementation of the university's original aims (Cheng 1949).

During the 1920s and 1930s, there was a wide variety of schools in existence, including government schools, missionary schools and private schools. In 1935, a government report on education, authored by E. Burney, estimated that only one third to one half of children of school age were actually receiving education. Of these, the vast majority received primary education in 'private vernacular schools', which received no government support. Very few schools were receiving government support at this time, which meant that access to education was severely restricted. As a result, varieties of 'pidginised' English continued to appear in Hong Kong up to the 1960s, according to Whinnom (1971), who explained the continued use of pidgin with reference to social class in Hong Kong, asserting that: 'The Chinese community in Hong Kong cannot be treated as a whole. There is, as it were, a "substrate section" of the community in which pidgin is maintained, most notably among servants, taxi-drivers, small shopkeepers, and the like' (1971: 102). Whinnom went on to note that '[m]iddle- and upper-class Chinese speak Chinese or English, but never pidgin, which they despise as the mark of a socially inferior class', adding that '[t]he rewards in Hong Kong for superior performance in English are considerable, and a good deal of very active language-learning and language-teaching must be one of the principal reasons for the slow decline in the use of pidgin' (1971: 102–3). Nevertheless, it was not until the 1970s and 1980s, as noted in chapter 2, that a system of universal education was established in the colony, which allowed the spread of English throughout the 'new middle class', on a scale hitherto unseen.

Chinese Englishes in South China, 1637 to the present

This chapter has attempted to trace the development of English in South China from the origins of cultural and linguistic contact in the early seventeenth century, through the era of the Canton trade, to 1950s and 1960s Hong Kong. As noted above, by far the most influential description of Chinese pidgin English was that of Leland (1876), an American who never visited China, and whose 'comic' description of the variety coincided with an era of western intrusion into China after the Second Opium War, as well as with violent anti-Chinese feelings and the exclusion of Chinese immigrants from the United States. From western sources, it would appear that 'pidgin English' was twice constructed by two very different types of discourse: first, as the voice of 'John Chinaman' in the popular magazine literature of the nineteenth century; and second, in the technically oriented literature of pidgin and creole studies, which began with Jespersen in the 1920s, gathered momentum with Reinecke (1937), and continues to the present with the work of Baker and Mühlhäusler (1990), among others.

At least two links might be made between these two opposing discourses. First, there is the use of a biologically or racially determined vocabulary, which is found to be multilevelled in both discourses. Thus the 'bastard' tongue of the layman's description becomes the 'hybridised' variety of the creolist. Second, both discourses seem to make an investment in describing pidgin English as a monoglossic and invariant system. In the earlier colonial accounts, pidgin English is seen as emblematic of both the problems of linguistic communication faced by the westerner in China and the sly, deceitful character of the 'heathen Chinee'. The argument that Chinese pidgin English was fixed and invariant, or 'stable', throughout most of its history is undermined by the history of events. It is perhaps easiest to claim some kind of stability for the system in its early stages. For example, when Wells Williams described it in 1836, he made the point that he was describing an extremely limited vocabulary, reporting that '[t]he number of words peculiar to the Canton-English, either in the word itself, or in the signification attached to it, is not great; perhaps there are fifty' (1836: 433).

In later decades, there is strong evidence that pidgin would have been regarded as a transitional variety by many learners of the language wishing to gain a wider competence in a fuller form of English. Fisher, a British army officer stationed at Canton in 1860, reported that many of the Chinese that he met were aware that there were two varieties of English in existence:

> Sing-chong used to think that we had, like them, a mandarin dialect and a vulgar tongue, the latter being that called pigeon ... All with whom we dealt appeared desirous to learn our mandarin dialect, and one officer gravely taught Lee-ching, a shopkeeper, whom we dealt with largely, to say to his customers when he wished to induce them to buy – 'I am aware that my prices are exorbitant', and the poor man learnt it quite in good faith. In writing, more time being given for deliberation than in speaking, their composition was much more careful. (Fisher 1863: 98)

The view that pidgin, rather than English, was the target of Chinese learners is also seriously challenged by the evidence of Tong's (1862) *Chinese and English Instructor*. The main function of Tong's book was as a dictionary and manual of *English*, and the evidence shows that the *fāanwáa*, or 'pidgin', was added as an afterthought. From the 1840s until the 1930s, there was increased social and linguistic contact between westerners and Chinese in Hong Kong and the other treaty ports, where an 'Anglo-Chinese', or 'China Coast' vocabulary of English developed. It is thus possible to argue that there is a line of historical development which begins with the jargon of 'Canton English' in the late eighteenth century, continues with 'China Coast English' (or 'Anglo-Chinese') in the late nineteenth and early twentieth centuries, and extends to the present in the English of contemporary Hong Kong.

4   The emergence of Hong Kong English as a 'new English'

For the British peoples, English is a birthright eagerly inherited. But for other nations it is a difficult acquisition. I sometimes wonder why they are anxious to learn it. I once set the question as an examination essay, and from more than one candidate got the answer because 'Americans use it'.   (Simpson 1933: 51)

New English or Old English, if Hong Kong wants English, then Hong Kong must make English its own.   (Harris 1989: 45–6)

We are the unwalled city . . . Don't you see? Here in Hong Kong, we were never inside the wall. We're like barbarians. Mongols at bay.
  (Albert Ho, talking to an American friend, the night of the 1997 handover in Xu Xi's 2000 novel *The Unwalled City*)

While Asian Englishes such as Indian English, Malaysian English, Philippine English and Singapore English have gained wide acceptance over the past twenty years, relatively little notice has been given to the notion of a distinct variety of 'Hong Kong English'. This chapter surveys the sociolinguistic background to the recognition of Hong Kong English, and considers the arguments in favour of a 'paradigm shift' which accommodates the emergence and recognition of Hong Kong English as a localised variety on a par with other 'outer-circle' Asian Englishes (see chapter 1).

World Englishes and the paradigm shift

Over the last fifteen years or so, Braj Kachru has suggested a model of global English in terms of 'three concentric circles': *the inner circle* (countries where English is the 'first language' of a majority of the population, for example, the USA, Britain, Australia and New Zealand); *the outer circle* (where English has the status of a 'second language', for example, India or the Philippines); and *the extending* (or 'expanding') *circle* (where English has the status of a 'foreign language', for example, China or Japan). In a sustained academic campaign for a non-Eurocentric approach to the study of World Englishes, Kachru has challenged a number of assumptions about the study of English as a global language.

In particular he has been eager to dispatch such sacred cows as the 'native speaker' versus 'non-native speaker' dichotomy, arguing for a 'pluricentric' approach to the acquisition and use of 'new' varieties of English or, more precisely, 'World Englishes' in such outer-circle areas as Bangladesh, Kenya, Malaysia, Nigeria, the Philippines and Singapore. This approach challenges the 'native speaker idealisation' myth, the 'native vs. nonnative speaker interaction' myth, the 'culture identity (or monoculture)' myth, the 'exocentric norm' myth and the 'interlanguage' myth (Kachru 1997: 10). Kachru also challenges the dominance of the Anglocentric literary canon, demanding the recognition of bilingual creativity in the 'new literatures' in English that have appeared in Africa, Asia and the Caribbean, and the extent to which these 'contact literatures in English' have undergone *nativisation* and *acculturation*. He argues that in South Asia, West Africa and Southeast Asia these literatures are thus 'both nativised and acculturated', as instanced by the work of Wole Soyinka from Nigeria and Raja Rao of India, and that the issue of bilingual creativity is an important area for linguistic, literary and pedagogical research (Kachru 1986c). The current sociolinguistic reality in World Englishes is that speakers of a wide range of first languages communicate with one another through English, and 'a speaker of a Bantu language may interact with a speaker of Japanese, a Taiwanese, an Indian, and so on'. As a result English has become acculturated in many 'un-English' sociolinguistic contexts – in societies where there is no shared Judaeo-Christian or European cultural heritage, or shared literary canon – and thus the English language has become 'multi-canonical' (Kachru 1991).

Kachru has further urged a rethink towards the teaching of English worldwide, calling for a two-fold 'paradigm shift' in approaches to English studies:

> First, a paradigm shift in research, teaching, and application of sociolinguistic realities to the functions of English. Second, a shift from frameworks and theories which are essentially appropriate only to monolingual countries. It is indeed essential to recognise that World Englishes represent certain linguistic, cultural and pragmatic realities and pluralism, and that pluralism is now an integral part of World Englishes and literatures written in Englishes. The pluralism of English must be reflected in the approaches, both theoretical and applied, we adopt for understanding this unprecedented linguistic phenomenon. (1992: 11)

In a (1997) paper on 'English as an Asian Language', Kachru notes that the English-using population of Asia totalled 350 million out of an estimated population of 3.5 billion; that India was the third largest English-using nation after the USA and the UK; that English was the language most in demand for acquisition of bilingualism/multilingualism in Asia; and that in some societies, including Singapore, English was assuming the role of first language, 'whatever we mean by that term' (1997: 7). He argues for an acceptance of 'English on Asian terms', noting that in Asia English has a potential as a liberating language. A language is liberated through its autonomy and thus its 'liberated' uses and functions have to be separated from its non-liberated uses. Again, Kachru emphasises the importance of literary creativity in this context, and argues for the acculturation of English to the needs and visions of Asian societies:

> The architects of each tradition, each strand, have molded, reshaped, acculturated, redesigned, and – by doing so – enriched what was a Western medium. The result is a liberated English which contains vitality, innovation, linguistic mix, and cultural identity. And, it is not the creativity of the monolingual and the monocultural – this creativity has rejuvenated the medium from 'exhaustion' and has 'liberated' it in many ways. (1997: 23)

In the case of Hong Kong, two related questions arise. First, is it possible to argue that the conditions now exist for a recognition of the 'autonomy' of Hong Kong English, on a par with other Englishes in the Asian region? Second, has the time also come to recognise the 'creativity' of English in Hong Kong, as evidenced by recent literary initiatives?

From Canton English to Hong Kong English

As shown in chapter 3, the origins of English in China, and of Hong Kong English itself, can be traced back to the early seventeenth century, when the first British trading ships reached Macao and Canton. In chapter 2, we saw that the social and political dynamics of 'modern Hong Kong', from the 1960s to the 1990s, helped create a modern cosmopolitan society, materially based on the dramatically expanding economy that allowed for the formation of a new middle class, who sought access to English either for themselves or for their children. The earlier system of elite schooling in English and 'elitist bilingualism' was replaced by a system of mass bilingualism (or folk bilingualism), which provided students with the opportunity to learn at least some English in 'Anglo-Chinese' secondary schools where English textbooks were used. University enrolment increased from around 2–4 per cent at the beginning of the 1980s to 17 per cent by 1996, with another 8 per cent studying overseas. Today there are eight local universities, compared with just two in 1980 and, at these, English is widely used as the language of lectures and textbooks. The educational reforms of the 1970s and 1980s led to the spread of English in 'modern' Hong Kong society, with the numbers of those in censuses claiming a knowledge of English rising from 9.7 per cent in 1961, to 38.1 per cent in 1996, and to 43 per cent in 2001.

During the 1990s, when an increased knowledge of English was spreading throughout society, official government language policy began to promote Chinese, both Cantonese and Putonghua, in the civil service, law and education. This policy was in part based on understandable concerns to provide a system of education accessible to all. In the years immediately prior to the 1997 handover, there also was a distinct tendency towards the greater use of Chinese in official domains such as the civil service, law and broadcasting. Post-1997, the use of spoken English in the Legislative Council and government press conferences, for example, has declined, but written English is still the language of internal documents within the civil service, the legal system and the police force. On the broader issue of the acquisition and use of English in the wider society, it is perhaps too soon to judge its prospects. Education is obviously a crucial domain, but although the 'firm policy' promoting Chinese-medium education was introduced in March 1997, there are already indications that this policy is being modified (see pp. 95–8 above). Whatever decisions are made at the secondary level, English remains the main language of textbooks and lectures at most universities in Hong Kong, although the exact balance of languages varies from institution to institution (Walters and Balla 1998).

In its 1999 policy address, the Hong Kong government announced its intention to strengthen the 'international' profile of the territory, and to promote Hong Kong as a 'world-class city' on a par with New York and London. Offered a choice between affirming Hong Kong's identity as a southern Chinese city or as a 'global' city, Hong Kong's Beijing-vetted government has opted for the latter. Such an identity choice inevitably involves the retention of English, if only for 'pragmatic' and 'business' considerations. In addition, at the time of writing, Hong Kong is also attempting to reposition itself as a centre of IT development and commerce. The government is now sponsoring a 64-acre 'Cyberport' initiative, which has received backing from Microsoft and other international IT companies. A recent policy address of the Hong Kong Special Administrative Region (HKSAR) government similarly emphasises a need for Hong Kong to restructure its economy to meet the needs of 'a knowledge-based era' (HKSAR Government 2001: 3). In the same document, the government affirms that:

> It is our policy to promote bi-literacy and tri-lingualism. Hong Kong is a cosmopolitan city, and it needs to promote the wider use of basic English. As part of China, Hong Kong people should also learn to speak fluent Putonghua. (2001: 13)

It seems, therefore, that in Hong Kong's rapidly changing society English is here to stay, although perceptions of its role have been crucially affected by a range of ideologies. Such ideologies have influenced the opinions of academics as well as those of the general public.

In chapter 2 (pp. 107–18 above), I characterised three sets of interlocking ideologies relating to English in the territory as 'the falling standards myth', the 'monolingualism myth' and the 'invisibility myth'. I have discussed the first two at some length, but perhaps more needs to be said about the third, which centrally involves a consideration of the notion of 'Hong Kong English'. At the core of this 'invisibility' myth is the argument that there is no such variety of English, because the specific demographics of English in Hong Kong dictate that Hong Kong Chinese will always opt to speak Cantonese or 'mixed code' to one another. Johnson, for example, claims that:

English is the means for dealing with and competing with expatriates, not for joining them... There is no social and cultural role for English to play among Hong Kong Chinese; it only has a role in their relations with expatriates and the outside world. (1994: 181–2)

Johnson is not alone in having such perceptions, nor are they confined to 'expatriate' academics. Li (1999) argues that there has been little change in the status of English in the last two decades, and that it does not fit into the usual ESL or EFL categorisation:

Its uniqueness lies in the fact that being an official language (along with Chinese since 1974), the presence of English can be felt from both from print and broadcast media to public means of transport, from business documents and school textbooks to street signs. It is therefore manifestly not a foreign language. On the other hand, unlike many post-colonial societies such as India, Nigeria and the Philippines, English is rarely used by Chinese Hongkongers for intra-ethnic communication. There is thus no societal basis for any nativised variety of 'Hong Kong English'. Instead the norms of correctness as referenced in the key domains of education, government, business and law follow those of standard English varieties, especially British English, hence 'exonormative'... (Li 1999: 95)

There are number of problems with this reasoning, the first of which is the implication that in societies such as the Philippines local norms are chiefly 'taught' rather than 'caught', as is the case in Hong Kong. I would rather suggest, however, that in both societies local norms of usage are largely covert rather than overt. Even though the notional 'target language' in a Hong Kong context may be 'standard (RP-accented) British English' only a very small minority of locally educated children ever approximate to such a norm (see pp. 206–9 below). At the same time, while it is true that linguists and educators in the Philippines now recognise the existence of 'Philippine English', norms of American English, particularly at a grammatical level, are still valued within education. The main issue in the Philippines perhaps (as in Hong Kong) relates to the recognition of English as one of the key languages of the society, as a language of Filipinos, not just of Americans or other foreigners. In this context, it is worth noting that it is not the case (as Li suggests above) that 'pure' English is widely used for conversational purposes on an intra-ethnic basis in the Philippines. Instead, the norm among English-knowing bilinguals is widespread code-switching and code-mixing, so that in Manila, for example, the use of 'Taglish' tends to be the unmarked code of choice (Rafael 2000).

In the Hong Kong context, Johnson's and Li's analyses above seem to be underpinned by the ideology that the ethnic and linguistic diversity of this society can be reduced to two groups – Chinese and the westerners – and that the degree of contact between such communities is minimal. Luke and Richards earlier claimed that the language situation in Hong Kong approximated to that of 'diglossia without bilingualism', and that Hong Kong was:

> a society where two or more languages are used, but in which (a) individual linguistic repertoires are largely confined to one of the languages of the society; (b) a single language is used for intragroup communication; (c) bilingualism is restricted to certain domains of intergroup contact; (d) the bilingual population is narrowly based, rather than being a broadly based population segment; (e) speech communities are marked by relatively impermeable group boundaries; (f) the society does not consist of a single speech community but two distinct speech communities; (g) intragroup monolingualism rather than bilingualism is the norm. With some exceptions, this could be a relatively accurate description of Hong Kong. (1982: 51)

They consider Hong Kong to be 'a case of societal bilingualism in which two largely monolingual communities coexist, with a small group of bilingual Cantonese functioning as "linguistic middle men"' (1982: 51). The problem here, however, is that the notion of 'two largely monolingual communities' divided by 'impermeable group boundaries' was empirically shaky even in 1983 and, by the late 1990s, completely untenable in view of an increasingly hybrid Hong Kong culture (see chapter 2).

Although such perceptions persist even (or perhaps especially) among academics, my own view is that, by the 1990s, Hong Kong had become increasingly multilingual and multicultural. The waves of emigration of the late 1980s and early 1990s coupled with the educational emigration of students to overseas universities have helped create a younger generation with a noticeably 'hip' international orientation. 'Returnee' children now account for 70 per cent of the student population in the previously 'expatriate' English Schools Foundation (ESF). Stay-at-home students have also become increasingly cosmopolitan over the last decade, negotiating their internationalism partly through English and 'mixed code', and increasingly through electronic media such as the internet.

Hong Kong's elite has long been multicultural, and an overseas education has been the norm for their children over almost thirty years. In local 'dynastic' families – the owners of banks and major Hong Kong companies – a degree of intermarriage with Europeans and Americans has been acceptable for decades. This is now true of other social classes as well, particularly if we consider that the notion of 'Eurasians' as a distinct class now seems distinctly dated. Until the 1930s, the Hong Kong government kept statistics on the number of Eurasians in the colony. Today, such statistics are no longer kept but, given the Hong Kong Chinese diaspora in Europe and North America, and the frequency of biracial marriages in the territory itself, there are probably many thousands of Hong Kong families with 'biracial' relatives. The notion of 'impermeable' racial boundaries now seems strangely quaint.

For many ordinary Hong Kong families, English has become part of their daily lives in a variety of different ways. Children of all ages devote hours of homework to the study of the language, and often older siblings are drafted by parents to help their younger brothers and sisters. A large proportion of undergraduates at the University of Hong Kong moonlight as English tutors, coaxing their young charges through their textbook exercises. Parents with a knowledge of the language and the time to spare often pitch in to help, or practise simple conversational skills with their children. In addition, there are now around 160,000 Filipina domestic helpers or 'amahs' working in the territory, who often use English as their main language and function as unofficial tutors to their charges.

Since 1993, the international revolution in electronic communications such as the internet and email has had an immense impact upon Hong Kong and Hong Kong students. A 2002 survey in the territory indicates that almost 60 per cent of Hong Kong households had a personal computer connected to the internet (Luk 2002). Patterns of language use in this context vary, and many of the local websites operate in Chinese, but among students at the University of Hong Kong there appears to be a decided preference for the use of English for email and online chat. The web is now used as an instructional medium in a range of disciplines throughout all the territory's universities, with the predominant language of academic access being English. For relaxation, many students surf bilingually and biculturally, accessing popular entertainment sites, music, film sites and other webpages in both Chinese and English. The restaurant and bar areas popular among young Hongkongers also attract resident British and Americans, ethnic Chinese from local international schools and returnee kids from Canadian and US universities. This kind of multicultural mix was virtually unknown twenty years ago, and the complete range of purposes for which young Hong Kong people 'need' English today varies from the mundane to the imaginative.

Many of the lower-middle-class and working-class children at local universities have parents who emigrated from mainland China to Hong Kong in the past few decades, and who have little or no knowledge of English themselves. In such families it is frequently true that the children have little chance to speak English, but when they graduate from university and begin work in the business sector, as the majority do, they often find an immediate use for both the spoken and written language. This is particularly the case if they manage to secure a job in one of the international companies based in the territory, where they will be working with colleagues from other Asian societies. Spoken English also serves an intraethnic communicative purpose between some Hong Kong Cantonese speakers and Putonghua speakers from mainland China.

Comparing Asian Englishes – recognition and legitimation

At all events, Johnson's and Li's contention that the recognition of Hong Kong English as an autonomous variety somehow depends on the use of 'pure' English between Hong Kong Cantonese speakers appears restrictive to say the least. An alternative view is that within the Asian region localised Englishes have assumed particular functions and roles related to the specifics of each speech community. For example, in Singapore English is used as an interethnic *lingua franca* between the majority Chinese population and sizeable minorities of Singaporean Malays and South Asians, which also has assisted the development of its intraethnic use. Those conditions do not exist in Hong Kong, however, and a better comparison might be with the Philippines, where the vast majority of English speakers share a command of the national language, Filipino, and/or regional languages such as Cebuano and Ilocano.

Philippine English started to achieve recognition as early as the late 1960s, with the publication of Teodoro Llamzon's (1969) pioneering study of *Standard Filipino English*. Llamzon and others have described the characteristics of Philippine English phonology, while at the same time endorsing the retention of 'General American' as a teaching model in the education system (Llamzon 1997). At the level of syntax, Gonzalez identifies such distinguishing features as the restructuring of the tense/aspect system, the use of articles, the sub-classification of verbs and nouns, the selectional restrictions or co-occurrence rules between verbs and nouns, verb and preposition combinations, and the use of two- and three-word verbs (Gonzalez 1983, 1997). Lexically, Bautista recently carried out a detailed study of Philippine English vocabulary items based on 'the English spoken by educated Filipinos', which includes new coinages in English as well as significant numbers of loans from Philippine languages (Bautista 1997).

Philippine linguists have argued for the recognition of a localised variety of English partly on linguistic grounds, by pointing to sets of features at the major levels of linguistic analysis, but also with reference to 'non-linguistic' factors. Llamzon (1983) identifies four other defining characteristics of 'new Englishes' namely, *ecological features*, *historical features*, *sociolinguistic features* and *cultural features*, notably the existence of a 'new literature' in the language. In many respects, the view that emerges from the literature, as well as from discussions with Philippine linguists and other Filipinos, is that Philippine English is now an energetic and maturing variety of Asian English in a society that has shed much of the baggage of the colonial past. At a 1996 conference in Manila, for example, the Philippine poet Gemino Abad asserted, 'The English language is now ours. We have colonized it too' (*Philippine Daily Inquirer* 1996).

While acknowledging the recognition accorded to Philippine English by international scholars, Gonzalez (1997) also notes that this variety also faces its own problems of 'legitimation', an issue that goes back at least as far as Prator's (1968) attack on the 'heresy in British TESL', authored with the Philippine situation in view. With reference to his own (1983) paper on the distinction between 'errors' and 'features', Gonzalez notes that the question of 'standards' in Asian Englishes is still controversial. In his view, '[t]here can be no doubt of the reality of local varieties of English in a society such as that of the Philippines, where the English language has been used as a second language by speakers of Philippine languages of Malayo-Polynesian/Austronesian provenance, which exhibit more or less the same structural features', but there are still issues of recognition that remain to be dealt with, and experience suggests that 'the stage of standardization is yet to be reached' (Gonzalez 1997: 209). A range of varieties is now heard and accepted on radio and television, including code-switched varieties of English. The issue for many teachers and educators, then, is whether only 'standard' American English be used in school materials, or whether the use of a local variety of English be permitted (Gonzalez 1997: 209).

Finally, Gonzalez suggests that a so-called 'error' may become a legitimate feature of Asian Englishes through the regularity of 'accepted custom', so that '[w]hen the speakers of the language use it often enough and in sufficient numbers to silence the prescriptors and gate-keepers, then the error becomes a legitimate feature' (1997: 210). In the case of the Philippines, it seems clear that Philippine English has achieved recognition but is still moving towards full 'legitimation'.

In Hong Kong, the first stage of the recognition of Hong Kong English is still wanting among some academics, although survey results indicate that the general Hong Kong public are aware of the existence of a distinct local variety. In fact, a number of questions on this issue were included in the 1993 Hong Kong sociolinguistic survey (Bacon-Shone and Bolton 1998). The first asked 'What variety were you taught at school?' and the second, 'Do you think there is a unique Hong Kong style of English?'. In answer to the first, 62.4 per cent responded 'English English', 30.4 per cent 'Hong Kong English' and 6.4 per cent 'American English'. In response to the second question, 67.2 per cent of the population answered affirmatively (that there is 'a unique style of Hong Kong English') and 32.5 per cent negatively.

These results are, of course, open to interpretation. The impression among the general public may be that the term 'Hong Kong English' refers to a 'substandard' variety of the language, somehow equivalent to 'bad English', but this may not always be the case. Even so, these results do indicate rather clearly an awareness among approximately two thirds of the population that there is a local 'style' of English in use in the community, however this may be defined. This latter point leads back to the issue of defining 'new Englishes'. Llamzon's 'essential features' taxonomy mentioned above is one of a number of suggested models.[1] The lexicographer Susan Butler of *The Macquarie Dictionary* has also written on this issue (Butler 1996, 1997a, b, 1999). Since the early 1990s, Butler has

---

[1] Platt, Weber and Ho (1984) highlight four defining characteristics of the 'new Englishes', i.e. (i) their development through the education system, both as a timetabled subject and as a teaching medium; (ii) their development in societies where there was no 'native' variety of English spoken by the majority of the population; (iii) their use for a range of functions in such communities, e.g., letter writing, in government, media and creative writing; and (iv) linguistic evidence of 'localisation' in language features 'such as sounds, intonation patterns, sentence structures, words, expressions' (Platt, Weber and Ho 1984: 2–3).

been working with the *Macquarie* team on developing a corpus of Asian English (*Asiacorp*) in preparation for a range of English dictionaries for the Southeast Asian region. Butler suggests the following characteristics help define varieties of World Englishes:

- a standard and recognizable pattern of pronunciation handed down from one generation to another (i.e. accent);
- particular words and phrases which spring up usually to express key features of the physical and social environment and which are regarded as peculiar to the variety (vocabulary);
- a history – a sense that this variety of English is the way it is because of the history of the language community;
- a literature written without apology in that variety of English (literary creativity); and
- reference works – dictionaries and style guides – which show that people in that language community look to themselves, not some outside authority, to decide what is right and wrong in terms of how they speak and write their English. (1997a: 106)

The Hong Kong accent

With reference to the first of Butler's criteria, Bolton and Kwok (1990) provide a description of segmental and suprasegmental features of the phonology of Hong Kong English (HK English), and investigate the reactions of university students to a number of English accents, including RP accents, US accents and Hong Kong accents through the use of a verbal guise technique. As part of this research, Bolton and Kwok transcribed the speech of a first-year student at the University of Hong Kong in the spring of 1987. This speaker was identified as a speaker of 'mid-range' Hong Kong English with a relatively 'broad' Hong Kong accent, acquired largely through her education at an Anglo-Chinese secondary school. A transcription of a sample of her speech, using a system of broad phonemic notation, following Platt, Weber and Ho (1983) and Trudgill and Hannah ([1982] 1994) is set out below. The following extracts of conversation were elicited in response to two prompts, the first eliciting a commentary on methods of English-language teaching, the second on her vacation job the previous summer.

Text 4.1 *A mid-range Hong Kong accent*

I   thinks if I have a chance to teach in secondary schoo(l), I, I   will
aɪ fɪŋks ɪf aɪ hæv ə tʃɑːns tu titʃ in sekənderi sku   aɪ aɪ wɪu

teach them step   by   step because they are, they're not   familiar with
titʃ ðem step˺ baɪ step˺ bikɒs ðeɪ ɑː ðeə   nɒt˺ fɛmiliə wɪv

English.
iŋgliʃ

And I will try to divi(de), divi(de) my lesson in grammar and (er)
ɛn aɪ wɪu traɪ tu diwaɪ   diwaɪ   maɪ lesən ən græmɑ   ən ɛ

oral speaking and listen, and listen to the English. And I think this
ɔ:rou spikiŋ   ɛn lɪsən ɛn lɪsən tu ði iŋglis   ɛn aɪ fiŋkˀ dɪs

aspec(t)s is qui(t)e importan(t) to to become (um) to speak English
æspeks ɪs kwaɪ   impɔtœn   tu tu bikʌm ɑm tu spikˀ iŋlis

fluently and know and how to read and write English.
fluəntli ɛn nou ɛn hau tu ridˀ ɛn raɪt iŋglis

[…]

Last summer holidays I, I was working in factory. (Um) I'm I'm no(t)
lɑ:st sʌmə   hɒlideɪs aɪ aɪ wəz wœkiŋ in fæktri əm   aɪm aɪm nɒ?

worked happily because the, the colleagues of mi(ne) is no(t) goo(d).
wœkt hæpɪli bikɒs   də də kɒligs   ɒf maɪ ɪs nɒ? gu?

They a(l)ways talk behin(nd) people and they, they are no(t), they are
deɪ ɔ:weɪs tɔk bihaɪ   pipou ɛn ðeɪ ðeə nɒ?   ðeə

very lazy and I trying to work har(d). They, um, they are no(t) like   me.
veri leɪsi ɛn aɪ traɪiŋ tu wœk hɑ:? deɪ   ɛm ðeə lɒ?   laɪkˀ mi

Therefore finally I left the factory and I fin(d) another work and it is
ðɛfɔ   faɪnəli aɪ left də fæktri ɛn aɪ faɪn ənʌðɑ   wœk ɛn it is

also a factory. (Um) I work for a month and the factory is very ho(t).
ɔsou ə fæktri ɛm aɪ wœk fɔ ə mʌnf ɛn ðə fæktəri is veri hɒ?

It's making do(ll)s and some toys, etcetera. And it's very dirty (um).
ɪs mɪkiŋ dɒs   ɛn sʌm tɔɪs eksetrɑ: ɛn ɪs veri dœti əm

(Er) finally I work for a month and I lef(t) and wait for my 'A' level
ɛ   faɪnəli aɪ wœk fɔ ə mʌnf ɛn aɪ lef   ɛn weɪt fɔ maɪ eɪ levou

resul(t).
risɐu
(Adapted from Bolton and Kwok 1990: 151–2)

Using this text and other data from their research, Bolton and Kwok present
an analysis of the Hong Kong accent in terms of segmental and suprasegmental
features. At the segmental level, differences between the HK and RP accents are
discussed with reference to the vowel system and the consonant system. With
reference to the *vowel system* the following points can be noted:

• a variable lack of contrast between RP /ɪ/ and /i:/ and the tendency to use
  /i/ for both RP phonemes;

- an absence of contrast between RP /e/ and /æ/ so that a vowel of intermediate quality /ɛ/ is frequently used for both RP phonemes;
- a frequent absence of contrast between RP /ɔ:/ and /ɒ/, with the tendency for both *port* and *pot* to be pronounced as /pɔt/;
- the reduction of RP /u:/ in *boot, food*, etc. to a shorter vowel in HK English in both *foot* /fut/ and *food* /fud/;
- the realisation of RP /ə:/ as the rounded central vowel /œ/;
- the realisation of the RP diphthong /əu/ as a rounded diphthong /ou/; and
- the unstressed RP schwa /ə/ is often stressed and given a 'fuller value' as /ɛ/, in /fɛmiliə/ for *familiar*, or /ɑ/ as in /græmɑ/ for *grammar*, or as /ɑ:/ in /tʃaɪnɑ:/ for *China*. (Bolton and Kwok 1990: 152)

With reference to the *consonant system*, patterns of 'substitution', 'non-release', 'deletion' and 'consonant cluster simplification' were identified. Typical substitutions include the replacement of RP /θ/ by /f/ as in /fɪŋks/ *thinks*; /ð/ by /d/ in initial position, as in /deɪ/ for *they*, and /ð/ by /v/ in final position as in /wɪv/ for *with*; /v/ by /w/, e.g. /diwaɪ/ for *divide*; /ʃ/ by /s/, as in /ɪŋglis/ for *English*; /l/ by /r/ as in /kɒrekˀ/ for *collect*, and /r/ for /l/ in other contexts; /l/ by /n/ and vice versa, as in /lit/ and /nɔŋ/ for *neat* and *long*; and the vocalisation of final /l/ (or 'dark l') as in /wiu/ for *will*, etc. Patterns of non-release and deletion include the non-release of /p/, /t/ and /k/ in final position, as in [stepˀ] for *step*, etc.; the glottalisation of final /t/ and /d/ as in [nɒʔ guʔ] *not good*; and the deletion of final consonants as in /diwaɪ/ for *divide* and /sku/ for *school*. Examples of the simplification of consonant clusters include the reduction /kts/ to /ks/ and /ft/ to /f/ (Bolton and Kwok 1990: 153–4).

In addition, Bolton and Kwok also identify accent features typical of North American English (Am. Eng.). These occurred both in the speech of mid- and upper-range speakers of English in Hong Kong, and included, in the speech of television presenters and radio newsreaders, the use of a 'flapped t' [ɖ] in medial position in words like *city*, etc.; the use of the Am. Eng. unrounded back vowel in /ɑ/ in *job, got*, etc.; and the use of the Am. Eng. /æ/ vowel instead of RP /ɑ:/, in words like *dance* and *banana*. At a suprasegmental level, features included the use of a high-rising intonation for all questions, including neutral wh-interrogatives; the levelling of the opposition between strong and weak syllables; and the lack of accent shift to achieve emphasis (1990: 154, 161).

Overall, Bolton and Kwok argue that 'Hong Kong English speakers typically share a number of localised features of a Hong Kong accent' (1990: 166), and that such features are not restricted to mid- or lower-range speakers, but cluster in varying proportions in the speech of locally educated upper-range speakers as well. The linguistic analysis in this paper was supplemented by attitudinal research, which suggested that the respondents 'identified' (Le Page and Tabouret-Keller 1985) with local speakers in a number of ways:

- they could recognise a Hong Kong accent relatively easily;
- they had difficulty in labelling other accents of English; and
- a substantial number of respondents (particularly male students) stated a preference for that accent of English associated with 'Hong Kong bilinguals'. (Bolton and Kwok 1990: 170)

This early study has been followed by more recent work (Hung 2000), which has led to the growing recognition of a distinct HK English accent. Support for the argument that a Hong Kong accent reflects a local identity again also emerged from the 1993 language survey (Bacon-Shone and Bolton 1998), where two related questions were asked: 'What sort of English should be taught in schools?' and 'When you speak English which accent would you most like to have?'. In response to the former question, 73.2 per cent answered 'English English', 15.7 per cent 'Hong Kong English' and 10.4 per cent 'American English', with 'Hong Kong English' evidently preferred as a target model over an American model. The results for the second question on accent indicated that 55 per cent favoured an English accent, 29.6 per cent a Hong Kong accent and 14.6 per cent an American accent. This result lent some support at least to the claim that 'many Hong Kong speakers of English . . . model their speech forms not on native-speaker stereotypes in North America or Britain but on the speech of educated bilinguals in Hong Kong' (Bolton and Kwok 1990: 164). The results also show a degree of support for an American English accent, and one might predict that future results will indicate an even higher level of support for a American accent of English.

Hong Kong vocabulary

A number of studies of a distinct Hong Kong vocabulary have been published in recent years, including Chan and Kwok (1985), a study of 'lexical borrowing from Chinese into English'; Taylor (1989) on the use of English in Hong Kong newspapers; Benson (1994) on 'political vocabulary of Hong Kong English'; and Carless (1995) on 'politicised expressions' in local newspapers. In addition, over the past ten years, Susan Butler and the *Macquarie Dictionary* team have compiled wordlists for Asian Englishes including Hong Kong English. Examples of Hong Kong words in the *Macquarie* database may be seen below in the form of entries for a new dictionary that *Macquarie* recently copublished with Grolier Publishers, the *Grolier International Dictionary: World English in an Asian Context* (Macquarie 2000c). This dictionary includes many vocabulary items from Asian Englishes, including the following from Hong Kong:

Text 4.2 *Sample entries from the* Grolier International Dictionary

ABC *noun* 1. an Australian-born Chinese 2. (especially in Hong Kong) an American-born Chinese

Ah *noun Hong Kong English* an informal term of address: *Ah Sam| Ah Chan*

almond cream *noun Hong Kong English* a sweet dessert of crushed almonds in a soup, usually served hot

AO *noun Hong Kong English* an abbreviation of 'administrative officer', a public servant in the most senior career grade in the Hong Kong Civil Service

astronaut *noun* 1. someone specially trained to travel in a spaceship 2. *Hong Kong English* a person whose family has emigrated abroad, for example to Australia or Canada, but who remains working in Hong Kong, and then spends a great deal of time flying between his or her family and Hong Kong

bak choi /bʌk 'tʃɔi/ *noun Hong Kong English* a variety of Chinese green and white cabbage □ *Other forms:* another spelling is **pak choi**

banana *noun* 1. a long curved fruit with a yellow skin 2. *Asian English* a westernised Chinese

BBC *noun Hong Kong English Informal* a British-born Chinese

beggar's chicken *noun* in Chinese cuisine, a chicken dish baked in lotus leaves and mud

big brother *noun Asian English* 1. a Chinese kinship term referring to the eldest male sibling in a family 2. a recruiter or protector in a Chinese secret society or triad

black hand *noun Hong Kong English* a behind-the-scenes mastermind who plans political or criminal activities

black society *noun Hong Kong English* a Chinese secret society or triad

bo lei /'boʊ 'leɪ/ *noun Hong Kong English* a variety of strong dark tea

Buddha's delight *noun* a vegetarian dish of bean curd, nuts, tiger lilies and a hair-like seaweed which is particularly popular at Chinese New Year, as the Cantonese name of the seaweed (*fat choi* or 'hair vegetable') sounds very similar to the New Year greeting wishing prosperity

cage *noun* 1. an enclosure made of wires or bars, in which animals or birds can be kept 2. anything that is like a prison 3. in Hong Kong, a partitioned bedspace in an apartment, rented by the very poor *verb* 4. to put someone or something in, or as if in, a cage: *The prisoner was caged in his cell.* The occupants of **a cage** (definition 3) are known as **cageman, cagewoman, cage dwellers or cage people** and it is short for cage house, the translation of the term in Chinese.

Canto- a prefix indicating the influence of the Cantonese language or culture, especially in books, film, television, or pop music: *Canto-drama | Canto-movie*

Canto-speak *noun Hong Kong English Informal* the Cantonese language

Canto star *noun Hong Kong English* a singer of Cantonese pop songs □ *Other forms:* you can also use **Canto-popstar**

char siew /tʃa 'sju/ *noun* Chinese-style roast pork □ *Other forms:* other spellings, in Hong Kong English, are **char siu** and **cha siu**

char siew bau /tʃa sju 'baʊ/ *noun Hong Kong English* a white bun containing spicy pork, a popular Cantonese snack □ *Other forms:* another spelling is **char siu bau**

cheeky *adjective* (**cheekier, cheekiest**) 1. rude or lacking respect, especially in a playful way: *Her cheeky behaviour annoyed the teacher.* 2. *Asian English Informal* behaving in a way that is overconfident and lacking respect for the opposite sex *phrase* 3. **Get cheeky with someone,** *Hong Kong English* to be insolent towards someone □ *Word family:* cheekily *adverb* –cheekiness *noun*

chicken *noun* 1. a young hen or rooster 2. the meat from this bird: *chicken for dinner* 3. *Informal* a coward: *He's too much of a chicken to climb that tree.* 4. *Hong Kong English Informal* a prostitute *-adjective Informal* 5. Cowardly *-phrase* 6. **Chicken out,** *informal* to back out because you are scared

China doll *noun Hong Kong English* a pretty young Chinese woman of submissive demeanour

Chinese banquet *noun* a dinner consisting of approximately a dozen courses, frequently attended by a large number of guests, as at a Chinese wedding banquet

Chinese broccoli /ˌtʃaɪniz ˈbrɒkəli/ *noun* → **kai lan**

Chinese cabbage *noun* → **bak choi**

Chinglish /ˈtʃɪŋglɪʃ/ *noun informal* **1.** any variety of English strongly influenced by Chinese **2.** any variety of Chinese featuring a high proportion of English loanwords

chit *noun Asian English* **bill**[1] (definition 1)

Chiu Chau /ˈtʃiu ˈtʃa/ *adjective Chinese and Hong Kong English* of or relating to people, objects and activities associated with the Chiu Chau dialect areas of Guangdong and Fukien province: *Chiu Chau food | Chiu Chau dialect* ☐ *Other forms:* other spellings are **Chiu Chow** and **Teo Chew**

choi sum /ˈtʃɔɪ sʌm/ *noun Asian English* a green leafy vegetable with tender white fleshy stems and yellow flowers ☐ *Other forms:* another spelling is **choy sum**

chop[1] *verb* (**chopped, chopping**) **1.** to hit with quick, strong blows using an axe or other sharp tool: *I chopped some wood for the fire. | They chopped the tree down.* **2.** to cut into smaller pieces: *You'd better chop that meat a bit smaller.* **3.** *Asian English* to hit (someone) with a chopper or knife ☐ *Word family:* **chopper** *noun*

chop[2] *Asian English noun* **1. a.** a personal seal or stamp, used to approve transactions, show that papers are official, etc. **b.** a design, corresponding to a brand or trademark, stamped on goods to indicate their special quality *verb* (**chopped, chopping**) **2.** to mark with such a stamp

cocktail /ˈkɒkteɪl/ *noun* **1.** a drink made from a mixture of alcoholic drinks and other ingredients such as fruit juice, cream, crushed ice, soft drink, etc. **2** *Hong Kong English* a party at which such drinks are served. [etc., etc.]

Since 1996, I have served as a consultant on Hong Kong vocabulary to *Macquarie*, and have studied the contemporary lexis of Hong Kong English in some detail, through personal observation, notetaking, computerised searches of local databases (particularly those of the *South China Morning Post*), consultation with *Macquarie* lexicographers and the use of *Macquarie*'s own database, *Asiacorp. Asiacorp* contains more than 10 million words from Southeast Asian and East Asian sources, including fiction, non-fiction and print media English-language texts from Hong Kong, Malaysia, Singapore, Thailand and the Philippines.

Some of the results of this research can be seen in appendix 5, which contains a glossary of 318 words of Hong Kong English vocabulary in contemporary use.[2] These may be regarded as 'Hong Kong items' in the sense that they are words used in Hong Kong to describe distinctive aspects of local life and culture, and have a limited currency in other varieties of English. Some of these words, however, are used in other communities in the region, notably Singapore and Malaysia, which have large Chinese communities (see pp. 214–15 below). In the next section, I have attempted to analyse these vocabulary items in terms of various processes of word-formation, with reference to current models of word-formation in the field of World Englishes.

---

[2] This glossary is not intended to provide a comprehensive list of all the vocabulary items that might be regarded as 'Hong Kong English' items, but represents a sample of various types of localised vocabulary currently used in the HKSAR.

Models of word-formation in World Englishes

The following categories are derived from a number of sources including Haugen (1950), Bautista (1997) and Cannon (1998). The model below involves five categories of word-formation:

coinage of new items, through a number of processes, including (a) analogical constructions, (b) clippings, (c) abbreviations, (d) total innovations, (e) new compounds, (f) prefixed compounds and (g) hybrid compounds, i.e. combinations of one English element with one borrowed element;

borrowing through (a) loanwords and (b) loan translations;

modified semantic reference, where items extend or narrow their meaning;

modified grammatical form, which refers to items whose grammatical forms are altered; and

preservation of 'archaic' usages.

Coinage

Examples of analogical constructions in HK English vocabulary include such items as *floormate*, *groupmate* and *hallmate*, which are formed by analogy to *classmate*. Other examples would include *mini-hall* and *mini-flat*, which may be formed by analogy with words like *mini-bus*, *mini-hifi*, etc. Another example with a Hong Kong attestation in the *South China Morning Post* (*SCMP*), and also found in other Southeast Asian countries, is *batchmate* ('a colleague recruited at the same time as others to a company or organisation').

Examples of clippings include *aircon* 'airconditioner'; *autopay* 'automatic payment' or 'standing order'; and *O'camp* 'orientation camp'. Abbreviations are very common in Hong Kong English, and those in the *Asiacorp* include *ABC* 'American-born Chinese'; *AO* 'administrative officer'; *BBC* 'British-born Chinese'; *BNO* 'British National Overseas'; *HKSAR* 'Hong Kong Special Administrative Region'; *II* 'illegal immigrant'; *LRT* 'Light Rail Transit'; *MTR* 'Mass Transit Rail'; and *OSCO* 'Organised and Serious Crimes Ordinance'.

Total innovations are a category suggested by Bautista, who states that '[t]his category may also use analogy and clipping, but the results stand out because they are so creative, so innovative' (1997: 62). Examples include *Canto*, and its related compounds, and *Chinglish*. The category of new compounds includes examples such as *ancestral home* 'place of origin of one's family's ancestors'; *Anglo-Chinese* 'related to Britain and China' or 'English-medium schools in HK'; *dough stick* 'a fried stick of wheat dough'; *foodstall* 'an open-air pavement restaurant'; *street hawker* 'an unlicensed street trader'; and *typhoon shelter* 'a sheltered area within a harbour'.

By far the most productive prefix in the prefixed compounds category is *Chinese*, although *China*, *dragon* and *mandarin* also have a certain productivity. For *Chinese*, examples from the *Macquarie* corpus include: *Chinese banquet, Chinese broccoli, Chinese cabbage, Chinese calendar, Chinese calligraphy, Chinese celery*, *Chinese character*, *Chinese chess*, etc.; for *China* and *dragon* examples include: *China doll*, *China hand*, *dragon boat*, *dragon dance*, *dragon throne*, *dragon's eye* and *dragonhead*; and for *mandarin*: *mandarin collar*, *mandarin fan*, *mandarin fish*, *mandarin hat* and *mandarin square*. Examples of hybrid compounds from the *Macquarie* corpus include *chim stick*, *Han Chinese*, *hoisin sauce*, *laisee packet*, *tan tan noodles*, *Tin Hau Festival* and *Yunnan ham*.

Borrowing

The second major category includes loanwords from Chinese, loanwords from other languages and loan translations or 'calques'. Loanwords from Chinese in the *Macquarie* corpus include *Ah*, *ai ya*, *amah*, *baak choy*, *bo lei*, *cha siu*, *cha siu bau*, *char siew*, *cheongsam*, *Ching Ming*, *Chiu Chau*, *choi sum*, *Chung Yeung*, *dai fei* and *dai lo*; loanwords from other languages include *brinjal*, *bungalow*, *catty*, *chit*, *chop*, *comprador*, *congee*, *coolie*, *garoupa*, *godown*, *lorcha*, *nullah*, *picul*, *praya*, *shroff* and *tael*; while loan translations include: *almond cream*, *astronaut*, *Bamboo Gang*, *banana*, *Basic Law*, *beggar's chicken*, *big brother*, *big circle*, *bitter melon*, *black hand*, *black society*, *blue lantern*, *boat people*, *Buddha's delight*, *cage*, *cagepeople*, *chicken*, *crystal bun*, *Double Tenth*, *drunken chicken*, etc.

Modified semantic reference

The third major category of word-formation includes words which exist in British and/or American English but have a modified meaning in Hong Kong English, including *aunty*, *bath*, *cheeky*, *chop* ('to wound with a cleaver'), *Christian*, *harsh*, *scold*, *send* and *uncle*. In an adult context, the word *cheeky* relates less to playful impudence and more to behaviour intended to, or resulting in, the provocation of violence. The word *harsh* when used of people denotes 'demanding, setting high standards'. Thus, at the University of Hong Kong, it is quite possible to hear a student comment that, 'She's a very nice teacher, but very harsh!'

Modified grammatical form

This essentially involves a change in the part of speech. The most frequent instance in Hong Kong English is the treatment as count nouns of what are mass nouns in British English. Examples include *alphabets*, *aircrafts*, *equipments*, *furnitures* and *staffs*. These forms occur very frequently in the essays of university students, but they also sometimes occur in the *South China Morning Post*. Other candidates for inclusion in this category are the forms *discuss about*, *list out*, *return back* and *stress on*, where the lexical verb is replaced by a phrasal verb construction not usually found in 'inner-circle' varieties.[3]

---

[3] The grammatical description of Hong Kong English has been hitherto under-researched, although various linguists have commented on a range of putative 'features' in addition to those noted here. These include copula omission; variable marking of plurals, third-person singular, past tense, and the definite and indefinite articles; the use of resumptive pronouns; and the distinctive patterning of relative clauses (see Platt 1982, Gisborne 2002, McArthur 2002).

Preservation of 'archaic' usages

There are relatively few examples in this category, notably *conservancy*, *Madam*, *subvent* and *teddy boy*. *Conservancy* is used as an alternative to *conservation*; *Madam* is used when referring to women in a position of authority ('Madam Lee', etc.) and also to female police officers in the full form (i.e. not 'ma'am'); *subvent* is often used as a transitive verb and adjectival participle in preference to 'subsidise' and 'subsidised'; and 'teddy boy' refers to members of street gangs associated with triads.

Categories of word-formation in Hong Kong English

An analysis of the sample of lexical data included in appendix 4 reveals that coinage accounts for around 37% of words in this sample, borrowing for 51%, modified semantic reference for 7%, modified grammatical form for 4% and archaic usage for around 1% of the data. However, a linguistic analysis of this kind is only one possible approach to the analysis of vocabulary data of this kind. Another approach would be to analyse the data according to semantic and situational categories. In this context, a number of categories seem salient including a category of 'China Coast' items which would include such items as *chit*, *chop*, *praya* and *shroff* which may be traced back to early varieties of Chinese English. Other items, however, relate to 'modern' Hong Kong life, especially the historical period that runs from the late 1960s to the present. Thus items such as *astronaut*, *banana*, *big brother*, *Canto-*, *chop* (in the sense of knife attack) etc. speak to the contemporary culture of life in an Asian metropolis, rather than that of the treaty-port past. A full inventory of the modern Hong Kong lexicon would include items across a wide range of different domains including food items (with both calques and phonetic borrowings), official terminology (names of institutions and organizations, particularly in the civil service), political vocabulary (e.g. 'one country, two systems'), police terms, place names, festivals, and flora and fauna. In addition to those items of vocabulary that are distinctly 'local', there are also a substantial number of terms that are used with modified semantic reference within the HKSAR. As Benson (2002) has pointed out, many Hong Kong words and usages are fully explicable only by reference to rather dense semantic and pragmatic relations that are internal to the Hong Kong context. This density can be seen in the semantic oppositions that exist (in the English mass media, for instance) between such terms as *pro-Beijing* versus *pro-Hong Kong*, *public housing* versus *private housing* and *economic migrants* versus *refugees*. Thus the analysis of Hong Kong vocabulary in structural linguistic terms above may be further extended by a finer-grained semantically based analysis.

Cross-currents in the vocabulary of Asian Englishes

A number of the loanwords above are of Anglo-Indian origin, including *brinjal*, *bungalow*, *chit*, *chop*, *congee*, *coolie*, *mango*, *monsoon* and *shroff*. Their existence and use in Hong Kong English provides evidence of the historical connections linking

India to Indian communities in Singapore, Malaya and colonial Hong Kong. British administrators often arrived in the Straits Settlements after serving in India, bringing with them Indian personnel as clerks and teachers (Hogue 1999). South Asians arrived in Hong Kong from the beginning of British rule, as soldiers (*sepoys*), sailors (*lascars*), merchants, traders and recruits for the police force. The total number of such Anglo-Indian items still in use in the territory is quite small, but the use of the terms *chit, chop, congee, coolie* and *shroff* is still quite distinctive.

Connections can be made across Asia in the other direction too. An initial analysis based on the Macquarie Dictionary's *Asiacorp* suggests that a substantial number of the words found in appendix 5 are also in use in Singapore and Malaysia, including:

> *ai ya, aircon, alphabets, ancestral home, aunty, banana, bar girl, batchmate, bath, Canto-pop, catty, cha siu, cheeky, cheongsam, Chinese broccoli, Chinese cabbage, Chinese calendar, Chinese medicine, Chinese New Year, Chinese tea, Chinese values, Chinese zodiac, Ching Ming, Chinglish, choi sum, chop, Christian, clan, clan association, congee, conservancy, coolie, curry puff, dim sum, dragon boat, dragon dance, essence of chicken, feng shui, Festival of the Hungry Ghosts, fish sauce, fishball, fishcake, fishpaste, food court, foodstall, fung shui, glutinous rice, godown, heaty, Hokkien, hundred-year-old-egg, Hungry Ghosts Festival, identity card, kai lan, Kitchen God, kowtow, lantern festival, lion dance, Lunar New Year, Mid-autumn Festival, Middle Kingdom, minibus, monsoon, mooncake, night market, overseas Chinese, piece, polyclinic, porridge, red packet, rice bowl, sampan, send, sticky rice, stress, tai chi, tai tai, tea money, Tiger Balm, uncle, yum seng*

There are historical and contemporary reasons for such an overlap. Historically, Hong Kong was a transit point for many Chinese emigrants from Guangdong and Fujian province who were recruited as part of the 'coolie' trade. At another level of society, Chinese merchants and traders in Singapore and the Straits Settlements had strong contacts with the Chinese merchant community in Hong Kong. More recently, the Singapore government has encouraged Hong Kong people to migrate to 'the Lion City', and many Hong Kong families now have relatives living there. A great deal of commercial business is transacted between the two cities, and with Malaysia. Many thousands of Singaporean and Malaysian Chinese visit Hong Kong every year, with similar numbers of Hongkongers shuttling to Singapore and Kuala Lumpur. When they meet they may speak varieties of Chinese, but English is used as well or instead.

History

The third criterion in Butler's taxonomy is that of 'history', in the sense that 'this variety of English is the way it is because of the history of the language community'. I have already discussed a wealth of material that demonstrates a series of historical connections, largely forgotten or obscured in the 'modern' debates on sociolinguistics in Hong Kong. It is evident that Hong Kong, and indeed China, has a history of linguistic contact with English that dates back to the seventeenth century, and that surprisingly little has been written on this topic, at least from a 'languages in contact' perspective. The various accounts of Chinese pidgin English (CPE) by expert creolists such as Baker and Mühlhäusler treat the topic as of relevance mainly to their particular research orientation and few connections with the current Hong Kong situation are made. One set of connections, as I have indicated, relates to the discussion of HK English vocabulary, as many of these items were first labelled as 'pidgin' words in the writings of Leland (1876) and others. Another set of connections might be made at a phonological level. For example, Baker and Mühlhäusler's account of CPE phonology (see pp. 162–3 above) shares at least four points of agreement with the Bolton and Kwok description of HK English phonology, and there are multiple connections between our analysis and Shi's (1991) account of CPE phonology with reference to 'the system of replacements' in the consonant system, and consonant cluster simplification.

In addition, there is the whole issue of 'languages in contact' and hybridisation in the various varieties of southern Chinese Englishes. The question of code-switching and code-mixing in Hong Kong has typically been seen as a very recent issue, even by established sociolinguists. Few Hong Kong academics have previously been able to relate the language debates of the contemporary period to the complex history of language contact in the South China region, with the exception of Pennington (1998c), who makes a number of connections between Chinese pidgin English, the Christian schools of nineteenth-century Hong Kong and the 'mixed mode' of language education in 1990s Hong Kong: 'The most significant fact about Hong Kong language in the present era is the vitality of the mixed code which has resulted from this process of linguistic flooding, diluting, and blending, and which in a sense carries on the traditions of the previous generations of pidgin speakers and linguistic middlemen' (1998c: 28).

From a broader perspective, the point might be made that throughout the past 200 years, only two of China's cities can lay claim to 'cosmopolitanism'. The first of these was Shanghai, which from around 1860 until 1949 was the most international city in China. By the 1930s, Shanghai was a centre of capitalism, commerce, crime, European and American colonialism, literary creativity, publishing, revolutionary political activity, translation and all the other constituents of developing Chinese modernity. After 1949, significant numbers of Shanghai Chinese relocated to Hong Kong, and the dynamics of a new modernity in turn fuelled the development of modern Hong Kong (see chapter 2). With a speed that virtually escaped notice at the time, somewhere during the 1980s and early 1990s, the cultural formations of late British colonialism redefined themselves into a global perspective, into a new 'cosmopolitanism' (Abbas 1997: 13). It is this new cosmopolitanism that holds the prospect of new cultural spaces in Hong Kong, not least in the area of literary creativity.

Literary creativity

Past commentaries on the literary history of Hong Kong have mirrored discourses on the English language in Hong Kong, often lamenting the absence of a Hong Kong literary tradition in English. Chan (1994) identifies three possible obstacles to the development of Hong Kong English writing: 'the language problem'; 'the psychological obstacle'; and the fact that 'there is no particular general urge to try writing poems, nor any particular prestige attached to the ability to do so' (Chan 1994: 407). Chan also suggests that there may not only be a lack of creative talent, but also a reluctance to use English as a literary medium, as 'linguistic competence is not necessarily coupled with creative talent', while '[e]ven those in whom creativity and linguistic facility meet may have no inclination whatsoever to write in a "borrowed tongue"' (1994: 407). Despite such pessimism, however, there have been some significant creative works published by local writers in recent years.

Examples include the poetry of Louise Ho (1994, 1997), Agnes Lam (1997), Leung Ping-kwan (1992, 1997) and Parkin and Wong (1997), as well as novels and short stories by Xu Xi (Sussy Komala/Chako). Louise Ho's poetry has won particular acclaim, and her ability to capture the rhythm and cadence of the changes in modern Hong Kong society has gained her the title of 'unofficial poet laureate' (Ho 2000). The novels of Xu Xi reflect a range of Hong Kong issues including the diasporic, the female and the cosmopolitan. In her latest novel, *The Unwalled City*, Xu Xi assembles an ensemble of Hong Kong characters including Andanna Lee, a young Hong Kong fashion model, Gail Szeto, a Eurasian business executive, Coleen Tang, an American woman married to a Hong Kong Chinese, and Vince da Luca, an expat Yank photographer. *The Unwalled City* describes the lives of these characters in the months before the 1997 handover, but the focus is not on the drama of politics, but on the real stuff of people's lives, work, relationships, marriages, children and love, or the lack of it (Xu Xi 2000). In a recent discussion of her work, Xu Xi comments that:

> Hong Kong readers (i.e. readers with a real, personal knowledge of Hong Kong through residence and work/life experience), both 'local' and 'foreign', find my work 'very Hong Kong', whatever that means. I only know my Hong Kong. It's the one I write about, and will continue to write about in fiction, in English. Someone else can decide what that English is. (2000: 18)

There has been a remarkable growth in local writing in English over the last decade. Recent initiatives include the appearance of a new literary journal *Dim Sum*, and the expansion of creative writing programmes at City University and the University of Hong Kong. In addition, there are works of fiction by Hong Kong writers in translation, notably *Hong Kong Collage*, edited by Cheung (1998). All this indicates a literary culture with a much greater vitality than previously existed, or was recognised, which promises much for the future creativity of English in the HKSAR. A recently published anthology now surveys Hong Kong English creative writing from 1945 to the present (Xu and Ingham 2003).

Reference works

With regard to Butler's final criterion, at present there are few reference works, e.g. dictionaries and style guides, that acknowledge the existence of local varieties of English. Nevertheless, developments are underway, and there now are plans for a dictionary of Chinese and Hong Kong English in the near future. Bolton, Hung and Nelson (in progress) are also compiling a database of around 1 million words of English in Hong Kong as part of the worldwide ICE (International Corpus of English) project. At present, the *South China Morning Post* serves as a *de facto* reference point for local usage, particularly vocabulary.

Criteria revisited – bubbling up from below

Whether this discussion of criteria is sufficiently persuasive or powerful to render visible a distinct Hong Kong variety is perhaps less important than the desire to create a new space for discussion and discourse on Hong Kong English. Such a space would encompass not only the global and cosmopolitan, but also the local and ludic, not just one variety of localised English but, one hopes, a range of different voices. For example, as Hong Kong 'moves forward', to cite a much-used phrase in local political speeches, its government is now promoting their vision of the HKSAR as a 'world-class city'. As part of this reimaging of Hong Kong society as an Asian Manhattan, the business community wants to improve standards of English in the domains of business and tourism, but linguistic creativity finds expression in other ways. One example is the explosion in popularity among the territory's computer-savvy young of internet communication, particularly the use of so-called ICQ ('I seek you') software for online chat. The most common language of ICQ is English, sometimes of a distinctly code-mixed and hybrid variety, as in the extract below (varieties of English, it is often said, are not only created from above, but also 'bubble up from below').

The following is an example of an online ICQ conversation between two university students, recorded and transcribed in 1998. At the time 'Billy' and 'Amy' were both postgraduates in their early twenties studying in the University of Hong Kong. The context of the e-mail conversation is that Amy is at home using her personal computer, while Billy is working at his part-time job, teaching at a local tutorial centre.

> Billy: knock. . . . knock. . anyone in??
> Amy: yup, what's up?
> Billy: No ar!! Just to make u type some words!! hehe
> Amy: u r really 'mo liu'[a]
> Amy: should find a gf quick ma!

Billy: No. So up till now no one suits me. I am too bad and eye corner high[b] ar!!!

Amy: i don't think u can find them easily. u know, good looking girls are difficult to find nowadays la!

Billy: Haha. . . . that's true. One day I have to go back to China to find a perfect one. . . . . . hehe north mui[c]!!!!

Amy: but most of the 'dai luk mui'[d] are materialistic ah! i don't want u to cry in front of me some day!

Billy: Sometimes I think I am a bad man. I cheat women.

Amy: how?

Billy: By words lor . . . I am often mouth flower[e] and tell lies to them kar.

Amy: ai ya, how can u say u r a good man then?

Amy: where r u now?

Billy: In my company.

Amy: having lesson now?

Billy: yes

Amy: so when u r teaching the students, how can u play icq ah? they pay money ga, be more responsible la!!!

Amy: u r really very impolite! what's the name of ur tutorial centre? i'll call to 'kam yat tei chun d'[f] n 'sing si chun ging'[g]!

Amy: What presents will you buy for my birthday?

Billy: ok lor. I am your servant for one day. U can order me to do anything for u!!

Amy: no ah! i want presents ah!!!!

Billy: Uh . . . five time flower six time change[h] kar u!!

Amy: ok thks in advance. take care la!

Amy: how's your girlfriend?

Billy: She stays at her out-home[i] these nights lar . . . I feel pretty comfortable these days

Billy: Hey, what do u ususally do on Sundays ?

Amy: y r u so nosy???

Billy: I am nosy cos I have a nose . . .

Amy: ha ha . . . very funny . . . CRAZY!!!

Billy: Yum cha[j] lor . . .

Amy: ai . . . got no breath[k] to talk to u la!;-p

Billy: I am going to sleep lar . . . zzzzzzz

Amy: ha ha . . . go out to wet[l] lor!

Billy: no. I prefer to be dry tonight. . . .

Amy: wow, unexpected wor[m]!

Key:

a. Mo liu – Cantonese *mòuh liuh*, 'nonsense'.

b. Eye corner high – Cantonese *ngáahn gok gōu* [eye corners high], 'to be very demanding'.

c. North mui – Cantonese *bāk mūi* [northern sister], 'girl from the PRC'.
d. Dai luk mui – Cantonese *daaihluhk mūi*, 'girl from the PRC'.
e. Mouth flower – Cantonese *háu fāa fāa*, 'sweet talk'.
f. Kam yat tei chun d – Cantonese *gāmyaht tái jān dī*, ATV programme, 'Today's investigative reporting'.
g. Sing si chun ging – Cantonese *sìhngsíh jēui gīk*, TVB programme, 'City news latest'.
h. Five time flower six time change – Cantonese *ńgh sìh fāa luhk sìh bin*, [You like flowers at 5 o'clock, but you've changed your mind by 6], 'you're always changing your mind'.
i. Out-home – Cantonese *ngoihgāa* [out home], 'a married woman's parental home'.
j. Yum cha – Cantonese *yámchàh* [drink tea], Hong Kong English, *yum cha*, 'go to the restaurant for snacks'.
k. No breath – Cantonese *móuh hei*, 'there's no point in going on'.
l. Go out to wet – Cantonese *heui wēt*, 'go out and have fun'.
m. Ah, ar, kar, la, lar, lor, wor – Cantonese particles *aa, aa, gaa, laa, laa, lo, wo*, used for varying degrees of intimacy and various expressions of attitude.

The attitudinal dimension

Issues related to language attitudes have also been significant in recent years. This can been seen in the number of 'language attitudes' studies carried out in the territory in the years 1980–97 (see chapter 2). In addition to academically motivated studies employing a social-psychological methodology, however, 'attitudes' in a more general sense have had a powerful effect on language ideologies in the community.

Sociolinguistic studies of language attitudes

From the 1970s onwards, many language attitude studies have been carried out by local researchers. These might be considered in two distinct groups, those carried out in the 1970s and 1980s by researchers from the Chinese University of Hong Kong such as Fu and Pierson, and those carried out at City University by Pennington, Yue and associates.

Fu (1975) carried out one of the earliest studies on attitudes to English. The study's results indicated deeply conflicted attitudes to English among local secondary schoolchildren: on the one hand, the children recognised the pragmatic benefits of proficiency in English but, on the other, they registered varying degrees of unease about using the language with Chinese people inside and outside the classroom. Respondents also gave their opinions about 'English-speaking westerners', and Fu elicited a large number of responses that negatively characterised westerners as being *cold, conceited, contemptuous, pompous, racist, rude, scornful, self-centred, sly* and *unfriendly*.

Pierson, Fu and Lee (1980) investigated linguistic attitudes among Cantonese-speaking secondary students in Hong Kong and reported that, in spite of their desire to learn good English, the respondents expressed very strong agreement with such statements as 'If I use English, it means I am not patriotic'; 'At times I fear that by using English I will become like a foreigner'; and 'When using English, I do not feel that I am Chinese any more'. Chinese people were rated highly on stereotypes related to community solidarity, including *conservative in outlook, loyal to one's family, trustworthy, hardworking, gentle and graceful* and *able and far-sighted*. Westerners, in contrast, received higher ratings on the stereotypes *cool and clear-headed, frank and honest, easy to get along with, successful, humble and polite, presentable in appearance, self-confident* and *like to help others*. What is most evident about this research is that the community is obviously seen in terms of a 'Chinese' versus 'western' opposition, with no mention of 'Hong Kong people' as a sociological or cultural group.

A decade or so later, Pennington and Yue (1994) replicated Pierson *et al.*'s earlier studies and gathered a significantly different set of results. This time, their respondents most strongly agreed with the following statements: 'I wish that I could speak fluent and accurate English'; 'The command of English is very helpful in understanding foreigners and their culture'; 'I do not feel awkward when using English'; and 'I would take English even if it were not a compulsory subject in school', results that Pennington and Yue interpreted as displaying 'a strong motivation to learn English'. Their secondary students disagreed most strongly with statements such as 'If I use English, it means that I am not patriotic' and 'At times I fear that by using English, I will become like a foreigner', a reaction which suggested that 'the students did not feel that use of English threatened their ethnolinguistic identity, nor were they in favor of abolishing the use of English in the schools' (Pennington and Yue 1994: 10–11). The findings of this research strongly refuted a number of key findings of earlier studies, particularly those relating to ethnolinguistic insecurities. The researchers explain such radical differences in terms of the changed social and political climate in the runup to 1997:

> With the strength of the local English-based culture now substantially reduced and the Chinese takeover only a few years away, there is less of a social, cultural, or political need to assert Chinese ethnolinguistic identity, since it is clearly established as a strong norm... With so many relatives abroad and with so many others thinking of emigrating in the next few years, it would seem almost inevitable for Hong Kong people to be less locally focused and less tied to the local culture than in the past. (1994: 13)

Pennington and Yue also speculate that 'the overall pattern of positive and negative attitudes of the students in the present study may show a movement towards a view of English not as a local language, but as a foreign language or an international language of wider communication' (1994: 14).

Other studies in the 1990s tend to confirm Pennington and Yue's results, including that by Axler, Yang and Stevens (1998), who conclude that 'it is entirely possible that Hong Kong people see themselves as a distinct . . . and characteristically bilingual group of pragmatic Chinese who do not feel "un-Chinese" when called on to use English' (1998: 337).

Language attitudes and language ideologies

In addition to the above studies, there were other indications of attitude from outside the local academy. Within public discussions of 'language issues', a great deal of energy was devoted by journalists, businessmen, politicians and educators to the public criticism of the linguistic performance of Hong Kong students.

In the early 1990s, a *Time* magazine article suggested that 'many [secondary school] students are not very good at either Chinese or English', and that 'the decline in English standards is clearly visible at the University of Hong Kong' (*Time* 16 September 1991). By 1996, according to a *Far Eastern Economic Review* special feature, the situation had deteriorated still further, and the University of Hong Kong was once again the whipping-boy (or girl):

> Founded in 1911 and still the colony's premier institution of higher learning, the university today has become a symbol of the decline in local English standards in Hong Kong. At a time when other parts of Asia are trying to boost their skills, on the surface, the battle for English on this campus appears to be a losing one . . . There are a number of factors at work here. To begin with, at least since the 1970s, Hong Kong's English-speaking middle class has been steadily sending its children to overseas universities. A Hong Kong government decision, announced in 1989 in reaction to the loss of confidence following Tiananmen Square, exacerbates the effect of this trend: to democratize Hong Kong's system of higher education, the government expanded enrolment to 18% of the relevant age group from about 7%. Here at the University of Hong Kong, that has meant a jump to 12,965 students today from about 7,000 only 10 years ago . . . And because the university no longer reflects simply the cream of Hong Kong society, the general level of English has declined as the numbers have increased. (McGurn 1996: 43)

McGurn's sociological analysis is in part accurate, but this piece was penned a year or so before the 1997 change in sovereignty, at a time when the international media were inclined to publish copy that fitted into a preset agenda for 'handover coverage'.

Journalistic attitudes to falling standards were often matched by those of local academics and educators. Yu and Atkinson, for example, suggest that 'Hong Kong students suffer from an inferiority complex and identity conflict which prevent them from learning English effectively and being fluent in Chinese'

(Yu and Atkinson 1988b: 320). Another academic, Yee (1989), quotes a local banker (and Hong Kong University Council member), Mr David Li:

> [We are] dissatisfied with the educational level of the people (we) are forced by necessity to employ – whether products of our secondary schools, colleges or universities. The main grievance is the poor level of English. But complaints extend to the breadth and depth of knowledge. The constituency's consensus seems to be that Hong Kong students have been schooled to memorise what will get them through examinations and, thus, lack analytical skills. (Li 1989, cited in Yee 1989: 228–9)

The empirical basis about judgements on 'falling standards' is dubious at best, as I have indicated in chapter 2. In the long term, the notion that standards of language have 'fallen' is clearly risible if we pause to reflect that in 1931 only 18 per cent of females could read and write Chinese (compared to 69 per cent of males), and around only 6 per cent of the Chinese population could speak English (Bacon-Shone and Bolton 1998). The public debates on language standards indicate that 'attitudes' took on an ideological edge that seemed to scapegoat the very people intended to benefit from education in Hong Kong, i.e. the many thousands of schoolchildren and college students undergoing public education. This seems to point to a 'pathology' in the local language debates of a particularly perverse nature (Harris 1989: 41), where the scorn of educators and community leaders was aimed at the children of the community, who were routinely scolded for their linguistic shortcomings.

Students arrive at university burdened by years of complaint about their deteriorating language standards. One area in particular where Kachru's 'paradigm shift' is badly needed is in this convoluted tangle of language attitudes. Notions of linguistic proficiency and linguistic potential may need to be revised to accommodate both the 'sociolinguistic realities' of Hong Kong and the need for sensitive and imaginative agendas for language education. What those agendas might involve is outside the scope of this present discussion, but one would hope for a revitalised attitude to the teaching of English that is fully prepared to accept and utilise the power of creativity and intellectual inspiration that the study of the language can provide.

The first professor of English in the University of Hong Kong was Robert K. M. Simpson. Simpson served as Professor of English from the late 1920s until the early 1950s, spending the war years in the Stanley internment camp as a prisoner of the Japanese. He reflected on the problems of Chinese students learning the language, noting that:

> For the British peoples, English is a birthright eagerly inherited. But for other nations it is a difficult acquisition. I sometimes wonder why they are anxious to learn it. I once set the question as an examination essay, and from more than one candidate got the answer because 'Americans use it'. (1933: 51)

Some seventy years on, perhaps the time may have finally arrived when Hong Kong can move on to create a space for its own use and discourses of English, with a place for the language as *one* of Hong Kong's languages, in a diverse and pluralistic society. As Kachru himself notes, '[i]n culturally, linguistically, and ideologically pluralistic societies, there is a complex hybridity ... I believe linguistic and cultural hybridity is our identity', and 'our major strategy is to acculturate the language in our contexts of use, on our terms, Asian terms' (1997: 22). In Hong Kong, it remains to be seen just what the terms for Hong Kong English will be. In his October 1999 policy address, the Chief Executive of the HKSAR, Tung, Chee-hwa, highlighted the vision of Hong Kong as a world-class city, explaining that 'Hong Kong should not only be a major Chinese city, but could become the most cosmopolitan city in Asia, enjoying a status comparable to that of New York in North America and London in Europe.' Tung restated the effectiveness of mother-tongue instruction, but announced 'a territory-wide publicity campaign to promote the use of English' and thus halt 'a decline in the English standards of our younger generation since the early 1990s' (Hong Kong Government 1999).

At the height of the language debate in the late 1980s, Roy Harris, then Professor of English at the University of Hong Kong, gave his own blunt assessment of the language choices for the government and educational leaders in the territory, and challenged the government at that time to promote a 'bilingual community which can function as the cultural and economic bridge between East and West in the twenty-first century' (Harris 1989: 45). That challenge remains today, and Harris' final remarks bear repeating:

> The language or languages a community uses must be its own; and communities, like individuals, have the ability to make a language their own. For communities, like individuals, are not just language users: they are language makers. New English or Old English, if Hong Kong wants English, then Hong Kong must make English its own. Otherwise it will surely lose it. (1989: 45–6)

The central argument presented in this chapter is that, with reference to those criteria applied to other Asian societies, the sociolinguistic conditions associated with the emergence of a 'new English' are now evident in the community, and that Hong Kong English now can claim recognition as one of the 'World Englishes' in the Kachruvian paradigm. It is also argued that such recognition has been blocked by a cluster of attitudes and ideologies that have previously denied the space for a new and creative discourse on the English language in Hong Kong.[4]

The exploration of the sociohistorical background to English in South China, presented in chapters 2 and 3, points to the ways in which historical and cultural

---

[4] These issues, among others, are discussed in some detail in a recent special issue of the journal *World Englishes*, entitled 'Hong Kong English: Autonomy and Creativity' (Bolton 2000d); an expanded version has been published in book form (Bolton 2002).

issues impinge on and define discussions of linguistics and language issues. In particular, the history of English in South China illustrates the multilevelled force of modernity in creating discourses on language as well as 'languages' themselves. In the South China context, in Macao and Canton (Guangzhou), there developed between the late sixteenth and early twentieth centuries powerful discourses on language and linguistics. The history of the sinicisation of English in Canton and Hong Kong provides only part of the picture. Other histories exist, including that of the 'Englishisation' of Cantonese (see chapter 2), as well as the history of the part that western languages and western linguists played in the formation of the modern Chinese language (Masini 1993).

In his book *Lost Words and Lost Worlds* (1990), Allan Pred discusses the impact of modernity on the language of Stockholm during the years 1880–1900, relating the changes in language at the time to the burgeoning capitalism of late nineteenth-century Sweden, patterns of rural–urban migration, population growth, human dislocation and class stratification. In such times of radical social reconstruction, new words and new discourses enter languages, while '[o]ld meanings are likewise disrupted or altered, defeated or disfigured'. Thus, he argues, 'to uncover lost words, no longer durable meanings and expressions, to retrieve elements from no longer spoken dialects, jargons, and slangs, is to lift the lid from a treasure chest of past social realities, to reveal fragments shimmering with the reflections of lost worlds of everyday life' (Pred 1990: 7 8).

A central theme of this book is that in the three hundred and more years following Peter Mundy's visit to Macao in 1637, many new words were created and used by westerners in China (and by Chinese in contact with westerners) in the context of China trade, and the western settlements in treaty-port enclaves and colonial Hong Kong. As a result of western modernity's intrusion into late Qing China, language is renegotiated and reordered, not only the Chinese language, through the modernising influences of missionary and colonial language scholars, but also English, where by the late nineteenth century it is possible to identify a distinct lexicon of what I have referred to earlier as 'China Coast English'. Following Pred's argument, it is also possible to see the growth and development of such varieties as 'Canton English', 'China Coast English' and 'Hong Kong English' not only in terms of words borrowed, invented and gained, but also in terms of words and discourses discarded, lost and forgotten. In the final decades of colonial Hong Kong, linguists and others were engaged with issues related to 'language contact' and 'mixed languages', while the experiences and debates of much earlier eras were forgotten or ignored.

The relevance of the historical to the 'new Englishes' is simple and direct. As Kachru states, 'the use of the term "new" is a misnomer: in a historical and linguistic sense these varieties are not new ... the "newness" of these varieties lies in the recent recognition of their linguistic and literary institutionalization' (1994: 2787).

5   Hong Kong, China and Chinese Englishes

My fellow students, you and I have studied in this English colony and in an English University, and we must learn by English examples. We must carry the English example of good government to every part of China.

> (Sun Yat-sen 1923, cited in Ingrams 1952: 261–2)

I have Chairman Mao's works, You have Chairman Mao's works. He has Chairman Mao's works, too. We study Chairman Mao's works hard.

> (1977 English textbook, cited in Adamson and Morris 1997: 17)

As this century ends and the 21st century approaches, what do we need now? We need heroes. What else do we need? English . . . Make me an international fighter! Make me a hero! I want to be somebody someday!

> (Li Yang, in Zhang Yuan's 2000 film, *Crazy English*)

Hong Kong becoming Xiang Gang

At midnight on 30 June 1997, Hong Kong ceased to be a British colony. The handover ceremony took place at the Convention and Exhibition Centre in Wanchai, on the northern waterfront of Hong Kong Island. The British representatives at the ceremony included Christopher Patten, the last governor of Hong Kong, the Foreign Secretary Robin Cook, Prime Minister Tony Blair and Prince Charles. Chinese government officials included President Jiang Zemin, Prime Minister Li Peng, Vice-Premier Qian Qichen, People's Liberation Army General Zhang Wannian and Tung Chee-hwa, the first Chief Executive of the HKSAR.

In his speech to the 400 guests and assembled world media at the ceremony, President Jiang Zemin commented on the historical significance of the event, declaring in Putonghua that:

> The national flag of the People's Republic of China and the regional flag of the Hong Kong Special Administrative Region of the People's Republic of China have now solemnly risen over this land. The return of Hong Kong to the motherland after going through a century of vicissitudes indicates

that from now on, the Hong Kong compatriots have become true masters of this Chinese land and that Hong Kong has now entered a new era of development. (Matheson 1997: 3)

Jiang Zemin concluded his speech by restating the commitment of the PRC government to the 'one country, two systems' concept, with its promise of 'a high degree of autonomy' for the executive, legislative and judicial branches of the Hong Kong government. At the end of the ceremony, in the words of the *South China Morning Post*, 'the two groups of principal officials stood, shook hands and descended from the stage into history' (Matheson 1997: 3).

Some five years on, Hong Kong's history has been less political than economic. By 1998, the recession that hit other Asian economies began to bite Hong Kong and the following five years have seen unprecedented budget deficits, increasing unemployment and the halving of residential property values. Ironically, in the years before 1997, a favourite trope of journalists and other commentators had hinged on the nature of the transition, and whether Hong Kong's economy and lifestyle would 'take over' the mainland, rather than the reverse.

All economic indicators for the territory have plunged while those of the PRC, led by the resurgent financial powerhouse of Shanghai, have risen sharply. On 12 October 2001, the World Trade Organisation granted full entry to China as an equal member of the world's leading capitalist trade organisation. As capitalism 'with Chinese characteristics' spreads throughout mainland China, a number of commentators, both local and international, have voiced concerns that Hong Kong's position as a leading business and financial centre might soon be superseded by Shanghai.

As China's business and trading communities adapt to international markets, the popularity of English seems to have reached a new high with government policy-makers, educationalists and the Chinese public. A recent news article from Shanghai reported on a sustained campaign to promote English throughout the city involving 'English days' for schools and self-study courses for police, restaurant staff and taxi-drivers:

> At many Shanghai schools, Wednesday is English day. Dormitories wake up to broadcasts of recorded English news and stories. All day, students make their own radio shows, study math, search the internet, and watch movies – in English. They sing the Back Street Boys and Jennifer Lopez songs in class, and view '*Sesame Street*' after school on Shanghai TV . . . In addition to English day in schools, they've passed out English tapes and books to other sectors of society likely to encounter English-speaking visitors, such as taxi-drivers. (Johnson 2001: 7)

The article claims that 'Shanghai's accent on English skills also reflects a longer-term desire to overtake rival Hong Kong as a Chinese, and Asian financial hub', and speculates that 'Shanghai's economy was on track to equal Hong Kong's in 15 years, if present growth rates continue' (2001: 7).

The broad picture now seems to show the PRC is out-performing most other Asian and western economies, with an estimated annual economic growth rate of around 7 to 9 per cent. And, in the minds of many, English seems inextricably linked to the nation's continued economic growth. When Deng Xiao-ping emerged as China's leader in the aftermath of the Cultural Revolution, the government adopted an 'Open-Door' policy towards the West that brought with it a renewed interest in the learning of foreign languages, particularly English.

Precise figures are hard to come by, but some statistics are available. These indicate a dramatic and rapid spread of English throughout China in the last forty years or so. For example, in 1957, at the height of Russian's popularity in schools, it is estimated that there were only 850 secondary-school English teachers in the whole country. By 2000, this figure had risen to about 500,000, and the government is planning to extend the teaching of English language to all primary schools (Adamson 2002). Current estimates of the numbers of English speakers in China have recently put the figure at over 200 million and rising, with 50 million secondary schoolchildren now studying the language (Zhao and Campbell 1995; Adamson 2002).

Hong Kong's reunification with mainland China has raised a vast number of issues related to the economic, political and social development of the HKSAR, some of which I have considered in earlier sections of this book, notably chapter 2. But linguistic issues obviously are present in this process as well. The Basic Law of Hong Kong broadly stipulated that the Hong Kong way of life would remain largely unaltered through a system of 'one country, two systems' for a period of fifty years, but the 'convergence' of the HKSAR with the People's Republic has already begun. In the previous chapter, the case was made for a recognition of the autonomy of 'Hong Kong English', as being on a par with the other Englishes of Asia, and part of the rationale for this paradigm shift is historically constructed. In chapter 2, the links between Canton jargon and Hong Kong English are described in some detail, as I argue that Hong Kong English has its own forgotten pasts in the South China context. As Hong Kong now becomes 'Hong Kong, China', with the prospect of becoming '*Xiang Gang, Zhong Guo*' over the next few decades, it is perhaps apposite to consider other aspects of China's forgotten, or at least partially remembered, history of English.

Visitors to the University of Hong Kong (HKU) who walk through the main building erected in 1911–12, with its balconies, cloisters, columns and fishponds, are often struck by the apparent uniqueness of this monument to British colonial education in China. The photographs of the university that appear in newspaper and television reports are invariably those of the main building (or 'Loke Yew Hall' as it is sometimes known), which tends to reinforce the image of the institution as a British colonial edifice in the minds of the Hong Kong media and public. This is despite the fact that over the past fifty years, the university has built scores of other more modern buildings, both on adjacent sites and in a number of other locations some distance from the original campus.

In the imagined history of the university, its colonial past plays an ambivalent role in its negotiation with the present, and recently the university's senior management have gone to some pains to 'reposition' the institution as a research-oriented international university located in Hong Kong. Its faculty at present are approximately 60 per cent Chinese, and represent a range of sino-ethnicities, including Hong Kong Chinese, Taiwanese, mainland Chinese, Chinese-Americans, etc., and 40 per cent international, including Americans, Australians, British, Canadians, New Zealanders, Singaporeans and South Asians, together with smaller numbers of other nationalities. The reality of the university today is that it is a complex multilingual and multicultural institution, where English is predominantly retained as the medium of lectures, but Cantonese and other varieties of Chinese are also used in less formal situations. Nevertheless, the belief that the university was, historically, a singular centre for western learning and a unique English-medium university in China is still widely held in the academic, as well as the general, community.

While this may have been largely true in the years since the establishment of the PRC government in 1949, it was by no means the case in the early decades of the twentieth century. In fact, when the University of Hong Kong was built, there were already a sizeable number of western universities established in China and, by the 1920s, HKU was linked to a loosely established system of western colleges that stretched across China (Forster 1932).[1] Unlike HKU, however, which was established explicitly as a secular institution, those on the mainland were predominantly Protestant missionary institutions known as the 'Chinese Christian colleges'. Like the system of missionary schools that fed them, these colleges were to play a crucial role in the spread of English throughout China in the late nineteenth and early twentieth centuries.

Missionary schools and colleges in China

As we saw in chapter 3, the very earliest missionary schools were established in South China, in Macao and Hong Kong. Prominent amongst these were the Morrison Education Society School (opened at Macao in 1839 and transferred to Hong Kong in 1842) and the Anglo-Chinese College (which moved to Hong Kong from Malacca in 1843). The Morrison Education Society School lasted only ten years, but in that time educated a number of early Chinese modernisers. The first headmaster of the Morrison Education Society School was an American missionary, Samuel R. Brown, a Yale graduate. The school's students included the entrepreneurial Tong King-sing 唐景星 (1832–1892), the author of the *Chinese and English Instructor* (pp. 172–8 above), Yung Wing 容閎 (1828–1912) and Wong

---

[1] For details of the establishment and early development of the University of Hong Kong, see Mellor (1980, 1992).

Fun 黄欵 (1828–78), believed to be the first Chinese graduates of western universities. Yung was the first Chinese to graduate from Yale, in 1854, while Wong graduated with a degree in medicine from Edinburgh in 1857 (Smith 1985).

Yung Wing was later influential in establishing the Chinese Educational Mission, which between 1872 and 1881 sent over 120 Chinese students to America for their education. This initiative began in 1870, when Yung Wing was summoned to a conference with highly placed government officials to discuss what measures the government might adopt to modernise China. At the same conference, the first steps were taken to establish a domestic steamship company, which was later to become the China Merchants' Steamship Navigation Company, in which Tong King-sing would play a leading role. Although the Chinese Educational Mission was abandoned in 1881, its 'returnee' students took up positions in the government, in the military and navy, and in many commercial organisations (Yung 1939). In this and other ways, the graduates of the Morrison Education Society School played a direct role in the 'self-strengthening' movement promoted by Chinese intellectuals in the last years of the nineteenth century.

In Hong Kong, a number of other influential missionary schools were established throughout the nineteenth century, including St Paul's College (1851), the Diocesan Native Female Training School (1860) and St Joseph's College (1876). The Hong Kong government's first secondary school, the Central School (later renamed Queen's College), was established in 1862. By the end of the nineteenth century, Queen's College was increasingly engaged in educating the sons of the Chinese elite in Hong Kong, and produced a number of celebrated graduates. The most famous of these was Sun Yat-sen 孫逸仙, leader of the 1911 revolution that overthrew the Manchu-led Qing dynasty, who studied there from 1884 to 1886. After Queen's College, Sun Yat-sen was one of the first students at the Hong Kong College of Medicine. He graduated in 1892, before embarking on a political career which culminated in his gaining the presidency of China in 1912. In 1923, Sun returned to Hong Kong and addressed a group of students, saying:

> Where and how did I get my revolutionary and modern ideas? I got my ideas in this very place; in the colony of Hong Kong. More than 30 years ago I was studying in Hong Kong and spent a great deal of spare time in walking the streets of the Colony. Hong Kong impressed me a good deal because there was orderly calm and because there was artistic work being done without interruption.. My fellow students, you and I have studied in this English colony and in an English University, and we must learn by English examples. We must carry the English example of good government to every part of China. (Sun Yat-sen, 1923, cited in Ingrams 1952: 261–2)

Elsewhere in China, missionary education began to expand after the end of the Second Opium War in 1860, due to the rapid expansion in the numbers of treaty ports and Protestant missionary efforts to convert the Chinese. Initially, progress was slow, and by the 1870s there were only twenty mission schools, with around 230 students. After the Boxer Rebellion of 1900, the numbers of missionaries grew very rapidly and, by 1925, more than 250,000 children were being educated in 7,000 Christian elementary schools, and around 26,000 in middle schools (Deng 1997).[2]

China's Christian colleges

The thirteen Protestant Christian colleges that were set up at the turn of the century also had a profound influence on Chinese education. These were St John's University in Shanghai (from 1879), Hangchow University (1897), Soochow University (from 1901), Shantung Christian University (also known as 'Cheeloo' University, from 1902), Lingnan University (previously 'Canton Christian College', from 1903), the University of Shanghai (1906), the University of Nanking (1910), West China Union University (1910) at Chengdu, Yenching University (at Beijing, from 1912), Fukien Christian University (1915), Ginling College (1915), Hwa Nan Women's College (at Fuzhou, from 1921) and Hua Chung University (at Wuhan, from 1927).[3] After the establishment of the PRC government in 1949, foreign missionaries were expelled from China, and the Christian colleges were renamed or merged with other institutions. The names in brackets in map 5.1 refer to the current titles of these institutions in the PRC.

The numbers of students attending these colleges were typically quite small. At the height of their influence, their total enrolment was in the order of some 12,000 students, while the numbers at St John's and Yenching were around 500 at each. In addition to these thirteen colleges, there was also Yale-in-China or

---

[2] Other important sources for the history of western missionary schools and colleges in China include Latourette (1929), Lutz (1971) and Ng (1996).

[3] St John's University was planned by Samuel I. J. Schereschewsky, an Episcopalian, modelled itself on an American university, and was founded in 1879. Hangchow University began as an American Presbyterian boarding school in 1845. Shantung Christian University (Cheeloo University) began as Tengchow College, founded in 1882 by the American Presbyterian Calvin W. Mateer, first attaining university status in 1902. Lingnan University began its collegiate life as 'Canton Christian College', established by American Presbyterians around 1904, while the University of Shanghai was set up by Northern and Southern Baptists from the USA in 1906. The University of Nanking was set up with funding from the Methodists in 1910. West China Union University was founded as a joint enterprise (i.e. 'union') between American, British and Canadian missionary groups in 1910. Soochow University was founded through the efforts of Southern Methodists in 1911, and Yenching University was established by various Protestant groups in 1912, including Methodists, Presbyterians Congregationalists (an early vice-president was the Henry W. Luce, the father of the founder of *Time* magazine). Fukien Christian University was established at Foochow in 1915 through a union between American and British missionary groups, and in the same year Ginling College was founded by Baptists, Methodists, Presbyterians and other nonconformist groups. Hwa Nan at Foochow (Fuzhou) was founded by the Methodist Episcopal Church, and became a university in 1921. Huachung University (the 'Central China University') at Wuhan was created in 1927 by the amalgamation of a number of colleges, including the Yale-in-China (or *Yali*) college at Changsha (Erh and Johnson 1998). Catholic institutions of higher learning at this time included the Aurora University in Shanghai, Tientsin College of Industry and Commerce and the Catholic University of Peking (Fu Jen) (Li 1954).

Map 5.1 China's Christian colleges, c. 1880–1952

'Yali' at Changsha and Tsinghua University, set up in 1911 with money from the Boxer Indemnity Fund (reparations the Chinese government was forced to pay after the 1900–1 rebellion). This institution was partly staffed by western missionaries, and run along American lines. The influence of such schools and colleges on society was felt throughout the 1920s and 1930s, when increasing numbers of middle-class parents sent their children to them to be educated:

> Mission schools could be viewed two ways. From the point of view of rad-ical Chinese nationalists, they were tools of Western cultural imperialism because they disseminated values of the Judeo-Christian culture among the Chinese people.. On the other hand, mission schools made undeni-able contributions to China's modernization, not only in technological terms, but in social and political terms as well. Christian colleges answered the need of Chinese youth for western learning and pioneered instruc-tion in practical fields such as medicine, nursing, agriculture, sociology, economics, and law. (Deng 1997: 69)

The mission schools were pioneers in female education, especially the Bridgman Girls' School in Beijing (1864) and the Shanghai Chinese–Western School for Girls (1890). By 1905, around 7,000 girls were being taught at the primary level, and 2,700 in secondary schools. Women's colleges followed, including Hwa Nan College in Fuzhou and Ginling College in Nanjing. A number of the Christian colleges were also innovators in certain specialist fields of study. The University of Nanking and Lingnan University (Canton Christian College) in Guangzhou were known for work on agriculture and pest control, Soochow University for legal studies, St John's and Hangchow for business, and Yenching University in Beijing for journalism and sociology. Medicine was strong at St John's and the North China Union Medical College (Deng 1997).

Missionary language debates

Many of the colleges taught English, although this was a subject of continual controversy and debate. Most of the colleges opted for the use of English as a teaching medium, although the management of languages tended to vary from college to college. At Peking University (the forerunner to Yenching University), the curriculum offered two parallel streams of study, the first through the Chinese 'vernacular', and the second using English as a teaching medium for all courses apart from Chinese studies. In 1888, the main objective of the English-medium programme was expressed thus:

> It will be our aim to give the student a critical and practical knowledge of the English language such as will open up to him all the treasures of Theology, of Science and Philosophy, and enable him, by the aid of current literature, to keep abreast of the times and render him fit to be a leader among the millions of his people to whom all this is a sealed book. (Edwards 1959: 20)

When Yenching University was founded in 1912, much emphasis was placed on Chinese studies at the college, especially after the establishment of the Harvard–Yenching Institute, whose brief was, *inter alia*, to function as a centre for the cataloguing and study of Chinese literature (Edwards 1959). The institute survives to the present day at Harvard University, Massachusetts.

Some universities became particularly well known for the quality of their graduates' command of English, and of these St John's in Shanghai gained an outstanding reputation. Under the leadership of its missionary principal, Dr Francis L. H. Pott, English became the main teaching medium at the college, so that 'St John's began to be known as the English training center of China' (Xu 1994: 22). Pott's own attitude to English was spelled out in his 1887 report to the Board of Missions, where he enumerated the benefits of English teaching as follows:

(1) By teaching students English we are doing something of the same character in educating the Chinese mind, as Greek and Latin accomplish for the foreign boy. The analysis of the words, the close study of their meaning, the drill in syntax, all tend toward developing the analytical powers of their mind; (2) We are doing our little toward helping in the civilization of China, preparing men capable of coming in contact with foreigners, and of filling important positions in business; (3) We are doing something toward breaking down the prejudice against everything foreign, so strong in the Chinese mind; (4) We are proving that we are acting on the ground that Christianity teaches us to prepare men to play their part well in this life, as well as teaching them about a life to come: and (5) China wishes now, and must have, at least in her open ports, natives acquainted with English. It is better to allow them to acquire English in schools where they receive Christian instruction than in schools totally of a secular character. (Pott 1887, cited in Xu 1994: 21)

Such institutional enthusiasm for English was by no means the norm at all Christian colleges. At Shantung University (or 'Cheeloo'), a debate about English was fiercely fought over a number of decades. Calvin W. Mateer and his wife Ada were convinced advocates of Chinese as a teaching medium. Other teachers at Shantung included Henry W. Luce and Samuel Couling, the author of a celebrated guide to sinology, the *The Encyclopaedia Sinica* (1917). The opposition of Mateer and like-minded colleagues to the teaching of English was motivated by their belief that a knowledge of the language would lure their charges away from Bible study and the church into commerce and money-making. Mateer and his wife were accomplished Chinese linguists, and published a number of dictionaries and guides to the language.

Demand for English was so strong, however, that in November 1906 the students at Shangtung organised a student strike and petitioned the faculty for a more modern approach to Chinese studies and the introduction of English as a subject of study (Corbett 1955). The Secretary of the Presbyterian Board in New York, Arthur J. Brown, was willing to consider such a proposal, but it was firmly opposed by Mateer and others:

If introduced at the beginning of the course, as is done in nearly all the schools that teach English at all, it would rapidly secularize the school and so defeat the chief aim for which the College exists. Second, it would make adequate education in Chinese, such as is now given in the College, impossible of realization, and third, it would be ministering to a demand that is based almost wholly on a desire for money – higher salaries for all graduates, and through them wealth for the Church. If introduced near the end of the course it would largely fail of its commonly avowed purpose of making English effective help in literary or scientific pursuits, while it would put in the way of students a temptation to use their education for purely mercenary purposes, which, as experience has shown, the average young man is generally unable to resist. (Mateer and Burt, cited by Corbett 1955: 77–8)

After Mateer's retirement in 1907, the school's directors finally agreed to the introduction of English, but subject to severe restrictions, including the payment of an extra $30 per year, which effectively doubled tuition fees for those who took this option. These restrictions were so severe that in 1909 only 16 out of 246 students were able to study the language. Just as these changes were being introduced in 1908, Mateer died aged 72, his antipathy for English as strong as ever:

> The faith of the long old centuries is passing rapidly away, but what shall the new faith be? This is the great Christian question of the hour. The young men of China are mad to learn English, because there is money in it. With English come books and newspapers, sowing the seeds of agnoticism [*sic*], and skepticism and rationalism and so forth. The cry is, Who will champion the truth? Who will administer the antidote? Who will uphold the cross? Who will testify for Christ? . . Young men, it is time to be up and doing! The march of events will not wait your tardiness. Who will hear the Master's trumpet call? (Mateer 1908, cited by Corbett 1955: 83–4)

Mateer's worries may have been premature, as Shantung University was able to maintain its emphasis on Chinese at least for the next decade or so, although the debates between missionaries on this topic persisted. In a 1915 article in the missionary journal *The Chinese Recorder* entitled 'The Place of English in Education in China', one A.W. March pointed out that 'Shantung University has to-day the largest enrollment in the college department of any mission school in China, and Chinese is the medium of instruction' (March 1915: 110). March then went on to argue strenuously against the use of English as a teaching medium, asserting that the benefits of using Chinese included far greater efficiency in training teachers and administrators, and the effective running of schools through the preparation of teaching materials and the fixing of terminology. In comparison, the use of English was inefficient, as it largely benefited that minority of students who were intending to study abroad, its use hindered cooperation with Chinese educational authorities, and it also weakened the religious influence of the school.

A year later, the *Recorder* published a rejoinder from a Canton Christian College teacher named House, who put the case for English in his own institution where his students, he claimed, also attained high standards ('almost classical') in their Chinese studies. At his college, he reported, English was taught well, as 'the young American instructor, fresh from his college life, full of vigor, and enthusiastic for fellowship, athletics and sport, enters, a live wire into the spirit of student life around them . . It is "the man up against the boy" that counts and it is the proper use of English that makes this possible' (House 1916: 100). House went on to conclude enthusiastically that:

For a dozen years and more the deep desire of the Chinese for English
and a Western education has presented a perfect opportunity for laying
hold of China's youth, for winning the cooperation and gifts of the best
Chinese, and for quickly and thoroughly educating an adequate Christian
leadership. This opportunity, to our everlasting discredit, is still passing
unmet because of the delay in making proper use of English, an instrument
at hand, perfectly suited to the task and of which we ourselves are masters.
(1916: 103)

Such an American 'can do' attitude was not untypical of the Protestant Christian Colleges, as the impetus for their foundation and development came mainly
from American not British missionary societies. Hayhoe comments that 'it is
striking how limited was the British influence on Chinese education, especially at the tertiary level', and explains this with reference to the fact that very
few of the British missionaries had received a university education themselves
(1996: 18).

The backlash against missionary education

Not all westerners in China were enamoured of the missionary approach to
education. Bertrand Russell (1872–1970) visited China in the academic year
1920–1, and was dismayed at many aspects of the American influence he saw
there. On his arrival at Peking University, he began his first lecture with the words,
'I am a communist', and then proceeded to extol the virtues of communism to
an audience of 1,500 (Moorehead 1992: 326).[4] Russell also visited Tsinghua, and
thought the education there 'thorough and good', noting that 'One great merit,
which belongs to American institutions generally is that the students are made
to learn English' (Russell [1922] 1966: 218). At the same time, however, Russell
had grave doubts about the civilising zeal of American missionaries:

The Chinese have a civilization and a national temperament in many ways
superior to those of the white men. A few Europeans ultimately discover
this, but Americans never do. They remain always missionaries – not of
Christianity, though they often think that is what they are preaching, but
of Americanism. What is Americanism? 'Clean living, clean thinking, and
pep', I think an American would reply. This means, in practice, the substitution of tidiness for art, cleanliness for beauty, moralizing for philosophy,
prostitutes for concubines (as being easier to conceal), and a general air
of being fearfully busy for the leisurely calm of the traditional Chinese.
Voltaire – that hardened old cynic – laid it down that the true ends of

---

[4] In similar vein, when George Bernard Shaw visited China in 1933, he is reported to have told
Hong Kong University students: 'If you read, read real books and steep yourself in revolutionary
books. Go up to your neck in Communism, because if you are not a revolutionist at twenty, you
will be at fifty an impossible fossil' (cited in Gray 1985: 216).

life are '*aimer et penser*'. Both are common in China, but neither is compatible with 'pep'. The American influence, therefore, inevitably tends to eliminate both. If it prevailed it would, no doubt, by means of hygiene, save the lives of many Chinamen, but would at the same time make them not worth saving. It cannot therefore be regarded as wholly and altogether satisfactory. (1922: 221)

He further concluded that 'One can never rid oneself of the feeling that the education controlled by white men is not disinterested: it seems always designed, unconsciously in the main, to produce convenient tools for the capitalist penetration of China by merchants and manufacturers of the nation concerned', but he spoke highly of modern Chinese universities such as Peking, where the students 'to a man' were socialists, 'as are most of the best among their Chinese teachers' (1922: 222).

In a rather different vein, Reginald F. Johnston (1874–1938), the English tutor to Pu Yi 溥儀, the 'Last Emperor' of Manchu China, was also critical of the missionary influence in China, which he saw as irrational and pernicious. Johnston authored an extended critique of missionaries entitled *A Chinese Appeal to Christendom* under the pseudonym of Lin Shao-yang, in which he lambasted their 'bigotry and ignorance' (Lin 1911: 288). He also made the case for a rational and secular approach to education, one that paid due respect to traditional Chinese philosophy and religions, arguing that 'The wisest of them [Christians] now know – and the wisest among Chinese know too – that perfection and absolute truth are to be found neither in the systems of the West nor in those of the East' (1911: 311). A number of other British intellectuals also played important roles in teaching English language and literature in China in the republican period, including Harold Acton (1904–94), William Empson (1906–84) and Ivor Armstrong Richards (1893–1979), who all did teaching stints at universities in Beijing during the interwar years. In this period, I. A. Richards devoted much time and energy to promoting his and C. K. Ogden's 'Basic English' project to the Nationalist government, and it was probably only the advent of war that prevented its adoption in the national education system (Tong 1999).

As early as 1922, however, missionary education came under heavy fire from university students and teachers working in Chinese colleges such as Peking University, Peking Higher Normal College, Peking Normal School, Communications University and Nankai University. Soon after, anti-Christian organisations were set up in Guangzhou, Nanjing, Hangzhou and Beijing, and campaigns against Christianity gathered momentum over the next five years, drawing support from the 'New Thought' movement, as well as nationalism and communism (Yamamoto and Yamamoto 1953). The manifesto of the pro-communist Anti-Christian Student Federation which was issued in March 1922 argued that Christianity and the Christian church were 'devils' who supported 'a looting and oppressing class' against 'the looted and oppressed class' (Yamamoto and Yamamoto 1953: 144). The manifesto further asserted that:

The world's capitalism which has grown and matured is now on the verge of collapse. Accordingly, capitalists of every country – whether in England, America, Japan or France – have become panic-stricken, and have used all possible means to seek a bare chance of survival. Whereupon they have all flocked to China one after another, and carried out an economic invasion. Modern Christianity and the Christian church are the vanguards of this economic invasion. (cited in Yamamoto and Yamamoto 1953: 144)

May Fourth and beyond

The defining moment for student radicalism in China had occurred three years earlier, on 4 May 1919, when Peking students protested against the terms of the Treaty of Versailles which handed German holdings in Shandong to Japan. There were also student demonstrations in Christian colleges throughout China, including Ginling, Hangchow, St John's and Shantung. These protests marked the beginnings of movements in politics, literature and creative writing that would influence Chinese intellectuals for generations to come across a number of political spectra, including both communists and nationalists. Further troubles followed the 30 May incident of 1925, when a Chinese worker was shot and killed and others injured during a demonstration in the British concession in Shanghai. Many students quit the Christian colleges, and there were demonstrations and other protests at St John's, Lingnan and Yali (Yale-in-China). Increasingly, mission schools and colleges were seen as bastions of foreign control and privilege that were at add odds with the creation of national pride and identity (Deng 1997).

In 1924–5, the Peking government introduced new regulations requiring the registration of missionary secondary schools, to safeguard the 'educational rights' of Chinese people. It was also mandated that the principals of such schools be Chinese citizens, that religious instruction be optional, and that their teaching should follow the guidelines issued by the government. Similar regulations were issued by the nationalists in Canton. In the years that followed, the Christian colleges began to comply with these regulations, and to transfer administrative posts to their Chinese colleagues. In some parts of China, including Nanjing, the tension between the nationalists and the missionaries spilled over into violence between Kuomintang troops and missionaries, and an estimated 3,000 missionaries left China at this time. By the end of 1928, many of the most important administrative positions in the Christian colleges had been taken over by Chinese staff. Many missionary elementary and secondary schools were secularised, although, ironically, the number of mission secondary school students continued to rise substantially until 1936 (Deng 1997).

The nationalist government established at Nanjing in 1927 attempted to integrate the mission schools into the national education system and appointed political instructors to mission schools, to ensure that teachers implemented government policy. Mission schools were allowed to continue teaching, but compulsory religious teaching was forbidden, and the administration of schools and colleges sinicised. Outside the treaty ports such reforms were accepted, but in cities like Shanghai there was resistance to such policies. With the onset of war against the Japanese in 1937, however, the relationship between the missionary schools and the government improved. From 1937–41, a number of colleges, including Cheeloo, Soochow and Yenching, continued to operate in Japanese-controlled areas, while others moved to Chengdu in Sichuan province (Deng 1997).

After the defeat of the Japanese, many of the missionary colleges attempted to resume their work, but their campuses rapidly became the site of renewed disturbances between nationalists and communists, who were gaining ground at universities such as St John's, Soochow and Yenching. A wave of anti-American feeling swept through many campuses, and many student activists from the colleges joined the communists. After 1949, many Christian teachers had stayed on at the colleges, but in the subsequent reorganisation, all foreign missionaries were expelled from China. Deng's assessment of missionary education emphasises its role in modernising China in the early decades of the twentieth century: by 1947, he states, Christian colleges were educating 15 to 20 per cent of university students in the country, and had made a substantial contribution to Chinese society.

> Christian education was not totally a foreign operation but involved many Chinese Christians. It received support from the Chinese government, through the Ministry of Education, and from the Chinese gentry class. At Christian schools, the best of the West and East met. And, despite the religious bias of their founders and home societies, mission schools represented the charitable side of Western culture. In the formative years of modern China, Christian education provided the much needed information on Western science, and many ideas that became constructs of a new culture. (Deng 1997: 86)

By the Republican period, however, in addition to missionary initiatives in English studies, there had developed an indigenous tradition of English-language teaching, which began in the late Qing era and extended into the years of the nationalist government.

Chinese initiatives in teaching English, 1862–1911

After the end of the Second Opium War in 1860, a number of Chinese officials and intellectuals, including Prince Kung 恭親王 (1833–98) and Li Hung-Chang 李鴻章 (1823–1901), became increasingly concerned at the western intrusion into China. They recognised the need for China to modernise its military and technical knowledge in order to combat the threat from European and American powers. This initiative became known as 'the self-strengthening movement', and its proponents argued that the learning of European languages, especially

English, was necessary for educational reform. Accordingly, Prince Kung and a number of his advisors petitioned the Emperor:

> We request Your Majesty to order Canton and Shanghai each to send to Peking two men who understand foreign spoken and written languages to be commissioned and consulted. We note that in any negotiations with foreign nations, the prerequisite is to know their nature and feelings. At present, their speech cannot be understood and their writing can hardly be deciphered. Everything is impeded. (Prince Kung *et al.*, cited in Teng and Fairbank 1967: 74)

Following this, in 1862, an interpreters' college, the *Tongwen Guan* 同文館, was established in Beijing and attached to the Office of Foreign Affairs, the *Zongli Yamen* 總理衙門. This latter institution had been set up to deal with the foreign envoys to China, permitted to reside in the capital by the Treaty of Tianjin in 1860. Although the *Tongwen Guan* was initially conceived as a purely patriotic and Chinese venture, some foreign teachers were employed at the school. These included the missionary William Alexander Parsons Martin (1827–1916), who was to play an important role in its development over the following decades. In addition, Robert Hart (1835–1911), the Inspector-General of China's Imperial Maritime Customs, was recruited to help manage the school. The *Tongwen Guan* gradually began to teach technical subjects in addition to languages, offering courses in anatomy, chemistry, geology, mineralogy and physics.

Similar schools were then established in other parts of China, including Shanghai and Guangzhou. At Shanghai's Foreign Language School (*Waiguo Yuyan Wenzi Xueguan* 外國語言文字學館), the American missionary Young J. Allen was recruited to teach English. The school offered a range of courses relevant to the needs of Shanghai's expanding business community, including Chinese studies, history and foreign languages. The school was later renamed the School for Dispersing Languages (*Guang Fangyan Guan* 廣方言館) and was merged with the Jiangnan Arsenal 江南製造局, which trained students in armaments, mechanical engineering and shipbuilding. Ross (1993) ascribes the school's success largely to the fact that the majority of the teaching staff were Chinese:

> In contrast to the overwhelmingly foreign composition of the Beijing Tongwen Guan's teaching and administrative staff, 24 of Shanghai's 29 teachers were Chinese. They were able to adapt their curriculum to Shanghai's uniquely cosmopolitan character, invoking Confucian tradition for institutional legitimacy and stability, yet meeting the competition they faced for qualified students from a growing number of modern schools established in Shanghai... 'Western studies' were attractive to Shanghai youths not just as the second-best vehicle for social mobility but because of the alternatives to tradition they presented. (1993: 27)

Despite the strong attraction of western studies, however, there was, almost from the outset, a concern that such studies should not undermine the educational basis of Chinese culture. This brought with it the perceived need to make a clear distinction between Chinese and western systems of learning. After China's defeat in the Sino-Japanese War of 1895, Zhang Zhidong 張之洞 (1837–1909) urged increased emphasis on the learning of foreign languages, but also made much of the distinction between Chinese and western values in education. Zhang's philosophy was expressed in the saying 'Chinese learning for fundamental principles, Western learning for practical application' (*Zhongxue wei ti, xixue wei yong* 中學為體，西學為用). Zhang explained this thus:

> In relations between China and the outside world, commercial affairs are the *t'i* [foundation] and armed force is the *yong* [technique]. Understanding regulations embodied in treaties and having a thorough knowledge of various countries' mining production, trade conditions, border defenses, administration orders, schools, military equipment, public laws and statutes are fundamental. The gateway is an understanding of the languages of other nations. (Zhang, cited in Ross 1993: 28)

Zhang reasoned that one should attempt to combine the substance of Chinese civilisation (*ti* 體) with the functional means of the West (*yong* 用), although he also argued that a detailed knowledge of the Chinese classics was a prerequisite for foreign-language study, as '[t]o know foreign countries and not know China is to lose one's conscience' (Zhang, cited in Ross 1993: 28).

However, institutions such as *Tongwen Guan* and Jiangnan Arsenal were relatively short-lived. After the Sino-Japanese War and Boxer Rebellion, the Qing government introduced new educational reforms, including the introduction of a national system of education based on the Japanese system (1902) and the abolition of the imperial examinations (1905). After 1898, the *Tongwen Guan* was merged with Peking University. Ross argues that Zhang Zhidong's attempt to maintain 'Chinese substance' was simply unfeasible, that the self-strengtheners were caught between a doomed Confucian order and western modernity and that, eventually, 'foreign-language proficiency became identified with foreign substance as well as function' (1993: 30). This again points to a fault line in English-language teaching in China which persists to the present: simply stated, how China might learn from the West, and yet at the same time preserve the integrity of Chinese culture, however defined.

English teaching in the Republican period (1911–49)

In the last decades of the Qing dynasty, large numbers of Chinese-run 'modern schools' (*xuetang* 學堂) were established in cities like Shanghai in competition with the mission schools, in response to a growing nationalism across China. According to the new national syllabus introduced in 1903, the three core subjects to be taught in schools were Chinese, mathematics and foreign languages. The number of government-funded schools increased very rapidly and soon outstripped the mission schools. By the 1920s, education in all its aspects increasingly came under the control of nationalist governments, operating mainly from Guangzhou in the early period of the Republic, and later from Nanjing.

In nationalist secondary schools wide provision was made for foreign-language studies, although the usual method was that of 'grammar translation', which typically meant exercises in 'intensive reading', memorising and the grammatical analysis of sentences (Ross 1993: 33). Whereas students in the mission schools and Christian colleges typically acquired English through regular contact with foreign teachers and a variety of English-language literature, English teaching in the Chinese schools was usually based on a detailed comparison with Chinese and methods that emphasised translation rather than composition. As a result, 'translation exercises required that the acquisition of the foreign-language capability take place with constant reference to the native language, while composition exercises freed the students to seek self-expression in accordance with newly acquired foreign norms' (Yeh 1990: 14–15). 'Returnee students' who had studied abroad added another dimension to language teaching in this period. Between the late nineteenth century and the early 1950s, it was estimated that around 50,000 Chinese students were educated in the United States alone, and many of these returned to China as academics and teachers, and took part in the educational debates of the time (Chao 1953).

At the core of many such arguments was the issue of how Chinese values might best be protected from the onslaught of the West. The issue of English was invoked by many Chinese educators:

> Some concluded that the enduring 'spiritual' qualities of Chinese civilization must act as a counterbalance to the utilitarian but destructive power of the 'material' West. Others, including Marxists and pragmatists, denied this division and sought to adopt Western scientific and political values wholesale or adapt them in the service of social change. Foreign languages became an indirect vehicle for both the liberal's gradual cultural reformation and the leftist's radical socio–political activism. (Ross 1993: 33)

By 1927, as noted above, the climate of Chinese opinion had turned against mission schools, which were increasingly seen as 'a source of cultural and psychological disunity', and an example of 'inner imperialism' (Ross 1993: 34). The government introduced measures to recover 'educational rights', including a series of regulations requiring the registration of all private schools in China, and the appointment of Chinese administrators to oversee them.

Lin Yutang and Shanghai English

In spite of various movements against foreigners in the nationalist period, an indigenous English-language intellectual culture did develop in the late 1920s and 1930s. This was based in that most literary of cities, Shanghai, and, once more, the memories of this period are largely forgotten, or, at best, only partly remembered, in the literature on this period.

One key figure among English-speaking Chinese intellectuals in Shanghai at this time was Lin Yutang 林語堂 (1895–1976), whose own intellectual development owed much to the influence of missionary educators. The son of a Chinese Presbyterian minister from Fujian province, Lin had his secondary education in Amoy (Xiamen), where he studied both Chinese and English. At the age of sixteen, he was admitted into St John's University Shanghai, which was, in his own words, 'the best school for studying English in China' (Sohigian 1991: 128). Once there, Lin read widely, including Darwin, Lamarck and Haekel on evolution theory, Westermarck on anthropology and H. S. Chamberlain on history. Initially intending to study theology, once at university he became increasingly sceptical and dropped his divinity studies. Lin also found that his Chinese studies suffered greatly at St John's, but he later went to some lengths to improve his knowledge of Chinese language and literature. When he graduated from St John's in 1916, he took up the post of professor of English at Tsinghua University and married Liao Cui-feng 廖翠鳳. In 1919, Lin went to the United States for graduate study, but financial difficulties forced him to move to Leipzig, where he enrolled for a PhD in linguistics. He gained his doctorate on *Altchinesische Lautlehre* ('Old Chinese phonetics') in 1923, and in the same year returned to China to take up a teaching post in the English Department of Peking University.

Lin stayed in Beijing from 1923 to 1926, but, after the city was taken over by warlords, he and a number of other colleagues, including Lu Xun 魯迅, decided to decamp to Amoy (Xiamen) University. After one year in Xiamen, followed by another working for the liberal faction of the Nationalist party at Hankou, Lin finally returned to Shanghai in 1928, where he immediately started writing, in both Chinese and English (Sohigian 1991). His Chinese writings established his popularity as a comic writer and satirist, and earned him the title of 'king of humour'. He also started contributing articles to two English-language publications, first the weekly *China Critic* 中國評論週報 and then *T'ien Hsia Monthly* 天下.

What is fascinating about both publications is that they were written in English by Chinese bilingual intellectuals for, as far as one can tell, a bilingual Chinese as well as an international audience. Shanghai's literati in the late 1920s fell into three groups, according to their educational background: the 'English-language group' (educated in England, the USA, or universities such as St John's, Tsinghua and Yenching); the 'French–German group' (often educated at Aurora Catholic University in Shanghai); and the 'Japanese-language group' which included those like Lu Xun who had studied in Japan (Lee 1999: 129). Those in the first category included Wen Yuan-ning 溫源寧, Wu Jing Xiong 吳經熊, Sun Fo 孫科 and Lin Yutang, all members of the editorial board of *T'ien Hsia Monthly*. They were representatives of a Chinese academic class who had been educated by missionaries in China and the West, were engaged in debate with westerners and other Chinese intellectuals, and were speaking for a modern China in an intellectual dialogue between East and West.

Wen, the chief editor, had studied at Cambridge University, where he caused a slight stir by taking his manservant with him. On his return to China he taught at Peking University from 1923 to 1934 before coming to Shanghai, and later served as the Chinese ambassador to Greece in the postwar period. According to Gill's (2001) fascinating account of the *T'ien Hsia* group, its 'most brilliant' member was arguably Wu Ching-hsiung (1899–1986), or John C. H. Wu, as he was known to English speakers.

The son of a prominent banker, Wu completed his undergraduate law degree at Soochow University in 1920, and then underwent postgraduate training at the University of Michigan for one year. While at Michigan, John Wu established a close personal friendship with Oliver Wendell Holmes, then eighty. On his return to China in 1924 he took up a legal career in Shanghai, first as professor of law, then principal, at his alma mater, Soochow University's Comparative Law School of China. In 1927 he became a judge and, in 1929 president of the Special High Court at Shanghai and a member of the Legislative Yuan. In 1936, he singlehandedly prepared the first draft of a new national constitution in just four weeks. After years of delay and revisions the constitution was finally adopted in 1946. Its first clause stated: 'The republic of China, founded on the Three People's Principles, is a democratic republic of the people, by the people and for the people.'

In 1935, John Wu took on the post of managing editor at *T'ien Hsia* at the request of Sun Fo, the son of Sun Yat-sen. In spite of the demands of his legal career, Wu was an enthusiast for the cultural and literary pursuits, and even published an introductory textbook on the study of English literature. The introduction to the first issue of *T'ien Hsia Monthly* was written by Sun Fo, then president of the Legislative Yuan, who entered a plea for 'international goodwill' and 'cultural understanding': 'Culture traffics in ideas. It has no national boundaries, it enriches itself just as much by what it gives as what it takes ... Culture has always maintained an Open Door policy. There is only one condition for entry – the humility to learn' (Sun 1935:4). Sun then went on to add that 'being a Chinese-run organ', the journal's editorial policy was aimed at interpreting China to the West rather than the reverse, and that while 'current political controversies' were to be avoided, all else was permitted, citing one of his father's favourite quotations *Tian xia wei gong* 天下為公 ('The universe is for everyone').

Wu was a convinced humanist and internationalist, who himself published essays on both Chinese and western literature, including 'The Four seasons of Tang poetry' and 'Shakespeare as a Taoist'. T. K. Chuan wrote on 'Descartes and pseudo-intellectualism' and 'William James', and Wen Yuan-ning penned articles on 'A. E. Housman's poetry', 'Walter De La Mare's poetry' and 'Notes on four contemporary British poets'.

There were also articles by westerners on Chinese literature and culture, including Harold Acton on 'The creative spirit in modern Chinese literature' and a large number of essays by John C. Ferguson on Chinese fine arts. Other contributors were John Blofeld, C. R. Boxer, J. M. Braga, Lawrence Durrell, William Empson, Louis Golding, Emily Hahn, Henry Miller, Herbert Read,

Osbert Sitwell and Arthur Waley, and every issue also contained at least one translation from classical and contemporary Chinese literature. In one of Wu's essays appropriately titled, 'Un mélange', he extols the virtues of universalism in culture, remarking that one of the best books on Buddhism is written by Alan Watts, an Englishman; and one of the most informative books on the origin of China by an American, H. G. Creel. He continues:

> I have learned much about the American political institutions from DeTocqueville and James Bryce, and much about English literature from Taine and Legouis. It was Liang Ch'i-ch'ao who first initiated me into the western ways of thinking. It was G. Lowes Dickinson who opened my eyes to the lovableness of the Chinese outlook. Laotze taught me the philosophy of Shakespeare. Freud and Marx have helped me to a better appreciation of Mencius. (Wu 1937: 256)

Lin Yutang contributed a large number of articles and translations to *T'ien Hsia*, particularly in the early years of the journal. These included the articles 'Feminist thought in ancient China' (1935), 'The aesthetics of Chinese calligraphy' (1935) and 'Contemporary Chinese periodical literature' (1936). He also wrote a number of translations, including 'Six chapters of a floating life' (1935). During this period he completed and published his first book in English, *My Country and My People* (1935), which was an immediate success in North America and Europe.

Lin moved to New York in 1936 and continued writing articles and books in English, including *The Importance of Living* (1937), *The Birth of a New China* (1939) and a novel, *A Moment in Peking* (1939). He based himself and his family in the United States, writing novels, essays, plays, travel books and translations. Later novels included *A Leaf in the Storm* (1942), *Chinatown Family* (1948), *The Vermilion Gate* (1953), *Lady Wu* (1947) and *The Red Peony* (1961). He also penned and edited a wide range of other writings on subjects including philosophy, religion and the Chinese language. In the United States, Lin Yutang soon became established as the 'Emerson of China', arguably the best-known and most prolific Chinese writer in English of the twentieth century (Sohigian 1991: 668).

John Wu's own writings in *Tsien H'sia* are remarkable for their passionate commitment to international tolerance and understanding. In an essay entitled 'Beyond East and West', he asserts that: 'East and West are thoroughly interpenetrated with each other. Differences of colour are skin-deep. Down in their hearts, men of all races are one. Shakespeare is a first-rate Taoist, and Robert Burton is a full-fledged Buddhist' (1937: 15). He further vows that:

> The East has come to learn more and more from the West and to adore it; the West has come to understand and appreciate the East to a degree never before known. In the seventeenth and eighteenth centuries, Europeans began to be attracted by Oriental culture, but I suspect it was more the

attraction of distance than the appreciation of what was familiar that then prevailed. It was a mere infatuation, a passing fad. But now things are quite different . . . To be born yellow and to be educated white is a privilege that Aristotle himself would have coveted. No, dear Aristotle, thou shalt not covet thy neighbour's treasure. And what a treasure it is to be able to feel like a Chinese and to think like a Westerner! And what an ideal, to be as tender-hearted as a woman, and at the same time as tough-minded as a man! (1937: 16–17)

Wu's optimism extends to the century itself, and he concludes that, long after the evils of the epoch had passed, 'this century will be looked back upon as the herald of a new Civilization, the turning point in which men begin to be transformed into Man' (1937: 16–17).

Despite this optimism, Wu's life changed very rapidly over the course of the next few years. In 1938, along with Emily Hahn and a number of other members of the Shanghai circle, Wu moved to Hong Kong, where he continued editing the *T'ien Hsia Monthly* until the Japanese invaded in December 1941. Wu was interned by the Japanese, but then managed to return to China and spent the war in Guilin, Guiyang and Chongqing. In 1949, he moved to the United States, first to Hawaii and then, in 1951, to Seton Hall University, where he was appointed professor of law, and where he remained until he relocated to Taiwan in 1967. Like Lin Yutang, who died in 1976 in Hong Kong, John Wu was to spend most of the rest of his life outside the China that he evidently loved so deeply (Howard 1967–79, vol. III).

English in China after the revolution (1949–present)

A number of trends emerged in foreign-language teaching after the establishment of the People's Republic in 1949. Up until the 1990s, Chinese education would experience a roller-coaster ride of changing policy directives, most dictated by the prevailing political winds. Immediately after the revolution, Russian began to replace English as the major foreign language in schools. By the beginning of the 1960s, however, with the weakening of the Soviet influence, English was reintroduced as a school language, but, shortly after, its resurgence was abruptly halted by the Cultural Revolution (1966–76), which devastated not only the national education system, but the whole of the Chinese nation.[5] Many English teachers were attacked, physically and otherwise, during this period, for various crimes including spying, and 'worshipping everything foreign' (Adamson and Morris 1997: 15).[6]

---

[5] The Cultural Revolution was preceded by a cataclysmic famine in the years 1958 to 1962 which claimed an estimated 30 million lives. If one then factors in the devastation of the Cultural Revolution, it is possible to arrive at a conservative total of 40 million 'unnatural deaths' during Mao's rule. The non-conservative estimate is in the region of 80 million people (Becker 1996: 274).

[6] See also Troutner (1996) for a fascinating and carefully researched account of this period.

Politically, the years between the end of the Cultural Revolution and the 1997 handover were dominated by the need to implement the 'four modernisations' in agriculture, industry, defence and science and technology. By the early 1980s, English had begun to receive increased attention in the national curriculum, particularly in major urban schools, as it was seen as increasingly necessary for university studies and employment and was widely referred to as 'the language of international communication and commerce' (Ross 1993: 40). At the same time, anxiety about the 'spiritual pollution' associated with foreign cultures and languages persisted, and the 1978 English syllabus was justified politically in the following terms:

> English is a very widely used language throughout the world. In certain aspects, English is a very important tool: for international class struggle; for economic and trade relationships; for cultural, scientific and technological exchange; and for the development of international friendship... To uphold the principle of classless internationalism and to carry out Chairman Mao's revolutionary diplomacy effectively, we need to nurture a large number of 'red and expert' people proficient in a foreign language and foreign disciplines. (1978 English syllabus, cited in Adamson & Morris 1997: 17)

When the syllabus was revised in 1982, the emphasis was changed from politics to economics, sentiments that were reiterated in the 1993 English syllabus for junior secondary schools which stipulated that:

> A foreign language is an important tool for interacting with other countries and plays an important role in promoting the development of the national and world economy, science and culture. In order to meet the needs of our Open Door Policy and to accelerate socialist modernization, efforts should be made to enable as many people as possible to acquire command of one or more foreign languages. (1993 English syllabus, Adamson & Morris 1997: 21)

The aims of the 1993 syllabus also include the fostering of communication, and the acquisition of knowledge of foreign cultures (Adamson & Morris 1997: 22), aims which were repeated in the revised 2000 English syllabus for junior secondary schools.

The changing styles of official English teaching over the last thirty years may be illustrated by the changes in English-language textbooks in this period. Figures 5.1 and 5.2 below are taken from a People's Educational Press (PEP) primary English textbook of 1960, and graphically illustrate the political content of the textbooks of that period. The copperplate handwriting beneath the printed text provides an interesting contrast to the stark slogans of communism. It is also worth noting that 'Peking' has not yet been regularised to the pinyin 'Beijing'. One can compare these two illustrations with a page from a more recent PEP

Figure 5.1 Driving a train (PEP 1960: 3)

Lesson 11

Paper tiger, paper tiger.
U.S. imperialism is a paper tiger.
We are not afraid of it.
Look! We crush it at one blow!

U. S. imperialism

is a paper tiger.

Figure 5.2 Paper tiger (PEP 1960: 15)

secondary textbook, shown in figure 5.3 below, which discusses the subject of Christmas. This is taken from a course book called *Junior English for China*, and is representative of more culturally open approaches to textbook design.

The inclusion of such a passage in a recent textbook seems genuinely indicative of the liberalisation of aspects of education in the contemporary PRC. It would have been unthinkable to have printed such a culturally loaded text in earlier books in the post-1949 era. In the supplementary text that follows Lesson 54, even Jesus Christ receives a mention:

> What does Christmas mean? Christmas Day is the birthday of Jesus Christ. When Christ was born nearly two thousand years ago, many people, rich and poor, gave him presents. So today, people still do the same thing to each other. Of course, everyone likes presents. But Mr Green says: 'It is better to give than to receive.' What do you think? (People's Educational Press 1992: 55)

Other lessons in the same textbook discuss such topics as the life of a British family resident in China, the biography of Thomas Edison, life in Australia, soccer and the spread of English as an international language.

Today, despite the fact that English continues to grow in importance as a school subject throughout China, attitudes to the language vary. Zhao and Campbell (1995) report that many students resent having to learn the language, and only do so because of the importance of the language for educational advancement, learning English 'purely because they have to'. They claim that 'most Chinese learners of English are not learning English for international communication but for social and economic mobility' (1995: 383, 385). Despite this, the importance of English in education is increasing and, in the last ten years, a number of colleges and universities on the Chinese mainland have experimented with the use of English as a teaching medium. For example, the Guangdong Education Commission recently announced its intention to establish English-medium courses in selected schools 'to equip Guangdong students in urban and Pearl Delta areas with the same command of English as their counterparts in Hong Kong and other Southeast Asian countries by 2005' (Yow 2001: 2). The same article reported that there were also plans to employ 'native-speaker' teachers in many of the best schools in the province.

Outside the national education system, the study of English has continued to spread. Over the past twenty years, successive 'English crazes' have found expression in a range of ways: in the English-speaking corners that were set up in many cities; in the growing popularity of certification of various kinds, including the TOEFL examination and Business English diplomas; and in various other activities associated with learning the language. English is a strong second language within the Chinese media, and several English-language newspapers and magazines are published for domestic as well as international consumption, including the *China Daily* 中國日報, the *Beijing Review* 北京週報 and a

Lesson 54

▭ Read

Christmas is an important festival in Britain and many other parts of the world. Read the passage below very quickly and find out "Who is Father Christmas?" Then read it again and answer the questions on page 54 of your workbook.

CHRISTMAS DAY

On Christmas Eve — the night before Christmas Day — children all over Britain put a stocking at the end of their beds before they go to sleep. Their parents usually tell them that Father Christmas will come during the night.

Father Christmas is very kind-hearted. He lands on top of each house and climbs down the chimney into the fireplace. He fills each of the stockings with Christmas presents.

Of course, Father Christmas isn't real. In Jim and Kate's house, "Father Christmas" is really Mr Green. Mr Green doesn't climb down the chimney. He waits until the children are asleep. Then he quietly goes into their bedrooms, and fills their stockings with small presents. When they were very young, Mr Green sometimes dressed up in a red coat. But he doesn't do that now. The children are no longer young, and they know who "Father Christmas" really is. But they still put their stockings at the end of their beds.

Use your dictionary

1 Try to guess what these words mean:
   Britain   stocking   chimney   kind-hearted   top
2 Now look up the words in a dictionary.

Read the end of the text in the next lesson for homework.

Figure 5.3 'Christmas Day' in a recent English textbook (PEP 1992: 54) range of smaller publications in cities such as Beijing, Guangzhou and Shanghai. English-language books are widely available from bookshops, and include reprints of western 'canonical' texts as well as Chinese literature in English translation. English-language radio programmes for language learning have had a large following for many years, as do such news channels as the Voice of America. In addition, China Central Television Station (CCTV) now has regular broadcasts in English. The increasing availability of the internet in China has also opened further channels for communication in English, as has the growing popularity of e-mail communication (Li 2000).

Another factor has been the popularity of overseas study in English-speaking countries. In the last twenty years, hundreds of thousands of Chinese students have travelled to the United States, Britain and Australia in order to take degree-level or postgraduate courses in a wide range of university subjects. Again, exact statistics are not easily available, but one 1997 report indicated that between 1978 and 1997, 270,000 mainland Chinese students had gone abroad to study, 40 per cent of them to the United States (Tang 1997: 10). The same article noted that after the Tiananmen Square 'crackdown' many Chinese students had opted to stay abroad, and 53,000 young Chinese had succeeded in gaining their green cards to remain in the United States. A more recent report from the *People's Daily* 人民日报 claims that more than 400,000 Chinese students studied abroad between 1978 and 2000, and notes that some 110,000 have subsequently returned to China to start their careers (Yan 2001).

Such figures might also be compared to those of a much earlier era, when the first generations of students went abroad in the late Qing and Republican eras. In the years 1847–1953, for example, it was calculated that the total number of Chinese students who had studied in the United States amounted to only 50,000 (Chao 1953). In 2000, according to the *New York Times* there were 50,000 Chinese students in the United States in that year alone, with 'more students at American universities from China than from any other country' (Rosenthal 2001). Many of the young men and women currently studying in the United States, Canada, Britain and other English-speaking countries stay abroad for varying lengths of time, and may eventually decide to join the international diaspora of overseas Chinese in North America and Europe. Others will return to China as 'English-knowing bilinguals' and use their experiences, education and knowledge of English to make their way in the rapidly changing society of the People's Republic.

For those remaining in China to study, there are now a number of alternatives to English teaching in state schools, including a small but growing number of private schools and tutorial centres (Lai 2001). But the most radical approach to English teaching in the late 1990s has been a nationwide campaign by a charismatic English teacher named Li Yang 李阳, who claims to have lectured to over 13 million people nationwide. His approach is known everywhere throughout China by the striking name of *Feng kuang ying yu* 疯狂英语 or 'Crazy English'.

Li Yang's 'Crazy English'

The 1999 documentary film *Crazy English* produced and directed by Zhang Yuan provides a fascinating insight into Li Yang's popularity, as it follows the celebrity English teacher on a nationwide tour from sports stadium to university to school to government enterprise.[7] Li Yang is a youthful thirty-something with a popstar image and entourage to match, who has turned his teaching method into a multi-million business. No mean feat for a self-confessed educational failure.

His method relies on a small number of basic principles, which are constantly drilled into audiences of various sizes, but which can number up to several thousand. Three core principles are 'speak as loudly as possible', 'speak as quickly as possible' and 'speak as clearly as possible'. The training sessions he provides on tour are actually fairly simple sessions of elementary English practice, where he instructs his audiences in pronunciation techniques using a modified 'total physical response' technique in combination with mnemonic hand signals. Interestingly enough, his own pronunciation is characterised by a marked American accent.

In addition to his public appearances, Li also earns money from the sale of books and tapes, but the key to his success is the accompanying psychological pitch, which is geared to the aspirations of his audience. In many of his public appearances, Li relates his own earlier difficulties in mastering the language, urging his devotees to follow his own example of determination and will-power in overcoming adversity, and teaching his audiences such slogans as 'I enjoy losing face!', 'Welcome setbacks!', 'Relish suffering!' and 'Seek success!'. In a radio broadcast that occurs early in the film, Li Yang puts across a message of self-help and self-improvement:

> Hello everybody! My name is Li Yang. This probably sounds strange. People have asked if I've fabricated my hardships. My parents, classmates and teachers will testify that I lacked confidence. I didn't know where to end up. I had an inferiority complex, felt ignorant. I didn't feel capable of anything. I was always telling myself to be determined: I'll start tomorrow! I'll start tomorrow! Everyone wants to succeed, I want to serve as an example. My Crazy English consists of many philosophies of life and success . . . Money is no longer a problem. In one day, I could make 20 to 30 grand, 30 to 40 grand. That time is past. I've moved onto another stage. Once I've accomplished something, it becomes dull. I think I've found a bigger goal. To tell thousands of people about my process of struggle. Everyone needs to do his work well. Because Chinese people lack confidence. Chinese people need to put their noses to the grindstone.

[7] The film *Crazy English* is produced by Chen Ziqiu and Zhang Yuan, and is directed by Zhang Yuan. The video version in VCD format is distributed by Asia Video Publishing Co., Ltd.

These exhortations are repeated and elaborated throughout many of his public appearances. In a conversation with his team of assistants, Li also indicates an acute awareness of the nature of his appeal to his constituency:

> Our enterprise can gather thousands of people in the freezing cold to listen to my lecture. Why? American General Powell said something once. No matter what country you're from or your religion, there's only one touching story on earth and that is pulling yourself up by your bootstraps with an unremitting determination. Starting from having nothing to being successful... Li Yang failed 13 college exams, he failed 3 semesters of English in a row. People will see themselves in this story. Others say he has succeeded because he is gifted. But after hearing this simple story, they will know: he used to be like what we are now. But now he is different from us. He has experienced struggle and overcome himself. It is not because of his family, his opportunity or his luck, nor because of who his father is. He has risen from an ordinary person to a social hero. This is what we want to spread. As this century ends and the 21st century approaches, what do we need now? We need heroes. What else do we need? English. These two factors continue to make Li Yang's Crazy English.

Li Yang's message of hope also combines with a message of monetary gain that seems to capture the spirit of the state-sanctioned materialism ('to get rich is glorious') of the late 1990s. Occasionally, however, this crosses all boundaries of the possible, as on the occasion when he tells Tsinghua University students of the money to be made teaching English abroad:

> For teaching English in Japan, the highest salary is US$30,000 per hour. Native speakers from America who go to Japan to teach for Sony, Toshiba, Sharp and National, earn up to US$30,000 per hour... My advertising slogan is already thought out. To learn English, look for a Chinese person. Where I'd advertise? *Yomiuri Shimbun* and *Asahi Shimbun* [two leading Japanese newspapers]. The market for English teachers in Japan is large. This is good news... So with this idea in mind, for the sake of making money, start to learn English tonight. Money is the biggest motivation for studying. How do you come to repay your parents in the future? Buy them an airplane ticket around the world. 'Go travel around the world!' This is the best way to repay your parents. This is one of the biggest motivations for studying.

Another important element of the Crazy English philosophy is a sharp and focused nationalism which Li expresses in a number of ways, including the repetition of patriotic slogans such as 'Never let your country down!', and the employment of a chubby, balding and buffoonish American as an onstage butt. In some performances, Li Yang's self-help philosophy is extended from the individual to the nation:

Figure 5.4 'How're you doing?'

What's the US industry and agriculture output for 1995? Almost 7,400 billion US dollars. How about for China? 550 billion US dollars. This is just small change for America. There's a Japanese bank called Mitsubishi Bank. One bank's deposit is 700 billion US dollars. More than that of all the banks in China combined. There's another American company, Microsoft. Bill Gates' Microsoft Company. Its value has exceeded 200 billion US dollars. There's another American company, General Electric, whose value will reach 400–600 billion US dollars by the year 2000. The value of one company is almost equal to the GNP of China. I'm telling you all of this, hoping you will remember it. Don't be blinded by the claim 'China's the biggest market'. We should teach our children that China is by no means the biggest market. Where is the biggest market? America, Japan, Europe! What is China's aim? To occupy these three markets, right? Here is a question for everybody. What's the purpose of studying English? Repeat after me. Occupy . . . America . . . Japan . . . Europe . . . these three big markets. Make money internationally! Say it loudly! Make money . . . internationally! Make money internationally!

In the two stills from the film reproduced as figures 5.4 and 5.5, Li Yang is standing on the Great Wall of China, giving instruction to a few hundred soldiers from the People's Liberation Army (PLA). In the film, the PLA soldiers are being trained to chant in unison such useful phrases as 'How're you doing?', 'Never let your country down!', 'I have been looking forward to meeting you!', 'Brilliant!', 'No pain, no gain!', 'Nineteen ninety-seven!' and 'The PLA is great!'

Figure 5.5 'The PLA is great!'

In this final chapter of this book, I have attempted to explore the notion of 'Chinese Englishes' from a historical viewpoint, in order to establish a number of connections between the pasts of Hong Kong and South China and the dramatically changing and developing present of the PRC, but much more might also be said about other lines of discussion, linguistic and otherwise. An important strand to the World Englishes paradigm is its potential for pluralism and pluricentricity. Pluricentricity in the Chinese context may involve a reconsideration of the discourses of both Chinese and English, and Hong Kong, with its localised Cantonese and English, provides a test case for both. A second important element in the World Englishes paradigm is that of the universalism (the 'we'-ness) of Kachruvian theory. Given the often controversial political history of English in China, it would be naïve to expect the uncritical reception of such sentiments. Yet, faced with a choice between the huckster nationalism of Li Yang and the gentle liberal humanism of Lin Yutang and John C. H. Wu, it is hard to resist nostalgia for this forgotten era of cultural and linguistic contact. It is similarly difficult to dismiss all hope of genuine cultural and intellectual understanding, however vulnerable such approaches may be to the critical analyses of cultural theory and postcolonialism.

A further challenge is that of the 'Chinese–English interface' throughout China and the world. As McArthur has pointed out, in terms of numbers of speakers and a range of other factors, English and Chinese represent two of the most important language traditions and cultures in the world today (McArthur 2000). A recent study by Dalby (2001) places Chinese as the most widely spoken language in the world, with 1,155 million speakers worldwide, of whom 800 million speak Mandarin as a first language, and 200 million speak the variety as a second language. In addition, it is estimated that there are 85 million speakers of Wu dialects (Shanghainese, etc.) and 70 million speakers of Yue dialects (Cantonese, etc.). English is in second place with a total of 1 billion speakers. Of these, 400 million are first-language speakers, and 600 million are second-language speakers. Much more could be said, and doubtless will be said and written, about the linguistic and cultural contacts between these two traditions, and the growing 'interface' between them (McArthur 2000). On the literary front, the recent 'bilingual creativity' of émigré Chinese writers such as Ha Jin (*Waiting*), Anchee Min (*Red Azalea*, *Becoming Madam Mao*) and Annie Wang (*Lili: a Novel of Tiananmen*) may in time extend to include creative writing in English from within China. But such developments belong to the possible futures of Chinese Englishes hinted at in the Preface. For myself, my main hope is that in this book I have succeeded at least in demonstrating that cultural and linguistic contact between these two linguistic traditions has had a long and complex history.

In the earlier sections of this chapter, I attempted to explain the connections between Hong Kong English and Chinese Englishes by referring to the colonial modernity of pre-1949 China, a type of modernity which persists to the present in many of the HKSAR's educational, social and political institutions. In the case of Li Yang's 'Crazy English', we see another modernity at work, that of a rapidly industrialising China in which capital and capitalism serve the needs of Maoist Marxist-Leninism reinvented as 'socialism with Chinese characteristics'. Creolists explain Canton 'jargon' as an early variety of 'business English' and, as China enters the World Trade Organisation, Li Yang's approach appears to give voice to the material hopes of millions of Chinese in a variety of brash English that twangs American but rings global with its exhortation 'Make the voice of China be widely heard all over the world!'.

In 1637, Peter Mundy lamented the financial losses of the Weddell expedition, as they were forced out of China, 'leaving a great part of our Coiveall [capital] beehind us, and a Farre greater yet uninvested' (Temple 1919: 301). The earliest attestation for 'capital' as in 'capitalism' in the *Oxford English Dictionary* is 1709, and yet we find this item some seventy years earlier in Mundy's account of one of the very first capitalist ventures put together by a British joint-stock company.[8] Almost 200 years later, in the Guangzhou of 1835, we find the first crude chapbooks written for the learning of English, at a time when the opium trade in that

---

[8] Temple's explanatory footnote to this item of vocabulary comments: 'Cavidall, Capital, in goods or money . . . it appears to have come through the Portuguese *cabedal*'(Temple 1919: 301).

city was the single largest trade of any commodity in the world (Shipp 1997). One hundred and seventy years further on, Li Yang bombards his audiences with strings of inspirational phrases in English, such as 'Feel the fear and do it anyway!', 'You can speak good English!', 'Storms make trees take deeper roots!' and 'Make money internationally!'. From the forgotten pasts of southern China, we move to the unexpected present of Chinese Englishes today.

Appendix 1   Chinese dialects in China

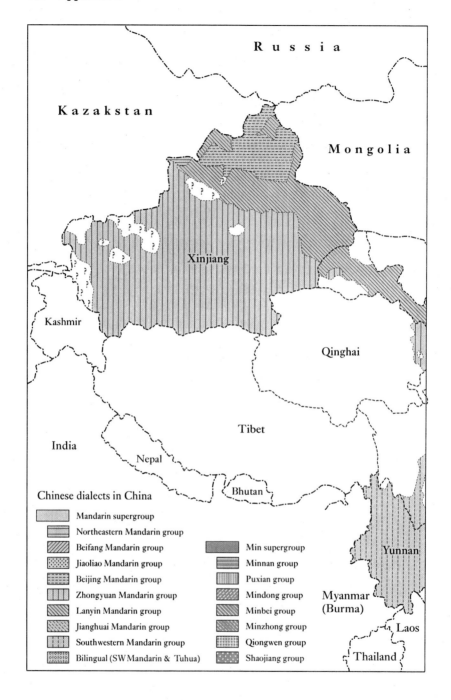

Chinese dialects in China

- Mandarin supergroup
- Northeastern Mandarin group
- Beifang Mandarin group
- Jiaoliao Mandarin group
- Beijing Mandarin group
- Zhongyuan Mandarin group
- Lanyin Mandarin group
- Jianghuai Mandarin group
- Southwestern Mandarin group
- Bilingual (SW Mandarin & Tuhua)
- Min supergroup
- Minnan group
- Puxian group
- Mindong group
- Minbei group
- Minzhong group
- Qiongwen group
- Shaojiang group

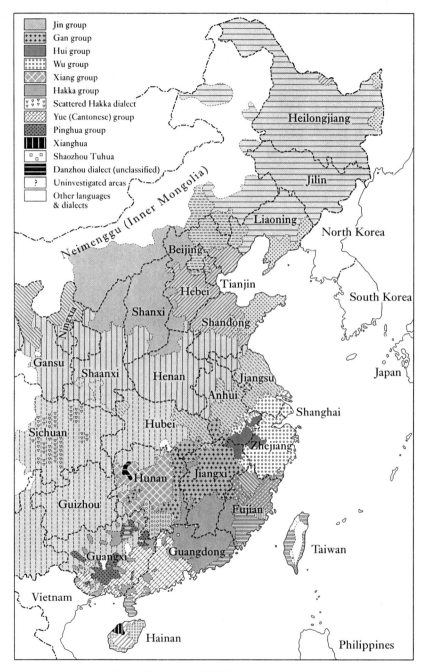

Adapted from Würm *et al*. (1987)

Appendix 2 Chinese dialects in Guangdong (Canton) province

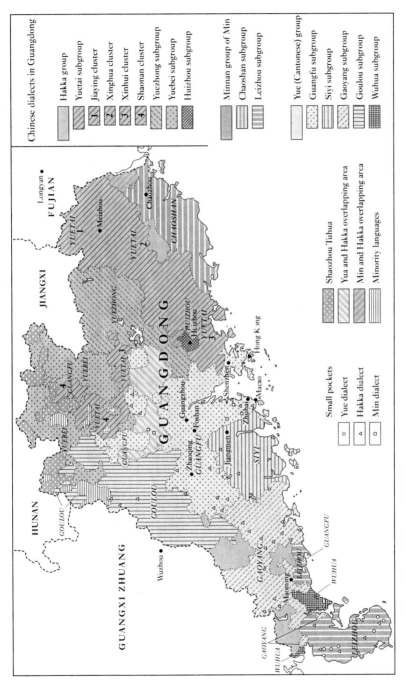

Adapted from Würm et al. (1987)

Chinese dialects in Guangdong

Hakka group
Yuetai subgroup
1 Jiaying cluster
2 Xinghua cluster
3 Xinhui cluster
4 Shaonan cluster
Yuezhong subgroup
Yuebei subgroup
Huizhou subgroup

Minnan group of Min
Chaoshan subgroup
Leizhou subgroup

Yue (Cantonese) group
Guangfu subgroup
Siyi subgroup
Gaoyang subgroup
Goulou subgroup
Wuhua subgroup

Shaozhou Tuhua
Yua and Hakka overlapping area
Min and Hakka overlapping area
Minority languages

Small pockets
○ Yue dialect
△ Hakka dialect
□ Min dialect

Appendix 3   The Yale system for transcribing Cantonese

Table A3.1 *Correspondences between the Yale and IPA systems for transcribing Cantonese*

Yale notation	IPA symbol
1. Initial consonants:	
b	p
p	p^h
m	m
f	f
d	t
t	t^h
n	n
l	l
g	k
k	k^h
ng	ŋ
h	h
j	ts
ch	ts^h
s	s
y	j
gw	kw
kw	kw^h
w	w
2. Final consonants:	
m	m
n	n
ng	ŋ
p	p
t	t
k	k

Yale notation	IPA symbol
3. Vowels:	
i	iː and /e/
yu	yː
u	uː and /o/
e	ɛː
o	ɔː
eu	œː and /θ/
a (aa)	ɐ and /aː/
iu	iw
eui	eɥ
ui	uɥ
ei	ej
oi	ɔj
ou	ow
ai	ɐj
au	ɐw
aai	aːj
aau	aːw

Table A3.2 *The tones of Cantonese in Yale notation*

Tone	Example notations
high tone	*mān*
mid-rising	*mán*
mid-level	*man*
low-level	*mahn*
low-rising	*máhn*
low-falling	*màhn*

Appendix 4   The Common Foreign Language of the Redhaired People (1835)

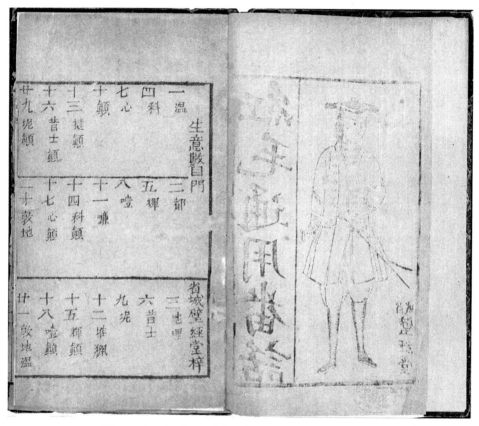

The section headings of the glossary read vertically down the right-hand side and the entries read vertically in columns running from right to left. A transcription and translation of the glossary is given below on pages 276–88. Correspondences between the illustrations and the transcription are indicated beneath each illustration. This page corresponds to section 1, items 1–21 of the transcription.

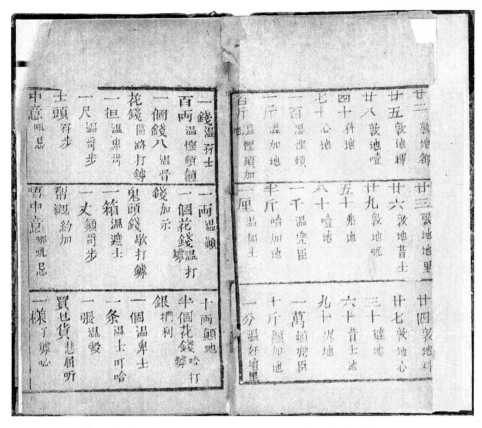

Items 46–69   Items 22–45

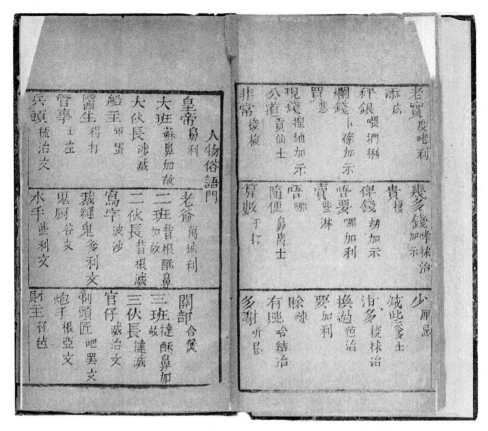

Section 2, items 94–114   Items 70–93

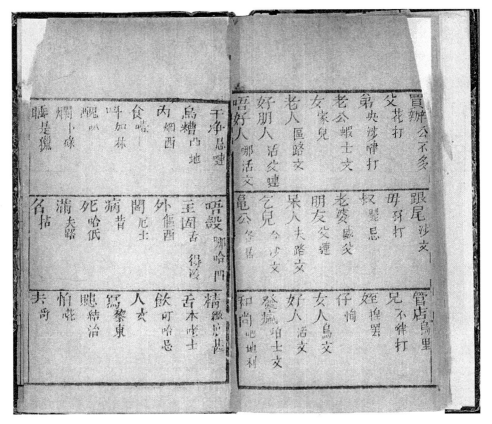

Items 139–162   Items 115–138

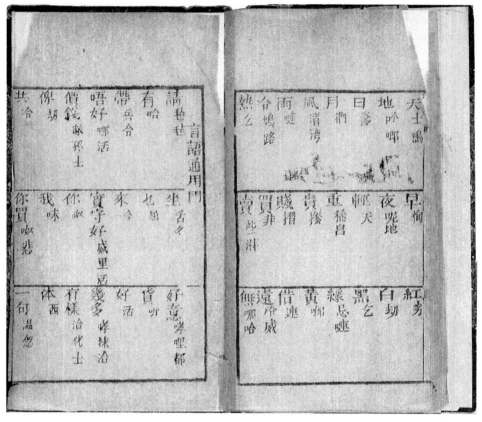

Section 3, items 187–207   Items 163–186

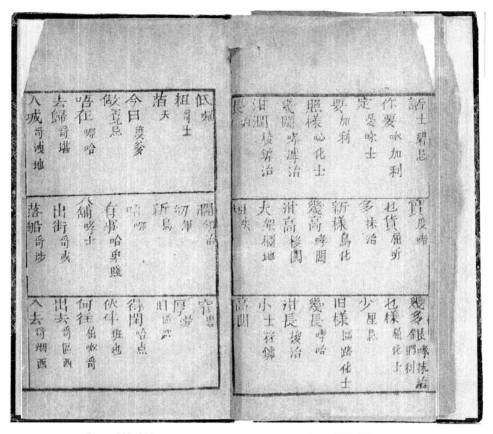

Items 232–255   Items 208–231

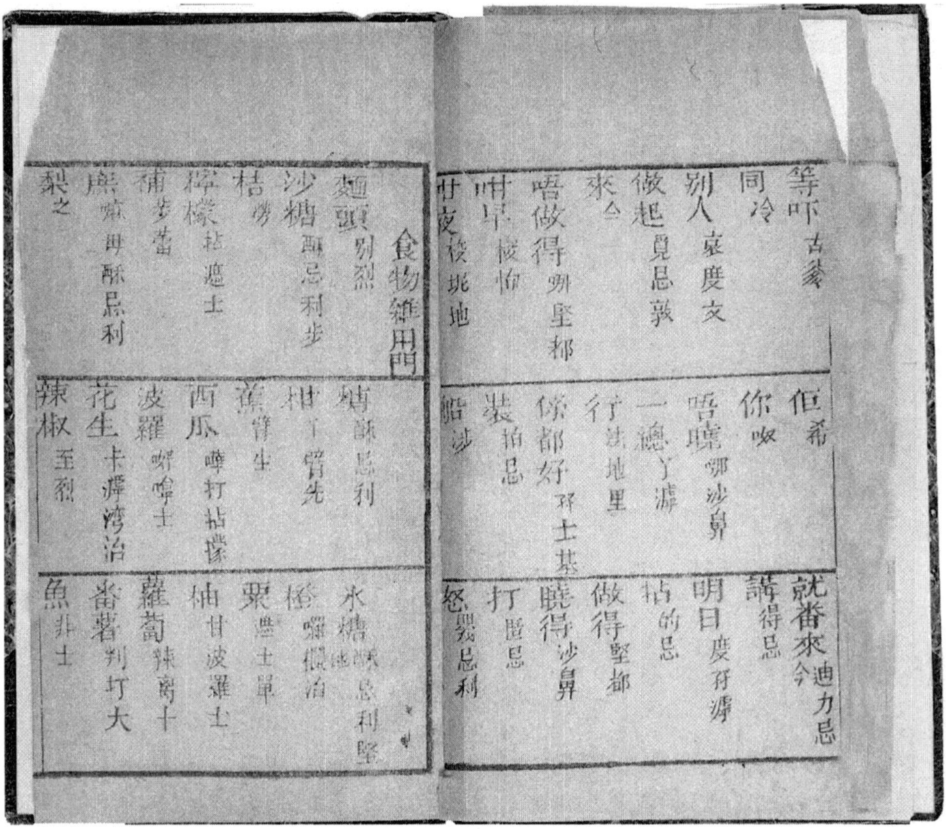

食物雜用門

梨之
廉嚇毑酥忌利
檸檬
補步蕾
桔
沙糖
麵頭別烈
辣椒
花生卡痺灣治
西瓜
蕉骨生
柑丁㗎先
魚
番薯
蘿蔔
柚甘波羅士
㗎打拮㗎
㗎糖
怪㗎假泊
聚㗎士單

等吓
同冷
別人
做起
唔做得
唔早
甘友後挑地

佢希
你唉
唔聽哪沙鼻
行地里
一總濾
傍都好
裝怕
船沙

就番來
誤得
明日慶
的
做得堅都
曉得沙鼻
打瞌
怒罵

Section 4, Items 280–300　　　　　Items 256–279

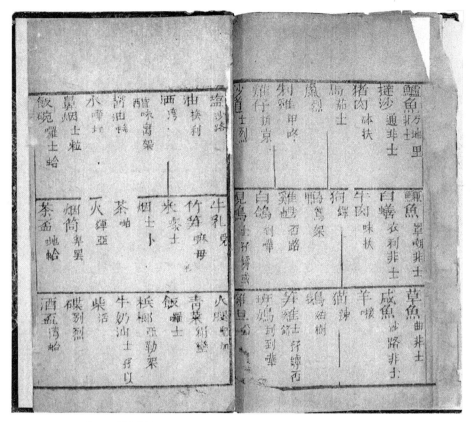

Items 325–348   Items 301–324

Items 349–372

Transcription and translation of the *Redhaired* glossary

The entries in this glossary are transcribed according to the Yale (Cantonese) system.

[Section 1] 生意數目門 Sāangyi soumuhk mùhn [Numbers used in business section]

(i) Chinese item(s)	(ii) English translation of (i)	(iii) Chinese characters used to indicate English pronunciation	(iv) Yale transcription indicating the sound of Chinese characters in (iii)	(v) Written form of English or pidgin indicated by transcription in (iv)
1. 一	one	溫	wān	one
2. 二	two	都	dōu	two
3. 三	three	地理	deih léih	three
4. 四	four	科	fō	four
5. 五	five	輝	fāi	five
6. 六	six	昔士	sīk sih	sixee
7. 七	seven	心	sām	seven
8. 八	eight	噎	yit	eight
9. 九	nine	呢	nàih	nine
10. 十	ten	顛	dīn	ten
11. 十一	eleven	嗹	lìhm	eleven
12. 十二	twelve	推猍 [*sic*,猵]	tēui lihp	twelve
13. 十三	thirteen	捷顛	taat dīn	thirteen
14. 十四	fourteen	科顛	fō dīn	fourteen
15. 十五	fifteen	輝顛	fāi dīn	fifteen
16. 十六	sixteen	昔士顛	sīk sih dīn	sixteen
17. 十七	seventeen	心顛	sām dīn	seventeen
18. 十八	eighteen	噎顛	yit dīn	eighteen
19. 廿九*	nineteen	呢顛	nàih dīn	nineteen
20. 二十	twenty	敦地	dēun deih	twenty
21. 廿一	twenty-one	敦地溫	dēun deih wān	twenty-one
22. 廿二	twenty-two	敦地都	dēun deih dōu	twenty-two
23. 廿三	twenty-three	敦地地里	dēun deih deih léih	twenty-three
24. 廿四	twenty-four	敦地科	dēun deih fō	twenty-four
25. 廿五	twenty-five	敦地輝	dēun deih fāi	twenty-five
26. 廿六	twenty-six	敦地昔士	dēun deih sīk sih	twenty-sixee
27. 廿七	twenty-seven	敦地心	dēun deih sām	twenty-seven
28. 廿八	twenty-eight	敦地噎	dēun deih yit	twenty-eight
29. 廿九	twenty-nine	敦地呢	dēun deih nàih	twenty-nine
30. 三十	thirty	捷地	taat deih	thirty
31. 四十	forty	科地	fō deih	forty
32. 五十	fifty	弗地	fāt deih	fifty

(*cont.*)

(i) Chinese item(s)	(ii) English translation of (i)	(iii) Chinese characters used to indicate English pronunciation	(iv) Yale transcription indicating the sound of Chinese characters in (iii)	(v) Written form of English or pidgin indicated by transcription in (iv)
33. 六十	sixty	昔士地	sīk sih deih	sixee day
34. 七十	seventy	心地	sām deih	seventy
35. 八十	eighty	噎地	yit deih	eighty
36. 九十	ninety	㖿地	nàih deih	ninety
37. 一百	one hundred	溫慳頓	wān hāan deuhn	one hundred
38. 一千	one thousand	溫兜臣	wān dāu sàhn	one thousand
39. 一萬	ten thousand	顛兜臣	dīn dāu sàhn	ten thousand
40. 一斤	one catty	溫加地	wān gāa deih	one catty
41. 半斤	half a catty	哈加地	hāa gāa deih	ha cattee
42. 十斤	ten catties	顛加地	dīn gāa deih	ten cattee
43. 百斤	one hundred catties	溫慳頓[加]地	wān hāan deuhn [gāa] deih	one hundred [ca]ttee
44. 一厘	one cash	溫加士	wān gāa sih	one cas(h)ee
45. 一分	one candareen	溫奸地里	wān gāan deih léih	one candeelee
46. 一錢	one mace	溫孖士	wān māa sih	one mahsee
47. 一兩	one tael	溫顛 [sic,地]	wān dīn [deih]	one tael
48. 十兩	ten taels	顛地	dīn deih	ten taels
49. 百兩	one hundred taels	溫慳頓顛 [sic,地]	wān hāan deuhn dīn [deih]	one hundred taels
50. 一個花錢	one flowery dollar	溫打喇	wān dāa laa	one dollar
51. 半個花錢	half a flowery dollar	哈打嘞	hāa dāa laa	ha(lf) dollar
52. 一個錢八	*unclear*	溫骨	wān gwāt	one quarter
53. 錢	cash	加示	gāa sih	cas(h)ee
54. 銀	money	捫利	mùhn leih	money
55. 花錢	flower(y) dollar	區路打嘞	āu louh dāa laa	olo dollar
56. 鬼頭錢	ghost head dollar	歇打嘞	hit dāa laa	head dollar
57. 一個	one piece	溫卑士	wān bēi sih	one piecee
58. 一担	one picul	溫卑哥	wān bēi gō	one picul
59. 一箱	one chest	溫遮士	wān jē sih	one ches(t)ee
60. 一条	one string	溫士叮哈 [sic,哈]	wān sih dīng hāa [ling]	oncee dingling
61. 一尺	one covado	溫哥步	wān gō bouh	one corebo[a]

(i) Chinese item(s)	(ii) English translation of (i)	(iii) Chinese characters used to indicate English pronunciation	(iv) Yale transcription indicating the sound of Chinese characters in (iii)	(v) Written form of English or pidgin indicated by transcription in (iv)
62. 一丈	ten covados	顚哥步	dīn gō bouh	ten corebo[b]
63. 一張	one length	溫 [unclear]	wān [unclear]	one [unclear]
64. 士頭	master	孖步 [sic,沙]	māa bouh [sāa]	massa
65. 幫襯	to buy	約加	yeuk gāa	unclear
66. 買乜貨	buy what thing	患屈听	bēi wāt ting	buy what ting
67. 中意	like	吶忌	láih geih	likee
68. 唔中意	not like	哪吶忌	náh láih geih	nah likee
69. 一樣	the same	丫鑞心	āa laa sām	alla same
70. 老實	honest	度唛利	douh lóuh leih	truly
71. 幾多錢	how much money	哮抹治加示	hāau mut jih gāa sih	how muchee cashee
72. 少	a little	厘忌	lèih geih	unclear
73. 添	more	庅	mō	more
74. 貴	expensive, dear	揢	dē	dear
75. 減些	less	爹士	dē sih	lessee
76. 秤銀	weigh money	喂捫捔	wai mùhn leih	weigh money
77. 俾錢	pay money	翈加示	gip gāa sih	give cashee
78. 泔多	so much	梭抹治	sō mut jih	so muchee
79. 爛錢	broken money	卜磦加示	būk lūk gāa sih	broken cashee
80. 唔要	do not want	哪加利	náh gāa leih	nah carei[c]
81. 換過	exchange	毡治	jīn jih	changee
82. 買	buy	患	bēi	buy
83. 賣	sell	些淋	sē làhm	sellum
84. 要	want	加利	gāa leih	carei[d]
85. 現錢	now money	揎地加示	lihp deih gāa sih	ready cash
86. 唔	no(t)	哪	náh	nah [no]
87. 賒	lend	唪	lìhn	lend
88. 公道	fair, honest	貢仙士	gung sīn sih	consinsi[e]
89. 隨便	please	箅离士	beih lèih sih	pleasee
90. 有聽	have [unclear]	哈結治	hāa git jih	ha catchee
91. 非常	extremely	捘梭 [sic,梭梭]	sō sō	so so
92. 算數	account	干打	gōn dāa	conta[f]
93. 多謝	thank you	听忌	ting geih	tinkee

[Section 2] 人物俗語門 Yáhnmaht juhkyúh mùhn [Colloquial language about people and things section]

(i) Chinese item(s)	(ii) English translation of (i)	(iii) Chinese characters used to indicate English pronunciation	(iv) Yale transcription indicating the sound of Chinese characters in (iii)	(v) Written form of English or pidgin indicated by transcription in (iv)
94. 皇帝	emperor	[...] 鼻利	beih leih	[. . .] peror
95. 老爺	mandarin	萬地利	maahn deih leih	mandarin
96. 關部	Hoppo	合煲	hahp bōu	Hoppo
97. 大班	supercargo	蘇鼻加故	sōu beih gāa gu	supercargo
98. 二班	second supercargo	昔根酥鼻加故	sīk gān sōu beih gāa gu	second supercargo
99. 三班	third supercargo	撻酥鼻加故	taat sōu beih gāa gu	third supercargo
100. 大伙長	ship's mate	涉滅	sip miht	ship's mate
101. 二伙長	second mate	昔根滅	sīk gān miht	second mate
102. 三伙長	third mate	撻滅	taat miht	third mate
103. 船主	captain	帀[*sic.*冚]蛋	káhm dáan	captain
104. 寫字	clerk	波沙	bō sāa	purser
105. 官仔	midshipman	滅治文	miht jih màhn	midshipman
106. 醫生	doctor	得打	dāk dáa	doctor
107. 裁縫鬼	tailor	爹利文	dē leih màhn	tailor man
108. 剃頭匠	barber	吧罢文	bāa bah màhn	barber man
109. 管事	steward	士左	sih jó	steward
110. 鬼廚	cook	谷文	gūk màhn	cook man
111. 炮手	gunner	根亞文	gān aa màhn	gunner man
112. 兵頭	soldier	梳治文	sō jih màhn	soldier man
113. 水手	sailor	些利文	sē leih màhn	sailor man
114. 財主	merchant	孖毡	māa jīn	merchant
115. 買辦	comprador	公不多	gūng bāt dō	comprador[g]
116. 跟尾	servant	沙文	sāa màhn	servant
117. 管店	coolie	烏里	wū léih	coolie
118. 父	father	花打	fāa dáa	father
119. 母	mother	孖打	māa dáa	mother
120. 兄	brother	不律打	bāt leuht dáa	brother
121. 弟	younger brother	央涉律打	yēung sip leuht dáa	younger brother
122. 叔	uncle	罌忌	āng geih	uncle
123. 姪	nephew	揑罢	nihp bah	nipper
124. 老公	husband	蝦士文	hāa sih màhn	hasiman
125. 老婆	wife	威父	wāi fuh	wifoo
126. 仔	son	恂	sēun	son
127. 女	girl	家兒	gāa yìh	girlee

(i) Chinese item(s)	(ii) English translation of (i)	(iii) Chinese characters used to indicate English pronunciation	(iv) Yale transcription indicating the sound of Chinese characters in (iii)	(v) Written form of English or pidgin indicated by transcription in (iv)
128. 朋友	friend	父嚥	fuh lìhn	friend
129. 女人	woman	烏文	wū màhn	woman
130. 老人	old man	區路文	āu louh màhn	olo man
131. 呆人	fool	夫路文	fū louh màhn	foolo man
132. 好人	good man	活文	wuht màhn	good man
133. 好朋人	good friend	活父嚥	wuht fuh lìhn	good friend
134. 乞兒	beggar	今沙文	gām sāa màhn	cumshaw man
135. 發瘋	be crazy	拍士文	paak sih màhn	poxy man
136. 唔好人	not good man	哪活文	náh wuht màhn	nah [no] good man
137. 龜公	pimp	各 [unclear]	gok [unclear]	unclear
138. 和尚	monk	吧地利	bāa deih leih	padre[h]
139. 干淨	clean	忌嚥	geih lìhn	clean
140. 唔較	not enough	哪哈凹	náh hāa nāp	no ha (e)nough
141. 精	handsome	緻宸[sic, 痕]甚	hàhn sahm	handsome
142. 烏糟	dirty	凸地	daht deih	dirty
143. 主固	unclear	舌得冷	sit dāk láahng	strong
144. 舌	tongue	本咥士	bún lóuh sih	unclear
145. 丙[sic,內]	inside	烟西	yīn sāi	insi(d)e
146. 外	outside	傴西 [sic, 區西]	yū yáuh [āu sāi]	outsi(d)e
147. 飲	drink	叮哈[sic,哈]忌	dīng hāa [ling] geih	drinkee
148. 食	eat	嘻	yit	eat
149. 問	ask	厄士	āk sih	askee
150. 人	man	文	màhn	man
151. 叫	call	加林	gāa làhm	callum
152. 病	sick	昔	sīk	sick
153. 寫	write	黎東	làih dūng	write down
154. 醜	ugly	叭	bet	bad
155. 死	die	哈低	hāa dāi	ha die
156. 慇	profit	結治	git jih	catchee
157. 爛	broken	卜碌	būk lūk	broke
158. 滿	full	夫路	fū louh	fullo
159. 怕	fear	呢	fā	fear
160. 睡	sleep	是獵	sih lihp	sleep
161. 名	name	拈	nīm	name
162. 去	go	哥	gō	go
163. 天	sky	士鳴 [sic. 鳴]	sih mìhng [gāi]	sky

(cont.)

(i) Chinese item(s)	(ii) English translation of (i)	(iii) Chinese characters used to indicate English pronunciation	(iv) Yale transcription indicating the sound of Chinese characters in (iii)	(v) Written form of English or pidgin indicated by transcription in (iv)
164. 早	soon	恂	sēun	soon
165. 紅	red	劣	lyut	red
166. 地	earth	吤哪	gó lòhng	ground
167. 夜	night	呢地	nīh deih	nightee[i]
168. 白	white	切	gip	*unclear*
169. 日	day	爹	dē	day
170. 輕	light	天	tīn	thin
171. 黑	black	乞	hāt	black
172. 月	moon	捫	mùhn	moon
173. 重	heavy	稀島 [sic, 鼻]	hēi [beih]	heavy
174. 綠	green	忌嗹	geih lìhn	green
175. 風	wind	渭灣	waih wāan	wind
176. 貴	dear	抒	dē	dear
177. 黃	yellow	啷	lòhng	*unclear*
178. 雨	rain	嗹	lìhn	rain
179. 賤	cheap	摺哈	jip	cheap
180. 借	lend	連	lìhn	lend
181. 冷	cold	鳩路	gāu louh	cold
182. 買	buy	非 [sic, 悲]	fēi [bēi]	buy
183. 遠	distant	哈威	láahng wāi	long way
184. 熱	hot	乞	hāt	hot
185. 賣	sell	些淋	sē làhm	sellum
186. 無	not have	哪哈	náh hāa	nah ha

[Section 3] 言語通用門 Yìhnyúh tūngyuhng mùhn [Everyday language section]

(i) Chinese item(s)	(ii) English translation of (i)	(iii) Chinese characters used to indicate English pronunciation	(iv) Yale transcription indicating the sound of Chinese characters in (iii)	(v) Written form of English or pidgin indicated by transcription in (iv)
187. 請	please	毡毡	jīn jīn	chin chin
188. 坐	sit	舌夕 [sic, 冬]	sit jihk [dūng]	sit down
189. 好意	how do you do	嘮哩都	hāau léih dōu	howlay do
190. 有	have	哈	hāa	ha

(i) Chinese item(s)	(ii) English translation of (i)	(iii) Chinese characters used to indicate English pronunciation	(iv) Yale transcription indicating the sound of Chinese characters in (iii)	(v) Written form of English or pidgin indicated by transcription in (iv)
191. 乜	what	屈	wāt	what
192. 貨	thing	听	ting	ting
193. 帶	bring	兵令	bīng lihng	bring
194. 來	come	今	gām	come
195. 好	good	活	wuht	good
196. 唔好	not good	哪活	náh wuht	nah good
197. 實守好	very good	威里活	wāi léih wuht	welly good
198. 幾多	how much	哮拺洽 [sic,治]	hāau mut hāp [jih]	how muchee
199. 價錢	price	敝孻士	baih lāai sih	prices
200. 你	you	呶	lòuh	you
201. 有樣	have something	洽化士	hāp faa sih	hab fashion
202. 俾	give	刧	gip	gib
203. 我	I/me	味	meih	me
204. 体*	see	西	sāi	see
205. 共	together	冷	láahng	(a)long
206. 你買	you buy	呶悲	lòuh bēi	you buy
207. 一句	one phrase	溫忽 [sic,忽]	wān chūng [fāt]	unclear
208. 話	speak	士碧忌	sih bīk geih	speakee
209. 實	true	度呶	douh lóuh	true
210. 幾多銀	how much money	哮拺治捫利	hāau mut jih mùhn leih	how muchee money
211. 你要	you want	呶加利	lòuh gāa leih	you carei[j]
212. 乜貨	what goods	屈听	wāt ting	what ting
213. 乜樣	what way	屈化士	wāt faa sih	what fashion
214. 定	deposit	晏咪士	aan mei sih	unclear
215. 多	more, much	拺治	mut jih	muchee
216. 少	little	厘忌	léih geih	unclear
217. 要	want	加利	gāa leih	carei[k]
218. 新樣	new way	鳥化 [士]	níuh faa [sih]	new fashion
219. 舊樣	old way	區路化士	āu louh faa sih	olo fashion
220. 照樣	same way	心化士	sām faa sih	same fashion
221. 幾高	how high	哮閐	hāau haai	how high
222. 幾長	how long	哮哈 [sic,冷]	hāau [láahng]	how long
223. 幾闊	how wide	哮淳[sic,鋹]治	hāau fū [laa] jih	how largee
224. 泔高	so tall	梭閐	sō haai	so high
225. 泔長	so long	梭治 [sic,冷]	sō jih [láahng]	so long

(cont.)

(i) Chinese item(s)	(ii) English translation of (i)	(iii) Chinese characters used to indicate English pronunciation	(iv) Yale transcription indicating the sound of Chinese characters in (iii)	(v) Written form of English or pidgin indicated by transcription in (iv)
226. 沰濶	so wide	梭觸治	sō laa jih	so largee
227. 大	big	架欄地	gaa làahn deih	grande[l]
228. 小	small	士孖觸	sih māa laa	small
229. 長	long	治 [sic,冷]	jih [láahng]	long
230. 短	short	失	sāt	short
231. 高	high	閐	hāai	high
232. 低	low	嚕	lō	low
233. 濶	wide	觸治	laa jih	largee[m]
234. 窄	narrow	碧	bīk	unclear
235. 粗	coarse	哥士	gō sih	coarsee
236. 切	fine	渾	fāi	fine
237. 厚	thick	惕	tīk	thick
238. 筘	thin	天	tīn	thin
239. 新	new	鳥	níuh	new
240. 旧	old	區路	āu louh	olo
241. 今日	today	度爹	douh dē	today
242. 唔	no(t)	哪	náh	nah [no]
243. 得閒	to have free time	哈点	hāa dím	ha tim
244. 做	make	覓忌	mihk geih	makee
245. 有事	busy	哈卑賤	hāa bēi jihn	ha pigeon
246. 伙伴	partner	班也	bāan yáh	partner[n]
247. 唔在	not here	哪哈	náh hāa	nah ha
248. 舖	trading house	哮士	hāau sih	housee
249. 何往	where go	屈呶哥	wāt lòuh gō	what you go
250. 去歸	go home	哥堪	gō hām	go home
251. 出街	go for a walk	哥或	gō waahk	go walk
252. 出去	go outside	哥區西	gō āu sāi	go outside
253. 入城	go to the city	哥泄地	gō sit deih	go citee
254. 落船	go aboard ship	哥涉	gō sip	go ship
255. 入去	go inside	哥烟西	gō yīn sāi	go inside
256. 等吓	wait a moment	古爹	gú dē	unclear
257. 佢	he	希	hēi	he
258. 就番來	come back soon	迪力忌今	dihk lihk geih gām	directly come
259. 同	together	冷	láahng	(a)long

(i) Chinese item(s)	(ii) English translation of (i)	(iii) Chinese characters used to indicate English pronunciation	(iv) Yale transcription indicating the sound of Chinese characters in (iii)	(v) Written form of English or pidgin indicated by transcription in (iv)
260. 你	you	啵	lòuh	you
261. 講	talk	得忌	dāk geih	talkee
262. 別人	other people	哀度文	ōi douh màhn	other man
263. 唔曉	not understand	哪沙鼻	náh sāa beih	nah savvy[o]
264. 明日	tomorrow	度孖滹 [sic, 滹]	douh māa fū [laa]	tomorrow
265. 做起	finished	覓忌敦	mihk geih dēun	makee done
266. 一總	altogether	丫滹 [sic, 滹]	āa fū [laa]	alla
267. 拈	take	的忌	dīk geih	takee
268. 來	come	今	gām	come
269. 行	business	法地里	faat deih léih	factory[p]
270. 做得	able to do	堅都	gīn dōu	can do
271. 唔做得	unable to do	哪堅都	náh gīn dōu	nah can do
272. 係都好	is also good	孖士基	māa sih gēi	maskee[q]
273. 曉得	understand	沙鼻	sāa beih	savvy[r]
274. 咁早	so early	梭恂	sō sēun	so soon
275. 裝	pack	拍忌	paak geih	packee
276. 打	hit	匿忌	līk geih	lickee
277. 咁夜	so late	梭岷地	sō làih deih	so lightee
278. 船	ship	涉	sip	ship
279. 怒	angry	罌忌利	āng geih leih	angry

[Section 4] 食物雜用門 Sihkmaht jaahpyuhng mùhn [Food and miscellaneous section]

(i) Chinese item(s)	(ii) English translation of (i)	(iii) Chinese characters used to indicate English pronunciation	(iv) Yale transcription indicating the sound of Chinese characters in (iii)	(v) Written form of English or pidgin indicated by transcription in (iv)
280. 麵頭	bread	別烈	biht liht	bread
281. 糖	sugar	酥忌利	sōu geih leih	sugar
282. 冰糖	rock sugar	酥忌利堅地	sōu geih leih gīn deih	sugar candy
283. 沙糖	granulated sugar	酥忌利步	sōu geih leih bouh	sugar powder

(i) Chinese item(s)	(ii) English translation of (i)	(iii) Chinese characters used to indicate English pronunciation	(iv) Yale transcription indicating the sound of Chinese characters in (iii)	(v) Written form of English or pidgin indicated by transcription in (iv)
284. 柑	small orange	丫臂先	āa bei sīn	apelsin[s]
285. 橙	orange	囉欄治	lō làahn jih	lolanchee[t]
286. 桔	mandarin orange	勞	lòuh	*unclear*
287. 蕉	banana	臂生	bei sāng	pisang[u]
288. 栗	chestnut	遮士單	jē sih dāan	chestnut
289. 檸檬	lemon/lime	拈遮士	līm jē sih	lemon [or lime] juice
290. 西瓜	water melon	嘩打拈檬	wàh dāa nīm mūng	water melon
291. 柚	pomelo	甘波羅士	gām bō lòh sih	pombolosee
292. 補	plum	步蕾[sic,㾸]	bouh léuih [lām]	plum
293. 波羅	pineapple	烞嗱士	hóu nàh sih	ananas[v]
294. 蘿蔔	radish	辣脷+[sic,士]	laaht lèih sahp [sih]	radish
295. 庶	sugar cane	嘛母酥忌利	màh móuh sōu geih leih	mamou [bamboo] sugar
296. 花生	peanut	卡溽灣治	kāa fū wāan jih	cavalance
297. 番薯	sweet potato	判打大	pun dāa daaih	potato
298. 梨	pear	之	jī	*unclear*
299. 辣椒	chili	至烈	ji liht	chili
300. 魚	fish	非士	fēi sih	fishee
301. 鱸魚	*lòuh* fish	萬地里非士	maahn deih léih fēi sih	mandarin fishee
302. 鯪魚	*lìhm* fish	罩嘲非士	jaau jāau fēi sih	chow chow fishee
303. 草魚	*chóu* fish	曲非士	kūk fēi sih	cook fishee
304. 撻沙	sole	通非士	tūng fēi sih	tongue fishee
305. 白鱔	eel	衣利非士	yī leih fēi sih	eelee fishee
306. 咸魚	salted fish	沙路非士	sāa louh fēi sih	sarlo fishee
307. 豬肉	pork	砵扶	būt fùh	pork
308. 牛肉	beef	味扶	meih fùh	beef
309. 羊	sheep	嗩	jīp	sheep
310. 馬	horse	茄[sic,荷]士	ké [hòh] sih	horsee
311. 狗	dog	鐸	dohk	dog
312. 貓	cat	辣	laaht	cat
313. 鼠	rat	烈	liht	rat
314. 鴨	duck	莴架	āng gaa	anka[w]
315. 鵝	goose	姑樹	gū syuh	goosoo
316. 刉雞	capon	甲咚	gaap dūng	capon
317. 雞乸	fowl	否路	fáu louh	fowlo

(i) Chinese item(s)	(ii) English translation of (i)	(iii) Chinese characters used to indicate English pronunciation	(iv) Yale transcription indicating the sound of Chinese characters in (iii)	(v) Written form of English or pidgin indicated by transcription in (iv)
318. 筍雞	bamboo chicken	士孖鮮否絡 [sic,路]	sih māa laa fáu míhng [louh]	small fowlo
319. 雞仔	chicken	折京	jit gīng	chicken
320. 白鴿	pigeon	到嗱	dou wāa	dove
321. 班鳩	turtle dove	到到嗱	dou dou wāa	turtle dove
322. 沙道	snipe	士烈	sih liht	snipe
323. 蜆鴨	small duck	士孖鮮或	sih māa laa waahk	small duck
324. 雞旦	egg	喴	yīk	egg
325. 鹽	salt	沙路	sāa louh	sarlo
326. 牛乳	milk	覔	mihk	milk
327. 火腿	ham	聖加	sing gāa	skinka[x]
328. 油	oil	挨利	ōi leih	oilee
329. 竹筍	bamboo shoot	嘛母	màh móuh	mamu [bamboo][y]
330. 青菜	green vegetables	絹望	gyun lyùhn	greens
331. 酒	wine	湾	wāan	wine
332. 米	uncooked rice	嚟士	làih sih	licee [ricee]
333. 飯	cooked rice	囉士	lō sih	lorsi[z]
334. 醋	vinegar	味脷架	meih lèih gaa	vinegar
335. 烟	smoke	士卜	sih būk	smoke
336. 檳榔	areca nut	亞勒架	aa lahk gaa	areca
337. 醬油	sauce	*unclear*	*unclear*	*unclear*
338. 茶	tea	哋	deih	tea
339. 牛奶油	butter	士孖以	sih māa yíh	s mör[aa]
340. 水	water	嗱打	wāa dáa	water
341. 火	fire	揮亞	fāi aa	fire
342. 柴	firewood	活	wuht	wood
343. 鼻烟	snuff	士粒	sih nāp	snuff
344. 烟筒	pipe	卑裂	bēi bah	pipa[bb]
345. 碟	plate	别烈	biht liht	plate
346. 飯碗	rice bowl	囉士蛤	lō sih gahp	lorsi cup
347. 茶盃	tea cup	哋蛤	deih gahp	tea cup
348. 酒盃	wine glass	清蛤	wāan gahp	wine cup
349. 紙	paper	地罢	deih bah	paper
350. 筆	pen	边	bīn	pen
351. 墨	ink	英忌	yīng geih	inkee
352. 硯盒	ink box	英忌	yīng geih	inkee

(cont.)

(i) Chinese item(s)	(ii) English translation of (i)	(iii) Chinese characters used to indicate English pronunciation	(iv) Yale transcription indicating the sound of Chinese characters in (iii)	(v) Written form of English or pidgin indicated by transcription in (iv)
353. 郜	book	卜	būk	book
354. 鎖	lock	勒	lahk	lock
355. 床	bed	必	bīt	bed
356. 枱	table	嗲步	dē bouh	table
357. 儍	bench	嚀	māang	*unclear*
358. 椅	chair	遮士	jē sih	chairsee
359. 被	quilt	丐亞	koi aa	coia[cc]
360. 蓆	mat	乜	māt	mat
361. 帳	curtain	吉殿	gāt dihn	curtain
362. 衫	coat	葛	got	coat
363. 褲	breeches	壁力遮士	bīk lihk jē sih	breechesee
364. 帽	hat	乞	hāt	hat
365. 鞋	shoe	酥	sōu	shoe
366. 襪	stocking	土[sic,士]得件	tóu [sih] dāk gihn	stocking
367. 手巾	handkerchief	興忌治	hīng geih jih	handkerchief
368. 扇	fan	番	fāan	fan
369. 刀	knife	坭父	nàih fuh	knifoo
370. 有	have	梭	sō	*unclear*
371. 鞭竿	walking stick	堅	gīn	cane
372. 鞋扣	shoe buckle	酥卜	sōu būk	shoe buckle

[a] Port. *covado* ('covid')
[b] Port. *covado* ('covid')
[c] Port. *não querer* ('no want')
[d] Port. *querer* ('want')
[e] Port. *consciencia* ('honest')
[f] Port. *conta* ('account')
[g] Port. *comprador* ('compradore')
[h] Port. *padre* ('father')
[i] Port. *noite* ('night')
[j] Port. *querer* ('want')
[k] Port. *querer* ('want')
[l] Port. *grande* ('large')
[m] Port. *largo* ('broad')
[n] Port. *companha* ('partner')
[o] Port. *não sabe* ('not understand')
[p] Port. *feitoria* ('trading establishment')
[q] Port. *mas que* ('never mind')
[r] Port. *sabe* ('understand')

^s Swedish *apelsin* ('orange')

^t Port. *laranja* ('orange')

^u Malay *pisang* ('banana')

^v Port. *ananas* ('pineapple')

^w Swedish *anka* ('duck')

^x Swedish *skinka* ('ham')

^y Possibly from Indo-Portuguese *mambu* ('bamboo')

^z Possibly from Port. *arroz* ('cooked rice')

^{aa} Swedish *smör* ('butter')

^{bb} Swedish *pipa* ('pipe')

^{cc} Possibly from Port. *colcha* ('blanket')

Note: The asterisk in column (i) indicates a typographical error in the original. In the other columns, similar errors are indicated by the use of *sic*, followed by the 'correct' Chinese character. In some instances, words or meanings that defy explanation or transcription are simply marked *unclear*.

Appendix 5   The vocabulary of Hong Kong English

Word	Short gloss
ABC	an American-born Chinese; Australian-born Chinese [abbr.]
Ah	an informal address term (*Ah Sam*, *Ah Chan*, etc.)
ai ya	an interjection, an exclamation of surprise, etc.
aircon	an airconditioner [abbr.]
aircraft [as count noun]	a plane, helicopter etc.
almond cream	a sweet dessert
alphabet [as count noun]	a letter of the alphabet
amah	a female domestic helper
ambassador	a person working as a public relations assistant
ancestral home	a place where one's ancestors were born or lived
Anglo-Chinese	related to Britain and China, or English-medium schools in Hong Kong
AO	a senior civil service grade [abbr. of 'administrative officer']
astronaut	an émigré often flying between the host country and Hong Kong
aunty	a female friend of the family (also *auntie*)
Australian-Chinese	an Australian citizen of Chinese descent or ethnicity
autopay	an automatic payment
baak choy	a variety of cabbage (also *bak choy*, *Chinese cabbage*)
back	currently in the office or having arrived at work; used instead of *in*, e.g. *He's not back yet* for *He's not in yet.*
Bamboo Gang	a Taiwanese secret society or 'triad' society
banana	a westernised Chinese
bar fine	the fee paid for the services of a female hostess
bar girl	a hostess or dancer who works in a bar

bar hostess	→ bar girl
Basic Law	the post-1997 Hong Kong constitution
batchmate	a colleague recruited at the same time as others to a company or organisation
bath	a shower or a bath
bat gwa	an ornamental eight-sided fung shui mirror (also *pat kwa*)
BBC	a British-born Chinese [abbr.]
beggar's chicken	chicken baked in lotus leaves and clay
big brother	a recruiter or protector in a Chinese triad or secret society
big circle	a group of gangsters from mainland China
bird's nest	a sweet soup made from swallows' nests
bitter melon	a variety of vegetable
black hand	a behind-the-scenes criminal mastermind
black society	a Chinese secret society or triad
blue lantern	a junior member of a triad
BNO	a type of passport [abbr. of 'British National Overseas']
bo lei	a variety of tea
boat people	1. boat dwellers 2. category of Vietnamese refugee
brinjal	an aubergine or eggplant
Buddha's delight	a Chinese vegetarian dish
bungalow	a large house in the colonial style
cage	a partitioned space with a bed in a shared apartment
cagepeople	residents of bedspaces (*cageman, cagewoman, etc.*)
can	an emphatic affirmative, e.g. *Can you do this? – can!*
Canadian-Chinese	a Canadian citizen of Chinese descent or ethnicity
Canto, Canto-	an abbreviation for 'Cantonese' (*Canto-phrasebook, etc.*)
Canto star	a Cantonese pop-star
Canto-pop	a style of Cantonese popular music
Canto-pop prince	a male Cantonese popstar
Canto-pop queen	a popular female Cantonese popstar
Canto-speak	the Cantonese language
Category Three	the adult-viewing film classification used by the Hong Kong censor
catty	a unit of weight approx. 0.625kg
Certificate of Identity	a type of travel document used by Hong Kong people
cha siu	roasted pork slices (also *char siu, char siew*)
cha siu bau	a white bun containing spicy pork
char siew	→ cha siu
cheeky	arrogant, provoking violence

cheongsam	a traditional Chinese dress of embroidered silk
chi	vital spiritual energy (also *qi*)
chicken	a prostitute
chim sticks	fortune-telling sticks
China doll	a pretty young woman of submissive demeanour
China hand	a long-time China resident
Chinese banquet	a formal Chinese dinner
Chinese broccoli	a type of green vegetable (also *gai lan*, *kai lan*)
Chinese cabbage	a variety of cabbage (also *baak choy*, *bak choy*)
Chinese calendar	the Chinese lunar calendar
Chinese calligraphy	the practice and art of writing Chinese characters
Chinese celery	a variety of celery
Chinese character	a written symbol in the Chinese writing system
Chinese chess	a form of chess played in China
Chinese cobra	a variety of snake
Chinese cucumber	a variety of vegetable
Chinese doughnut	a fried stick of wheat dough (*dough stick*)
Chinese dragon	a mythical creature in Chinese folk mythology
Chinese kale	a variety of green vegetable
Chinese medicine	a medical practice based on herbs, etc.
Chinese national	a citizen of the People's Republic of China
Chinese New Year	the new year celebration according to the lunar calendar (also *Lunar New Year*, *Chinese Spring Festival*)
Chinese noodles	a common item of Chinese cuisine
Chinese pink dolphin	a breed of dolphin (also called *Chinese white dolphin*)
Chinese sausage	a spicy sausage made from pork or liver
Chinese secret society	a sworn brotherhood association; a triad
Chinese silk road	the trade route used by silk traders during the Middle Ages
Chinese tea	varieties of tea grown and drunk in China
Chinese turnip	a white root vegetable (also *Chinese radish*)
Chinese Valentine's Day	a festival on the 15th of the first month of the Lunar New Year
Chinese values	a 'Confucianistic' ethical system
Chinese-Vietnamese	a Vietnamese citizen of Chinese descent or ethnicity
Chinese zodiac	the astrological signs of the Chinese calendar
Ching Ming	a spring festival in the Chinese calendar
Chinglish	various mixtures of Chinese and English
chit	a written note or bill, etc.
Chiu Chau	of the Chiu Chau dialect areas of Guangdong and Fukien province, e.g. *Chiu Chau food* (also *Chiu Chow*, *Teo Chew*)

choi sum	a variety of green vegetable (also *choy sum*, *Chinese flowering cabbage*)
chop	1. a seal or stamp 2. wound with a large knife or cleaver
chow fan	fried rice
chow mein	fried noodles
Christian	Protestant (as opposed to Catholic)
Chung Yeung	an autumn festival
clan	a group of family members, or dialect speakers
clan association	an association of members of a Chinese clan
cocktail	a cocktail party
comprador	a financial middleman
congee	a type of liquid rice dish (also *rice gruel*, *rice porridge*)
conservancy	conservation, e.g. *water conservancy*
coolie	a labourer or unskilled worker
crystal bun	a sweet, ball-shaped dumpling
curry puff	a food item sold in bakeries
dai fei	a powerful speedboat used for smuggling people or goods
dai lo	a protector in a Chinese triad (also *big brother*)
dai luk	mainland China
dau	a generic term for many varieties of beans
dau miu	a type of green vegetable (also *dou miao*)
dim sum	various food snacks served in Chinese restaurants during the daytime (also *yum cha*)
discuss about (something)	to discuss (a topic)
dissident	an opposition political activist in mainland China
district officer	a senior civil servant grade
domestic helper	an employed homeworker
Double Tenth	10 October; Taiwan's National Day
dough stick	a fried stick of wheat dough (*Chinese doughnut*)
dragon boat	a narrow boat with dragon's head at the prow
dragon dance	a dance performed at festivals, weddings, etc.
dragon throne	the emperor in imperial China
dragon's eye	a variety of fruit (also *lungan* or *longan*)
dragonhead	the leader of a Chinese secret society or triad
drunken chicken	cooked chicken marinated in rice wine, served cold
emphasise on (something)	to emphasise something (cf. *stress on*)
equipment [as count noun]	a piece of equipment
essence of chicken	a health-food preparation

faan	cooked rice as in *faan hap*, 'rice box'
faat choy	black hair-like seaweed (also *fat choy*)
fan gwai	a derogatory term for a white person or westerner (also *fan kwai*)
feng shui	a system of geomancy (also *fung shui*)
Festival of the Hungry Ghosts	a festival in early autumn (also *Hungry Ghosts Festival*)
fish sauce	a sauce prepared from fish extract
fishball	a type of food dish and snack
fishball girl	a type of sex worker
fishball stall	1. a type foodstall 2. a type of sex establishment
fishcake	a cake of shredded fish, often in soup
fishpaste	crushed fish meat used to prepare fish balls
flatted factory	factory space located in an industrial building
food court	an area in a shopping mall selling various kinds of cooked food
foodstall	an open-air pavement restaurant
Fourteen K (14K)	a type of secret society or triad
fung shui	→ feng shui
gai lan	a type of green vegetable (also *kai lan, Chinese broccoli*)
garoupa	a grouper (type of fish)
gluten ball	a small ball of deep-fried wheat gluten, often in soup
glutinous rice	a food item (also *sticky rice*)
godown	a warehouse
golden mushroom	a variety of long-stemmed mushroom
golden rice bowl	a secure job (cf. *iron rice bowl*)
grass jelly	a gelatinous food dish
griffin	1. a new horse on the racetrack 2. a newly arrived westerner
guanxi	contacts and 'relationships' in business, etc.
guk fa cha	a variety of tea using chrysthanthemum leaves
gwailo	a derogatory term for a western man, literally 'ghost man' (also *gweilo*)
gwaipo	a derogatory term for a western woman, literally 'ghost woman' (also *gweipo*)
H shares	PRC shares listed on the Hong Kong Stock Exchange
ham sap	lecherous or salacious
Han Chinese	the dominant ethnicity in the PRC
har gau	a shrimp dumpling snack
harsh	of people, strict and demanding
hawker	a street vendor (also *hawker stall, food*)

heaty	used of food, etc. that stimulates heat
helper	→ domestic helper
heung ha	→ ancestral home
HKSAR	Hong Kong Special Administrative Region [abbr.]
hoisin sauce	a sauce prepared from fish extract
Hokkien	the word in the Fujian language for 'Fujian' (Md.), i.e. Chinese people from Fujian province, and/or the associated dialect (in Cant. *Fukien*)
hong	a large corporation based in Hong Kong
Hong Kong Chinese	a Hong Kong resident of Chinese descent
Hongkonger	a Hong Kong resident or Hong Kong person
Hong Kong side	on Hong Kong island
hundred-year-old egg	a type of preserved egg (elsewhere *century egg*)
Hungry Ghosts Festival	→ Festival of the Hungry Ghosts
ICAC	Independent Commission Against Corruption [abbr.]
I-Ching	a book of fortune-telling and philosophy
identity card	a card used for personal identification (also *ID card*)
II	an illegal immigrant [abbr.]
iron rice bowl	a secure job (cf. *golden rice bowl*)
kai lan	→ gai lan
kaifong	a neighbour
kaito	a small ferry used around Hong Kong
Kitchen God	a mythological deity presiding over kitchens
KIV	keep in view [abbr.]
Kowloon side	on the Kowloon peninsula
kowtow	to bow down on bended knees
kumquat	a variety of small orange (also *cumquat*)
kungfu	a variety of tea
kut	a bushy green plant with small round oranges
Kwan Tai	the god of triads, police and property agents
laisee	a packet of money placed in a special red envelope and given as a gift at Chinese New Year, weddings, etc.
laisee packet	a 'red envelope'
lantern festival	1. a festival on Chinese Valentine's Day 2. festivities at the Mid-autumn Festival
lap sap	rubbish or refuse
lion dance	a performance by costumed dancers dressed as a lion
list out	to verbally list (a number of things, points, etc.)
lo shui	a spicy variety of soya sauce
local	a Hong Kong Chinese person

lotus seed	the seed of a lotus plant
LRT	Light Rail Transit [abbr.], a rail transport system in Hong Kong's New Territories
lucky money	money placed inside a 'red envelope'
Lunar New Year	→ **Chinese New Year**
lychee	a variety of fruit (also *lichee*)
Macao sole	a variety of sea fish, *Cynoglocans trulla*, found in southern China
madam	an address term used for women in authority, including police officers
mafoo	1. a stable boy 2. a prostitute's pimp or protector
mah jai	a male subordinate or lackey (also *ma chai*)
mandarin collar	a collar worn on a traditional Chinese dress
mandarin fan	a type of antique Chinese fan
mandarin fish	a type of fish, *Synchiropus splendidus*
mandarin hat	a type of circular hat
mandarin square	an embroidered patch on Chinese robes
mansion	a generic name for many apartment buildings
mao tai	a variety of spirits distilled from rice
Mid-autumn Festival	a festival held in the eighth month (also *Moon Festival*, *Mooncake Festival*)
Middle Kingdom	a name for China
milk tea	tea with milk
minibus	a small bus with seats for 16 people (also *public light bus*)
Monkey God	a mythological deity
monsoon	in Hong Kong, a northeast or southwest wind
Moon Festival	→ **Mid-autumn Festival**
mooncake	a round cake containing lotus paste and egg, eaten at the time of the *Mid-autumn Festival*
Mooncake Festival	→ **Mid-autumn Festival**
MTR	Mass Transit Railway [abbr.], the 'underground' in Hong Kong
mummy	female supervisor of bar hostesses
night market	an illuminated street market trading at night
nightclub hostess	a hostess working in a Hong Kong nightclub
nullah	an open watercourse or drain
officiate [as trans. verb]	to perform official duties (of a ceremony, etc.)
one-woman brothel	a vice-establishment with a single prostitute
oolong	a variety of Chinese tea
OSCO	Organised and Serious Crimes Ordinance [abbr.]
overseas Chinese	people of Chinese birth or Chinese descent living abroad
pai kau	a form of dominos played in Hong Kong

panel	a school department, e.g. *the English panel*
pat kwa	→ bat gwa
Peking cabbage	a variety of cabbage
Peking duck	a dish of roasted duck
piece	an item, e.g. *one piece of essay*
polyclinic	a medical group-practice
porridge	→ congee, e.g. *rice porridge, teochew porridge*
praya	a waterfront street or road
public light bus	→ minibus
Punti	the Cantonese language (*archaic* but still used by HK law courts)
qigong	a practice of meditation, martial arts, etc.
raise up	to raise, e.g. *I'd like to raise up a new issue*
red capitalist	an executive, etc. of a mainland Chinese business corporation
red chips	the shares of mainland China corporations active in the HKSAR
red envelope	a special type of red paper envelope used to contain 'lucky money'
red packet	→ laisee
red pole	the rank of 'fighter' or 'enforcer' in a triad society
return back	to return, e.g. *let's return back home*
rice bowl	a means of earning a living
rice box	a prepared rice meal, usually served in a polystyrene box
rice dumplings	steamed rice wrapped in lotus leaves
rice wine	various kinds of spirits distilled from rice
sago pudding	a popular dish served for dessert
sam foo	an outfit of white jacket and black trousers (also *samfoo, sam fu*)
sampan	a type of wooden boat
San Yee On	a type of triad society (also *Sun Yee On*)
scold	to reprimand, or upbraid, e. g. *the boss scolded his staff*
scroll painting	a traditional form of Chinese painting
send	to accompany, e.g. *I'll send you downstairs*
Shantung	a variety of silk
shark's fin	the fin of the shark used as the main ingredient in *shark's fin soup*
shoe shine	to ingratiate oneself with a superior
shoe shiner	a person who seeks advancement through flattery, etc.
shroff	an office or kiosk, e.g. in car parks
sitting-out area	a small paved park in a built-up area

siu mai	a snack of pork and shrimp dumplings
snakehead	the leader of a human smuggling ring
Special Administrative Region (SAR)	a province or region in the People's Republic of China which is allowed a degree of administrative and political autonomy
Special Economic Zone (SEZ)	a region of China with a degree of economic independence
spirit money	money offered as appeasement to gods
Spring Festival	the Lunar New Year festivities
staff [as count noun]	a member of staff
sticky rice	→ glutinous rice
stir-fry	a cooking method
straw mushroom	a variety of mushroom
street hawker	an unlicensed street trader
stress on something	to stress, e.g. *He stressed on several points in his talk*
subvent	to subsidise
tael	a unit of weight used in Hong Kong
tai chi	a type of martial arts exercise
tai tai	a rich woman of leisure, usually married
taipan	in Hong Kong, the CEO of a large company
tan tan noodles	a Sichuan dish of spicy noodles
tea gathering	a kind of tea party, or soft drinks party
tea house	a teashop selling teas and snacks
tea money	a tip, bribe, or other form of *ex gratia* payment
teddy boy	a male member of a Hong Kong street gang
Tiger Balm	a mentholated medicinal ointment
Tin Hau festival	a festival honouring Tin Hau, the Goddess of the Sea
treaty ports	Chinese cities 'opened' to western powers in the nineteenth century, including Canton (Guangzhou), Amoy (Xiamen), etc.
triad	1. a criminal secret society, such as the *14K triad society*, etc. 2. a member of a triad society
typhoon shelter	a sheltered area within a harbour
uncle	a term of address used for a male friend of the family
vermicelli	a variety of Chinese noodles
villa	1. a low-rise house 2. a flat or house used for prostitution
waah	an exclamation of surprise or wonder
wah kiu	people of Chinese ethnicity living outside mainland China
wallah-wallah	a small boat used to ferry passengers
wan yee	a type of medicinal fungus used in cooking
white paper fan	rank of advisor in a triad society

Wo Hop To	one of the four major secret societies or triads in Hong Kong
Wo Shing Wo	one of the four major secret societies or triads in Hong Kong
yamen	in Qing China, the office of mandarin officials (*archaic*)
yang	the male or 'positive' principle in cosmology
yin	the female or 'negative' principle in cosmology
yum cha	→ dim sum
yum sing	a toast, approx. 'cheers!' (also *yum seng*)
Yunnan ham	a variety of spicy ham popular in Chinese cuisine

References

The publisher has used its best endeavours to ensure that the URLs for external websites referred to in this book are correct and active at the time of going to press. However, the publisher has no responsibility for the websites and can make no guarantee that a site will remain live or that the content is or will remain appropriate.

Abbas, Ackbar (1992). The last emporium: verse and cultural space. In P. K. Leung (ed.), *City at the End of Time*. Hong Kong: Twilight Books, 2–18.

Abbas, Ackbar (1997). *Hong Kong: Culture and the Politics of Disappearance*. Originally published by the University of Minnesota Press. Hong Kong: Hong Kong University Press.

Adamson, Bob (2002). Barbarian as a foreign language: English in China's schools. In *World Englishes* special issue on English in China. Forthcoming.

Adamson, Bob & Morris, Paul (1997). The English curriculum in the People's Republic of China. *Comparative Education Review* 41.1: 3–26.

Afendras, Evangelos A. (1998). The onset of bilingualism in Hong Kong: language choice in the home domain. In M. C. Pennington (ed.), *Language in Hong Kong at Century's End*. Hong Kong: Hong Kong University Press, 113–41.

Allen, Jamie (1997). *Seeing Red: China's Uncompromising Takeover of Hong Kong*. Singapore: Butterworth-Heinemann Asia.

Allsopp, Richard (1996). *The Dictionary of Caribbean English Usage*. Oxford: Oxford University Press.

Anderson, Aeneas (1795). *A Narrative of the British Embassy to China, in the Years 1792, 1793, and 1794: Containing the Various Circumstances of the Embassy, with Accounts of Customs and Manners of the Chinese, and a Description of the Country, Towns, Cities, &c., &c.* London: Debrett.

Anderson, Benedict R. (1983 [1995]). *Imagined Communities: Reflections on the Origin and Spread of Nationalism*. London: Verso.

Anon (1835). *Hùhng mòuh tūng yuhng fāanwáa* (*The Common Foreign Language of the Redhaired People*). Sāang sihng bīk gīng tòhng (Canton: Wall Documents Hall publishers).

Anon (1857). Canton-English. *Household Words* 15: 450–52.

Anson, George (1748). *A Voyage Round the World: in the Years MDCCXL, I, II, III, IV*. In R. Walter & B. Robins (eds.) (1974). London: Oxford University Press.

298

Apple, Michael (1986). *Teachers and Texts*. New York: Routledge and Kegan Paul.

Ashcroft, Bill, Griffiths, Gareth & Tiffin, Helen (1989). *The Empire Writes Back*. London: Routledge.

Avis, Walter S. (1967). *A Dictionary of Canadianisms on Historical Principles*. Toronto: Gage.

Axler, Maria, Yang, Anson & Stevens, Trudy (1998). Current language attitudes of Hong Kong Chinese adolescents and young adults. In M. C. Pennington (ed.), *Language in Hong Kong at Century's End*. Hong Kong: Hong Kong University Press, 329–38.

Bacon-Shone, John & Bolton, Kingsley (1998). Charting multilingualism: language censuses and language surveys in Hong Kong. In M. C. Pennington (ed.), *Language in Hong Kong at Century's End*. Hong Kong: Hong Kong University Press, 43–90.

Bailey, Nathan (1721). *An Universal Etymological English Dictionary*. London: Printed for E. Bell [and 9 others].

Baker, Philip (1987). Historical developments in Chinese pidgin English and the nature of the relationships between the various pidgin Englishes of the Pacific region. *Journal of Pidgin and Creole Languages* 2: 163–207.

Baker, Philip & Mühlhäusler, Peter (1990). From business to pidgin. *Journal of Asian-Pacific Communication* 1: 87–115.

Bakhtin, Mikhail M. (1981). *The Dialogic Imagination*, ed. Michael Holmquist. Austin: University of Texas Press.

Balfour, S. F. (1941). Hong Kong before the British. *T'ien Hsia Monthly* 11: 330–464.

Ball, Dyer J. (1888). *Cantonese Made Easy*. Hong Kong: Kelly and Walsh.

Ball, Dyer J. (1903). *Things Chinese; or, Notes Connected with China*. Hong Kong: Kelly and Walsh.

Banjo, Ayo & Young, Peter (1982). On editing a second-language dictionary: the proposed Dictionary of West African English (DWAE). *English World-Wide* 3: 87–91.

Barber, Katherine (1999). *The Canadian Oxford Dictionary*. Oxford: Oxford University Press.

Barr, Pat (1970). *Foreign Devils*. Harmondsworth: Penguin.

Barrère, Albert & Leland, Charles G. (1889). *A Dictionary of Slang, Jargon & Cant, Embracing English, American, and Anglo-Indian Slang, Pidgin English, Tinker's Jargon, and Other Irregular Phraseology*. London: Ballantyne Press.

Barreto, Luis F. (1997) The cultural frontier. *Macau*. Macao: Government Media Bureau, 58–72.

Bartlett, John Russell (1848). *Dictionary of Americanisms: a Glossary of Words and Phrases Usually Regarded as Peculiar to the United States*. New York: Bartlett and Welford.

Bauer, Robert (1984). The Hong Kong Cantonese speech community. *Language Learning and Communication* 3: 289–315.

Bauer, Robert S. & Benedict, Paul K. (1997). *Modern Cantonese Phonology*. Berlin and New York: Mouton de Gruyter.

Bautista, Maria Lourdes S. (1997). The lexicon of Philippine English. In M. L. S. Bautista (ed.), *English is an Asian language: the Philippine Context*. Manila: Macquarie Library, 49–72.

Bawden, Charles Roskelly (1954). An eighteenth century Chinese source for the Portuguese dialect of Macao. Silver Jubilee Volume of the *Zinbun-Kagaku-Kenkyusyo*, 12–33.

Becker, Jasper (1996). *Hungry Ghosts: China's Secret Famine*. London: John Murray.

Bell, Daniel A. (1998). Hong Kong's transition to capitalism. *Dissent* 45: 15–23.

Bell, Roger T. (1981). *An Introduction to Applied Linguistics*. Batsford Academic and Educational Ltd.

Benson, Phil (1993). Localised vocabulary in Hong Kong English and Australian English. In R. Pemberton & E. Tsang (eds.), *Studies in Lexis: Proceedings from a Seminar*. Hong Kong University of Science and Technology, 99–111.

Benson, Phil (1994). The political vocabulary of Hong Kong English. *Hong Kong Papers in Linguistics and Language Teaching* 17: 63–81.

Benson, Phil (1997). The lexicography of English in the world: the treatment of China in four British dictionaries. PhD thesis. University of Exeter.

Benson, Phil (2000). Hong Kong words: variation and context. Special issue of *World Englishes* on 'Hong Kong English: Autonomy and Creativity' 19. 3: 373–80.

Benson, Phil (2001). *Ethnocentrism and the English Dictionary*. London and New York: Routledge.

Bhatia, Tek K. & Ritchie, William C. (eds.) (1989). Special issue of *World Englishes*, on 'Code-mixing: English Across Languages', 8.3.

Bickers, Robert (1999). *Britain in China*. Manchester: Manchester University Press.

Blount, Thomas (1656). *Glossographia [. . .]*. London: Thomas Newcomb.

Bolton, Kingsley (1983). Review of Hughes & Trudgill (1979), *English Accents and Dialects*. *Language Learning and Communication* 2: 124–6.

Bolton, Kingsley (1992). Sociolinguistics today: Asia and the West. In K. Bolton & H. Kwok (eds.), *Sociolinguistics Today: International Perspectives*. London: Routledge, 5–66.

Bolton, Kingsley (2000a). The sociolinguistics of English in Hong Kong. *World Englishes* 19.3: 265–85.

Bolton, Kingsley (2000b). Researching Hong Kong English: a guide to bibliographical sources. *World Englishes* 19.3: 445–52.

Bolton, Kingsley (2000c). Language and hybridization: Pidgin tales from the China coast. *Interventions* 2.1: 35–52.

Bolton, Kingsley (ed.) (2000d). Special issue of *World Englishes*, on 'Hong Kong English: Autonomy and Creativity', 19.3: 265–85.

Bolton, Kingsley (2001a). The life and lexicography of Robert Morrison (1782–1834). Introduction to *Vocabulary of the Canton Dialect*. Macao: East India Company Press. Reprinted, London: Ganesha Press.

Bolton, Kingsley (2001b). Ernst Johann Eitel (1838–1908) and *A Chinese–English Dictionary in the Cantonese Dialect*. Introduction to *A Chinese–English Dictionary in the Cantonese Dialect*, 2nd edn., 1910–11. Reprinted, London: Ganesha Publishing.

Bolton, Kingsley (ed.) (2002). *Hong Kong English: Autonomy and Creativity*. Hong Kong: Hong Kong University Press.

Bolton, Kingsley, Hung, Joseph & Nelson, Gerald (Forthcoming). *The International Corpus of English Project in Hong Kong*.

Bolton, Kingsley & Hutton, Christopher (1999). Linguistics in cross-cultural communication: from the *Chinese Repository* to the 'Chinese Emerson'. *Asian Pacific Communication* 9.1 and 2: 145–63.

Bolton, Kingsley & Kwok, Helen (1990). The dynamics of the Hong Kong accent: social identity and sociolinguistic description. *Journal of Asian Pacific Communication* 1: 147–72.

Bolton, Kingsley & Luke, Kang-kwong (1999). *Language and Society in Hong Kong: the Social Survey of Languages in the 1980's*. Hong Kong: Social Sciences Research Centre.

Bolton, Kingsley & Tong, Q. S. (eds.) (2002). Special issue of *World Englishes*, on 'English in China: Interdisciplinary Perspectives', 21.2: 177–355.

Bolton, Whitney F. (ed.) ([1966] 1973). *The English Language: Essays by English and American Men of Letters*. Cambridge: Cambridge University Press.

Bolton, Whitney F. & Crystal, David (eds.) (1969). *The English Language: Essays by Linguists and Men of Letters 1858–1964*. Cambridge: Cambridge University Press.

Boorman, Howard L. & Howard, Richard C. (1967–79). *Biographical Dictionary of Republican China*. New York : Columbia University Press, 3: 421–2.

Boxer, Charles R. (1968). *Fidalgos in the Far East*. Hong Kong: Oxford University Press.

Boyle, Joseph (1997a). Imperialism and the English language in Hong Kong. *Journal of Multilingual and Multicultural Development* 18.3: 169–81.

Boyle, Joseph (1997b). Changing attitudes to English. *English Today* 13: 3–6.

Boyle, Joseph (1997c). The use of mixed-code in Hong Kong English language teaching. *System* 25: 83–9.

Boyle, Joseph P. (1997d). Native-speaker teachers of English in Hong Kong. *Language and Education* 11: 163–81.

Boyle, Joseph & Boyle, Linda (1991). *Common Spoken English Errors in Hong Kong*. Hong Kong: Longman.

Branegan, Jay (1991). Finding a proper place for English. *Time*. 16 September, 27.

Branford, William (ed.) (1987). *The South African Pocket Dictionary*. Cape Town: Oxford University Press.

Branford, William, et al. (1976) *Voorloper. An Interim Presentation of Materials for a Dictionary of South African English on Historical Principles*. Grahamstown: Rhodes University.

Bratt-Paulston, Christina (1980). *Bilingual Education: Theories and Issues*. Rowley, Mass.: Newbury House.

Bridgman, Elijah C. (1833). Introductory remarks. *Chinese Repository* 2: 1–9.

Bridgman, Elijah C. (1841). *A Chinese Chrestomathy in the Canton Dialect*. Macao: S.W. Williams.

Brown, Kimberleg (2002). World Englishes and the classroom: research and practice agendas for the year 2000. In E. Thumboo (ed.), *The Three Circles of English*. Singapore: Uni Press, 371–82.

Bruce, Nigel (1996). *Language in Hong Kong Education and Society: a Bibliography*. Hong Kong: English Centre, University of Hong Kong.

Brumfit, Christopher (ed.) (1982). *English of International Communication*. Oxford: Pergamon Press.

Brutt-Griffler, Janina (2002). *World English: a Study of its Development*. Clevedon: Multilingual Matters.

Bullokar, John (1616). *An English Expositor [. . .]*. London: John Legatt.

Bullokar, William (1580, 1586). *Booke at Large (1580) and Bref Grammar for English (1586)*. Facsimile reproductions. Delmar, New York: Scholars' Facsimiles & Reprints, 1977.

Bunton, David (1989). *Common English Errors in Hong Kong*. Hong Kong: Longman.

Bunton, David (1991). A comparison of English errors made by Hong Kong students and those made by non-native learners of English internationally. In *Institute of Language in Education Journal*. Special issue no. 2: 9–22.

Bunton, David (1994). *Common Social English Errors in Hong Kong*. Hong Kong: Longman.

Burchfield, Robert W. (1985). *The English Language*. Oxford: Oxford University Press.

Butler, Susan (ed.) (1981). *The Macquarie Dictionary*. Sydney: Macquarie Dictionary Company Ltd.

Butler, Susan (1996). World English in an Asian context: the Macquarie Dictionary project. *World Englishes* 15: 347–57.

Butler, Susan (1997a). Corpus of English in Southeast Asia: implications for a regional dictionary. In M. L. S. Bautista (ed.), *English is an Asian Language: the Philippine Context*. Manila: Macquarie Library, 103–24.

Butler, Susan (1997b). Selecting South-East Asian Words for an Australian Dictionary: how to choose in an English not your own. In E. Schneider (ed.), *Englishes Around the World*, Vol. 2: *Caribbean, Africa, Asia, Australasia*. Amsterdam: John Benjamins, 273–86.

Butler, Susan (1999). The needs of dictionary users in Southeast Asia. In M. Newbrook (ed.), *English is an Asian Language: the Thai Context*. Sydney: Macquarie Library, 80–94.

Cameron, Deborah (1990). Demythologizing sociolinguistics: Why language does not reflect society. In J. E. Joseph & T. J. Taylor (eds.), *Ideologies of Language*. London: Routledge, 79–83.

Cameron, Nigel (1970). *Barbarians and Mandarins*. Hong Kong: Oxford University Press.

Cannon, Garland (1998). Chinese borrowings in English. *American Speech* 63: 3–33.

Cannon, P. S. (1936). The 'Pidgin English' of the China Coast. *Journal of the Army Educational Corps* 13: 137–40.

Carless, David R. (1995). Politicised expressions in the *South China Morning Post*. *English Today* 42: 18–22.

Cassidy, Frederic G. (1985). *Dictionary of American Regional English*. Cambridge, Mass.: Harvard University Press.

Cassidy, Frederic G. & Le Page, Robert (1967). *Dictionary of Jamaican English*. Cambridge: Cambridge University Press.

Castells, Manuel (1986). The Shek Kip Mei syndrome: public housing and economic development in Hong Kong. Hong Kong: Centre of Urban Studies & Urban Planning. Working paper 15.

Chako, Sussy [Xu Xi] (1995). Wah Kiu wanderer. *Asia Magazine*. March. The Sting column, 30.

Chan, Brian H. S. (1998). How does Cantonese-English code-mixing work? In M. C. Pennington (ed.), *Language in Hong Kong at Century's End*. Hong Kong: Hong Kong University Press, 43–90.

Chan, Mimi (1994). Hong Kong. In A. Dingwall (ed.), *Traveller's Literary Companion to South-East Asia*. Brighton: In Print Publishing, 405–43.

Chan, Mimi & Kwok, Helen (1982). *A Study of Lexical Borrowing from English in Hong Kong Chinese*. Hong Kong: Centre for Asian Studies.

Chan, Mimi & Kwok, Helen (1985). *A Study of Lexical Borrowing from Chinese into English with Special Reference to Hong Kong*. Hong Kong: Centre of Asian Studies.

Chan, Victor H. F. (1999). Hong Kong English and the Internet. MA dissertation, University of Hong Kong.

Chan, Yuen-ying (2000). The English-language media in Hong Kong. *World Englishes* 19.3: 323–35.

Chao, Sankey C. (1953). *The Teaching of English to Cantonese Students: a Critical Study of Some Cultural and Linguistic Forms*. Teachers College, Columbia University.

Charter, David (2000). London children share 307 languages. *The Times*. 22 January, 8.

Chen, Hoi-Ying (1998). Norms of pronunciation and the sociolinguistics of Cantonese in Hong Kong. M. Phil thesis, University of Hong Kong.

Cheng, Chin-chuan (1983). Chinese varieties of English. In B. B. Kachru (ed.), *The Other Tongue: English Across Cultures*. Oxford: Pergamon Institute of English, 125–40.

Cheng, Tien-mu & Pasierbsky, Fritz (1988). China. In U. Ammon, N. Dittmar & K. J. Matteier (eds.), *Sociolinguistics: an International Handbook of the Science of Language and Society*. Berlin: Walter de Gruyter, 2: 1274–82.

Cheng, Tung-choy (1949). The education of overseas Chinese: comparative study of Hong Kong, Singapore, and the East Indies. MA thesis, University of London.

Cheshire, Jenny (ed.) (1991a). *English Around the World: Sociolinguistic Perspectives*. Cambridge: Cambridge University Press.

Cheshire, Jenny (1991b). Introduction: sociolinguistics and English around the world. In J. Cheshire (ed.), *English Around the World: Sociolinguistic Perspectives*. Cambridge: Cambridge University Press, 1–12.

Cheung, Anne (1997). Language rights and the Hong Kong courts. *Hong Kong Journal of Applied Linguistics* 2: 49–75.

Cheung, Chi-fai (1999). School language choice urged senior pupils should have option for English-medium learning. *South China Morning Post*. 2 November, 4.

Cheung, Chi-fai (2000). Population set to top seven million. *South China Morning Post*. 16 February, 1.

Cheung, Martha P. (ed.) (1998). *Hong Kong Collage: Contemporary Stories and Writing*. Hong Kong: Oxford University Press.

Chin, James K. (2001). A critical survey of the Chinese sources on early Portuguese activities in China. In Jorge M. dos Santos Alves (ed.), *Conferências nos encontros de história Luso-Chinesa – Portugal e a China*. Lisbon: Fundação Oriente, 317–56.

Chin, Wan-kan (1997). From dialect to grapholect: written Cantonese from a folkloristic viewpoint. *Hong Kong Journal of Applied Linguistics* 2: 77–91.

China Daily (1992). Li: work to standardize language. *China Daily*. 26 September, 1.

Chinese Government (1992). *The Basic Law of the Hong Kong Special Administrative Region of the People's Republic of China*. Hong Kong: One Country, Two Systems Economic Research Institute.

Ching, Frank (1994). Growing pains. *South China Morning Post*. 8 January. Review, 4.

Coates, Austin F. H. (1978). *A Macao Narrative*. Hong Kong: Heinemann.

Cocker, Mark (1998). *Rivers of Blood, Rivers of Gold: Europe's Conflict with Tribal Peoples*. London: Jonathan Cape.

Cockeram, Henry (1623). *The English Dictionarie: or, An Interpreter of Hard English words*. London: Printed [by Eliot's Court Press] for Nathaniel Butter.

Cohn, Bernard S. (1996). *Colonialism and Its Forms of Knowledge: the British in India*. New Jersey: Princeton University Press.

Conrad, Andrew W. (1996). The international role of English: the state of the discussion. In J. A. Fishman, A. W. Conrad & A. Rubal-Lopez (eds.), *Post-imperial English*. Berlin and New York: Mouton de Gruyter, 13–36.

Corbett, Charles Hodge (1955). *Shangtung Christian University (Cheeloo)*. New York: United Board for Christian Colleges in China.

Cortazzi, Martin & Jin, Lixian (1996). English teaching and learning in China. *Language Teaching* 29: 61–80.

Couling, Samuel (1917). *The Encyclopaedia Sinica*. Shanghai: Kelly and Walsh.
Cowles, Roy T. (1914). *A Pocket Dictionary of Cantonese*. Reprinted 1986. Hong Kong: Hong Kong University Press.
Craddock, Percy (1994). *Experiences of China*. London: John Murray.
Craigie, William A. & Hulbert, James R. (1938–44). *A Dictionary of the Older Scottish Tongue*. Aberdeen: Aberdeen University Press.
Crystal, David (1969). *Prosodic Systems and Intonation in English*. Cambridge: Cambridge University Press.
Crystal, David (1975). *The English Tone of Voice: Essays in Intonation, Prosody and Paralanguage*. London: Edward Arnold.
Crystal, David (1988). *The English Language*. London: Penguin Books.
Crystal, David (1995). *The Cambridge Encyclopedia of the English Language*. Cambridge: Cambridge University Press.
Crystal, David (1997). *English as a Global Language*. Cambridge: Cambridge University Press.
Crystal, David & Quirk, Randolph (1964). *Systems of Prosodic and Paralinguistic Features in English*. The Hague: Mouton.
Cuthbert, Alexander R. (1985). Architecture, society and space: the high-density question re-examined. *Progress in Planning* 24: 71–160.
Da Silva, Beatriz (1998). *Cronologia de historia de Macau: século XIX*. Macao: Fundação Macau.
Dalby, David (2001). The linguasphere: kaleidoscope of the world's languages. *English Today* 17.1: 22–6.
Dawson, Raymond (1967). *The Chinese Chameleon*. London: Oxford University Press.
DeFrancis, John (1950). *Nationalism and Language Reform in China*. New York: Octagon Books.
DeFrancis, John (1984). *The Chinese Language: Fact and Fantasy*. Honolulu: University of Hawaii Press.
Deng, Peng (1997). *Private Education in Modern China*. London: Praeger.
Dennys, Nicholas B. (1870). Pidgin English. *Nation* 11: 118–19.
Dennys, Nicholas B. (1878). 'Pidgin' English. *Journal of the Straits Branch of the Royal Asiatic Society* 2: 168–74.
Dennys, Nicholas B. (1894). *A Descriptive Dictionary of British Malaya*. London: London and China Telegraph Office.
Downs, Jacques M. (1997). *The Golden Ghetto: the American Commercial Community at Canton and the Shaping of American China Policy, 1784–1844*. Bethlehem: Lehigh University Press.
Dzau, Yulin Francis (ed.) (1990). *English in China*. Hong Kong: API Press.
Eagleton, Terry (1996). *Literary Theory: an Introduction*. 2nd edn. Oxford: Blackwell.
Edwards, Dwight W. (1959). *Yenching University*. New York: United Board for Christian Higher Education in Asia.
Eggington, William G. & Wren, Helen (1997). *Language Policy: Dominant English, Pluralist Challenges*. Amsterdam and Canberra: John Benjamins and Language Australia.
Eitel, Ernest J. (1877). *A Chinese Dictionary of the Cantonese Dialect*. London: Trübner; Hong Kong: Lane & Crawford.
Elder, Chris (ed.) (1999). *China's Treaty Ports: Half Love and Half Hate*. Hong Kong: Oxford University Press.
Elliott, Dorinda & Strasser, Steven (1996). Hong Kong's American tune. *Time*. 30 December, 27–30.

Elliott, Elsie (1971). *The Avarice, Bureaucracy and Corruption of Hong Kong*. Hong Kong: Friends Commercial Printing Factory.

Ellis, Paul (1998). Hong Kong's emerging tertius role in the global economy. *Business Horizons* 41: 37–43.

Erh, Deke & Johnston Tess (1998). *Hallowed Halls: Protestant Colleges in Old China*. Hong Kong: Old China Hand Press.

Evans, Grant, & Tam, Maria S. M. (eds.) (1997). *Hong Kong: the Anthropology of a Chinese Metropolis*. Surrey: Curzon Press.

Evans, Stephen, Jones, Rodney, Rusmin, Ruru S. & Cheung, Oi Ling (1998). Three languages: one future. In M. C. Pennington (ed.), *Language in Hong Kong at Century's End*. Hong Kong: Hong Kong University Press, 43–90.

Fairbank, John K. (1953). *Trade and Diplomacy on the China Coast: the Opening of the Treaty Ports 1842–1854*. Cambridge, Mass.: Harvard University Press.

Faraclas, Nicholas (1991). The pronoun system in Nigerian pidgin: a preliminary study. In J. Cheshire (ed.), *English Around the World: Sociolinguistic Perspectives*. Cambridge: Cambridge University Press, 509–17.

Farmer, John S. (1889). *Americanisms Old & New. A Dictionary of Words, Phrases and Colloquialisms Peculiar to the United States, British America, the West Indies &c, &c*. London: Poulter.

Farrington, Anthony (2002). *Trading Places: the East India Company and Asia*. London: British Library.

Fasold, Ralph (1984). *The Sociolinguistics of Society*. Oxford: Basil Blackwell.

Faure, David (1996). Becoming Cantonese, the Ming Dynasty transition. In T. T. Liu & D. Faure (1996), *Unity and Diversity: Local Cultures and Identities in China*. Hong Kong: Hong Kong University Press, 37–50.

Fisher, Arthur A. (1863). *Personal Narrative of Three Years' Service in China*. London: Bentley.

Fishman, Joshua A. (1964). *Language Loyalty in the United States*. The Hague: Mouton.

Fishman, Joshua A. (1965). Who speaks what language to whom and when? *Linguistique* 2: 67–88.

Fishman, Joshua A. (1968). *Language Problems of Developing Nations*. New York: Wiley.

Fishman, Joshua A. (1972). *Language and Nationalism: Two Integrative Essays*. Rowley, Mass.: Newbury House.

Fishman, Joshua A. (1977). Knowing, using and liking English as an additional language. In J. A. Fishman, R. L. Cooper & A. W. Conrad, *The Spread of English: The Sociology of English as an Additional Language*. Rowley, Mass.: Newbury House, 302–10.

Fishman, Joshua A. (1989). *Language and Ethnicity in Minority Sociolinguistic Perspective*. Clevedon, Phil.: Multilingual Matters.

Fishman, Joshua A. (1996a). Introduction: some empirical and theoretical issues. In J. A. Fishman, A. W. Conrad & A. Rubal-Lopez (eds.), *Post-imperial English*. Berlin and New York: Mouton de Gruyter, 3–12.

Fishman, Joshua A. (1996b). Summary and interpretation: post-imperial English 1940–1990. In J. A. Fishman, A.W. Conrad & A. Rubal-Lopez (eds.), *Post-imperial English*. Berlin and New York: Mouton de Gruyter, 623–41.

Fishman, Joshua A., Conrad, Andrew W. & Rubal-Lopez, Alma (eds.) (1996). *Post-imperial English*. Berlin and New York: Mouton de Gruyter.

Fishman, Joshua A., Cooper, Robert L. & Conrad, Andrew W. (eds.) (1977). *The Spread of English: the Sociology of English as an Additional Language*. Rowley, Mass.: Newbury House.

Fishman, Joshua A., Cooper, Robert L. & Rosenbaum, Yehudit (1977). English around the world. In J. A. Fishman, R. L. Cooper. & A. W. Conrad (eds.), *The Spread of English: the Sociology of English as an Additional Language*. Rowley, Mass.: Newbury House, 77–107.

Fishman, Joshua A., Ferguson, Charles & Das Gupta, Jyotirinda (eds.) (1968). *Language Problems of Developing Nations*. New York: J. Wiley.

Foley, Joseph (ed.) (1988). *New Englishes: the Case of Singapore*. Singapore: Singapore University Press.

Forster, Lancelot (1932). *The Universities Along the Yangtze*. Hong Kong: South China Morning Post.

Frank, André G. (1998). *Reorient: Global Economy in the Asian Age*. California: University of California Press.

Freeborn, Dennis (1992). *From Old English to Standard English*. Basingstoke: Macmillan.

Fu, Gail S. (1975). *A Hong Kong Perspective: English Language Learning and the Chinese Student*. Comparative Education Dissertation Series No. 28, University of Michigan.

Fu, Gail S. (1987). The Hong Kong bilingual. In R. Lord & Helen N. L. Cheng (eds.), *Language Education in Hong Kong*. Hong Kong: Chinese University Press, 27–50.

Fuchs, Walter (1931). Remarks on a new 'Hua-I-I-Yü'. *Bulletin No. 8 of the Catholic University of Peking*, 91–9.

Fung, Daniel R. (1996). International commercial confidence in Hong Kong in the run-up to 1997 and beyond. Transcript of a speech given at the Swiss Business Council in Hong Kong. 7 November.

Fung, Wai-kong & Wong, Lok (1995). Democrats dominate Legco. *South China Morning Post*. 19 September, 1.

Furber, Holden (1976). *Rival Empires of Trade in the Orient, 1600–1800*. Minneapolis: University of Minnesota Press.

Gallagher Louis J. (1942). *China in the Sixteenth Century*. [Incomplete reference] In C. Mackerras (1989), *Western Images of China*. Hong Kong: Oxford University Press.

Galtung, Johan (1980). *The True Worlds: a Transnational Perspective*. New York: Free Press.

Gibbons, John (1979a). Code-mixing and koineising in the speech of students at the University of Hong Kong. *Anthropological Linguistics* 21: 113–23.

Gibbons, John (1979b). U-gay-wa. In R. Lord (ed.), *Hong Kong Language Papers*. Hong Kong: Hong Kong University Press, 3–43.

Gibbons, John (1982). The issue of the medium of instruction in the lower forms of Hong Kong secondary schools. *Journal of Multilingual and Multicultural Development* 3: 117–28.

Gibbons, John (1983). Attitudes towards language and code-mixing in Hong Kong. *Journal of Multilingual and Multicultural Development* 4: 129–47.

Gibbons, John (1984). Interpreting the English proficiency profile in Hong Kong. *RELC Journal* 15: 64–74.

Gibbons, John (1987). *Code-mixing and Code Choice: a Hong Kong Case Study*. Clevedon: Multilingual Matters Ltd.

Gidumal, R. (1998). Race discrimination in HK. Hong Kong Human Rights Monitor Newsletter, February. http://www.hkhrm.org.hk/English/le ports/enw/enw/oz98c.htm. Accessed 6 Jan. 2000.

Giles, Herbert A. (1886). *A Glossary of Reference on Subjects Connected with the Far East.* Hong Kong: Messrs. Lane, Crawford & Co.

Gill, Alexander (1621). *Logonomia Anglica.* Reprinted 1968. Menston, Yorks.: Yorks Scolar Press.

Gill, Ian (2001). Billie's Ballad. Unpublished manuscript.

Gillingham, Paul (1983). *At the Peak: Hong Kong between the Wars.* Hong Kong: Macmillan.

Girborne, Nikolas (2002). Relative clauses in Hong Kong English. In K. Bolton (ed.), *Hong Kong English: Antonomy and Creativity.* Hong Kong: Hong Kong University Press, 141–60.

Gomes, Luis G. (1950). *Monografia de Macau.* Macao: Imprensa Nacional.

Gonzalez, Andrew B. (1983). When does an error become a distinctive feature of Philippine English? In R. B. Noss (ed.), *Varieties of English in Southeast Asia.* Singapore: Singapore University Press, 150–72.

Gonzalez, Andrew B. (1997). Philippine English: a variety in search of legitimation. In W. Schneider (ed.), *Englishes around the World.* Amsterdam: John Benjamins, 2: 205–12.

Gonzalez, Andrew B. & Bautista, Maria Lourdes S. (1986). *Language Surveys in the Philippines (1966–1984).* Manila: De La Salle University Press.

Görlach, Manfred (1980). Editorial. *English World-Wide* 1: 3–7.

Görlach, Manfred (1988). English as world language – the state of the art. *English World-Wide* 9: 1–32.

Görlach, Manfred (1989). Word-formation and the ENL: ESL: EFL distinction. *English World-Wide* 10: 279–313.

Görlach, Manfred (1990). Dictionaries of transplanted Englishes. In F. J. Hansmann et al. (eds.), *Wörterbücher. Dictionaries. Dictionnaires,* 3 vols. Berlin: de Gruyter, 2: 1475–99.

Görlach, Manfred (1991). *Introduction to Early Modern English.* Cambridge: Cambridge University Press.

Görlach, Manfred (1995a). Innovation in new Englishes. In M. Görlach (ed.), *More Englishes: New Studies in Varieties of English 1988–1994.* Amsterdam and Philadelphia: John Benjamins, 39–60.

Görlach, Manfred (1995b). Dictionaries of transplanted Englishes. In M. Görlach (ed.), *More Englishes: New Studies in Varieties of English 1988–1994.* Amsterdam and Philadelphia: John Benjamins, 124–63.

Görlach, Manfred (1996). And is it English? *English World-Wide* 17: 153–74.

Görlach, Manfred (1998). *Even More Englishes: Studies 1996–1997.* Amsterdam and Philadelphia: John Benjamins.

Graddol, David (1997). *The Future of English?* London: British Council.

Gramsci, Antonio (1985). *Selections from Cultural Writings,* ed. D. Forgacs & G. Nowell-Smith. Cambridge, Mass.: Harvard University Press.

Gray, Piers (1985). Hong Kong, Shanghai, the great wall: Bernard Shaw in China. In Rodelle Weintraub (ed.), *Shaw Abroad.* University Park: Pennsylvania State University Press, 211–38.

Green, Owen M. (1934). Pidgin English. *Fortnightly* 142: 331–9.

Greenbaum, Sidney (ed.) (1985). *The English Language Today.* Oxford: Pergamon.

Greenbaum, S. (ed.) (1986). *Comparing English Worldwide: the International Corpus of English.* Oxford: Clarendon Press.

Guldin, Gregory E. (1997). Hong Kong ethnicity of folk models and change. In G. Evans & M. S. M. Tam (eds.), *Hong Kong: the Anthropology of a Chinese Metropolis*. Richmond: Curzon Press, 25–50.

Gupta, Anthea F. (1994). *The Step-tongue: Children's English in Singapore*. Clevedon: Multilingual Matters.

Gupta, Anthea F. (1995). Discussion on linguistic human rights. Linguist list. http://www.emich.edu/~linguist/issues/6/6-1381.html. 5 October 1995, accessed 18 October 2001.

Hall, Robert A. (1944). Chinese pidgin English grammar and texts. *Journal of the American Oriental Society* 64: 95–113.

Halliday, Jon (1974). Hong Kong: Britain's Chinese colony. *New Left Review* 91–112.

Halliday, Michael A. K. (1978). *Language as a Social Semiotic: the Social Interpretation of Language and Meaning*. London: Edward Arnold.

Halliday, Michael A. K., MacIntosh, Angus & Strevens, Peter (1964). *The Linguistic Sciences and Language Teaching*. London: Longmans.

Hamlett, Tim (1997). English in Hongkong: the future. *English Today* 13: 10–11.

Hao, Keki (1988). The view from China. *English Today* 4.1: 50–2.

Hao, Yen-p'ing (1970). *The Comprador in Nineteenth Century China: Bridge between East and West*. Cambridge, Mass.: Harvard University Press.

Harris, Peter B. (1983). *Public Administration and Public Affairs in Hong Kong*. Hong Kong: Heinemann Asia.

Harris, Roy (1989). The worst English in the world? *Supplement to the Gazette* 36: 37–46. Hong Kong: University of Hong Kong.

Haugen, Einar (1950). The analysis of linguistic borrowing. In A. S. Dil (ed.) (1972), *The Ecology of Language*, 79–109. Stanford: Stanford University Press. Originally published in *Language* 26:231.

Haugen, Einar (1966). National and international languages. In A. S. Dil (ed.) (1972), *The Ecology of Language*. Stanford: Stanford University Press, 255–64. Originally published as *Voice of America Forum Series 10*.

Hawkins, R. E. (1984). *Common Indian Words in English*. Delhi: Oxford University Press.

Hayhoe, Ruth (1996). *China's Universities 1895–1995: a Century of Cultural Conflict*. New York: Garland.

Hickey, William ([1769] 1975). *Memoirs of William Hickey*, ed. Peter Quennell. London: Routledge & Kegan Paul.

Hill, A. P. (1920). *Broken China: a Vocabulary of Pidgin English*. Shanghai: A. P. Hill & C. B. Weiss.

HKSAR Government (2001). *Building on our Strengths Investing in our Future*. Hong Kong: Printing Department, Hong Kong Special Administrative Region Government.

Ho, Louise (1994). *Local Habitation*. Hong Kong: Twilight Books Company.

Ho, Louise (1997). *New Ends Old Beginnings*. Hong Kong: Asia 2000.

Ho, Louise (2000). Hong Kong writing and writing Hong Kong. Special issue of *World Englishes* on 'Hong Kong English: Autonomy and Creativity', 19.3: 381–6.

Hogue, Cavan (1999). The influence of Indian English on the Englishes of Southeast Asia. Manuscript.

Holborrow, Marnie (1999). *The Politics of English: a Marxist View of Language*. London: Sage.

Holm, John (1982). *Dictionary of Bahamian English*. Cold Spring, New York: Lexik House (with A. W. Shilling).

Holm, John (1988). *Pidgins and Creoles*, Vol. 1: *Theory and Structure*. Cambridge: Cambridge University Press.

Holm, John (1989). *Pidgins and Creoles*, Vol. 2: *Reference Survey*. Cambridge: Cambridge University Press.

Hong Kong Education Commission (1986). *Education Commission Report No.2*. Hong Kong: Government Printer.

Hong Kong Education Commission (1994). *Report of the Working Group on Language Proficiency*. Hong Kong: Government Printer.

Hong Kong Government (1981). *1981 Population Census: Preliminary Report on Labour Force Composition*. Hong Kong: Census and Statistics Department.

Hong Kong Government (1982). *A Perspective on Education in Hong Kong: Report by a Visiting Panel*. Hong Kong: Government Printer.

Hong Kong Government (1996). *1996 Population By-census: Summary Results*. Hong Kong: Census and Statistics Department.

Hong Kong Government (1999). The 1999 Policy Address. October 1999. http://www.info. gov.hk/pa99/english/speech.htm. Accessed 22 February 2000.

Hong Kong Government (2001). *2001 Population Census: Summary of Results*. Hong Kong: Hong Kong Special Administrative Region Government, Census and Statistics Department.

Hong Kong University (1985). *A Profile of New Students*. Hong Kong: Office of Student Affairs, University of Hong Kong.

Horwill, Herbert William (1935). *A Dictionary of Modern American Usage*. Oxford: Clarendon Press.

Hosillos, Lucila (1982). Breaking through the Wayang Screen: literary interdependence among new literatures in Southeast Asia. In B. Bennct, T. H. Ee & R. Shepherd (eds.), *The Writer's Sense of the Contemporary: Papers in Southeast Asian and Australian Literature*. Nedlands: Centre for Studies in Australian Literature, 59–62.

House, Herbert E. (1916). English in education in China. *Chinese Recorder* 47: 98–103.

Huang, Parker Po-fei (1970). *Cantonese Dictionary: Cantonese–English, English–Cantonese*. New Haven: Yale University Press.

Huang, Zhenhua (1999). The impact of globalisation on English in Chinese universities. In D. Graddol & U. H. Meinhof (eds.), *English in a Changing World*. Guildford: Association Internationale de Linguistique Appliquée (AILA), 79–88.

Hudson, Richard A. (1980). *Sociolinguistics*. Cambridge: Cambridge University Press.

Hughes, Arthur & Trudgill, Peter (1979). *English Accents and Dialects*. London: Edward Arnold.

Human Rights Monitor (1999). Response to the Education Commission Consultation Document: 'The Aims of Education'. http://www.hkhrm. org.hk/english/reports/education. html. Hong Kong: Hong Kong Human Rights Monitor. Accessed 6 January 2000.

Hung, Tony T. N. (2000). Towards a phonology of Hong Kong English. *World Englishes* 19.3: 337–56.

Hunter, Duncan B. (1974). Bilingualism and Hong Kong English. *The Educationalist* 5: 15–18.

Hunter, William C. (1882). *The 'fan kwae' at Canton before Treaty Days, 1825–1844*. London: K. Paul, Trench & Co.

Hutton, Christopher (2001). The search for a total dictionary of Chinese: Samuel Wells Williams' *Syllabic Dictionary* (1874). Introduction to Samuel Wells Williams' *A Syllabic Dictionary of the Chinese Language Arranged According to the Wu-Fang Yuen Yin with the Pronunciation of the Characters as Heard in Peking, Canton, Amoy, and Shanghai*. Shanghai: American Presbyterian Press, 1874. Reprinted, London: Ganesha Publishing.

Ingrams, Harold (1952). *Hong Kong*. London: Her Majesty's Stationery Office.

Iyer, Pico (1993). The empire writes back. *Time*. 8 February, 48–53.

Jacoby, Russell (1995). Marginal returns: the trouble with post-colonial theory. *Lingua Franca*. September/October, 32.

Jao, Yu-ching (1985). The monetary system and the future of Hong Kong. In Y. C. Jao, C. K. Leung, P. Wesley-Smith & S.L. Wong (eds.), *Hong Kong and 1997: Strategies for the Future*. Hong Kong: University of Hong Kong, 361–98.

Jin, Ha (1999). *Waiting*. New York: Pantheon Books.

Johnson, Christopher (2001). Shanghai puts the accent on English. *Christian Science Monitor* 93. 227: 7.

Johnson, Robert K. (1983). Bilingual switching strategies: a studying of the modes of teacher-talk in bilingual secondary school classrooms in Hong Kong. *Language Learning and Communication* 2: 249–350.

Johnson, Robert K. (1994). Language policy and planning in Hong Kong. *Annual Review of Applied Linguistics* 14: 177–99.

Johnson, Robert K. & Cheung Yat-shing (1995). *Reading Literacy in Hong Kong: an IEA World Literacy Project on the Reading Proficiency of Hong Kong Students in Chinese and English*. Hong Kong: Department of Chinese and Bilingual Studies, Hong Kong Polytechnic University.

Johnson, Robert K. & Lee, Paul L. M. (1987). Modes of instruction: teaching strategies and student responses. In R. Lord & H. N. L. Cheng (eds.), *Language Education in Hong Kong*. Hong Kong: Chinese University Press, 99–121.

Johnson, Robert Keith, Shek, Cecilia K. W. & Law, Edmond H. F. (1993). *Using English as a Medium of Instruction*. Hong Kong: Longman.

Johnson, Samuel (1755). *A Dictionary of the English Language*. London: Printed by W. Strahan, for J. and P. Knapton [etc.].

Johnson, Samuel (1773). Preface. *A Dictionary of the English Language*. In W. F. Bolton (ed.) (1966), *The English Language*. Cambridge: Cambridge University Press, 1: 129–56.

Joseph, John E. (1997). English in Hong Kong: emergence and decline. In S. Wright & H. K. Holmes (eds.), *One Country, Two Systems: Changing Language Use in Hong Kong*. Clevedon, Phil.: Multilingual Matters.

Kachru, Braj B. (1965). The *Indianness* in Indian English. *Word* 21: 391–410.

Kachru, Braj B. (1980). The new Englishes and old dictionaries: directions in lexicographical research on non-native varieties of English. In L. Zgusta (ed.), *Theory and Method in Lexicography: Western and Non-western Perspectives*. Columbia, SC: Hornbeam Press, 71–104.

Kachru, Braj B. (1983). *The Indianisation of English: the English Language in India*. New Delhi: Oxford University Press.

Kachru, Braj B. (1985). Standards, codification and sociolinguistic realism: the English language in the outer circle. In R. Quirk & H.G. Widdowson (eds.), *English in the World*. Cambridge: Cambridge University Press and the British Council, 11–30.

Kachru, Braj B. (1986a). *The Alchemy of English: the Spread, Functions, and Models of Non-native Englishes*. Oxford: Pergamon Press. Reprinted 1990, Urbana, Ill.: University of Illinois Press.

Kachru, Braj B. (1986b). Socially-realistic linguistics: the Firthian tradition. *International Journal of the Sociology of Language* 31: 65–89.

Kachru, Braj B. (1986c). The bilingual's creativity and contact literatures. In B. B. Kachru, *The Alchemy of English: the Spread, Functions, and Models of Non-native Englishes*. Oxford: Pergamon Press, 159–73. Reprinted 1990, Urbana, Ill.: University of Illinois Press.

Kachru, Braj B. (1990). World Englishes and applied linguistics. *World Englishes* 9: 3–30.

Kachru, Braj B. (1991). Liberation linguistics and the Quirk concern. *English Today* 25: 3–13.

Kachru, Braj B. (1992). World Englishes: approaches, issues and resources. *Language Teaching* 25: 1–14.

Kachru, Braj B. (1994). New Englishes. In R. E. Asher & E. F. Koerner (eds.), *The Encyclopedia of Language and Linguistics*. Oxford: Pergamon Press, 2787–91.

Kachru, Braj B. (1996). World Englishes: agony and ecstasy. *Journal of Aesthetic Education* 30: 135–55.

Kachru, Braj B. (1997). English as an Asian language. In M. L. S. Bautista (ed.), *English is an Asian language: the Philippine Context*. Manila: The Macquarie Library, 1–23.

Kachru, Braj B. (ed.) (1982). *The Other Tongue: English across Cultures*. Urbana, Ill.: University of Illinois Press. 2nd rev. edn, 1992.

Kachru, Braj B. and Nelson, Cecil (1996). World Englishes. In S. L. Mackay and N. H. Hornberger (eds.), *Sociolinguistics and Language Teaching*. Cambridge: Cambridge University Press.

Kachru, Braj B. & Smith, Larry E. (1985). Editorial. *World Englishes* 4: 209–12.

Kachru, Braj B. & Smith, Larry E. (1988). World Englishes: an integrative and cross-cultural journal of WE-ness. In *Robert Maxwell and Pergamon Press: 40 Years' Service to Science, Technology and Education*. Oxford: Pergamon Press, 674–8.

Kale, Joan (1990). Controllers or victims: language and education in the Torres Strait. In Richard B. Baldauf Jr & Allan Luke (eds.), *Language Planning and Education in Australasia and the South Pacific*. Clevedon, Phil.: Multilingual Matters, 106–26.

Kang, Jianxiu (1999). English everywhere in China. *English Today* 15.2: 46–8.

Kass, G. V. (1980). An exploratory technique for investigating large quantities of categorical data. *Applied Statistics* 29.2: 119–27.

Kennedy, Graeme (1998). *An Introduction to Corpus Linguistics*. London: Longman.

Kersey, John (1702). *The New English Dictionary*. Reprinted by the Scolar Press, Menston (Yorks.), 1969. Facsimile reprint of 1st edn. London: Printed for H. Bonwicke & R. Knaplock.

King, Anthony D. (1990). *Global Cities*. London: Routledge.

King, Bruce (ed.) (1974). *Literature of the World in English*. London: Routledge & Kegan Paul.

King, Rex (1987). Why pupils are facing testing time. *South China Morning Post*. 24 February, 17.

Koerner, E. F. Konrad & Asher, Ronald E. (1995). *Concise History of the Language Sciences*. Oxford: Pergamon Press.

Kwo, Ora W. Y. (1992). The teaching of Putonghua in Hong Kong Schools: language education in a changing economic and political context. In G. A. Postiglione (ed.), *Education and Society in Hong Kong*. Hong Kong: Hong Kong University Press, 203–13.

Kwok, Edmond S. T. (1982). From 'the Campaign for Chinese to be an Official Language' to 'the Second Chinese Language Campaign'. In J. Y. S. Cheng (ed.), *Hong Kong in the 1980s*. Hong Kong: Summerson Eastern Publishers Ltd, 32–44.

Kwok, Helen & Chan, Mimi (1972). Where the twain do meet: a preliminary study of the language habits of university undergraduates in Hong Kong. *General Linguistics* 12: 63–79.

Kwok, Helen & Chan, Mimi (1975). Creative writing in English: problems faced by undergraduates in the English Department, University of Hong Kong. *Topics in Culture Learning*. Honolulu: East-West Centre, University of Hawaii, 3: 27–38.

Kwok, Shirley (1997). New rule will halve schools using English. *South China Morning Post*. 22 March, 7.

Kwong, Ki Chiu (1923). *English and Chinese Dictionary*. Hong Kong: Kelly and Walsh.

L. (1893). English as she is spoke in China. *China Review* 20: 203–4.

Labov, William (1972a). *Language in the Inner City: Studies in the Black English Vernacular*. Philadelphia: University of Pennsylvania Press.

Labov, William (1972b). *Sociolinguistic Patterns*. Philadelphia: University of Pennsylvania Press.

Lai, Eva (2001). Teaching English as a private enterprise in China. *English Today* 17.2: 32–6.

Lam, Agnes (1997). *Woman to Woman and Other Poems*. Hong Kong: Asia 2000.

Landry, Donna & Maclean, Gerald (1996). *The Spivak Reader*. New York, London: Routledge.

Latourette, Kenneth S. (1929). *A History of Christian Missions in China*. London: Society for Promoting Christian Knowledge.

Lau, Chi-kuen (1986). Political excuse for poor studies. *South China Morning Post*. 16 December, 4.

Lau, Chi-kuen (1995). Language of the future. *South China Morning Post*. 18 September, 19.

Lau, Sidney (1977). *A Practical Cantonese-English Dictionary*. Hong Kong: Government Printer.

Lau, Siu-kai (1982). *Society and Politics in Hong Kong*. Hong Kong: Chinese University Press.

Le Page, Robert B. (1966). *Intercomprehensibility between English-language Using Communities: a Preliminary Study* (mimeographed). 14 [Cited by Prator, 1968].

Le Page, Robert B. (1986) Acts of identity. *English Today* 8: 21–4.

Le Page, Robert B. & Tabouret-Keller, Andrée (1985). *Acts of Identity: Creole-based Approaches to Language and Ethnicity*. Cambridge: Cambridge University Press.

Lee, Gregory B. (1996). *Troubadours, Trumpeters, Troubled Makers*. London: Hurst & Company.

Lee, Leo Ou-fan (1999). *Shanghai Modern: the Flowering of a New Urban Culture in China, 1930–1945*. Cambridge, Mass.: Harvard University Press.

Lee, M. K. (1982). Emerging patterns of social conflict in Hong Kong society. In J. Y. S. Cheng (ed.), *Hong Kong in the 1980s*. Hong Kong: Summerson, 23–31.

Lee, Naomi (1996). Fujian school expands to cope with growing demand. *South China Morning Post*. 20 August, 6.

Lee, Siu-lun Cedric (1996). A sociolinguistic study of code-mixing in Hong Kong. M. Phil. thesis, Chinese University of Hong Kong.

Lee, Wing-on (1998). Social class, language and achievement. In G. A. Postiglione & W. O. Lee (eds.), *Schooling in Hong Kong*. Hong Kong: Hong Kong University Press, 155–74.

Leland, Charles G. (1876). *Pidgin English Sing-Song*. London: Kegan Paul, Trench, Trubner & Co. Ltd.

Lelyveld, David (1993). The fate of Hindustani: colonial knowledge and the project of a national language. In C. A. Breckenridge & P. van der Veer (eds.), *Orientalism and the Postcolonial Predicament*. Philadelphia: University of Pennsylvania Press, 189–214.

Lepschy, Giulio (1994). *History of Linguistics*. London: Longman.

Lethbridge, Henry J. (1978). *Hong Kong: Stability and Change*. Hong Kong: Oxford University Press.

Leung, Benjamin K. P. (1996). *Perspectives on Hong Kong Society*. Hong Kong: Oxford University Press.

Leung, Ping-kwan (1992). *City at the End of Time*. Hong Kong: Twilight Books Company. With Gordon T. Osing.

Leung, Ping-kwan (1997). *Foodscape*. Hong Kong: The Original Photography Club Limited. With Lee Ka-sing & Martha Cheung.

Li, Anthony C. ([1954] 1997). *The History of Privately Controlled Higher Education in the Republic of China*. Westport, Conn.: Greenwood Press.

Li, David C. S. (1996). *Issues in Bilingualism and Biculturalism: a Hong Kong Case Study*. New York: Peter Lang.

Li, David C. S. (1998). The plight of the purist. In M. C. Pennington (ed.), *Language in Hong Kong at Century's End*. Hong Kong: Hong Kong University Press, 161–89.

Li, David C. S. (1999). The functions and status of English in Hong Kong: a post-1997 update. *English World-Wide* 20: 67–110.

Li, Dong (1995). English in China. *English Today* 11.1: 53–6.

Li, Yongyan (2000). Surfing e-mails. *English Today* 16.4: 30–4.

Lim, Shirley (1984). Gods who fall: ancestral religions in the new literatures in English from Malaysia and Singapore. *Commonwealth-Novel-in-English*, Bluefield, WV (CNIE). Spring–Summer 3: 39–55.

Lin, Angel Mei Yi (1996). Bilingualism or linguistic segregation? Symbolic domination, resistance and code-switching in Hong Kong schools. *Linguistics and Education* 8: 49–84.

Lin, Angel Mei Yi (1997). Analyzing the 'language problem' discourses in Hong Kong: how official, academic, and media discourses construct and perpetuate dominant models of language, learning, and education. *Journal of Pragmatics* 28: 427–40.

Lin, Angel Mei Yi & Detaramani, Champa (1998). By carrot and by rod: extrinsic motivation and English language attainment of Hong Kong tertiary students. In

M. C. Pennington (ed.), *Language in Hong Kong at Century's End*. Hong Kong: Hong Kong University Press, 43–90.

Lin, Shao-yang (1911). *A Chinese Appeal to Christendom Concerning Christian Missions*. London: Watts.

Lindsay, Hugh H. (1840). An adventure in China. In J. J. Robert & H. H. Lindsay (eds.), *Oriental Miscellanies*. Wigan: C. S. Simms.

Liu, Kwang-ching (1982). A Chinese entrepreneur. In M. Keswick (ed.), *The Thistle and the Jade*. London: Octopus Books Limited, 103–27.

Livingstone, David N. (1992). *The Geographical Tradition*. Oxford: Blackwell.

Llamzon, Tesdoro, A. (1969). *Standard Filipino English*. Manila: Ateneo University Press.

Llamzon, Tesdoro, A. (1983). Essential features of new varieties of English. In R. B. Noss (ed.), *Varieties of English in Southeast Asia*. Singapore: Regional Language Centre, 92–109.

Llamzon, Teodoro A. (1997). The phonology of Philippine English. In M. L. S. Bautista (ed.), *English is an Asian Language: the Philippine Context*. Manila: Macquarie Library, 92–109.

Loh, Christine (1999). *Claiming the Hong Kong Advantage: Future-based and Ambition Driven*. Hong Kong: Citizens Party.

Lord, Robert (1974). English – how serious a problem for students in Hong Kong? *The English Bulletin* 4. 3: 1–10.

Lord, Robert (1987). Language policy and planning in Hong Kong: Past, present and (especially) future. In R. Lord & Helen N. L. Cheng (1987), *Language Education in Hong Kong*. Hong Kong: Chinese University Press, 3–24.

Lord, Robert & Cheng, Helen N. L. (eds.) (1987). *Language Education in Hong Kong*. Hong Kong: Chinese University Press.

Lord, Robert & T'sou, Benjamin K. (1985). *The Language Bomb*. Hong Kong: Longman (Far East).

Lowenberg, Peter H. (1984). English in the Malay archipelago: nativization and its functions in a sociolinguistic area. PhD thesis, University of Illinois.

Luk, Sidney (2002). Surfing swells to 500m online. *South China Morning Post*. Business News, 8 March, 11.

Luke, Kang Kwong & Nancarrow, Owen (1991). On being literate in Hong Kong. *Institute of Language in Education Journal* 8: 84–92.

Luke, Kang Kwong & Richards, Jack C. (1982). English in Hong Kong: functions and status. *English World-Wide* 3: 47–64.

Lutz, Jessie G. (1971). *China and the Christian Colleges, 1850–1950*. Ithaca: Cornell University Press.

Mackerras, Colin (1989). *Western Images of China*. Hong Kong: Oxford University Press.

Macquarie (2000a). Entries for Grolier Dictionary. November 1999.

Macquarie (2000b). Fact sheet on *Asiacorp*. March 2000.

Macquarie (2000c). *Grolier International Dictionary: World English in an Asian Context*. Sydney: Macquarie Dictionary Company Ltd.

Mahathir bin Mohamad (1970). *The Malay Dilemma*. Kuala Lumpur: Federal Publications.

Malcolm, Elizabeth L. (1973). The Chinese Repository and western literature on China 1800 to 1850. *Modern Asian Studies* 7.2: 165–78.

Maley, Alan (1986). Xanadu – 'A miracle of rare device': the teaching of English in China. In J. M. Valdes (ed.), *Culture Bound: Bridging the Cultural Gap in Language Teaching.* Cambridge: Cambridge University Press, 102–11.

March, A. W. (1915). The place of English in education in China. *The Chinese Recorder* 46: 109–21.

Masini, Federico (1993). *The Formation of Modern Chinese Lexicon and its Evolution toward a National Language: the Period from 1840 to 1898.* Journal of Chinese Linguistics Monograph series no. 6.

Mateer, Calvin W. (1878). Discussion on the importance of vernacular Christian literature. In the General Conference of the Protestant Missionaries of China (ed.), *Records of the General Conference of the Protestant Missionaries of China, held at Shanghai, May 10–24, 1877.* Shanghai: Presbyterian Mission Press.

Matheson, Ruth (1997). Dignity reigns as Britain lowers flags. *South China Morning Post.* 1 July, 3.

Mathews, Mitford M. (1951). *Dictionary of Americanisms on Historical Principles.* Chicago: Chicago University Press (*DA*).

Matthews, Stephen & Yip, Virginia (1994). *Cantonese: a Comprehensive Grammar.* London and New York: Routledge.

McArthur, Tom (1987). The English languages? *English Today* 11: 9–11.

McArthur, Tom (1992a). *The Oxford Companion to the English Language.* Oxford: Oxford University Press.

McArthur, Tom (1992b). New Englishes. In T. McArthur (ed.), *The Oxford Companion to the English Language.* Oxford: Oxford University Press, 688 9.

McArthur, Tom (1992c). Quirk, Randolph. In T. McArthur (ed.), *The Oxford Companion to the English Language.* Oxford: Oxford University Press, 835–6.

McArthur, Tom (1992d). Models of English. *English Today* 32: 12–21.

McArthur, Tom (1993). The sins of the fathers. *English Today* 35: 48–50.

McArthur, Tom (1998). *The English Languages.* Cambridge: Cambridge University Press.

McArthur, Tom (2000). The English–Chinese interface. Talk given at the University of Hong Kong, March 2000.

McArthur, Tom (2002). *The Oxford Guide to World English.* Oxford: Oxford University Press.

McCrum, Robert, Cran, William & MacNeil, Robert (1986). *The Story of English.* London: Faber & Faber, BBC Publications.

McGurn, W. (1996). Money talks. *Far Eastern Economic Review.* 21 March, 40–4.

Medhurst (1832). *A Dictionary of the Hok-këèn Dialect of the Chinese Language.*

Mellor, Bernard (1980). *The University of Hong Kong: an Informal History.* Hong Kong: Hong Kong University Press.

Mellor, Bernard (1992). *Lugard in Hong Kong.* Hong Kong: Hong Kong University Press.

Meyer, Benard F. & Wempe, Theodore F. (1947). *The Student's Cantonese–English Dictionary.* New York: Catholic Foreign Mission Society of America.

Meyer, Charles F. (2002). *English Corpus Linguistics: an Introduction.* Cambridge: Cambridge University Press.

Millward, Celia M. (1996). *A Biography of the English Language.* Fort Worth: Harcourt Brace College Publishers.

Min, Anchee (1999). *Red Azalea.* New York: Berkley Books.

Min, Anchee (2000). *Becoming Madame Mao.* Boston, Mass.: Houghton Mifflin.

Mok, Ka Lai, Cynthia (1998). The sociolinguistics of written Chinese in local comic book subculture: stigmatised language varieties in Hong Kong. M. Phil. thesis. Hong Kong: University of Hong Kong.

Mok, Man Cheung (1904). *English Made Easy*. Hong Kong.

Moorehead, Caroline (1992). *Betrand Russell: a Life*. New York: Viking.

Moody, Andrew J. (1996). Transmission languages and source languages of Chinese borrowings in English. *American Speech* 71.4: 405–20.

Moody, Andrew J. (1997). The status of language change in Hong Kong English. Ph.D. thesis. Ann Arbor, Michigan: UMI.

Morris, Edward E. (1898). *Austral English. A Dictionary of Australasian Words, Phrases and Usage*. London: Macmillan; reprinted Wakefield 1971.

Morrison, John R. (1834). A glossary of words and phrases peculiar to the jargon spoken at Canton. In J. R. Morrison (ed.), *A Chinese Commercial Guide Consisting of a Collection of Details Respecting Foreign Trade in China*. Canton: Albion Press, unnumbered.

Morrison, Robert (1815). *A Grammar of the Chinese Language*. Serampore: Mission-Press.

Morrison, Robert (1815–22). *A Dictionary of the Chinese Language*. Macao: East India Company's Press.

Morrison, Robert (1823). *Translation of the Bible*. 21 vols. Malacca.

Morrison, Robert (1828). *Vocabulary of the Canton Dialect*. Macao: East India Company's Press.

Morse, Hosea B. (1926). *The Chronicles of the East India Company Trading to China, 1635–1834*. Vol.1. Oxford: Clarendon Press.

Moser, Leo J. (1985). *The Chinese Mosaic*. Boulder, Col.: Westview Press.

Moy, Joyce (1998). Education chief wants 'radical' system review. *South China Morning Post*. 25 November, 1.

Mufwene, Salikoko S. (1997). Introduction: understanding speech continua. *World Englishes* 16: 181–4.

Mufwene, Salikoko S. (2001). *The Ecology of Language Evolution*. Cambridge: Cambridge University Press.

Mühlhäusler, Peter (1986). *Pidgin and Creole Linguistics*. Oxford: Blackwell.

Mühlhäusler, Peter (1996). *Linguistic Ecology*. London: Routledge.

Munby, John (1978). *Communicative Syllabus Design*. Cambridge: Cambridge University Press.

Mundy, Peter (1637 [1919]). *Itinerarium Mundii* [The travels of Peter Mundy]. Edited by R. C. Temple as *The Travels of Peter Mundy, in Europe and Asia, 1608–1667*. 5 volumes 1907–36. [Volume 3, part I, published in 1919 contains Mundy's journal relating to China.] Cambridge: Hakluyt Society.

Munn, Christopher C. (2001). *Anglo-China: Chinese People and British Rule in Hong Kong, 1841–1870*. London: Curzon Press.

Murray, James A. H. (1888). General explanations. From J. A. H. Murray (ed.), *A New English Dictionary on Historical Principles*. Vol. 1, in W. F. Bolton & D. Crystal, *The English Language*. Cambridge: Cambridge University Press, 2: 59–79.

Nelson, Gerald (1996). The design of the corpus. In Sidney Greenbaum (ed.), *Comparing English Worldwide: the International Corpus of English*. Oxford: Clarendon Press, 27–35.

Nevius, John L. (1872). *China and the Chinese*. New York: Harper & Brothers.

Ng, Christina & Tang, Eunice (1997). Teachers' needs in the process of EFL reform in China – a report from Shanghai. *Perspectives* 9.1: 63–85.

Ng, Peter T. M. (1996). Historical archives in Chinese Christian colleges from before 1949. *International Bulletin of Missionary Research* 20.3: 106–8.

Nist, John (1966). *A Structural History of English*. New York: St Martin's Press.

Noble, Charles F. (1762). *A Voyage to the East Indies in 1747 and 1748*. London: T. Becket and P. A. Dehondt.

Norman, Jerry (1988). *Chinese*. Cambridge: Cambridge University Press.

Noss, Robert B. (ed.) (1983). *Varieties of English in Southeast Asia*. Singapore: Regional Language Center.

O'Sullivan, Dan (1984). *The Age of Discovery 1400–1550*. London and New York: Longman.

Ohannessian, Sirarpi, Ferguson, Charles & Polomé, Edgar (1975). *Language Surveys in Developing Nations*. Arlington, Virginia: Center for Applied Linguistics.

Omar, Asmah Haji (1996). Post-imperial status of English in Malaysia. In J. A. Fishman, A. W. Conrad & A. Rubal-Lopez (eds.), *Post-imperial English*. Berlin, New York: Mouton de Gruyter, 513–33.

Orsman, Harry (1997). *The Dictionary of New Zealand English: a Dictionary of New Zealandisms on Historical Principles*. Auckland: Oxford University Press.

Pakir, Anne, Gopinathan, S., Ho Wah Kam & Saravanan, V. (1994). *Language, Society, and Education in Singapore: Issues and Trends*. Singapore: Times Academic Press.

Parkin, Andrew & Wong, Laurence (1997). *Hong Kong Poems*. Vancouver: Ronsdale Press.

Patri, Mrudula & Pennington, Martha C. (1998). Acculturation to English by an ethnic minority: the language attitudes of Indian adolescents in a Hong Kong international school. In M. Pennington (ed.), *Language in Hong Kong at Century's End*. Hong Kong: Hong Kong University Press, 339–62.

Pennel, Elizabeth R. (1906). *Charles Godfrey Leland: a Biography*. London: Archibald Constable & Co. Ltd.

Pennington, Martha C. (1995). Language diversity in bilingualism: preliminary speculations on varieties of Hong Kong English. *Language in Education Journal* 1: 1–19.

Pennington, Martha C. (ed.) (1998a). *Language in Hong Kong at Century's End*. Hong Kong: Hong Kong University Press.

Pennington, Martha C. (1998b). Perspectives on language in Hong Kong at Century's End. In M. C. Pennington (ed.), *Language in Hong Kong at Century's End*. Hong Kong: Hong Kong University Press, 3–40.

Pennington, Martha C. (1998c). The folly of language planning; or, a brief history of the English language in Hong Kong. *English Today* 54: 25–30.

Pennington, Martha C. & Yue, Francis (1994). English and Chinese in Hong Kong: pre-1997 language attitudes. *World Englishes* 13: 1–20.

Pennycook, Alastair (1994). *The Cultural Politics of English as an International Language*. London: Longman.

Pennycook, Alastair (1998). *English and the Discourses of Colonialism*. London and New York: Routledge.

Pennycook, Alastair (2001). *Critical Applied Linguistics*. New Jersey: Lawrence Erlbaum Associates.

People's Educational Press (1960). *Ying Yu*. Primary 3 textbook. Beijing: People's Educational Press.

People's Educational Press (1992). *Junior English for China*. Beijing: People's Educational Press.

Pettman, Rev. Charles (1913). *Africanderisms. A Glossary of South African Words and Phrases and of Place and Other Names*. London: Longmans, Green & Co.

Philippine Daily Inquirer (1996). 'English is now ours, we have colonized it'. 12 August, 13.

Philipps, Edward (1678). *New World of Words or a General English Dictionary*. London: printed by W. R. for Robert Harford at the Angel in Cornhill.

Phillipson, Robert (1992). *Linguistic Imperialism*. Oxford: Oxford University Press.

Pickering, John (1816). *A Vocabulary or Collection of Words and Phrases Which Have Been Supposed to be Peculiar to the United States of America*. Boston: Cummings and Hilliard.

Pierson, Herbert D. (1987). Language attitudes and language proficiency: A review of selected research. In R. Lord & H. Cheng, *Language Education in Hong Kong*. Hong Kong: Chinese University Press, 51–82.

Pierson, Herbert D. (1992). Cantonese, English, or Putonghua – unresolved communicative issue in Hong Kong's future. In G. A. Postiglione (ed.), *Education and Society in Hong Kong*. Hong Kong: Hong Kong University Press, 183–202.

Pierson, Herbert D. (1998). Societal accommodation to English and Putonghua in Cantonese-speaking Hong Kong. In M. C. Pennington (ed.), *Language in Hong Kong at Century's End*. Hong Kong: Hong Kong University Press, 43–90.

Pierson, Herbert D. & Fu, Gail S. (1982). Report on the linguistic attitudes project in Hong Kong and its relevance for second language instruction. *Language Learning and Communication* 1: 289–316.

Pierson, Herbert D., Fu, Gail S. & Lee, S.Y. (1980). An analysis of the relationship between language attitudes and English attainment of secondary students in Hong Kong. *Language Learning* 27: 1–27.

Pierson-Smith, A. (1997). English for promotional purposes. *English Today* 13: 6–8.

Platt, John (1977). The sub-varieties of Singapore English: their sociolectal and functional status. In W. Crewe (ed.), *The English Language in Singapore*. Singapore: Eastern University Press, 83–95.

Platt, John (1982). English in Singapore, Malaysia and Hong Kong. In R. W. Bailey and M. Görlach (eds.), *English as a World Language*. Ann Arbor: University of Michigan Press, 384–414.

Platt, John & Weber, Heidi K. (1980). *English in Singapore and Malaysia: Status, Features, Functions*. Kuala Lumpur: Oxford University Press.

Platt, John, Weber, Heidi & Ho, Mian-lian (1984). *The New Englishes*. London: Routledge.

Porter, Jonathan (1996). *Macau: the Imaginary City*. Boulder, Col.: Westview Press.

Postiglione, Gerald A. (1998). Schooling and social stratification. In G. A. Postiglione & W. O. Lee (eds.), *Schooling in Hong Kong*. Hong Kong: Hong Kong University Press, 137–53.

Potter, John (1992). *Common Business English Errors in Hong Kong*. Hong Kong: Longman.

Prator, Clifford (1968). The British heresy in TESL. In J. A. Fishman, C. Ferguson & J. Das Gupta (eds.), *Language Problems of Developing Nations*. New York: John Wiley and Sons, 459–76.

Pred, Allan (1990). *Lost Words and Lost Worlds: Modernity and the Language of Everyday Life in Late Nineteenth-century Stockholm*. Cambridge: Cambridge University Press.

Pride, John B. (ed.) (1982). *New Englishes*. Rowley, Mass.: Newbury House.

Pride, John B. & Liu, Ru-shan (1988). Some aspects of the spread of English in China since 1949. *International Journal of the Sociology of Language* 74: 41–70.

Pun, Shuk-han (1997). Hegemonic struggles in the language policy development of Hong Kong, 1982–1994. In W. O. Lee & M. Bray (eds.), *Education and Political Transition: Perspectives and Dimensions in East Asia*. Hong Kong: Comparative Education Research Centre, University of Hong Kong, 81–98.

Puttenham, George (1589). *The Arte of English Poesie*. London: Richard Field.

Quirk, Randolph (1962). *The Use of English*. London: Longman.

Quirk, Randolph (1972). *The English Language and Images of Matter*. Oxford: Oxford University Press.

Quirk, Randolph (1985). The English language in a global context. In R. Quirk & H. G. Widdowson (eds.), *English in the World: Teaching and Learning the Language and Literature*. Cambridge: Cambridge University Press, 1–30.

Quirk, Randolph (1990). Language varieties and standard language. *English Today* 21: 3–21.

Quirk, Randolph, Greenbaum, Sidney, Leech, Geoffrey & Svartvik, Jan (1972). *A Grammar of Contemporary English*. London: Longman.

Quirk, Randolph & Widdowson, Henry G. (eds.) (1985). *English in the World: Teaching and Learning the Language and Literature*. Cambridge: Cambridge University Press.

Radio Television Hong Kong (1997). *The Hong Kong Connection: Learning to Speak*. Radio Television Hong Kong television programme broadcast 8 April.

Rafael, Vincente L. (2000). *White Love and Other Events in Filipino History*. Manila: Ateneo De Manila University Press.

Rafferty, Kevin (1991). *City on the Rocks: Hong Kong's Uncertain Future*. London: Viking.

Ramsey, S. Robert (1987). *The Languages of China*. New Jersey: Princeton University Press.

Rao, G. Subba (1954). *Indian Words in English: a Study in Indo-British Cultural and Linguistic Relations*. Oxford: Clarendon.

Rao, Zhenhui (1996). Reconciling communicative approaches to the teaching of English with traditional Chinese methods. *Research in the Teaching of English* 30.4: 458–71.

Reinecke, John E. (1937). Marginal languages: a sociological survey of the creole languages and trade jargons. PhD dissertation, Graduate School, Yale University.

Ricento, Thomas (2000). *Ideology, Politics, and Language Policies: Focus on English*. Amsterdam and Philadelphia: John Benjamins.

Richards, Jack C. (1982). Rhetorical and communicative styles in the new varieties of English. In J. B. Pride (ed.), *New Englishes*. Rowley, Mass.: Newbury House, 227–48.

Richards, Stephen (1998). Learning English in Hong Kong: making connections between motivation, language use, and strategy choice. In M. C. Pennington (ed.), *Language in Hong Kong at Century's End*. Hong Kong: Hong Kong University Press, 43–90.

Romaine, Susanne (1994). *Language in Society: an Introduction to Sociolinguistics*. Oxford: Oxford University Press.

Romaine, Suzanne (1988). *Pidgin and Creole Languages*. London: Longman.

Romaine, Suzanne (1997). The British heresy in ESL revisited. In S. Eliasson & E. H. Jahr (eds.), *Language and its Ecology: Essays in Memory of Einar Haugen*. Berlin, New York: Mouton de Gruyter, 417–32.

Rosenthal, Elizabeth (2001). Tough US visa policy angers Chinese scholars. College Times supplement to *New York Times*. 10 September. http://college2.nytimes.com/guests/articles/2001/09/10/ 868954.xml.

Ross, Heidi A. (1993). *China Learns English: Language Teaching and Social Change in the People's Republic*. London: Yale University Press.

Rubinstein, Murray A. (1996). *The Origins of the Anglo-American Missionary Enterprise in China, 1807–1840*. Lanham, Md: Scarecrow Press.

Russell, Bertrand ([1922] 1966). *The Problem of China*. 2nd edn. London: George Allen & Unwin.

Saville-Troike, M. (1981). *Ethnography of Communication: an Introduction*. Oxford: Basil Blackwell.

Schiller, Herbert I. (1976). *Communication and Cultural Domination*. White Plains, New York: Sharpe.

Schneider, Edgar W. (1993). *A New Bibliography of Writings on Varieties of English, 1984–1992/93* (with B. Glauser & M. Görlach). Amsterdam and Philadelphia: John Benjamins.

Schneider, Edgar W. (1997a). Introduction. In E. W. Schneider (ed.), *Englishes Around the World*. Amsterdam and Philadelphia: John Benjamins, 1: 15–17.

Schneider, Edgar W. (1997b) (ed.). *Englishes Around the World*, vol. 1: *General Studies, British Isles, North America. Studies in Honour of Manfred Görlach*. Amsterdam and Philadelphia: John Benjamins.

Schneider, Edgar W. (1997c) (ed.). *Englishes Around the World*, vol. 2: *Caribbean, Africa, Asia, Australasia. Studies in Honour of Manfred Görlach*. Amsterdam and Philadelphia: John Benjamins.

Schneider, Edgar W. (2000). Corpus linguistics in the Asian context: exemplary analyses of the Kolhapur corpus of Indian English. In M. L. A. S. Bautista, T. A. Llamzon and B. P. Sibayan (eds.), *Parangalcang Brother Andrew: Festschrift for Andrew Gonzalez on His Sixtieth Birthday*. Manila: De La Salle University Press.

Schumann, John H. (1978). *The Pidginization Process: a Model for Second Language Acquisition*. Rowley, Mass.: Newbury House.

Schwab, Raymond (1984). *The Oriental Renaissance: Europe's Rediscovery of India and the East, 1680–1880*. New York: Columbia University Press.

Scott, C. P. G. (1896/97). The Malayan words in English. *Journal of the American Oriental Society* 17: 93–144; 18: 49–124.

Sebba, Mark (1997). *Contact Languages*. Basingstoke: Macmillan.

Selby, Anne & Selby, Stephen (1997). China coast pidgin English. *Journal of the Hong Kong Branch of the Royal Asiatic Society* 35: 113–41.

Serjeantson, Mary S. (1935). *A History of Foreign Words in English*. London: Routledge and Kegan Paul.

Seuren, Pieter A. M. (1998). *Western Linguistics: an Historical Introduction*. Oxford: Blackwell.

Shaw, Wilkinson J. (1897). Canton English. *The New Review* 16: 548–55.

Shi, Ding-xu (1986). Chinese Pidgin English: its origin and linguistic features. Unpublished MA long paper. Department of Linguistics, University of Pittsburgh.

Shi, Ding-xu (1991). Chinese Pidgin English: its origin and linguistic features. *Journal of Chinese Linguistics* 19: 1–40.

Shi, Ding-xu (1993). Learning pidgin English through Chinese characters. In F. Byrne & J. Holm (eds.), *Atlantic Meets Pacific: a Global View of Pidginization and Creolization*. Amsterdam: John Benjamins, 495–65.

Shipp, Steve (1997). *Macau, China: a Political History of the Portuguese Colony's Transition to Chinese Rule*. Jefferson, NC: McFarland & Co.

Sibayan, Bonifacio P. & Gonzalez, Andrew B. (1996). Post-imperial English in the Philippines. In J. A. Fishman, A. W. Conrad & A. Rubal-Lopez (eds.), *Post-imperial English*. Berlin and New York: Mouton de Gruyter, 139–72.

Siegel, Jeff (1997). Pidgin and English in Melanesia: is there a continuum? *World Englishes* 16: 185–204.

Silva, Penny (ed.) (1998). *A Dictionary of South African English on Historical Principles*. Oxford: Oxford University Press.

Simpson, Robert K. M. (1933). *The Student Reader*. Hong Kong.

Simpson, William (1873). China's future place in philology. *Macmillan's* 29: 45–8.

Sin, King-sui & Roebuck, Derek (1996). Language engineering for legal transplantation: conceptual problems in creating common law Chinese. *Language and Communication* 16: 235–54.

Singler, John V. (1997). The configuration of Liberia's Englishes. *World Englishes* 16: 205–31.

Siu, Yat-ming (1996). Population and immigration: with a special account on Chinese immigrants. In M. K. Nyaw & S. M. Li (eds.), *The Other Hong Kong Report 1996*. Hong Kong: Chinese University Press, 325–47.

Skeldon, Ronald (ed.) (1994). *Reluctant exiles? Migration from Hong Kong and the New Overseas Chinese*. Hong Kong: Hong Kong University Press.

Skeldon, Ronald (1996). Migration from China. *Journal of International Affairs* 49: 434–55.

Skutnabb-Kangas, Tove (2000). *Linguistic Genocide in Education, or Worldwide Diversity and Human Rights*. Maihwah, NJ, and London. Lawrence Erlbaum Associates.

Smith, Carl T. (1971). The formative years of the Tong brothers, pioneers in the modernization of China's commerce and industry. *Chung Chi Journal* 10: 81–95.

Smith, Carl T. (1985). The English-educated Elite in Nineteenth-century Hong Kong. In C. T. Smith, *Chinese Christians: Elites, Middlemen, and the Church in Hong Kong*. Hong Kong: Oxford University Press, 139–71.

Smith, George (1847). *A Narrative of an Exploratory Visit to Each of the Consular Cities of China and to the Islands of Hong Kong and Chusan in Behalf of the Missionary Society in the Years 1844, 1845, 1846*. London: Seely, Burnside & Seely.

Smith, Larry E. (ed.) (1981). *English for Cross-cultural Communication*. London: Macmillan.

Smith, Larry E. (1987). *Discourse across Cultures: Strategies in World Englishes*. New York: Prentice Hall.

So, Daniel (1992). Language-based bifurcation of secondary education in Hong Kong: past, present and future. In K. K. Luke (ed.), *Into the Twenty First Century: Issues of Language and Education in Hong Kong*. Hong Kong: Linguistic Society of Hong Kong, 69–95.

So, Daniel W. C. (1987). Searching for a bilingual exit. In R. Lord & H. N. L. Cheng (eds.), *Language Education in Hong Kong*. Hong Kong: Chinese University Press, 249–68.

Sohigian, Diran John (1991). The life and times of Lin Yutang. PhD thesis, New York: Columbia University; Ann Arbor: UMI Dissertation Services.

South China Morning Post (1984a). The Bermuda bombshell. *South China Morning Post*. 30 March, [Victor Su, Matthew Leung & Terry Cheng] 25.

South China Morning Post (1984b). Punters give approval to agreement. *South China Morning Post*. 20 December, [Staff reporters] Business News, 1.

South China Morning Post (1986a). Language project deserves applause. *South China Morning Post.* 1 November, [Editorial] 10.

South China Morning Post (1986b). Putonghua, not Cantonese in classes. *South China Morning Post.* 22 July, [Editorial] 16.

South China Morning Post (1987a). Need for far-sighted policy on languages. *South China Morning Post.* 25 January, [Editorial] 8.

South China Morning Post (1987b). Magic and wonderment of English must remain. *South China Morning Post.* 11 June, [Editorial] 28.

South China Morning Post (1989a). 92 per cent want more democracy for Hongkong, survey finds. *South China Morning Post.* 25 May, [Staff reporters] 1.

South China Morning Post (1989b). UK passports for 225,000 points system to favour private sector workers. *South China Morning Post.* 21 December, [Staff reporters] 1.

South China Morning Post (1989c). 'Worst' English tag should be eliminated. *South China Morning Post.* 27 February, [Editorial] 18.

South China Morning Post (1991). Liberals win 15, Independents 3. *South China Morning Post.* 16 September, [Staff reporters] 1.

South China Morning Post (1996). Ignorant. *South China Morning Post.* 11 February, letters page [letter from Chau Tak-hay] 11.

South China Morning Post (1999). Language lessons. *South China Morning Post.* 22 November, [Editorial] 16.

Spolsky, Bernard (1994). Fishman, Joshua A. (1926–). In R. E. Asher & E. F. K. Koerner (eds.), *The Encyclopaedia of Language and Linguistics.* Oxford: Pergamon, 3: 1265–6.

Stedman, Thomas L. & Lee, K. P. (1888). *Chinese-English Phrase Book in the Canton Dialect.* Washington, New York, Paris: Brentano's.

Strevens, Peter (1977). *New Orientations in the Teaching of English.* Oxford: Oxford University Press.

Strevens, Peter (1980). *Teaching English as an International Language.* Oxford: Pergamon.

Sun, Fo (1935) Foreword. *T'ien Hsia Monthly* 1. 1: 3–5.

Sun, Ruimei (1996). Teaching English in China: a brief history. *Language International* 8.3: 36–7.

Sweeting, Anthony (1997). Education policy and the 1997 factor: the art of the possible interacting with the dismal science. *Comparative Education* 33: 171–85.

Tang, Ivan (1997). Professor researches extent of brain drain. *South China Morning Post.* 8 March, 10.

Tay, Mary W. J. (1991). Southeast Asia and Hongkong. In Jenny Cheshire (ed.), *English Around the World: Sociolinguistic Perspectives.* Cambridge: Cambridge University Press, 319–32.

Taylor, Andrew (1989). Hong Kong's English newspapers. *English Today* 20: 18–24.

Temple, Richard C. (ed.) (1907). The travels of Peter Mundy, in Europe and Asia, 1608–1667, vol. I. Cambridge: Hakluyt Society.

Temple, Richard C. (ed.) (1919). The travels of Peter Mundy, in Europe and Asia, 1608–1667, vol. III, 1. Cambridge: Hakluyt Society.

Teng, Ssu-yü & Fairbank, John K. (1967). *China's Response to the West.* Cambridge, Mass.: Harvard University Press.

Tenney, C. D. (1889). The English language in Chinese educational work. *Chinese Recorder* 20: 469–71.

Thompson, Robert W. (1959). Two synchronic cross-sections in the Portuguese dialect of Macao. *Orbis* 8: 29–53.

Thornton, Richard H. (1912). *An American Glossary*. Philadelphia: J. B. Lippincott.

Todd, Loreto & Hancock, Ian (1986). *International English Usage*. London: Croom Helm.

Todd, Loreto (1984). *Modern Englishes: Pidgins and Creoles*. Oxford: Blackwell.

Todd, Loreto (1995). Tracking the homing pidgin: a millennium report. *English Today* 41: 33–43.

Tollefson, James W. (ed.) (1995). *Power and Inequality in Language Education*. Cambridge: Cambridge University Press.

Tollefson, James W. (ed.) (2002). *Language Policies in Education: Critical Issues*. Mahwah, NJ, and London: Lawrence Erlbaum Associates.

Tong, Qing Sheng (1999). The bathos of a universalism: I. A Richards and his basic English. In Lydia H. Liu (ed.), *Tokens of Exchange*. London: Duke University Press, 331–54.

Tong, Qing Sheng (2000). Inventing China: the use of Orientalist views on the Chinese language. *Interventions* 2.1: 6–20.

Tong, Ting-kü (1862). *The Chinese and English Instructor (Ying Ü Tsap Ts'ün)*. Canton.

Tongue, Ray & Waters, Dan (1978). English, HK-style. *South China Morning Post*. 29 September, 2.

Toreen, Olof (1771). *A Voyage to Suratte*. London: Printed for Benjamin White.

Troutner, Jennifer L.(1996). *Language, Culture and Politics: English in China, 1840s–1990s*. Michigan: UMI.

Trudgill, Peter (1978). Introduction: sociolinguistics and sociolinguistics. In P. Trudgill (ed.), *Sociolinguistic Patterns in British English*. London: Edward Arnold, 1–18.

Trudgill, Peter & Hannah, Jean ([1982] 1994). *International English: a Guide to Varieties of Standard English*. London: Arnold.

Tryon, Darrell T., Mühlhäusler, Peter & Baker, Philip (1996). English-derived contact languages in the Pacific in the 19th century (excluding Australia). In S. A. Würm, P. Mühlhäusler & D. T. Tryon (eds.), *Atlas of Languages of Intercultural Communication in the Pacific, Asia, and the Americas* 2: 497–522.

Tsang, Shu-ki (1999). The Hong Kong economy: opportunities out of the crisis. *Journal of Contemporary China* 8: 29–45.

T'sou, Benjamin K. (1985). Chinese and the cultural eunuch syndrome. In R. Lord & B. K. T'sou, *The Language Bomb*. Hong Kong: Longman (Far East), 15–19.

Tsui, Clarence (1999). Fading voices fight to be heard. *South China Morning Post*. 23 May, 3.

United Nations Economic and Social Commission for Asia and the Pacific (1974). *The Demographic Situation in Hong Kong*. Bangkok: ESCAP.

Van Dyke, Paul A. (2000). Pigs, chickens, and lemonade: the provisions trade in Canton, 1700 to 1840. Forthcoming in the *International Journal of Maritime History*, June 2000.

Van Dyke, Paul A. (2001). Port Canton, and the Pearl River delta, 1690–1845. PhD dissertation, University of Southern California.

Viereck, Wolfgang & Bald, Wolf-Dietrich (eds.) (1986). *English in Contact with Other Languages*. Budapest: Akademiai Kiado.

Wade, Geoff (2001). The Portuguese as represented in some Chinese sources of the Ming dynasty. In Jorge M. dos Santos Alves (ed.), *Conferências nos encontros de historia Luso-chinesa – Portugal e a China*. Lisbon: Fundacão Oriente, 263–316.

Wallis, John (1653). *Grammatica Linguae Anglicanae [. . .]*. Oxoniae: Typis L. Lichfield, et prostant venales apud John Crosley.

Walter, Richard & Robins, Benjamin ([1748] 1974). *A Voyage Round the World: in the Years MDCCXL, I, II, III, IV*, edited with an introduction by Glyndwr Williams. London: Oxford University Press.

Walters, Steve & Balla, John (1998). Medium of instruction: policy and reality at one Hong Kong tertiary institution. In M. C. Pennington (ed.), *Language in Hong Kong at Century's End*. Hong Kong: Hong Kong University Press, 365–89.

Wan, Cynthia (2000a). $60m in funds to bridge the education gap. *South China Morning Post*. 10 March, 6.

Wan, Cynthia (2000b). English schools body changes course. *South China Morning Post*. 13 March, 3.

Wang, Annie (2001). *Lili: a Novel of Tiananmen*. New York: Pantheon Books.

Wang, Yinquan (1999). 'College English' in China. *English Today* 15.1: 45–51.

Webster, Michael & Lam, William C. P. (1991). Further notes on the influence of Cantonese on the English of Hong Kong students. *ILE Journal*. Special issue no. 2: 35–42.

Webster, Michael, Ward, Alan & Craig, Kenneth (1987). Language errors due to first language interference (Cantonese) produced by Hong Kong students of English. *ILE Journal* (HK) 3: 63–81.

Webster, Noah (1789). *Dissertations on the English Language*. Boston: Isaiah Thomas; facsimile reprint, Menston: Scolar Press, 1967.

Webster, Noah (1806). *A Compendious Dictionary of the English Language*. New Haven.

Webster, Noah (1828). *An American Dictionary of the English language*. 2 vols. New York: S. Converse; facsimile reprint, San Francisco: Foundation for American Christian Education, 1967 (*ADEL*).

Wei, Sandy Tsz-shan (2000). The language of the law in Hong Kong. M.Phil. thesis, University of Hong Kong.

Wells, John C. (1982). *Accents of English*. 3 vols. Cambridge: Cambridge University Press.

Welsh, Frank (1993). *A History of Hong Kong*. London: HarperCollins.

Wharton, Jeremiah (1654). *The English grammar*. Facsimile reprint, 1970, of 1st edn. London: Printed by William Du-Gard for the Author. Menston: Scolar Press.

Whinnom, Keith (1971). Linguistic hybridization and the special case of pidgins and creoles. In D. Hymes (ed.), *Pidginization and Creolization of Languages*. Cambridge: Cambridge University Press, 91–115.

Whitworth, George Clifford (1885). *An Anglo-Indian Dictionary: a Glossary of Indian Terms Used in English, and of such English or Other Non-Indian Terms as have obtained Special Meanings in India*. London: Kegan Paul, Trench & Co.

Wild, Norman (1943–6). Materials for the study of the Ssu I Kuan. *Bulletin of the School of Oriental and African Studies* 9: 617–40.

Williams, Samuel Wells (1836). Jargon spoken at Canton. *Chinese Repository* 4 (January): 428–35.

Williams, Samuel Wells (1837). Hungmaou mae mae tung yung kwei kwa, or those words of the devilish language of the red-bristled people commonly used in buying and selling. *Chinese Repository* 6 (October): 276–9.

Williams, Samuel Wells (1848). *The Middle Kingdom*. New York: Charles Scribner's Sons.

Williams, Samuel Wells (1856). *Tonic Dictionary of the Chinese Language in the Canton Dialect*. Canton: Chinese Repository.

Williams, Samuel Wells (1874). *A Syllabic Dictionary of the Chinese Language*. Shanghai: American Presbyterian Mission Press.

Winchester, Simon (1999). Dueling dictionaries. *Wall Street Journal*. 17 September, 14.

Winford, Donald (1997). Re-examining Caribbean English Creole continua. *World Englishes* 16: 233–79.

Wong, Fanny (1992). Electoral proposals irresponsible, says China. *South China Morning Post*. 8 October, 1.

Wong, Luke S. K. (1989). Housing and residential environment. In T. L. Tsim and B. H. K. Luk (eds.), *The Other Hong Kong Report*. Hong Kong: Chinese University Press, 229–43.

Wood, Chris (1997). The 'cage people'. *Maclean's* 110: 38.

Wu, John C. H. (1937). Beyond the east and west. *T'ien Hsia Monthly* 4.1: 9–17.

Würm, Stephen A. et al. (1987). *Language Atlas of China*. Hong Kong: Longman.

Xu, Edward Yihua (1994). Religion and education: St John's University as an evangelizing agency. PhD thesis. Ann Arbor: UMI.

Xu Xi (2000). Writing the literature of non-denial. Special issue of *World Englishes* on 'Hong Kong English: Autonomy and Creativity', 19.3: 415–28.

Xu Xi and Ingham, Mike (eds.) (2003). *City Voices: Hong Kong Writing in English 1945 to the Present*. Hong Kong: Hong Kong University Press.

Yamamoto, Sumiko & Yamamoto Tatsuro (1953). The anti-Christian movement in China, 1922–1927. *The Far Eastern Quarterly* 12.2: 133–47.

Yan, Li (2001). Some 110,000 overseas students returned home for careers. *People's Daily*. Online edition. http://english.peopledaily.com.cn/200102/13/eng20010213_62241.html.

Yau, Man-siu (1989). The controversy over teaching medium in Hong Kong: an analysis of a language policy. *Journal of Multilingual and Multicultural Development* 10: 279–95.

Yau, Man-siu (1993). Functions of two codes in Hong Kong Chinese. *World Englishes* 12: 25–33.

Yee, Albert H. (1989). Cross-cultural perspectives on higher education in East Asia: psychological effects upon Asian students. *Journal of Multilingual and Multicultural Devleopment* 10: 213–32.

Yeh, Wen-Hsin (1990). *The Alienated Academy: Culture and Politics in Republican China, 1919–1937*. Cambridge, Mass.: Harvard University Press.

Young, John (1996). Changing identities in Hong Kong: from British colonialism to Chinese nationalism. A paper presented at the 110th Annual Meeting of the American Historical Association, 4–7 January.

Young, Robert J. C. (1990). *White Mythologies: Writing History and the West*. London: Routledge.

Young, Robert J. C. (1995). *Colonial Desire: Hybridity in Theory, Culture, and Race*. London: Routledge.

Yow, Sophia (2001). Guangdong to trial English as medium. *South China Morning Post*. 20 October, 2.

Yu, Vivienne W. S. and Atkinson, Paul A. (1988a). An investigation of the language difficulties experienced by Hong Kong secondary school students in English-medium schools: (I) The problems. *Journal of Multilingual and Multicultural Development* 9: 267–84.

Yu, Vivienne W. S. and Atkinson, Paul A. (1988b). An investigation of the language difficulties experienced by Hong Kong secondary school students in English-medium
schools: (II) Some causal factors. *Journal of Multilingual and Multicultural Development* 9: 307–22.

Yule, Henry & Burnell, Arthur Coke ([1886] 1969). *Hobson-Jobson*. London: John Murray.
New edition 1903, reprinted 1969, London: Routledge & Kegan Paul.

Yung, Shang Him (1939). The Chinese educational mission and its influence. *T'ien Hsia
Monthly* 9.3: 225–56.

Zhang, Ailing (2000). Language switches among Chinese/English bilinguals. *English
Today* 16.1: 53–6.

Zhao, Yong & Campbell, Keith P. (1995). English in China. *World Englishes* 14.3: 377–90.

Zuengler, Jane Ellen (1983). *Kenyan English*. In B. B. Kachru (ed.), *The Other Tongue:
English Across Cultures*. Oxford: Pergamon, 112–24.

Index